CLYMER®

MERCURY

OUTBOARD SHOP MANUAL
45-225 HP • 1972-1989

The World's Finest Publisher of Mechanical How-To Manuals

INTERTEC PUBLISHING

P.O. Box 12901, Overland Park, Kansas 66282-2901

Copyright ©1989 Intertec Publishing

FIRST EDITION
First Printing June, 1984
Second Printing February, 1985
Third Printing September, 1985

SECOND EDITION
Updated to include 1985-1986 models
First Printing May, 1986

THIRD EDITION
Updated to include 1987 models
First Printing April, 1987
Second Printing December, 1987
Third Printing June, 1988

FOURTH EDITION
Updated to include 1988-1989 models
First Printing June, 1989
Second Printing December, 1989
Third Printing April, 1990
Fourth Printing October, 1990
Fifth Printing November, 1991
Sixth Printing August, 1992
Seventh Printing June, 1993
Eighth Printing April, 1994
Ninth Printing January, 1995
Tenth Printing October, 1995
Eleventh Printing January, 1997
Twelfth Printing October, 1997
Thirteenth Printing January, 1999
Fourteenth Printing March, 2000
Fifteenth Printing June, 2001

Printed in U.S.A.

CLYMER and colophon are registered trademarks of Intertec Publishing.

ISBN: 0-89287-396-5

Tools shown in Chapter Two courtesy of Thorsen Tool, Dallas, Texas. Test equipment shown in Chapter Two courtesy of Dixson, Inc., Grand Junction, Colorado.

Technical illustrations courtesy of Mercury Marine with additional illustrations by Mitzi McCarthy and Diana Kirkland. With thanks to Marine Specialists, Sun Valley, California, and Ken's Boat Center, Burbank, California.

COVER: Photographed by Michael Brown Photographic Productions, Los Angeles, California. Assisted by Bill Masho.
- *Facilities, boats and motors courtesy of Mercury Marine Co.*
- *Wellcraft driven by Michael Allen.*
- *Photo boat driven by Dave Martin.*
- *Model—Jill Herendeen.*

CLYMER PUBLICATIONS
Intertec Directory & Book Division
Chief Executive Officer Timothy M. Andrews
President Ron Wall
Vice President, Directory & Book Division Rich Hathaway

The following books and guides are published by Intertec Publishing.

CLYMER SHOP MANUALS
Boat Motors and Drives
Motorcycles and ATVs
Snowmobiles
Personal Watercraft

ABOS/INTERTEC/CLYMER BLUE BOOKS AND TRADE-IN GUIDES
Recreational Vehicles
Outdoor Power Equipment
Agricultural Tractors
Lawn and Garden Tractors
Motorcycles and ATVs
Snowmobiles and Personal Watercraft
Boats and Motors

AIRCRAFT BLUEBOOK-PRICE DIGEST
Airplanes
Helicopters

AC-U-KWIK DIRECTORIES
The Corporate Pilot's Airport/FBO Directory
International Manager's Edition
Jet Book

I&T SHOP SERVICE MANUALS
Tractors

INTERTEC SERVICE MANUALS
Snowmobiles
Outdoor Power Equipment
Personal Watercraft
Gasoline and Diesel Engines
Recreational Vehicles
Boat Motors and Drives
Motorcycles
Lawn and Garden Tractors

Contents

Quick Reference Data

TUNE-UP SPECIFICATIONS (MERC 500 WITH LIGHTNING ENERGIZER SYSTEM)

Firing order	1-3-2-4
Spark plug	AC-V40FFM or Champion L77V
Spark plug gap	Not adjustable
Maximum advance	35° BTDC @ 5,200 rpm
Throttle primary pickup	7-9° BTDC
Throttle secondary pickup	@ 35° BTDC stop
Full throttle rpm	4,800-5,500 rpm
Idle rpm	550-600 rpm (3-5° ATDC) in FORWARD gear
Water pressure (at cylinder block)	3-5 psi (0.211-0.352 kg/cm²) @ 2,000 rpm

MERC 500 MAXIMUM SPARK ADVANCE

Engine rpm @ wide-open throttle	Maximum spark advance setting
2,000-4,000	38-39° BTDC
4,000-4,800	37-38° BTDC
5,200-5,500	35° BTDC

TUNE-UP SPECIFICATIONS (MERC 500 WITH DISTRIBUTOR-LESS IGNITION TO SERIAL NO. 4576236)

Firing order	1-3-2-4
Spark plug	AC-V40FFM or Champion L77V
Spark plug gap	Not adjustable
Maximum advance	30° BTDC @ 5,000 rpm
Throttle primary pickup	7-9° BTDC
Throttle secondary pickup	@ maximum stop (30° BTDC)
Full throttle rpm	4,800-5,500 rpm
Idle rpm	550-600 rpm (5° ATDC) in FORWARD gear
Water pressure (at cylinder block)	3-5 psi (0.211-0.352 kg/cm²) @ 2,000 rpm

TUNE-UP SPECIFICATIONS (MERC 500, 45 AND 50 [4-CYLINDER] ABOVE SERIAL NO. 4576236)

Firing order	1-3-2-4
Firing sequence	90° consecutive
Spark plug	AC-V40FFK or Champion L78V
Spark plug gap	Not adjustable
Maximum advance	30° BTDC @ 5,000 rpm
Throttle primary pickup	7-9° BTDC*
Throttle secondary pickup	@ maximum stop (30° BTDC)
Full throttle rpm	5,000-5,500 rpm
Idle rpm	550-600 rpm (5° ATDC) in FORWARD gear
Water pressure (at cylinder block)	3-5 psi (0.211-0.352 kg/cm²) @ 2,000 rpm

* With serial No. above 5632037 (U.S.), 7150562 (Canada), 8066280 (Australia) and 9265180 (Belgium): 0-2° ATDC.

TUNE-UP SPECIFICATIONS (MERC 650 DISTRIBUTOR-LESS IGNITION)

Firing order	1-2-3
Spark plug	AC-V40FFM or Champion L76V
Spark plug gap	Not adjustable
Maximum advance	23° BTDC @ 5,300 rpm
Throttle primary pickup	6-8° BTDC
Throttle secondary pickup	Not adjustable
Full throttle rpm	4,800-5,300 rpm
Idle rpm	550-600 rpm (6-8° ATDC) in FORWARD gear
Water pressure (at cylinder block)	3 or more psi (0.211 or more kg/cm²) @ 2,000 rpm

TUNE-UP SPECIFICATIONS (MERC 650 WITH DISTRIBUTOR CD IGNITION)

Firing order	1-2-3[1]
Spark plug	AC-V40FFM or Champion L77V
Spark plug gap	Not adjustable
Maximum advance	23° BTDC
Throttle primary pickup	3-5° BTDC[2]
Throttle secondary pickup	Not adjustable
Full throttle rpm	4,800-5,300 rpm
Idle rpm	550-600 rpm
Water pressure (at cylinder block)	3-5 psi (0.211-0.352 kg/cm²) @ 2,000 rpm

1. Firing order changed to 1-3-2 above serial No. 5467466 (U.S.), 7135987 (Canada), 8063334 (Australia) and 9238105 (Belgium).
2. Below serial No. 3552906, 0-2° BTDC.

TUNE-UP SPECIFICATIONS
(MERC 700/70 [PRIOR TO 1984]/60/50 [3-CYLINDER] WITH FLYWHEEL CD IGNITION)

Firing order	1-2-3*
Spark plug	AC-V40FFM or Champion L76V
Spark plug gap	Not adjustable
Maximum advance	23° BTDC @ 5,500 rpm
Throttle primary pickup	Not adjustable
Throttle secondary pickup	Maximum spark (static setting)
Full throttle rpm	5,000-5,500 rpm
Idle rpm	650-750 rpm (6-8° ATDC) in FORWARD gear
Water pressure (at cylinder block)	3 or more psi (0.211 or more kg/cm²) @ 2,000 rpm

* Firing order changed to 1-3-2 above serial No. 5467466 (U.S.), 7135987 (Canada), 8063334 (Australia) and 9238105 (Belgium).

TUNE-UP SPECIFICATIONS (1987-ON MERC 70, 80 AND 90)

Firing order	1-3-2
Spark plug	NGK-BUHW-2, Champion L78V or AC-V40FFK
Spark plug gap	Not Adjustable
Maximum advance	
Cranking	
Models 70 and 80 (Prior to serial No. B239242)	24° BTDC

(continued)

TUNE-UP SPECIFICATIONS (1987-ON MERC 70, 80 AND 90) (continued)

Models 70 and 80 (After serial No. B239241)	28° BTDC
Model 90	28° BTDC
Running	
Models 70 and 80 (Prior to serial No. B239243)	22° BTDC
Models 70 and 80 (After serial No. B239241)	26° BTDC
Model 90	26° BTDC
Idle timing	0-4° BTDC
Idle rpm in forward gear	650-700 rpm
Full throttle rpm	
Models 70 and 80	4750-5250 rpm
Model 90	5000-5500 rpm

TUNE-UP SPECIFICATIONS (MERC 850 WITH DISTRIBUTOR CD IGNITION)

Firing order	1-3-2-4
Spark plug	AC-V40FFM or Champion L76V
Spark plug gap	Not adjustable
Maximum advance	27° BTDC
Throttle primary pickup	3-5° BTDC
Throttle secondary pickup	27° BTDC
Full throttle rpm	4,800-5,500 rpm
Idle rpm	550-650 rpm
Water pressure (at cylinder block)	2-5 psi (0.141-0.352 kg/cm²) @ 2,000 rpm

TUNE-UP SPECIFICATIONS
(MERC 75/80 [PRIOR TO 1984] 800/850 WITH DISTRIBUTOR-LESS IGNITION)

Firing order	1-3-2-4
Spark plug	AC-V40FFK or Champion L78V
Spark plug gap	Not adjustable
Maximum advance	27° BTDC
Throttle primary pickup	2° BTDC-2° ATDC (1)
Throttle secondary pickup	Not adjustable
Full throttle rpm	5,000-5,500 rpm
Idle rpm	550-650 rpm (5-8° ATDC) in FORWARD gear
Water pressure (at cylinder block)	2-5 psi (0.141-0.352 kg/cm²) @ 2,000 rpm

* Below serial No. 4423112, 2-4° BTDC.

TUNE-UP SPECIFICATIONS
(MERC 900, 1150, 1400, 1500 AND 1500XS WITH DISTRIBUTOR CD IGNITION)

Firing order	1-4-5-2-3-6
Spark plug	AC-V40FFM or Champion L76V
Spark plug gap	Not adjustable
Maximum advance	21° BTDC
Throttle primary pickup	4-6° BTDC
Throttle secondary pickup	Not adjustable
Full throttle rpm	
Merc 900	4,500-5,000 rpm
Merc 1150	5,000-5,500 rpm
Merc 1400, 1500	5,300-5,800 rpm
Merc 1500 XS	5,800-6,300 rpm
Idle rpm	550-650 rpm in FORWARD gear
Water pressure (at cylinder block)	2-5 psi (0.141-0.352 kg/cm²) @ 2,000 rpm

TUNE-UP SPECIFICATIONS
(MERC 90-140 HP [6-CYLINDER] WITH DISTRIBUTOR-LESS IGNITION)

Firing order	1-4-5-2-3-6
Spark plug	AC-V40FFM or Champion L76V
Spark plug gap	Not adjustable
Maximum advance	18° BTDC*
Throttle primary pickup	4-6° BTDC
Throttle secondary pickup	
Merc 90	1-3° BTDC
Merc 115	5-7° ATDC
Merc 140	4-6° ATDC
Full throttle rpm	
Merc 90	4,500-5,000 rpm
Merc 115	5,000-5,500 rpm
Merc 140	5,300-5,800 rpm
Idle rpm	550-650 rpm in FORWARD gear
Water pressure (at cylinder block)	2-5 psi (0.141-0.352 kg/cm²) @ 2,000 rpm

* 20° @ cranking speed.

TUNE-UP SPECIFICATIONS (1988-ON MERC 100 AND 1989 MERC 115)

Firing order	1-3-2-4
Spark plug	NGK BUHW, Champion L76V or AC-V40FFM
Spark plug gap	Not adjustable
Maximum advance	
Cranking	
Model 100	27° BTDC
Model 115	25° BTDC
Running	23° BTDC
Idle timing	2-4° BTDC
Idle rpm in forward gear	
Model 100	600-700 rpm
Model 115	650-700 rpm
Full throttle rpm	4,750-5,250 rpm
Water pressure (at cylinder block)	1-5 psi @ 5,000 rpm

TUNE-UP SPECIFICATIONS (MERC 1750 V6, 1976-1977)

Firing order	1-2-3-4-5-6
Spark plug	AC-V40FFM or Champion L76V
Spark plug gap	Not adjustable
Maximum advance	15° BTDC[1]
Throttle primary pickup	8-10° ATDC[2]
Throttle secondary pickup	Not adjustable
Full throttle rpm	4,800-5,800 rpm
Idle rpm	550-650 rpm in FORWARD gear
Water pressure (at cylinder block)	8-11 psi (0.56-0.77 kg/cm²) @ 3,000 rpm

1. One punch mark.
2. Three punch marks.

TUNE-UP SPECIFICATIONS (MERC 1750 AND 175 V6 WITH 1978-ON)

Firing order	1-2-3-4-5-6
Spark plug	AC-V40FFM or Champion L76V
Spark plug gap	Not adjustable
Maximum advance	18° BTDC[1]
Throttle primary pickup	14° ATDC[2]
Throttle secondary pickup	Not adjustable
Full throttle rpm	5,300-5,800 rpm
Idle rpm	600-700 rpm in FORWARD gear
Water pressure (at cylinder block)	18-25 psi (1.27-1.76 kg/cm²) @ 5,000 rpm

1. 20° BTDC @ cranking speed.
2. Serial no. 6618751 and above; 7° ATDC.

TUNE-UP SPECIFICATIONS
(MERC 1500 AND 150 HP V6 BELOW SERIAL NO. 5203429
MERC 2000 AND 200 HP V6 BELOW SERIAL NO. 5363918)

1500 AND 150	
Firing order	1-2-3-4-5-6
Spark plug	AC-V40FFM or Champion L76V
Spark plug gap	Not adjustable
Maximum advance	16° BTDC[1]
Throttle primary pickup	7.5-8.5° ATDC
Throttle secondary pickup	Not adjustable
Full throttle rpm	5,000-5,500 rpm
Idle rpm	600-700 rpm (7.5-8.5° ATDC) in FORWARD gear
Water pressure (at cylinder block)	18-25 psi (1.27-1.76 kg/cm²) @ 5,000 rpm

2000 AND 200 HP	
Firing order	1-2-3-4-5-6
Spark plug	AC-V40FFM or Champion L76V
Spark plug gap	Not adjustable
Maximum advance	18° BTDC[2]
Throttle primary pickup	8-10° ATDC
Throttle secondary pickup	Not adjustable
Full throttle rpm	5,300-5,800 rpm
Idle rpm	550-650 rpm (12-15° ATDC) in FORWARD gear[3]
Water pressure (at cylinder block)	18-25 psi (1.27-1.76 kg/cm²) @ 5,000 rpm

1. 18° @ cranking.   2. 20° @ cranking.   3. Never exceed 800 rpm idle in gear.

TUNE-UP SPECIFICATIONS
(MERC 135 HP)
(MERC 150 HP V6 SERIAL NO. 5203429 AND ABOVE;
MERC 200 HP V6 SERIAL NO. 5363918 AND ABOVE)

135 HP AND 150 HP	
Firing order	1-2-3-4-5-6
Spark plug	AC-V40FFM or Champion L76V
Spark plug gap	Not adjustable
Maximum advance	16° BTDC[1]
Throttle primary pickup	11° ATDC
Throttle secondary pickup	Not adjustable
Full throttle rpm	5,000-5,500 rpm
Idle rpm	600-700 rpm
Water pressure (at cylinder block)	18-25 psi (1.27-1.76 kg/cm²) @ 5,000 rpm

200 HP	
Firing order	1-2-3-4-5-6
Spark plug	AC-V40FFM or Champion L76V
Spark plug gap	Not adjustable
Maximum advance	18° BTDC[2]
Throttle primary pickup	10° ATDC
Throttle secondary pickup	Not adjustable
Full throttle rpm	5,300-5,800 rpm
Idle rpm	600-700 rpm (12-15° ATDC) in FORWARD gear[3]
Water pressure (at cylinder block)	18-25 psi (1.27-1.76 kg/cm²) @ 5,000 rpm

1. 18° @ cranking.   2. 20° @ cranking.   3. Never exceed 800 rpm idle in gear.

TUNE-UP SPECIFICATIONS (MERC V150 XR2)

Firing order	1-2-3-4-5-6
Spark plug	NGK-BUHW, AC-V40FFM or Champion L76V
Spark plug gap	Not adjustable
Maximum timing	20° BTDC
	(22° BTDC @ cranking speed)
Throttle primary pickup	11° ATDC
Full throttle rpm	5,500-6,000 rpm
Idle rpm	600-700 in FORWARD gear

(MERC 150 XR4; V200[1] AND V225)	
Firing order	1-2-3-4-5-6
Spark plug	NGK-BUHW, AC-V40FFM or Champion L76V
Spark plug gap	Not adjustable
Maximum timing	22° BTDC @ cranking speed
	20° BTDC @ 5,400 rpm
	26° BTDC over 5,600 rpm[2]
Throttle primary pickup	
Below serial No. 657932	12° ATDC
Above serial No. 657933 or WH-28 carburetor	7° ATDC
Full throttle rpm	5,300-5,800 rpm
Idle rpm	600-700 in FORWARD gear

1. Serial No. 6073192 and above.
2. High speed spark advance module automatically advances maximum timing to 26° @ engine speed of 5,500 ± 100 rpm.

Introduction

This Clymer shop manual covers service and repair of all Mercury inline 3, 4 and 6 and V6 45-225 hp outboard motors from 1972-1989. Step-by-step instructions and hundreds of illustrations guide you through jobs ranging from simple maintenance to complete overhaul.

This manual can be used by anyone from a first-time amateur to a professional mechanic. Easy to read type, detailed drawings and clear photographs give you all the information you need to do the work right.

Having a well-maintained engine will increase your enjoyment of your boat as well as assuring your safety offshore. Keep this shop manual handy and use it often. It can save you hundreds of dollars in maintenance and repair bills and make yours a reliable, top-performing boat.

Chapter One

General Information

This detailed, comprehensive manual contains complete information on maintenance, tune-up, repair and overhaul. Hundreds of photos and drawings guide you through every step-by-step procedure.

Troubleshooting, tune-up, maintenance and repair are not difficult if you know what tools and equipment to use and what to do. Anyone not afraid to get their hands dirty, of average intelligence and with some mechanical ability, can perform most of the procedures in this book. See Chapter Two for more information on tools and techniques.

A shop manual is a reference. You want to be able to find information fast. Clymer books are designed with you in mind. All chapters are thumb tabbed and important items are indexed at the end of the book. All procedures, tables, photos, etc., in this manual assume that the reader may be working on the machine or using this manual for the first time.

Keep this book handy in your tool box. It will help you to better understand how your machine runs, lower repair and maintenance costs and generally increase your enjoyment of your marine equipment.

MANUAL ORGANIZATION

This chapter provides general information useful to marine owners and mechanics.

Chapter Two discusses the tools and techniques for preventive maintenance, troubleshooting and repair.

Chapter Three describes typical equipment problems and provides logical troubleshooting procedures.

Following chapters describe specific systems, providing disassembly, repair, assembly and adjustment procedures in simple step-by-step form. Specifications concerning a specific system are included at the end of the appropriate chapter.

NOTES, CAUTIONS AND WARNINGS

The terms NOTE, CAUTION and WARNING have specific meanings in this manual. A NOTE provides additional information to make a step or procedure easier or clearer. Disregarding a NOTE could cause inconvenience, but would not cause damage or personal injury.

A CAUTION emphasizes areas where equipment damage could result. Disregarding a CAUTION could cause permanent mechanical damage; however, personal injury is unlikely.

A WARNING emphasizes areas where personal injury or even death could result from negligence. Mechanical damage may also occur. WARNINGS *are to be taken seriously*. In some cases, serious injury or death has resulted from disregarding similar warnings.

TORQUE SPECIFICATIONS

Torque specifications throughout this manual are given in foot-pounds (ft.-lb.) and either Newton meters (N•m) or meter-kilograms (mkg). Newton meters are being adopted in place of meter-kilograms in accordance with the International Modernized Metric System. Existing torque wrenches calibrated in meter-kilograms can be used by performing a simple conversion: move the decimal point one place to the right. For example, 4.7 mkg = 47 N•m. This conversion is accurate enough for mechanics' use even though the exact mathematical conversion is 3.5 mkg = 34.3 N•m.

ENGINE OPERATION

All marine engines, whether 2- or 4-stroke, gasoline or diesel, operate on the Otto cycle of intake, compression, power and exhaust phases.

4-stroke Cycle

A 4-stroke engine requires two crankshaft revolutions (4 strokes of the piston) to complete the Otto cycle. **Figure 1** shows gasoline 4-stroke engine operation. **Figure 2** shows diesel 4-stroke engine operation.

2-stroke Cycle

A 2-stroke engine requires only 1 crankshaft revolution (2 strokes of the piston) to complete the Otto cycle. **Figure 3** shows gasoline 2-stroke engine operation. Although diesel 2-strokes exist, they are not commonly used in light marine applications.

FASTENERS

The material and design of the various fasteners used on marine equipment are not arrived at by chance or accident. Fastener design determines the type of tool required to work with the fastener. Fastener material is carefully selected to decrease the possibility of physical failure or corrosion. See *Galvanic Corrosion* in this chapter for more information on marine materials.

Threads

Nuts, bolts and screws are manufactured in a wide range of thread patterns. To join a nut and bolt, the diameter of the bolt and the diameter of the hole in the nut must be the same. It is just as important that the threads on both be properly matched.

The best way to determine if the threads on two fasteners are matched is to turn the nut on the bolt (or the bolt into the threaded hole in a piece of equipment) with fingers only. Be sure both pieces are clean. If much force is required, check the thread condition on each fastener. If the thread condition is good but the fasteners jam, the threads are not compatible.

Four important specifications describe every thread:

  a. Diameter.
  b. Threads per inch.
  c. Thread pattern.
  d. Thread direction.

Figure 4 shows the first two specifications. Thread pattern is more subtle. Italian and British

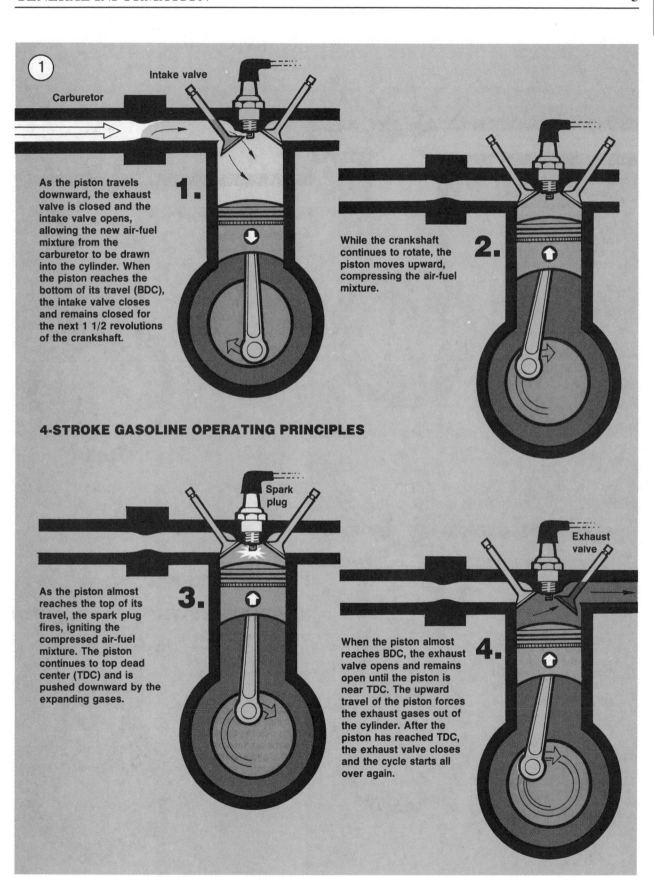

① Carburetor / Intake valve

1. As the piston travels downward, the exhaust valve is closed and the intake valve opens, allowing the new air-fuel mixture from the carburetor to be drawn into the cylinder. When the piston reaches the bottom of its travel (BDC), the intake valve closes and remains closed for the next 1 1/2 revolutions of the crankshaft.

2. While the crankshaft continues to rotate, the piston moves upward, compressing the air-fuel mixture.

4-STROKE GASOLINE OPERATING PRINCIPLES

Spark plug

3. As the piston almost reaches the top of its travel, the spark plug fires, igniting the compressed air-fuel mixture. The piston continues to top dead center (TDC) and is pushed downward by the expanding gases.

Exhaust valve

4. When the piston almost reaches BDC, the exhaust valve opens and remains open until the piston is near TDC. The upward travel of the piston forces the exhaust gases out of the cylinder. After the piston has reached TDC, the exhaust valve closes and the cycle starts all over again.

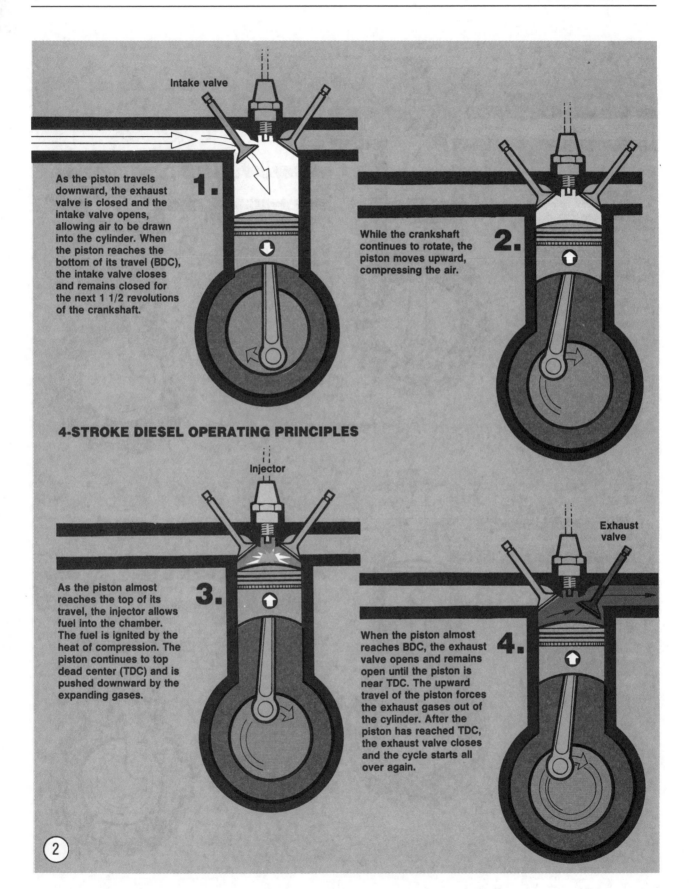

Intake valve

1. As the piston travels downward, the exhaust valve is closed and the intake valve opens, allowing air to be drawn into the cylinder. When the piston reaches the bottom of its travel (BDC), the intake valve closes and remains closed for the next 1 1/2 revolutions of the crankshaft.

2. While the crankshaft continues to rotate, the piston moves upward, compressing the air.

4-STROKE DIESEL OPERATING PRINCIPLES

Injector

3. As the piston almost reaches the top of its travel, the injector allows fuel into the chamber. The fuel is ignited by the heat of compression. The piston continues to top dead center (TDC) and is pushed downward by the expanding gases.

Exhaust valve

4. When the piston almost reaches BDC, the exhaust valve opens and remains open until the piston is near TDC. The upward travel of the piston forces the exhaust gases out of the cylinder. After the piston has reached TDC, the exhaust valve closes and the cycle starts all over again.

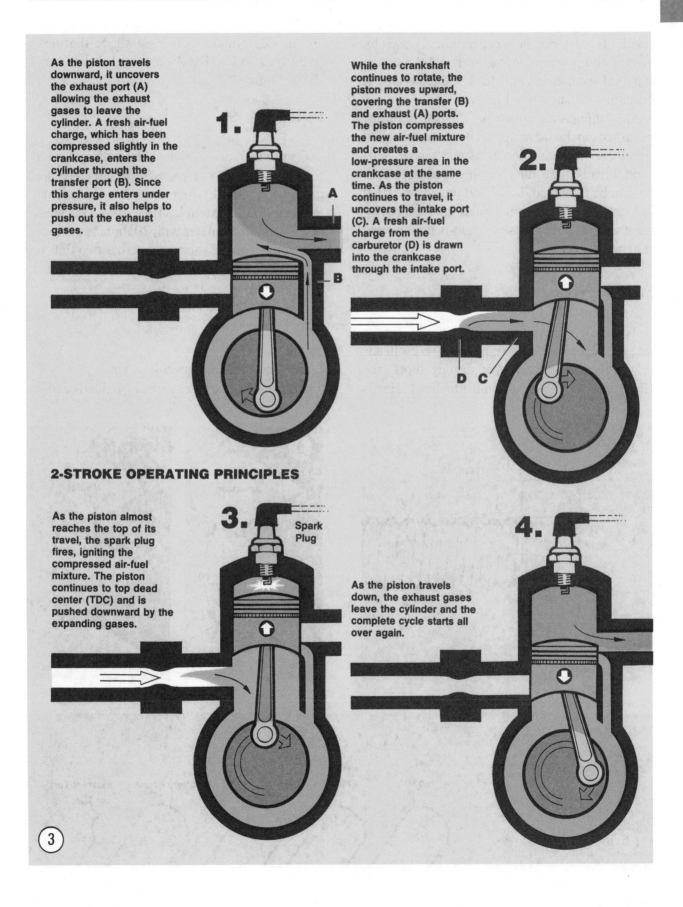

As the piston travels downward, it uncovers the exhaust port (A) allowing the exhaust gases to leave the cylinder. A fresh air-fuel charge, which has been compressed slightly in the crankcase, enters the cylinder through the transfer port (B). Since this charge enters under pressure, it also helps to push out the exhaust gases.

While the crankshaft continues to rotate, the piston moves upward, covering the transfer (B) and exhaust (A) ports. The piston compresses the new air-fuel mixture and creates a low-pressure area in the crankcase at the same time. As the piston continues to travel, it uncovers the intake port (C). A fresh air-fuel charge from the carburetor (D) is drawn into the crankcase through the intake port.

2-STROKE OPERATING PRINCIPLES

As the piston almost reaches the top of its travel, the spark plug fires, igniting the compressed air-fuel mixture. The piston continues to top dead center (TDC) and is pushed downward by the expanding gases.

Spark Plug

As the piston travels down, the exhaust gases leave the cylinder and the complete cycle starts all over again.

standards exist, but the most commonly used by marine equipment manufacturers are American standard and metric standard. The threads are cut differently as shown in **Figure 5**.

Most threads are cut so that the fastener must be turned clockwise to tighten it. These are called right-hand threads. Some fasteners have left-hand threads; they must be turned counterclockwise to be tightened. Left-hand threads are used in locations where normal rotation of the equipment would tend to loosen a right-hand threaded fastener.

Machine Screws

There are many different types of machine screws. **Figure 6** shows a number of screw heads requiring different types of turning tools (see Chapter Two for detailed information). Heads

are also designed to protrude above the metal (round) or to be slightly recessed in the metal (flat) (**Figure 7**).

Bolts

Commonly called bolts, the technical name for these fasteners is cap screw. They are normally described by diameter, threads per inch and length. For example, 1/4-20 × 1 indicates a bolt 1/4 in. in diameter with 20 threads per inch, 1 in. long. The measurement across two flats on the head of the bolt indicates the proper wrench size to be used.

Nuts

Nuts are manufactured in a variety of types and sizes. Most are hexagonal (6-sided) and fit

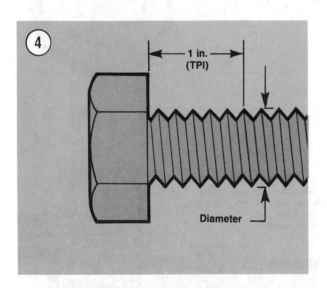

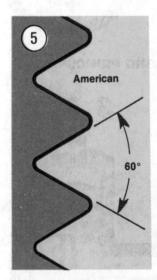

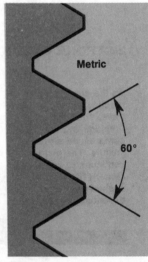

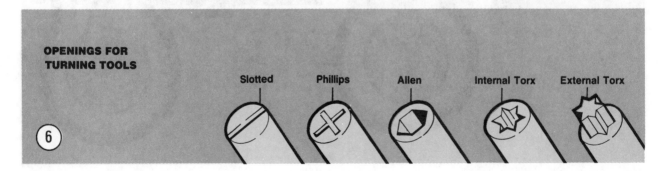

on bolts, screws and studs with the same diameter and threads per inch.

Figure 8 shows several types of nuts. The common nut is usually used with a lockwasher. Self-locking nuts have a nylon insert that prevents the nut from loosening; no lockwasher is required. Wing nuts are designed for fast removal by hand. Wing nuts are used for convenience in non-critical locations.

To indicate the size of a nut, manufacturers specify the diameter of the opening and the threads per inch. This is similar to bolt specification, but without the length dimension. The measurement across two flats on the nut indicates the proper wrench size to be used.

Washers

There are two basic types of washers: flat washers and lockwashers. Flat washers are simple discs with a hole to fit a screw or bolt. Lockwashers are designed to prevent a fastener from working loose due to vibration, expansion and contraction. **Figure 9** shows several types of lockwashers. Note that flat washers are often used between a lockwasher and a fastener to provide a smooth bearing surface. This allows the fastener to be turned easily with a tool.

Cotter Pins

Cotter pins (**Figure 10**) are used to secure special kinds of fasteners. The threaded stud

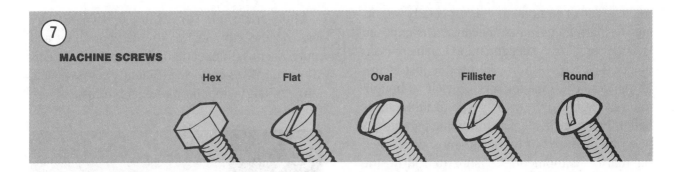

⑦ MACHINE SCREWS

Hex Flat Oval Fillister Round

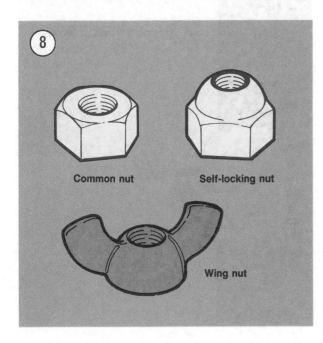

⑧

Common nut Self-locking nut

Wing nut

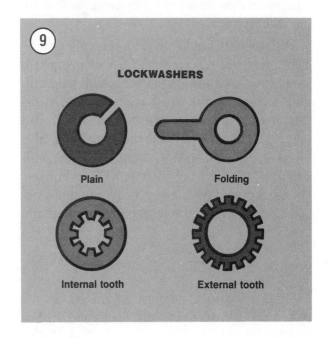

⑨ LOCKWASHERS

Plain Folding

Internal tooth External tooth

must have a hole in it; the nut or nut lock piece has projections that the cotter pin fits between. This type of nut is called a "Castellated nut." Cotter pins should not be reused after removal.

Snap Rings

Snap rings can be of an internal or external design. They are used to retain items on shafts (external type) or within tubes (internal type). Snap rings can be reused if they are not distorted during removal. In some applications, snap rings of varying thickness can be selected to control the end play of parts assemblies.

LUBRICANTS

Periodic lubrication ensures long service life for any type of equipment. It is especially important to marine equipment because it is exposed to salt or brackish water and other harsh environments. The *type* of lubricant used is just as important as the lubrication service itself; although, in an emergency, the wrong type of lubricant is better than none at all. The following paragraphs describe the types of lubricants most often used on marine equipment. Be sure to follow the equipment manufacturer's recommendations for lubricant types.

Generally, all liquid lubricants are called "oil." They may be mineral-based (including petroleum bases), natural-based (vegetable and animal bases), synthetic-based or emulsions (mixtures). "Grease" is an oil which is thickened with a metallic "soap." The resulting material is then usually enhanced with anticorrosion, antioxidant and extreme pressure (EP) additives. Grease is often classified by the type of thickener added; lithium and calcium soap are commonly used.

4-stroke Engine Oil

Oil for 4-stroke engines is graded by the American Petroleum Institute (API) and the So-

ciety of Automotive Engineers (SAE) in several categories. Oil containers display these ratings on the top or label (**Figure 11**).

API oil grade is indicated by letters, oils for gasoline engines are identified by an "S" and oils for diesel engines are identified by a "C." Most modern gasoline engines require SF or SG graded oil. Automotive and marine diesel engines use CC or CD graded oil.

Viscosity is an indication of the oil's thickness, or resistance to flow. The SAE uses numbers to indicate viscosity; thin oils have low numbers and thick oils have high numbers. A "W" after the number indicates that the viscosity testing was done at low temperature to simulate cold weather operation. Engine oils fall into the 5W-20W and 20-50 range.

Multi-grade oils (for example, 10W-40) are less viscous (thinner) at low temperatures and more viscous (thicker) at high temperatures. This allows the oil to perform efficiently across a wide range of engine operating temperatures.

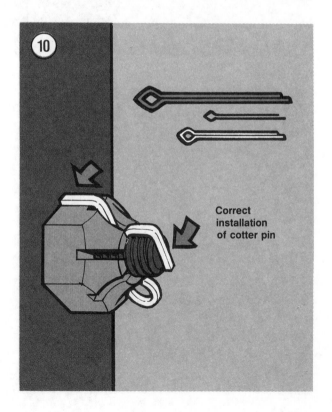

Correct installation of cotter pin

2-stroke Engine Oil

Lubrication for a 2-stroke engine is provided by oil mixed with the incoming fuel-air mixture. Some of the oil mist settles out in the crankcase, lubricating the crankshaft and lower end of the connecting rods. The rest of the oil enters the combustion chamber to lubricate the piston, rings and cylinder wall. This oil is then burned along with the fuel-air mixture during the combustion process.

Engine oil must have several special qualities to work well in a 2-stroke engine. It must mix easily and stay in suspension in gasoline. When burned, it can't leave behind excessive deposits. It must also be able to withstand the high temperatures associated with 2-stroke engines.

The National Marine Manufacturer's Association (NMMA) has set standards for oil used in 2-stroke, water-cooled engines. This is the NMMA TC-W (two-cycle, water-cooled) grade (**Figure 12**). The oil's performance in the following areas is evaluated:

a. Lubrication (prevention of wear and scuffing).
b. Spark plug fouling.
c. Preignition.
d. Piston ring sticking.
e. Piston varnish.
f. General engine condition (including deposits).
g. Exhaust port blockage.
h. Rust prevention.
i. Mixing ability with gasoline.

In addition to oil grade, manufacturers specify the ratio of gasoline to oil required during break-in and normal engine operation.

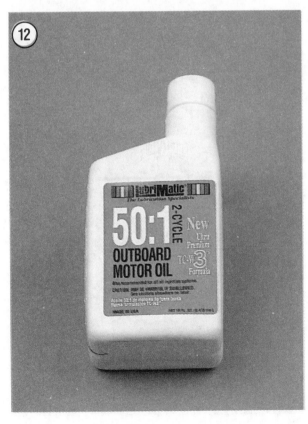

Gear Oil

Gear lubricants are assigned SAE viscosity numbers under the same system as 4-stroke engine oil. Gear lubricant falls into the SAE 72-250 range (**Figure 13**). Some gear lubricants are multi-grade; for example, SAE 85W-90.

Three types of marine gear lubricant are generally available: SAE 90 hypoid gear lubricant is designed for older manual-shift units; Type C gear lubricant contains additives designed for electric shift mechanisms; High viscosity gear lubricant is a heavier oil designed to withstand the shock loading of high-performance engines or units subjected to severe duty use. Always use a gear lubricant of the type specified by the unit's manufacturer.

Grease

Greases are graded by the National Lubricating Grease Institute (NLGI). Greases are graded by number according to the consistency of the grease; these ratings range from No. 000 to No. 6, with No. 6 being the most solid. A typical multipurpose grease is NLGI No. 2 (**Figure 14**). For specific applications, equipment manufacturers may require grease with an additive such as molybdenum disulfide (MOS^2).

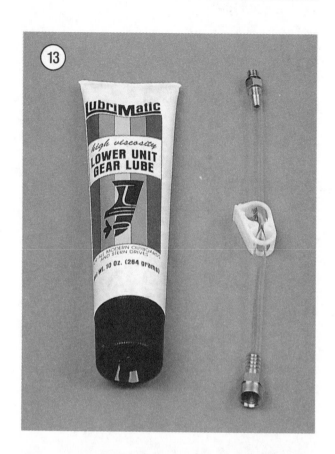

GASKET SEALANT

Gasket sealant is used instead of pre-formed gaskets on some applications, or as a gasket dressing on others. Two types of gasket sealant are commonly used: room temperature vulcanizing (RTV) and anaerobic. Because these two materials have different sealing properties, they cannot be used interchangeably.

RTV Sealant

This is a silicone gel supplied in tubes (**Figure 15**). Moisture in the air causes RTV to cure. Always place the cap on the tube as soon as possible when using RTV. RTV has a shelf life of one year and will not cure properly when the shelf life has expired. Check the expiration date

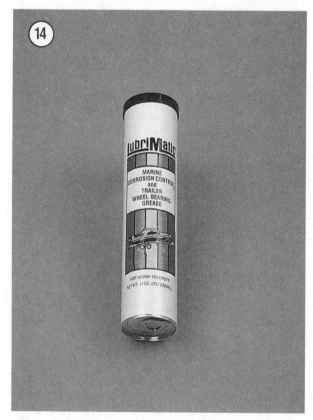

on RTV tubes before using and keep partially used tubes tightly sealed. RTV sealant can generally fill gaps up to 1/4 in. (6.3 mm) and works well on slightly flexible surfaces.

Applying RTV Sealant

Clean all gasket residue from mating surfaces. Surfaces should be clean and free of oil and dirt. Remove all RTV gasket material from blind attaching holes because it can create a "hydraulic" effect and affect bolt torque.

Apply RTV sealant in a continuous bead 2-3 mm (0.08-0.12 in.) thick. Circle all mounting holes unless otherwise specified. Torque mating parts within 10 minutes after application.

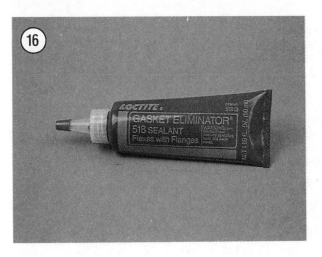

Anaerobic Sealant

This is a gel supplied in tubes (**Figure 16**). It cures only in the absence of air, as when squeezed tightly between two machined mating surfaces. For this reason, it will not spoil if the cap is left off the tube. It should not be used if one mating surface is flexible. Anaerobic sealant is able to fill gaps up to 0.030 in. (0.8 mm) and generally works best on rigid, machined flanges or surfaces.

Applying Anaerobic Sealant

Clean all gasket residue from mating surfaces. Surfaces must be clean and free of oil and dirt. Remove all gasket material from blind attaching holes, as it can cause a "hydraulic" effect and affect bolt torque.

Apply anaerobic sealant in a 1 mm or less (0.04 in.) bead to one sealing surface. Circle all mounting holes. Torque mating parts within 15 minutes after application.

GALVANIC CORROSION

A chemical reaction occurs whenever two different types of metal are joined by an electrical conductor and immersed in an electrolyte. Electrons transfer from one metal to the other through the electrolyte and return through the conductor.

The hardware on a boat is made of many different types of metal. The boat hull acts as a conductor between the metals. Even if the hull is wooden or fiberglass, the slightest film of water (electrolyte) within the hull provides conductivity. This combination creates a good environment for electron flow (**Figure 17**). Unfortunately, this electron flow results in galvanic corrosion of the metal involved, causing one of the metals to be corroded or eaten away by the process. The amount of electron flow (and, therefore, the amount of corrosion) depends on several factors:

a. The types of metal involved.

b. The efficiency of the conductor.

c. The strength of the electrolyte.

Metals

The chemical composition of the metals used in marine equipment has a significant effect on the amount and speed of galvanic corrosion. Certain metals are more resistant to corrosion than others. These electrically negative metals are commonly called "noble;" they act as the cathode in any reaction. Metals that are more subject to corrosion are electrically positive; they act as the anode in a reaction. The more noble metals include titanium, 18-8 stainless steel and nickel. Less noble metals include zinc, aluminum and magnesium. Galvanic corrosion

becomes more severe as the difference in electrical potential between the two metals increases.

In some cases, galvanic corrosion can occur within a single piece of metal. Common brass is a mixture of zinc and copper, and, when immersed in an electrolyte, the zinc portion of the mixture will corrode away as reaction occurs between the zinc and the copper particles.

Conductors

The hull of the boat often acts as the conductor between different types of metal. Marine equipment, such as an outboard motor or stern drive unit, can also act as the conductor. Large masses of metal, firmly connected together, are more efficient conductors than water. Rubber mountings and vinyl-based paint can act as insulators between pieces of metal.

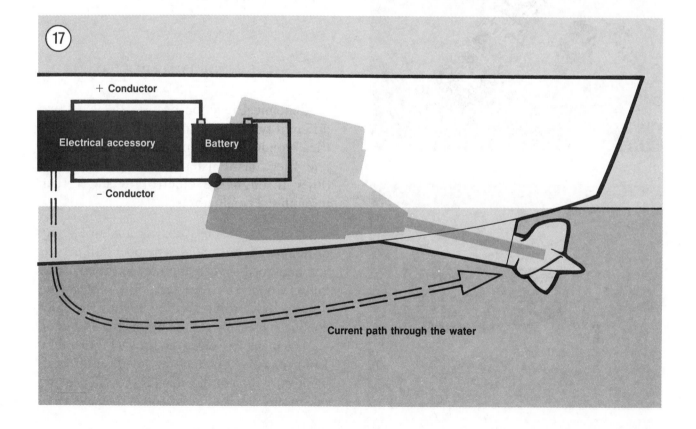

Electrolyte

The water in which a boat operates acts as the electrolyte for the galvanic corrosion process. The better a conductor the electrolyte is, the more severe and rapid the corrosion.

Cold, clean freshwater is the poorest electrolyte. As water temperature increases, its conductivity increases. Pollutants will increase conductivity; brackish or saltwater is also an efficient electrolyte. This is one of the reasons that most manufacturers recommend a freshwater flush for marine equipment after operation in saltwater, polluted or brackish water.

PROTECTION FROM GALVANIC CORROSION

Because of the environment in which marine equipment must operate, it is practically impossible to totally prevent galvanic corrosion. There are several ways by which the process can be slowed. After taking these precautions, the next step is to "fool" the process into occurring only where *you* want it to occur. This is the role of sacrificial anodes and impressed current systems.

Slowing Corrosion

Some simple precautions can help reduce the amount of corrosion taking place outside the hull. These are *not* a substitute for the corrosion protection methods discussed under *Sacrificial Anodes* and *Impressed Current Systems* in this chapter, but they can help these protection methods do their job.

Use fasteners of a metal more noble than the part they are fastening. If corrosion occurs, the larger equipment will suffer but the fastener will be protected. Because fasteners are usually very small in comparison to the equipment being fastened, the equipment can survive the loss of material. If the fastener were to corrode instead of the equipment, major problems could arise.

Keep all painted surfaces in good condition. If paint is scraped off and bare metal exposed, corrosion will rapidly increase. Use a vinyl- or plastic-based paint, which acts as an electrical insulator.

Be careful when using metal-based antifouling paints. These should not be applied to metal parts of the boat, outboard motor or stern drive unit or they will actually react with the equipment, causing corrosion between the equipment and the layer of paint. Organic-based paints are available for use on metal surfaces.

Where a corrosion protection device is used, remember that it must be immersed in the electrolyte along with the rest of the boat to have any effect. If you raise the power unit out of the water when the boat is docked, any anodes on the power unit will be removed from the corrosion cycle and will not protect the rest of the equipment that is still immersed. Also, such corrosion protection devices must not be painted because this would insulate them from the corrosion process.

Any change in the boat's equipment, such as the installation of a new stainless steel propeller, will change the electrical potential and could cause increased corrosion. Keep in mind that when you add new equipment or change materials, you should review your corrosion protection system to be sure it is up to the job.

Sacrificial Anodes

Anodes are usually made of zinc, a far from noble metal. Sacrificial anodes are specially designed to do nothing but corrode. Properly fastening such pieces to the boat will cause them to act as the anode in *any* galvanic reaction that occurs; any other metal present will act as the cathode and will not be damaged.

Anodes must be used properly to be effective. Simply fastening pieces of zinc to your boat in random locations won't do the job.

You must determine how much anode surface area is required to adequately protect the equipment's surface area. A good starting point is provided by Military Specification MIL-A-818001, which states that one square inch of new anode will protect either:

a. 800 square inches of freshly painted steel.
b. 250 square inches of bare steel or bare aluminum alloy.
c. 100 square inches of copper or copper alloy.

This rule is for a boat at rest. When underway, more anode area is required to protect the same equipment surface area.

The anode must be fastened so that it has good electrical contact with the metal to be protected. If possible, the anode can be attached directly to the other metal. If that is not possible, the entire network of metal parts in the boat should be electrically bonded together so that all pieces are protected.

Good quality anodes have inserts of some other metal around the fastener holes. Otherwise, the anode could erode away around the fastener. The anode can then become loose or even fall off, removing all protection.

Another Military Specification (MIL-A-18001) defines the type of alloy preferred that will corrode at a uniform rate without forming a crust that could reduce its efficiency after a time.

Impressed Current Systems

An impressed current system can be installed on any boat that has a battery. The system consists of an anode, a control box and a sensor. The anode in this system is coated with a very noble metal, such as platinum, so that it is almost corrosion-free and will last indefinitely. The sensor, under the boat's waterline, monitors the potential for corrosion. When it senses that

corrosion could be occurring, it transmits this information to the control box.

The control box connects the boat's battery to the anode. When the sensor signals the need, the control box applies positive battery voltage to the anode. Current from the battery flows from the anode to all other metal parts of the boat, no matter how noble or non-noble these parts may be. This battery current takes the place of any galvanic current flow.

Only a very small amount of battery current is needed to counteract galvanic corrosion. Manufacturers estimate that it would take two or three months of constant use to drain a typical marine battery, assuming the battery is never recharged.

An impressed current system is more expensive to install than simple anodes but, considering its low maintenance requirements and the excellent protection it provides, the long-term cost may actually be lower.

PROPELLERS

The propeller is the final link between the boat's drive system and the water. A perfectly

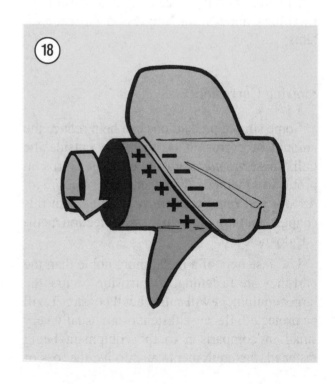

maintained engine and hull are useless if the propeller is the wrong type or has been allowed to deteriorate. Although propeller selection for a specific situation is beyond the scope of this book, the following information on propeller construction and design will allow you to discuss the subject intelligently with your marine dealer.

How a Propeller Works

As the curved blades of a propeller rotate through the water, a high-pressure area is created on one side of the blade and a low-pressure area exists on the other side of the blade (**Figure 18**). The propeller moves toward the low-pressure area, carrying the boat with it.

Propeller Parts

Although a propeller may be a one-piece unit, it is made up of several different parts (**Figure 19**). Variations in the design of these parts make different propellers suitable for different jobs.

The blade tip is the point on the blade farthest from the center of the propeller hub. The blade

tip separates the leading edge from the trailing edge.

The leading edge is the edge of the blade nearest to the boat. During normal rotation, this is the area of the blade that first cuts through the water.

The trailing edge is the edge of the blade farthest from the boat.

The blade face is the surface of the blade that faces away from the boat. During normal rotation, high pressure exists on this side of the blade.

The blade back is the surface of the blade that faces toward the boat. During normal rotation, low pressure exists on this side of the blade.

The cup is a small curve or lip on the trailing edge of the blade.

The hub is the central portion of the propeller. It connects the blades to the propeller shaft (part of the boat's drive system). On some drive systems, engine exhaust is routed through the hub; in this case, the hub is made up of an outer and an inner portion, connected by ribs.

The diffuser ring is used on through-hub exhaust models to prevent exhaust gases from entering the blade area.

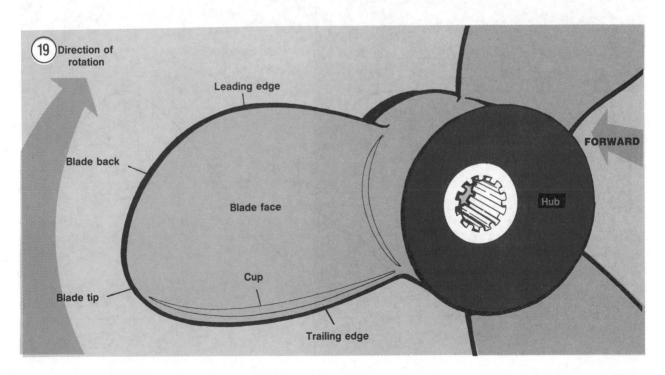

19   Direction of rotation

Leading edge

Blade back

Blade face

FORWARD

Hub

Cup

Blade tip

Trailing edge

Propeller Design

Changes in length, angle, thickness and material of propeller parts make different propellers suitable for different situations.

Diameter

Propeller diameter is the distance from the center of the hub to the blade tip, multiplied by

2. That is, it is the diameter of the circle formed by the blade tips during propeller rotation (**Figure 20**).

Pitch and rake

Propeller pitch and rake describe the placement of the blade in relation to the hub (**Figure 21**).

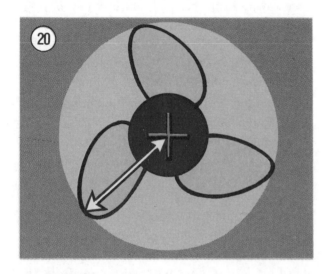

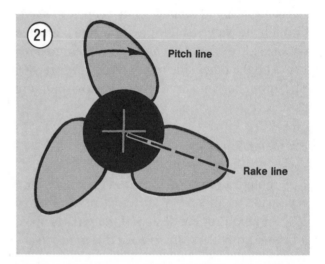

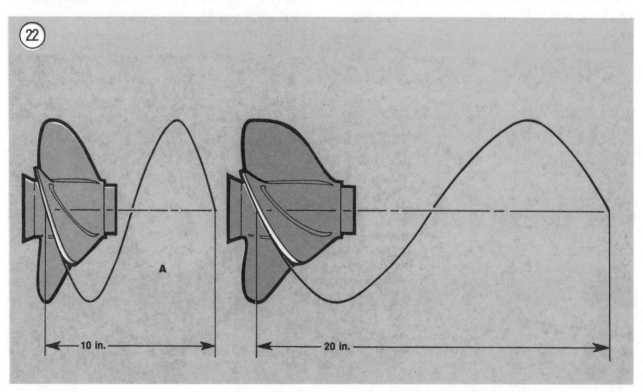

Pitch is expressed by the theoretical distance that the propeller would travel in one revolution. In A, **Figure 22**, the propeller would travel 10 inches in one revolution. In B, **Figure 22**, the propeller would travel 20 inches in one revolution. This distance is only theoretical; during actual operation, the propeller achieves about 80% of its rated travel.

Propeller blades can be constructed with constant pitch (**Figure 23**) or progressive pitch (**Figure 24**). Progressive pitch starts low at the leading edge and increases toward to trailing edge. The propeller pitch specification is the average of the pitch across the entire blade.

Blade rake is specified in degrees and is measured along a line from the center of the hub to the blade tip. A blade that is perpendicular to the hub (A, **Figure 25**) has 0° of rake. A blade that is angled from perpendicular (B, **Figure 25**) has a rake expressed by its difference from perpen-

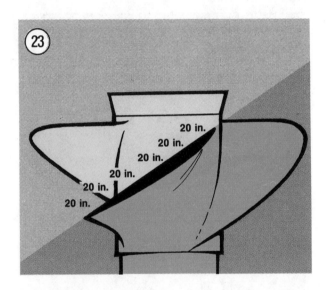

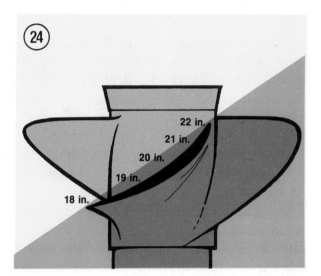

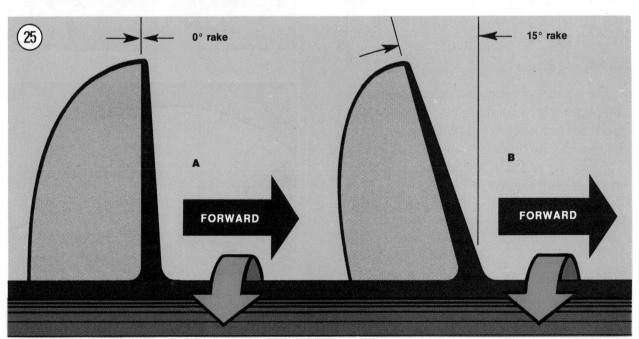

dicular. Most propellers have rakes ranging from 0-20°.

Blade thickness

Blade thickness is not uniform at all points along the blade. For efficiency, blades should be as thin as possible at all points while retaining enough strength to move the boat. Blades tend to be thicker where they meet the hub and thinner at the blade tip (**Figure 26**). This is to support the heavier loads at the hub section of the blade. This thickness is dependent on the strength of the material used.

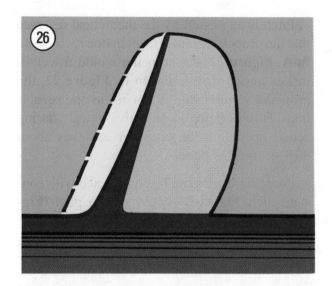

When cut along a line from the leading edge to the trailing edge in the central portion of the blade (**Figure 27**), the propeller blade resembles an airplane wing. The blade face, where high pressure exists during normal rotation, is almost flat. The blade back, where low pressure exists during normal rotation, is curved, with the thinnest portions at the edges and the thickest portion at the center.

Propellers that run only partially submerged, as in racing applications, may have a wedge-shaped cross-section (**Figure 28**). The leading edge is very thin; the blade thickness increases toward the trailing edge, where it is the thickest. If a propeller such as this is run totally submerged, it is very inefficient.

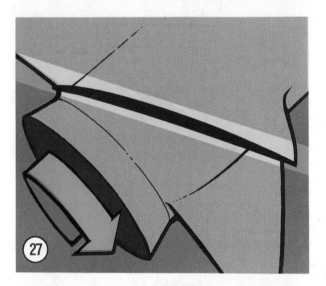

Number of blades

The number of blades used on a propeller is a compromise between efficiency and vibration. A one-blade propeller would be the most efficient, but it would also create high levels of vibration. As blades are added, efficiency decreases, but so do vibration levels. Most propellers have three blades, representing the most practical trade-off between efficiency and vibration.

Material

Propeller materials are chosen for strength, corrosion resistance and economy. Stainless steel, aluminum and bronze are the most commonly used materials. Bronze is quite strong but

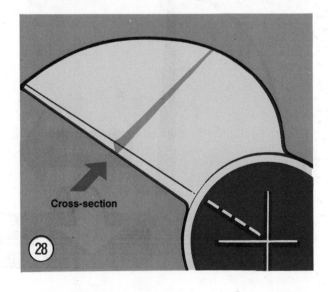

Cross-section

rather expensive. Stainless steel is more common than bronze because of its combination of strength and lower cost. Aluminum alloys are the least expensive but usually lack the strength of steel. Plastic propellers may be used in some low horsepower applications.

Direction of rotation

Propellers are made for both right-hand and left-hand rotation although right-hand is the most commonly used. When seen from behind the boat in forward motion, a right-hand propeller turns clockwise and a left-hand propeller turns counterclockwise. Off the boat, you can tell the difference by observing the angle of the blades (**Figure 29**). A right-hand propeller's blades slant from the upper left to the lower right; a left-hand propeller's blades are the opposite.

Cavitation and Ventilation

Cavitation and ventilation are *not* interchangeable terms; they refer to two distinct problems encountered during propeller operation.

To understand cavitation, you must first understand the relationship between pressure and the boiling point of water. At sea level, water will boil at 212° F. As pressure increases, such as within an engine's closed cooling system, the boiling point of water increases—it will boil at some temperature higher than 212° F. The opposite is also true. As pressure decreases, water will boil at a temperature lower than 212° F. If pressure drops low enough, water will boil at typical ambient temperatures of 50-60° F.

We have said that, during normal propeller operation, low-pressure exists on the blade back. Normally, the pressure does not drop low enough for boiling to occur. However, poor blade design

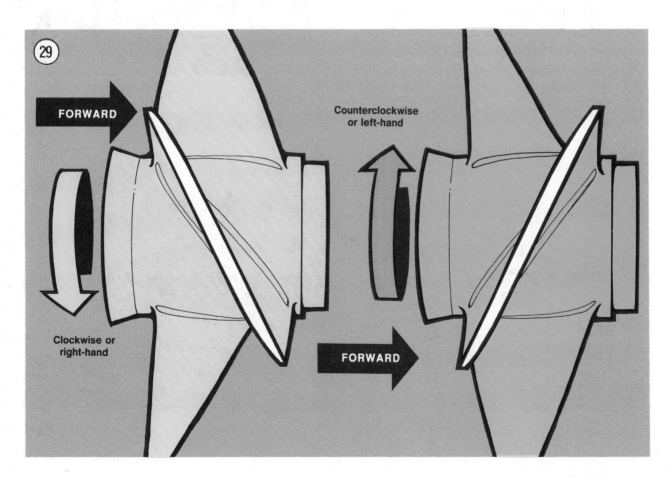

or selection, or blade damage can cause an un-usual pressure drop on a small area of the blade (**Figure 30**). Boiling can occur in this small area. As the water boils, air bubbles form. As the boiling water passes to a higher pressure area of the blade, the boiling stops and the bubbles col-lapse. The collapsing bubbles release enough energy to erode the surface of the blade.

This entire process of pressure drop, boiling and bubble collapse is called "cavitation." The damage caused by the collapsing bubbles is called a "cavi-tation burn." It is important to remember that cavi-tation is caused by a decrease in pressure, *not* an increase in temperature.

Ventilation is not as complex a process as cavi-tation. Ventilation refers to air entering the blade area, either from above the surface of the water or from a through-hub exhaust system. As the blades meet the air, the propeller momentarily over-revs, losing most of its thrust. An added complication is that as the propeller over-revs, pressure on the blade back decreases and massive cavitation can occur.

Most pieces of marine equipment have a plate above the propeller area designed to keep surface air from entering the blade area (**Figure 31**). This plate is correctly called an "antiventilation plate," although you will often *see* it called an "anticavitation plate." Through hub exhaust sys-tems also have specially designed hubs to keep exhaust gases from entering the blade area.

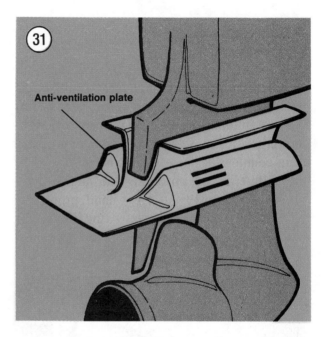

Anti-ventilation plate

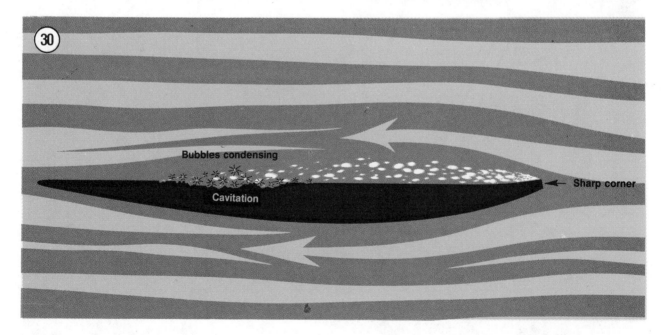

Bubbles condensing

Cavitation

Sharp corner

Chapter Two

Tools and Techniques

This chapter describes the common tools required for marine equipment repairs and troubleshooting. Techniques that will make your work easier and more effective are also described. Some of the procedures in this book require special skills or expertise; in some cases, you are better off entrusting the job to a dealer or qualified specialist.

SAFETY FIRST

Professional mechanics can work for years and never suffer a serious injury. If you follow a few rules of common sense and safety, you too can enjoy many safe hours servicing your marine equipment. If you ignore these rules, you can hurt yourself or damage the equipment.

1. Never use gasoline as a cleaning solvent.
2. Never smoke or use a torch near flammable liquids, such as cleaning solvent. If you are working in your home garage, remember that your home gas appliances have pilot lights.
3. Never smoke or use a torch in an area where batteries are being charged. Highly explosive hydrogen gas is formed during the charging process.

4. Use the proper size wrenches to avoid damage to fasteners and injury to yourself.
5. When loosening a tight or stuck fastener, think of what would happen if the wrench should slip. Protect yourself accordingly.
6. Keep your work area clean, uncluttered and well lighted.
7. Wear safety goggles during all operations involving drilling, grinding or the use of a cold chisel.
8. Never use worn tools.
9. Keep a Coast Guard approved fire extinguisher handy. Be sure it is rated for gasoline (Class B) and electrical (Class C) fires.

BASIC HAND TOOLS

A number of tools are required to maintain marine equipment. You may already have some of these tools for home or car repairs. There are also tools made especially for marine equipment repairs; these you will have to purchase. In any case, a wide variety of quality tools will make repairs easier and more effective.

Keep your tools clean and in a tool box. Keep them organized with the sockets and related drives together, the open end and box wrenches together, etc. After using a tool, wipe off dirt and grease with a clean cloth and place the tool in its correct place.

The following tools are required to perform virtually any repair job. Each tool is described and the recommended size given for starting a tool collection. Additional tools and some duplications may be added as you become more familiar with the equipment. You may need all standard U.S. size tools, all metric size tools or a mixture of both.

Screwdrivers

The screwdriver is a very basic tool, but if used improperly, it will do more damage than good. The slot on a screw has a definite dimension and shape. A screwdriver must be selected to conform with that shape. Use a small screwdriver for small screws and a large one for large screws or the screw head will be damaged.

Two types of screwdriver are commonly required: a common (flat-blade) screwdriver (**Figure 1**) and Phillips screwdrivers (**Figure 2**).

Screwdrivers are available in sets, which often include an assortment of common and Phillips blades. If you buy them individually, buy at least the following:

a. Common screwdriver—5/16 × 6 in. blade.
b. Common screwdriver—3/8 × 12 in. blade.
c. Phillips screwdriver—size 2 tip, 6 in. blade.

Use screwdrivers only for driving screws. Never use a screwdriver for prying or chiseling. Do not try to remove a Phillips or Allen head screw with a common screwdriver; you can damage the head so that the proper tool will be unable to remove it.

Keep screwdrivers in the proper condition and they will last longer and perform better. Always keep the tip of a common screwdriver in good condition. **Figure 3** shows how to grind the tip to the proper shape if it becomes damaged. Note the parallel sides of the tip.

Pliers

Pliers come in a wide range of types and sizes. Pliers are useful for cutting, bending and crimping. They should never be used to cut hardened objects or to turn bolts or nuts. **Figure 4** shows several types of pliers.

Each type of pliers has a specialized function. General purpose pliers are used mainly for holding things and for bending. Locking pliers are used as pliers or to hold objects very tightly, like a vise. Needlenose pliers are used to hold or bend small objects. Adjustable or slip-joint pliers can

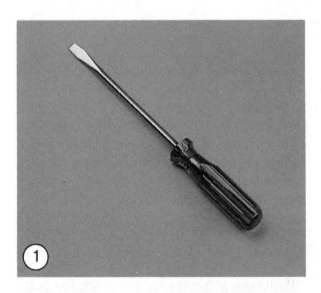

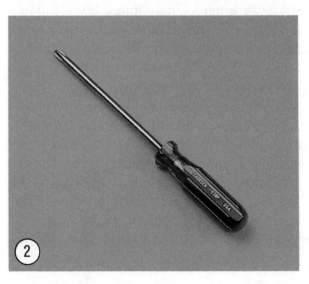

be adjusted to hold various sizes of objects; the jaws remain parallel to grip around objects such as pipe or tubing. There are many more types of pliers. The ones described here are the most commonly used.

Box and Open-end Wrenches

Box and open-end wrenches are available in sets or separately in a variety of sizes. See **Figure 5** and **Figure 6**. The number stamped near the end refers to the distance between two parallel flats on the hex head bolt or nut.

Box wrenches are usually superior to open-end wrenches. An open-end wrench grips the nut on only two flats. Unless it fits well, it may slip and round off the points on the nut. The box wrench grips all 6 flats. Both 6-point and 12-point openings on box wrenches are available. The 6-point gives superior holding power; the 12-point allows a shorter swing.

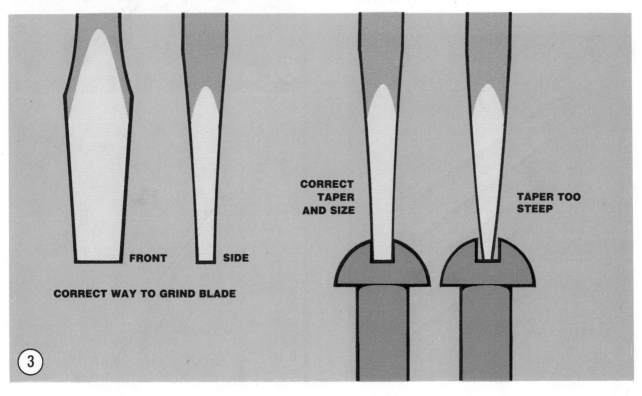

FRONT   SIDE

CORRECT WAY TO GRIND BLADE

CORRECT TAPER AND SIZE

TAPER TOO STEEP

Combination wrenches, which are open on one side and boxed on the other, are also available. Both ends are the same size.

Adjustable Wrenches

An adjustable wrench can be adjusted to fit nearly any nut or bolt head. See **Figure 7**. However, it can loosen and slip, causing damage to the nut and maybe to your knuckles. Use an adjustable wrench only when other wrenches are not available.

Adjustable wrenches come in sizes ranging from 4-18 in. overall. A 6 or 8 in. wrench is recommended as an all-purpose wrench.

Socket Wrenches

This type is undoubtedly the fastest, safest and most convenient to use. See **Figure 8**. Sockets, which attach to a suitable handle, are available with 6-point or 12-point openings and use 1/4, 3/8 and 3/4 inch drives. The drive size indicates

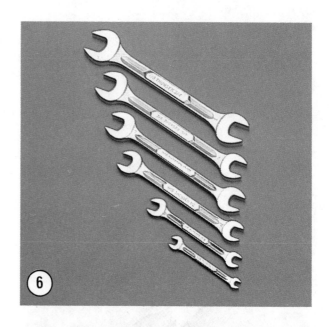

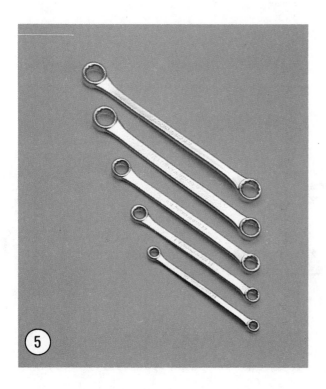

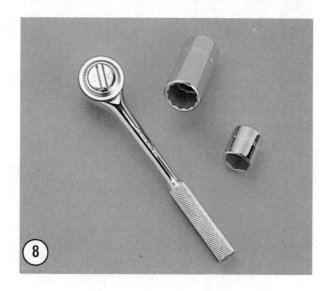

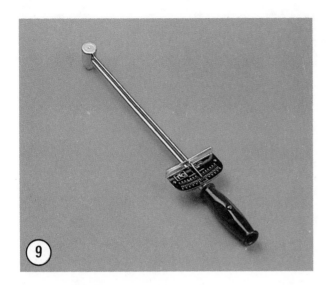

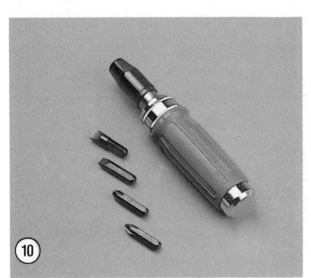

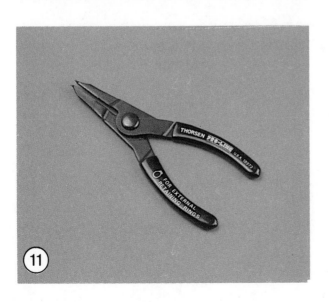

the size of the square hole that mates with the ratchet or flex handle.

Torque Wrench

A torque wrench (**Figure 9**) is used with a socket to measure how tight a nut or bolt is installed. They come in a wide price range and with either 3/8 or 1/2 in. square drive. The drive size indicates the size of the square drive that mates with the socket. Purchase one that measures up to 150 ft.-lb. (203 N•m).

Impact Driver

This tool (**Figure 10**) makes removal of tight fasteners easy and eliminates damage to bolts and screw slots. Impact drivers and interchangeable bits are available at most large hardware and auto parts stores.

Circlip Pliers

Circlip pliers (sometimes referred to as snap-ring pliers) are necessary to remove circlips. See **Figure 11**. Circlip pliers usually come with several different size tips; many designs can be switched from internal type to external type.

Hammers

The correct hammer is necessary for repairs. Use only a hammer with a face (or head) of rubber or plastic or the soft-faced type that is filled with buckshot (**Figure 12**). These are sometimes necessary in engine tear-downs. *Never* use a metal-faced hammer as severe damage will result in most cases. You can always produce the same amount of force with a soft-faced hammer.

Feeler Gauge

This tool has either flat or wire measuring gauges (**Figure 13**). Wire gauges are used to measure spark plug gap; flat gauges are used for all other measurements. A non-magnetic (brass) gauge may be specified when working around magnetized parts.

Other Special Tools

Some procedures require special tools; these are identified in the appropriate chapter. Unless otherwise specified, the part number used in this book to identify a special tool is the marine equipment manufacturer's part number.

Special tools can usually be purchased through your marine equipment dealer. Some can be made locally by a machinist, often at a much lower price. You may find certain special tools at tool rental dealers. Don't use makeshift tools if you can't locate the correct special tool; you will probably cause more damage than good.

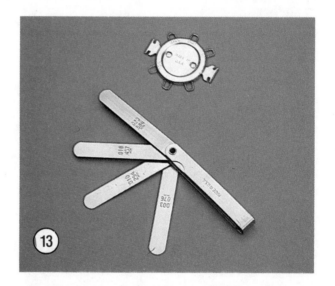

TEST EQUIPMENT

Multimeter

This instrument (**Figure 14**) is invaluable for electrical system troubleshooting and service. It combines a voltmeter, an ohmmeter and an ammeter into one unit, so it is often called a VOM.

Two types of multimeter are available, analog and digital. Analog meters have a moving needle with marked bands indicating the volt, ohm and amperage scales. The digital meter (DVOM) is ideally suited for troubleshooting because it is easy to read, more accurate than analog, contains internal overload protection, is auto-ranging (analog meters must be recalibrated each time the scale is changed) and has automatic polarity compensation.

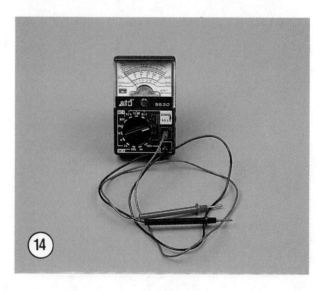

2

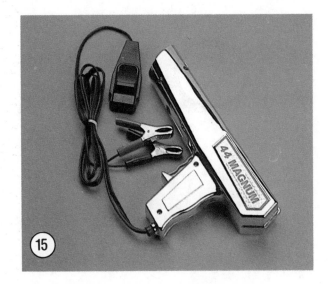

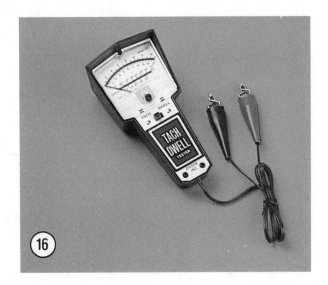

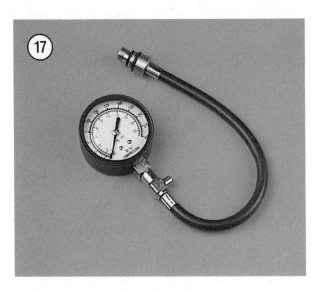

Strobe Timing Light

This instrument is necessary for dynamic tuning (setting ignition timing while the engine is running). By flashing a light at the precise instant the spark plug fires, the position of the timing mark can be seen. The flashing light makes a moving mark appear to stand still opposite a stationary mark.

Suitable lights range from inexpensive neon bulb types to powerful xenon strobe lights. See **Figure 15**. A light with an inductive pickup is best because it eliminates any possible damage to ignition wiring.

Tachometer/Dwell Meter

A portable tachometer is necessary for tuning. See **Figure 16**. Ignition timing and carburetor adjustments must be performed at the specified idle speed. The best instrument for this purpose is one with a low range of 0-1000 or 0-2000 rpm and a high range of 0-6000 rpm. Extended range (0-6000 or 0-8000 rpm) instruments lack accuracy at lower speeds. The instrument should be capable of detecting changes of 25 rpm on the low range.

A dwell meter is often combined with a tachometer. Dwell meters are used with breaker point ignition systems to measure the amount of time the points remain closed during engine operation.

Compression Gauge

This tool (**Figure 17**) measures the amount of pressure present in the engine's combustion chamber during the compression stroke. This indicates general engine condition. Compression readings can be interpreted along with vacuum gauge readings to pinpoint specific engine mechanical problems.

The easiest type to use has screw-in adapters that fit into the spark plug holes. Press-in rubber-tipped types are also available.

Vacuum Gauge

The vacuum gauge (**Figure 18**) measures the intake manifold vacuum created by the engine's intake stroke. Manifold and valve problems (on 4-stroke engines) can be identified by interpreting the readings. When combined with compression gauge readings, other engine problems can be diagnosed.

Some vacuum gauges can also be used as fuel pressure gauges to trace fuel system problems.

Hydrometer

Battery electrolyte specific gravity is measured with a hydrometer (**Figure 19**). The specific gravity of the electrolyte indicates the battery's state of charge. The best type has automatic temperature compensation; otherwise, you must calculate the compensation yourself.

Precision Measuring Tools

Various tools are needed to make precision measurements. A dial indicator (**Figure 20**), for example, is used to determine run-out of rotating parts and end play of parts assemblies. A dial indicator can also be used to precisely measure piston position in relation to top dead center; some engines require this measurement for ignition timing adjustment.

Vernier calipers (**Figure 21**) and micrometers (**Figure 22**) are other precision measuring tools used to determine the size of parts (such as piston diameter).

Precision measuring equipment must be stored, handled and used carefully or it will not remain accurate.

SERVICE HINTS

Most of the service procedures covered in this manual are straightforward and can be performed by anyone reasonably handy with tools.

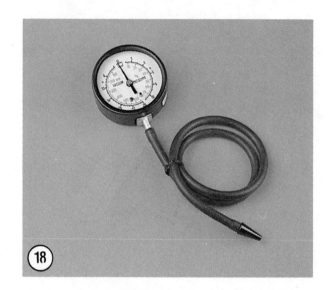

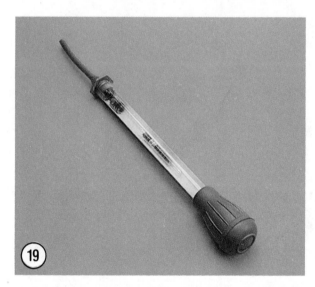

It is suggested, however, that you consider your own skills and toolbox carefully before attempting any operation involving major disassembly of the engine or gearcase.

Some operations, for example, require the use of a press. It would be wiser to have these performed by a shop equipped for such work, rather than trying to do the job yourself with makeshift equipment. Other procedures require precise measurements. Unless you have the skills and

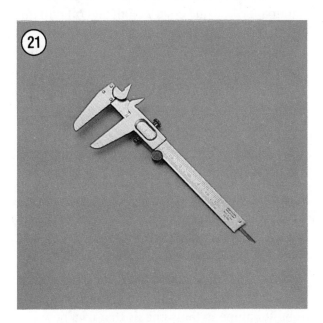

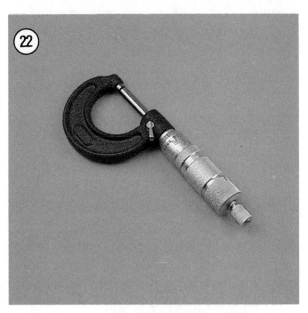

equipment required, it would be better to have a qualified repair shop make the measurements for you.

Preparation for Disassembly

Repairs go much faster and easier if the equipment is clean before you begin work. There are special cleaners, such as Gunk or Bel-Ray Degreaser, for washing the engine and related parts. Just spray or brush on the cleaning solution, let it stand, then rinse away with a garden hose. Clean all oily or greasy parts with cleaning solvent as you remove them.

> *WARNING*
> *Never use gasoline as a cleaning agent. It presents an extreme fire hazard. Be sure to work in a well-ventilated area when using cleaning solvent. Keep a Coast Guard approved fire extinguisher, rated for gasoline fires, handy in any case.*

Much of the labor charged for repairs made by dealers is for the removal and disassembly of other parts to reach the defective unit. It is frequently possible to perform the preliminary operations yourself and then take the defective unit in to the dealer for repair.

If you decide to tackle the job yourself, read the entire section in this manual that pertains to it, making sure you have identified the proper one. Study the illustrations and text until you have a good idea of what is involved in completing the job satisfactorily. If special tools or replacement parts are required, make arrangements to get them before you start. It is frustrating and time-consuming to get partly into a job and then be unable to complete it.

Disassembly Precautions

During disassembly of parts, keep a few general precautions in mind. Force is rarely needed to get things apart. If parts are a tight fit, such as a bearing in a case, there is usually a tool designed to separate them. Never use a screwdriver to pry apart parts with machined surfaces (such as cylinder heads and crankcases). You will mar the surfaces and end up with leaks.

Make diagrams (or take an instant picture) wherever similar-appearing parts are found. For example, head and crankcase bolts are often not the same length. You may think you can remember where everything came from, but mistakes are costly. There is also the possibility you may be sidetracked and not return to work for days or even weeks. In the interval, carefully laid out parts may have been disturbed.

Cover all openings after removing parts to keep small parts, dirt or other contamination from entering.

Tag all similar internal parts for location and direction. All internal components should be re-installed in the same location and direction from which removed. Record the number and thickness of any shims as they are removed. Small parts, such as bolts, can be identified by placing them in plastic sandwich bags. Seal and label them with masking tape.

Wiring should be tagged with masking tape and marked as each wire is removed. Again, do not rely on memory alone.

Protect finished surfaces from physical damage or corrosion. Keep gasoline off painted surfaces.

Assembly Precautions

No parts, except those assembled with a press fit, require unusual force during assembly. If a part is hard to remove or install, find out why before proceeding.

When assembling two parts, start all fasteners, then tighten evenly in an alternating or crossing pattern if no specific tightening sequence is given.

When assembling parts, be sure all shims and washers are installed exactly as they came out.

Whenever a rotating part butts against a stationary part, look for a shim or washer. Use new gaskets if there is any doubt about the condition of the old ones. Unless otherwise specified, a thin coat of oil on gaskets may help them seal effectively.

Heavy grease can be used to hold small parts in place if they tend to fall out during assembly. However, keep grease and oil away from electrical components.

High spots may be sanded off a piston with sandpaper, but fine emery cloth and oil will do a much more professional job.

Carbon can be removed from the cylinder head, the piston crown and the exhaust port with a dull screwdriver. *Do not* scratch either surface. Wipe off the surface with a clean cloth when finished.

The carburetor is best cleaned by disassembling it and soaking the parts in a commercial carburetor cleaner. Never soak gaskets and rubber parts in these cleaners. Never use wire to clean out jets and air passages; they are easily damaged. Use compressed air to blow out the carburetor *after* the float has been removed.

Take your time and do the job right. Do not forget that the break-in procedure on a newly rebuilt engine is the same as that of a new one. Use the break-in oil recommendations and follow other instructions given in your owner's manual.

SPECIAL TIPS

Because of the extreme demands placed on marine equipment, several points should be kept in mind when performing service and repair. The following items are general suggestions that may improve the overall life of the machine and help avoid costly failures.

1. Unless otherwise specified, use a locking compound, such as Loctite Threadlocker, on all bolts and nuts, even if they are secured with lockwashers. Be sure to use the specified grade

of thread locking compound. A screw or bolt lost from an engine cover or bearing retainer could easily cause serious and expensive damage before its loss is noticed.

When applying thread locking compound, use a small amount. If too much is used, it can work its way down the threads and stick parts together that were not meant to be stuck together.

Keep a tube of thread locking compound in your tool box; when used properly, it is cheap insurance.

2. Use a hammer-driven impact tool to remove and install screws and bolts. These tools help prevent the rounding off of bolt heads and screw slots and ensure a tight installation.

3. When straightening the fold-over type lock-washer, use a wide-blade chisel, such as an old and dull wood chisel. Such a tool provides a better purchase on the folded tab, making straightening easier.

4. When installing the fold-over type lock-washer, always use a new washer if possible. If a new washer is not available, always fold over a part of the washer that has not been previously folded. Reusing the same fold may cause the washer to break, resulting in the loss of its locking ability and a loose piece of metal adrift in the engine.

When folding the washer, start the fold with a screwdriver and finish it with a pair of pliers. If a punch is used to make the fold, the fold may be too sharp, thereby increasing the chances of the washer breaking under stress.

These washers are relatively inexpensive and it is suggested that you keep several of each size in your tool box for repairs.

5. When replacing missing or broken fasteners (bolts, nuts and screws), always use authorized replacement parts. They are specially hardened for each application. The wrong 50-cent bolt could easily cause serious and expensive damage.

6. When installing gaskets, always use authorized replacement gaskets *without* sealer, unless designated. Many gaskets are designed to swell when they come in contact with oil. Gasket sealer will prevent the gaskets from swelling as intended and can result in oil leaks. Authorized replacement gaskets are cut from material of the precise thickness needed. Installation of a too thick or too thin gasket in a critical area could cause equipment damage.

MECHANIC'S TECHNIQUES

Removing Frozen Fasteners

When a fastener rusts and cannot be removed, several methods may be used to loosen it. First, apply penetrating oil, such as Liquid Wrench or WD-40 (available at any hardware or auto supply store). Apply it liberally and allow it penetrate for 10-15 minutes. Tap the fastener several times with a small hammer; do not hit it hard enough to cause damage. Reapply the penetrating oil if necessary.

For frozen screws, apply penetrating oil as described, then insert a screwdriver in the slot and tap the top of the screwdriver with a hammer. This loosens the rust so the screw can be removed in the normal way. If the screw head is too chewed up to use a screwdriver, grip the head with locking pliers and twist the screw out.

Avoid applying heat unless specifically instructed because it may melt, warp or remove the temper from parts.

Remedying Stripped Threads

Occasionally, threads are stripped through carelessness or impact damage. Often the threads can be cleaned up by running a tap (for internal threads on nuts) or die (for external threads on bolts) through threads. See **Figure 23**.

Removing Broken Screws or Bolts

When the head breaks off a screw or bolt, several methods are available for removing the remaining portion.

If a large portion of the remainder projects out, try gripping it with vise-grip pliers. If the projecting portion is too small, file it to fit a wrench or cut a slot in it to fit a screwdriver. See **Figure 24**.

If the head breaks off flush, use a screw extractor. To do this, centerpunch the remaining portion of the screw or bolt. Drill a small hole in the screw and tap the extractor into the hole. Back the screw out with a wrench on the extractor. See **Figure 25**.

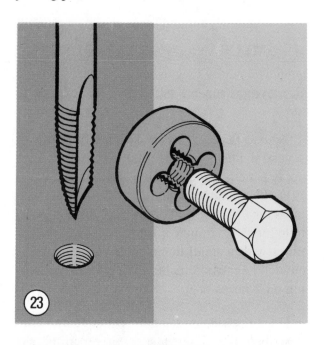

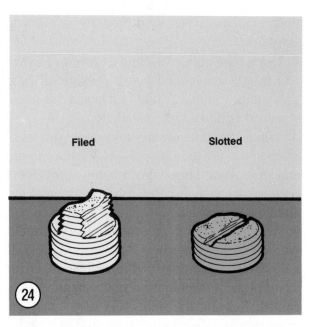

Filed   Slotted

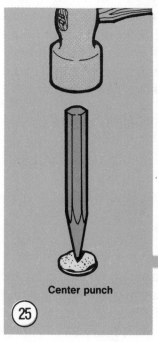

Center punch

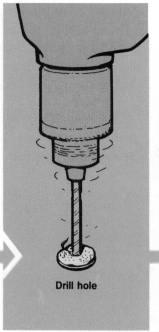

Drill hole

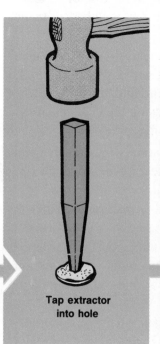

Tap extractor
into hole

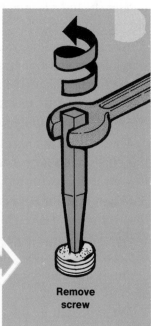

Remove
screw

Chapter Three

Troubleshooting

Troubleshooting is a relatively simple matter when it is done logically. The first step in any troubleshooting procedure is to define the symptoms as closely as possible and then localize the problem. Subsequent steps involve testing and analyzing those areas which could cause the symptoms. A haphazard approach may eventually solve the problem, but it can be very costly in terms of wasted time and unnecessary parts replacement.

Proper lubrication, maintenance and periodic tune-ups as described in Chapter Four will reduce the necessity for troubleshooting. Even with the best of care, however, an outboard motor is prone to problems which will require troubleshooting. This chapter contains brief descriptions of each operating system and troubleshooting procedures to be used. **Table 1** gives Mercury model designations. **Table 2** provides starter draw specifications. **Tables 3-6** present typical problems with their probable causes and solutions. **Tables 1-6** are at the end of the chapter.

OPERATING REQUIREMENTS

Every outboard motor requires 3 basic things to run properly: an uninterrupted supply of fuel and air in the correct proportions, proper ignition at the right time and adequate compression. If any of these are lacking, the motor will not run. The electrical system is the weakest link in the chain. More problems result from electrical malfunctions than from any other source. Keep this in mind before you blame the fuel system and start making unnecessary carburetor adjustments.

If a motor has been sitting for any length of time and refuses to start, check the condition of the battery first to make sure it has an adequate charge, then look to the fuel delivery system. This includes the gas tank, fuel pump, fuel lines and carburetor(s). Rust may have formed in the tank, obstructing fuel flow. Gasoline deposits may have gummed up carburetor jets and air passages. Gasoline tends to lose its potency after standing for long periods. Condensation may contaminate it with water. Drain the old gas and try starting with a fresh tankful.

STARTING SYSTEM

Description

High compression, multi-cylinder outboard motors use an electric starter motor (**Figure 1**). The motor is mounted vertically on the engine. When battery current is supplied to the starter motor, its pinion gear is thrust upward to engage the teeth on the engine flywheel (**Figure 2**). Once the engine starts, the pinion gear disengages from the flywheel. This is similar to the method used in cranking an automotive engine.

The starting system requires a fully charged battery to provide the large amount of electrical current required to operate the starter motor. The battery may be charged externally or by an alternator on the engine which will keep the battery charged while the engine is running.

The charging circuit on outboards equipped with a starter motor consists of the battery, an ignition switch, a solenoid to carry the heavy electrical current to the motor (**Figure 3**) and the starter motor. Turning the ignition switch to the START allows current to flow through the solenoid coil. The solenoid contacts close and allow current to flow from the battery through the solenoid to the starter motor. A neutral start switch in the circuit open prevents current flow through the solenoid coil if the shift control lever is not in NEUTRAL.

CAUTION
Do not operate the starter motor continuously for more than 30 seconds. Allow the motor to cool for at least 2 minutes between attempts to start the engine.

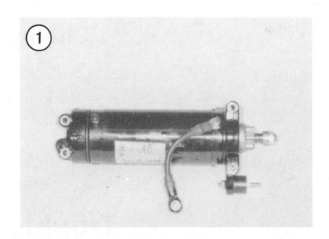

Troubleshooting

If the following procedures do not locate the problem, refer to **Table 3** for more extensive testing. Before troubleshooting the starting circuit, make sure that:

a. The battery is fully charged.
b. The shift control lever is in NEUTRAL.
c. All electrical connections are clean and tight.
d. The wiring harness is in good condition, with no worn or frayed insulation.
e. The fuse installed in the red lead between ignition switch and solenoid, if so equipped, is good.
f. The fuel system is filled with an adequate supply of fresh gasoline that

4. Use an ampere gauge (**Figure 4**) and check the current draw while cranking the engine. Refer to **Table 1** for specifications. If an excessive current draw is indicated, rebuild or replace the starter motor.

Starter Motor Does Not Turn Over

Refer to **Figure 5** and perform the following 7-test sequence.

NOTE
Test points at starter solenoid vary according to solenoid used, as shown in **Figure 5**.

Disconnect the yellow starter motor cable at the starter solenoid to prevent the engine from cranking.

On some cranking circuits, there may be a 20-amp fuse installed in the red lead between the ignition switch and starter solenoid (test points 5 and 6, **Figure 5**). Make sure the fuse is good on systems so equipped before proceeding with the test sequence.

Test No. 1

1. Disconnect the black ground wire at test point 2.
2. Connect a voltmeter between test point 2 and a good engine ground.
3. Turn the ignition key to the "START" position.
4A. If there is no voltage reading, proceed with *Test No. 2*.
4B. If the voltmeter reads 12 volts, check the black ground wire for an open circuit or poor connection. Reconnect wire to solenoid and proceed with *Test No. 6*.

Test No. 2

1. Connect the voltmeter between test point 3 and a good engine ground.
2. Turn the ignition key to START.
3A. If there is no voltage reading, proceed with *Test No. 3*.

has been properly mixed with Quicksilver 50-D 2-cycle outboard motor oil.

Starter Motor Turns Slowly

1. Make sure the battery is fully charged.
2. Check for corroded or loose electrical connections. Clean and tighten as required.
3. Check for proper size and length of battery cables. Replace cables that are undersize or relocate battery to shorten distance between battery and starter solenoid.

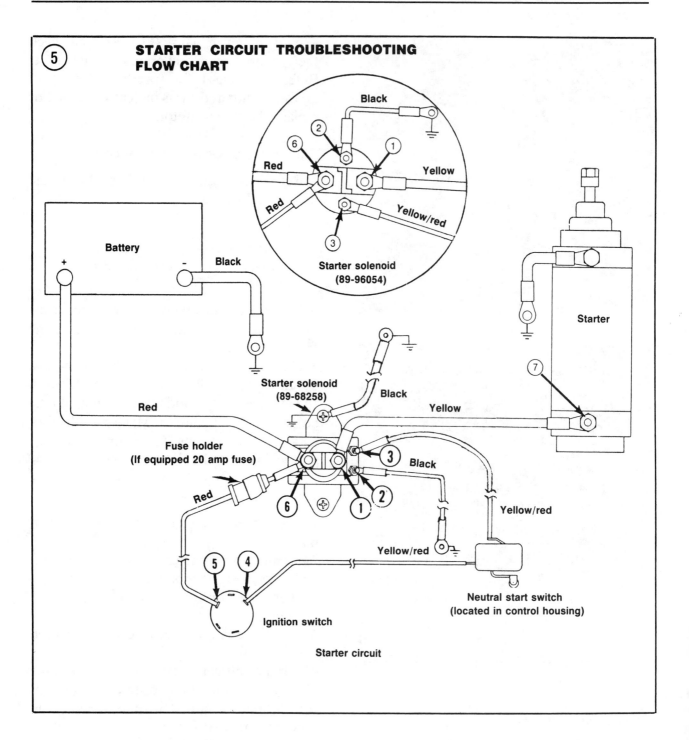

STARTER CIRCUIT TROUBLESHOOTING FLOW CHART

Black

Red

Red

Red

Yellow

Yellow/red

Starter solenoid (89-96054)

Battery

+   –   Black

Red

Fuse holder (If equipped 20 amp fuse)

Red

Starter solenoid (89-68258)

Black

Yellow

Starter

Black

Yellow/red

Yellow/red

Neutral start switch (located in control housing)

Ignition switch

Starter circuit

3B. If the voltmeter reads 12 volts, replace the starter solenoid.

Test No. 3

1. Connect the voltmeter between test point 4 and a good engine ground.
2. Turn the ignition key to START.

3A. If there is no voltage reading, proceed with *Test No. 4*.

3B. If the voltmeter reads 12 volts, check the neutral start switch for an open circuit. If the switch is satisfactory, the open circuit is in the yellow wire between test points 3 and 4.

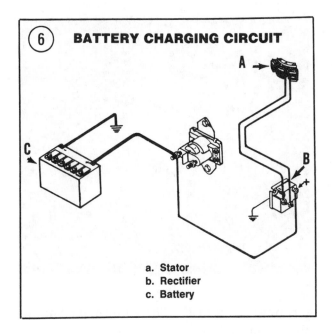

6. BATTERY CHARGING CIRCUIT

a. Stator
b. Rectifier
c. Battery

Test No. 4

1. Connect the voltmeter between test point 5 and a good engine ground.
2A. If there is no voltage reading, proceed with *Test No. 5.*
2B. If the voltmeter reads 12 volts, replace the ignition switch.

Test No. 5

1. Connect the voltmeter between test point 6 and a good engine ground.
2A. If there is no voltage reading, check the red wire between test point 6 and the positive battery terminal.
2B. If the voltmeter reads 12 volts, look for an open circuit between test point 5 and 6.

Test No. 6

1. Connect the voltmeter between test point 1 and a good engine ground.
2. Turn the ignition key to START.
3A. If there is no voltage reading, replace the starter solenoid.
3B. If the voltmeter reads 12 volts, the solenoid should also click in Step 2. Proceed to *Test No. 7.*

Test No. 7

1. Reconnect the yellow starter cable to the starter solenoid.
2. Connect the voltmeter between test point 7 and a good engine ground.
3. Turn the ignition key to START.
4A. If there is no voltage reading, check for a poor connection or open circuit in the yellow starter cable.
4B. If the voltmeter reads 12 volts and the starter motor does not turn over, replace the starter motor.

CHARGING SYSTEM

Description

The charging system consists of permanent magnets located within the flywheel, a stator assembly, a rectifier to change alternating current (AC) to direct current (DC), the starter solenoid, battery and connecting wiring. See **Figure 6**.

A malfunction in the battery charging system generally causes the battery to remain undercharged. Since the stator is protected by the flywheel, it is more likely that the battery, rectifier or connecting wiring will cause problems. The following conditions will cause rectifier damage:

a. Battery leads reversed.
b. Running the engine with the battery leads disconnected.
c. A broken wire or loose connection resulting in an open circuit.

System Inspection

Before performing the stator/rectifier tests, visually check the following.

1. Make sure the red cable is connected to the positive battery terminal. If polarity is reversed, check for a damaged rectifier.

3

A damaged rectifier will generally be discolored or have a burned appearance.

2. Check for corroded or loose connections. Clean or tighten as required.

3. Check battery condition. Clean and recharged as required.

4. Check wiring harness between stator and battery for cut, chafed or deteriorated insulation and corroded, loose or disconnected connections. Repair or replace as required.

Stator Test (Alternator Coils Only)

The stator can be checked without removal from the engine.

1. Disconnect yellow or yellow/red stator leads from the rectifier terminals. See **Figure 7** for diode type rectifier used on late models.

2. Connect an ohmmeter between the disconnected stator leads. With the ohmmeter set on the R×1 scale, the resistance should be less than one ohm.

3. Connect the red ohmmeter test lead to either stator lead. Connect the black ohmmeter test lead to a good engine ground. Set the ohmmeter on the R×1,000 scale. The ohmmeter should show no continuity.

4. If the stator does not provide the readings specified in Step 2 and Step 3, replace it.

Rectifier Test

The rectifier can be tested without removal from the engine. Disconnect the battery leads at the battery before performing this procedure. Refer to **Figure 8** for terminal connections.

1. Disconnect all leads from the rectifier terminals.

2. Set the ohmmeter on the R×1,000 scale.

3. Connect the red ohmmeter test lead to ground and the black test lead alternately to

terminals A and C. The ohmmeter should show continuity.

4. Connect the black ohmmeter test lead to ground and the red test lead alternately to terminals A and C. The ohmmeter should show no continuity.

5. Connect the black ohmmeter test lead to terminal B and the red test lead alternately to terminals A and C. The ohmmeter should show continuity.

6. Connect the red ohmmeter test lead to terminal B and the black test lead alternately to terminals A and C. The ohmmeter should show no continuity.

7. Replace the rectifier if the ohmmeter readings are not as specified in Steps 3-6.

IGNITION SYSTEM

The wiring harness used between the ignition switch and engine is adequate to handle the electrical needs of the outboard. It *will not* handle the electrical needs of accessories. Whenever an accessory is added, run new wiring between the battery and accessory, installing a separate fuse panel on the instrument panel.

If the ignition switch requires replacement, *never* install an automotive-type switch. A marine-type switch must always be used.

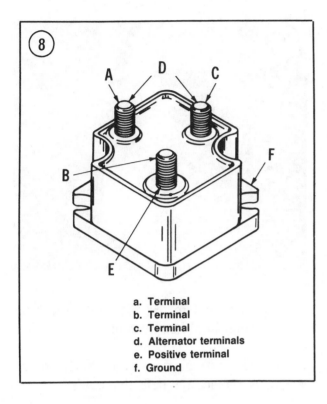

a. Terminal
b. Terminal
c. Terminal
d. Alternator terminals
e. Positive terminal
f. Ground

Description

Several different ignition systems have been used on Mercury outboards since 1972. See Chapter Seven for a full description of each. For the purposes of troubleshooting, the ignition systems can be divided into 3 types:

  a. The Lightning Energizer system used on 1975 Merc 500 models.

  b. A distributor-type capacitor discharge (CD) system used with 1975 Merc 650-850 and 1975-1976 Merc 1150-1500 models.

  c. A flywheel (alternator-driven) capacitor discharge (CD) system used on remaining Merc models covered in this book.

General troubleshooting procedures are provided in **Table 4**.

Troubleshooting Precautions

Several precautions should be strictly observed to avoid damage to the ignition system.

1. Do not reverse the battery connections. This reverses polarity and can damage the rectifier(s) and switchbox(es).

2. Do not "spark" the battery terminals with the battery cable connections to check polarity.

3. Do not disconnect the battery cables with the engine running.

4. Do not crank engine if switchbox(es) are not grounded to engine.

5. Do not touch or disconnect any ignition components when the engine is running, while the ignition switch is ON or while the battery cables are connected.

6. If you must run the engine on a distributor-less ignition system without the battery connected to the harness, disconnect the yellow alternator leads at the rectifier and tape them separately.

Troubleshooting Preparation
(All Ignition Systems)

1. Test the ignition switch and mercury switch as described in this chapter to make sure they are not causing the problem.

NOTE
To test the wiring harness for poor solder connections in Step 2, bend the molded rubber connector while checking each wire for resistance.

2. Check the wiring harness and all plug-in connections to make sure that all terminals are free of corrosion, all connectors are tight and the wiring insulation is in good condition.

3. Check all electrical components that are grounded to the engine for a good ground.

4. Make sure that all ground wires are properly connected and that the connections are clean and tight.

5. Check remainder of the wiring for disconnected wires and short or open circuits.

3

6. Make sure there is an adequate supply of fresh and properly mixed fuel available to the engine.

7. Check the battery condition. Clean terminals and recharge battery, if necessary.

8. Check spark plug cable routing. Make sure the cables are properly connected to their respective spark plugs.

9. Remove all spark plugs, keeping them in order. Check the condition of each plug. See *Spark Plug Removal,* Chapter Four.

10. Install a spark tester and check for spark at each cylinder. If a spark tester is not available, reconnect the proper spark plug cable to the plug. Lay the plug against the cylinder head so its base makes a good connection and turn the engine over. If there is no spark or only a weak one, check for loose connections at the coil and battery. If the connections are good, the problem is most likely in the ignition system.

TROUBLESHOOTING LIGHTNING ENERGIZER IGNITION SYSTEM

The switchbox cannot be checked satisfactorily without the use of a Quicksilver Thunderbolt Ignition Analyzer (part No. C-91-62563A1) follow the manufacturer's instructions when using the device.

Charging Coil Test

1. Disconnect the red, white and blue alternator driver leads from the switchbox terminals.

2. Connect an ohmmeter between the white and red leads. With the meter set on the R × 100 scale, it should read 3.4-4.5 (340-450) ohms.

3. Connect the ohmmeter between the white and blue leads. With the meter set on the R×1 scale, it should read 10-11 ohms.

4. Connect the ohmmeter between the red lead and a good ground. The meter should show no continuity.

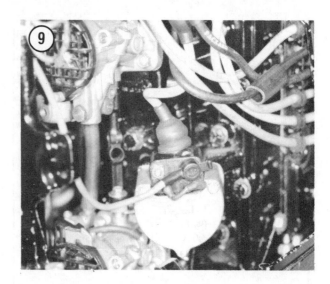

5. Repeat Step 4 to test the white and blue leads. There should be no continuity in either case.

6. If the system does not perform as specified, replace the defective coil(s).

DISTRIBUTOR-TYPE CD IGNITION SYSTEM TROUBLESHOOTING

The switchbox, ignition coil and trigger cannot be checked satisfactorily without the use of a Quicksilver Thunderbolt Ignition Analyzer (part No. C-91-62563A1). A quick test can be performed on the ignition coil with an ohmmeter. If the coil tests good in the following procedure, have the switchbox and trigger assemblies checked by a Mercury dealer.

Ignition Coil Test

Figure 9 shows one type of coil used; **Figure 10** shows the multiple coil arrangement used with 4- and 6-cylinder engines.

1. Disconnect the positive and negative leads at the coil terminals.

2. Remove the high tension lead from the coil tower.

3. Connect the ohmmeter test leads between the coil negative and positive terminals. With

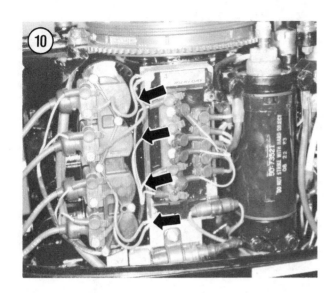

the meter set on the $R \times 1$ scale, it should read approximately 0.01-0.02 ohms.

4. Connect the ohmmeter leads between the coil tower and either the negative or positive coil terminals. With the meter set on the $R \times 1,000$ scale, it should show no continuity.

5. Connect the ohmmeter leads between the coil tower and a good engine ground. With the meter set on the $R \times 100$ scale, it should read approximately 57-73 ohms.

6. If the coil readings are not as specified in Steps 3-5, replace the coil.

FLYWHEEL CD IGNITION SYSTEM TROUBLESHOOTING

The switchbox(es) and ignition coils cannot be checked satisfactorily without the use of a Quicksilver Thunderbolt Ignition Analyzer (part No. C-91-62563A1). All other components can be tested with an ohmmeter. If the stator and trigger assembly test good in the following procedures, have the switchbox(es) and ignition coils checked by a Mercury dealer.

A change in the cylinder firing order on Merc 650 and 700 models requires a modification in the ignition firing order on certain engines whenever the power head or crankshaft is changed. When power head part No. 76785A80 or part No. 64933A75 or crankshaft part No. 462-7574A2 is installed on models with the following serial numbers, the ignition wiring must be modified:

U.S.—5467466 and below.
Canada—7135987 and below.
Australia—8063334 and below.
Belgium—9238105 and below.

3

Wiring Modifications

Power head installation
(part No. 76785A80)
crankshaft installation
(part No. 462-7574A2)

1. Remove and discard the green/red wire between the No. 3 cylinder ignition coil and switchbox.

2. Disconnect green/white wire from No. 2 cylinder coil and connect it to the No. 3 coil.

3. Connect the new green/red wire provided with the power head or crankshaft between the No. 2 coil and switchbox terminal marked "GREEN/RED."

Power Head Installation
(part No. 64933A75)

1. Disconnect the No. 2 and No. 3 cylinder spark plug leads at the distributor tower.

2. Connect the No. 2 plug lead to the distributor tower marked "3."

3. Connect the No. 3 plug lead to the distributor tower marked "2."

Stator Test

NOTE
Wire color abbreviations are embossed on switchbox at each terminal. To remove switchbox wires in the following procedures, unsnap the rubber cap and remove the nut holding each wire to be removed in place. Reinstall nut on terminal to prevent its loss.

45, 50 (4-cyl.), 75, 80 and 85 hp models

1. Disconnect the stator leads from the switchbox (**Figure 11**, typical).
2. Connect an ohmmeter between the blue and blue/white stator leads. With the meter set on the R×1,000 scale, it should read 5,700-8,000 ohms.
3. Connect the ohmmeter between the red and red/white stator leads. With the meter set on the R×1 scale, it should read 56-76 ohms.
4. Connect the ohmmeter between the blue stator lead and a good engine ground. With the meter set on the R×1,000 scale, there should be no continuity.
5. Repeat Step 4 with the red stator lead. There should be no continuity.
6. If the stator assembly performs as specified in each step, reconnect the leads to the switchbox. If it does not, replace the stator assembly.

50 (3-cyl.), 60, 65 and 70 (prior to 1984) hp models

1. Disconnect the stator leads from the switchbox (**Figure 11**, typical).
2. Connect an ohmmeter between the blue and red stator leads. With the ohmmeter set on the R×1,000 scale, it should read 5,400-6,200 ohms.
3. Connect the ohmmeter between the red stator lead and a good engine ground. With the meter set on the R×1 scale, it should read 125-175 ohms.
4. If the stator assembly performs as specified in each step, reconnect the leads to the switchbox. If it does not, replace the stator assembly.

70, 80 and 90 hp (1987-on) models

1. Disconnect the stator leads from the switchbox (**Figure 11**, typical).

2. Connect an ohmmeter between the blue and red stator leads. With the ohmmeter set on the RX1,000 scale, it should read 3,600-4,200 ohms.
3. Connect the ohmmeter between the red stator lead and a good engine ground. With the meter set on the RX1 scale, it should read 90-140 ohms.
4. If the stator assembly performs as specified in each step, reconnect the leads to the switchbox. If it does not, replace the stator assembly.

100 and 115 hp (4-cyl.) models

1. Disconnect the stator leads from the switchbox (**Figure 11**, typical).
2. Connect an ohmmeter between the blue and blue/white stator leads. With the meter set on the RX1,000 scale, it should read 6,000-7,000 ohms.
3. Connect the ohmmeter between the red and red/white stator leads. With the meter set on the RX1 scale, it should read 90-140 ohms.
4. Connect the ohmmeter between the blue stator lead and a good engine ground. With the meter set on the RX1,000 scale, there should be no continuity.
5. Repeat Step 4 with the red stator lead. There should be no continuity.
6. If the stator assembly performs as specified in each step, reconnect the leads to the switchbox. If it does not, replace the stator assembly.

90, 115 and 140 hp inline and all V6 models

The 6-cylinder inline and V6 models use 2 different types of stator assemblies:

a. Type 1—grounds directly to the engine through the stator mounting plate.

b. Type 2—grounds to the engine through a black ground wire.

When testing Type 2 stators, make sure that the black ground wire is connected to the engine.

1. Remove 2 screws holding outer switchbox to inner switchbox (**Figure 12**). Separate the switchboxes.

2. Disconnect the blue/white and red/white stator leads from the outer switchbox. Disconnect the blue and red stator leads from the inner switchbox.

3. Connect an ohmmeter between the blue and red stator leads. With the meter set on the $R \times 1,000$ scale, it should read 5,400-6,200 ohms.

4. Connect the ohmmeter between the blue/white and red/white stator leads. With the meter set on the $R \times 1,000$ scale, it should read 5,400-6,200 ohms.

5. Connect the ohmmeter leads between the red stator lead and a good engine ground. With the meter set on the $R \times 1$ scale, it should read 125-175 ohms.

6. Connect the ohmmeter leads between the red/white stator lead and a good engine ground. With the meter set on the $R \times 1$ scale, it should read 125-175 ohms.

7. If the stator assembly performs as specified in each step, reconnect the leads to the switchboxes and reassemble the switchboxes to the engine. If it does not, replace the stator assembly.

Trigger Assembly Test

> *NOTE*
> *The resistance values specified in the following procedures are for engines being tested at room temperature. The resistance values will be slightly greater if the engine has recently been run and has not completely cooled down when tested.*

45, 50 (4-cyl.), 75, 80, 85, 100 and 115 (4-cyl.) hp models

1. Disconnect all trigger leads from the switchbox (**Figure 11**, typical).

2. Connect an ohmmeter between the brown and the white/black trigger leads. With the meter set on the $R \times 100$ scale, it should read 700-1,000 ohms.

3A. 45, 50, 75, 80 and 85 hp models — Connect the ohmmeter between the white and violet trigger leads. With the meter set on the RX100 scale, it should read 700-1,000 ohms.

3B. 100 and 115 hp models — Connect the ohmmeter between the white and white/black trigger leads. With the meter set on the RX100 scale, it should read 700-1,000 ohms.

4. If the trigger assembly performs as specified in each step, reconnect the leads to the switchbox. If it does not, replace the trigger assembly.

50 (3-cyl.), 60, 65, 70, 80 and 90 (3-cyl.) hp models

1. Disconnect all trigger leads from the switchbox (**Figure 11**, typical).

2. Connect an ohmmeter between the brown and the white/black trigger leads. With the meter set on the R×100 scale, it should read 1,100-1,400 ohms.

3. Connect the ohmmeter between the white and the white/black trigger leads. With the meter set on the R×100 scale, it should read 1,100-1,400 ohms.

4. Connect the ohmmeter between the violet and the white/black trigger leads. With the meter set on the R×100 scale, it should read 1,100-1,400 ohms.

5. If the trigger assembly performs as specified in each step, reconnect the leads to the switchbox. If it does not, replace the trigger assembly.

90, 115 and 140 hp inline and all V6 models

1. Remove 2 screws holding outer switchbox to inner switchbox (**Figure 12**). Separate the switchboxes and disconnect all trigger leads.

2. Connect an ohmmeter between the brown (without yellow sleeve) and the white (with yellow sleeve) trigger leads. With the meter set on the R×100 scale, it should read 1,100-1,400 ohms.

3. Connect the ohmmeter between the white (without yellow sleeve) and the violet (with yellow sleeve) trigger leads. With the meter set on the R×100 scale, it should read 1,100-1,400 ohms.

4. Connect the ohmmeter between the violet (without yellow sleeve) and the brown (with yellow sleeve) trigger leads. With the meter set on the R×100 scale, it should read 1,100-1,400 ohms.

5. If the trigger assembly performs as specified in each step, reconnect the leads to the switchboxes and reassemble the switchboxes to the engine. If it does not, replace the trigger assembly.

Ignition Coil Test

Resistance tests can detect only some coil problems. If a coil passes this procedure but is still suspected of causing the problem, have the coil tested on a Quicksilver Ignition Analyzer or Merc-o-tronic Magneto Analyzer by a dealer. See **Figure 9** and **Figure 10** for typical coil configurations.

1. Disconnect the positive and negative leads at the coil terminals.

2. Remove the high tension lead from the coil tower.

3. Connect the ohmmeter test leads between the coil negative and positive terminals. With the meter set on the R×1 scale, it should read approximately 0.02-0.04 ohms.

4A. Orange colored coils:

  a. Connect the ohmmeter leads between the coil tower and either the positive or negative coil terminal. With the meter set on the R×100 scale, it should show no continuity.

  b. Connect the ohmmeter leads between the coil tower and engine ground (if mounted) or the pigtail lead on the rear of the coil (if removed). With the meter set on the R×100 scale, it should read approximately 800-1,100 ohms.

4B. Blue colored coils—Connect the ohmmeter leads between the coil tower and either the positive or negative coil terminal. With the meter set on the R×100 scale, it should read approximately 800-1,100 ohms.

5. If the coil readings are not as specified in Step 3 and Step 4, replace the coil.

Mercury Switch Test

See **Figure 13** for a typical mercury switch installation.

1. Remove the screw holding the mercury switch and its black ground lead to the engine.

NOTE
On some models, the orange lead specified in Step 2 may be black/yellow in color.

2. Connect an ohmmeter between the black ground lead and the orange switch lead. Set the meter on the R×1 scale.
3. Hold the mercury switch as it would be positioned if the engine were in the "down" position. The meter should show no continuity.
4. Hold the mercury switch in the "up" position and tap it on its end with a finger. The meter should show continuity.
5. Replace the switch if it does not perform as specified in Step 3 and Step 4.

Ignition Switch Test

The ignition switch is most easily tested at the remote control assembly wiring harness connector. Refer to the wiring diagram for your model at the end of the book for terminal location and identification according to the appropriate procedure below.

90-140 hp models

1. Disconnect the negative battery lead, then the positive lead.
2. Disconnect remote control wiring harness and instrument panel connector.
3. Connect an ohmmeter between terminals D and E. With ignition switch at STOP, meter should indicate continuity.
4. Connect the ohmmeter between terminals A and D. With ignition switch at RUN, meter should indicate continuity.

5. Place shift lever in NEUTRAL. Connect the ohmmeter between terminals A and B. The meter should indicate continuity.
6. Remove and replace switch if it does not perform as specified.

V6 models (1976-1978)

1. Disconnect the negative battery lead, then the positive lead.
2. Disconnect remote control wiring harness and instrument panel connector.
3. Connect an ohmmeter between terminals 7 and 4 of the remote control harness connector. With ignition switch at STOP, meter should indicate continuity.
4. Connect the ohmmeter between terminal 1 of the remote control harness connector and terminal A of the instrument panel connector. With ignition switch at RUN, meter should indicate continuity.
5. Place shift lever in neutral position. Connect the ohmmeter between terminals 1 and 3 of the remote control harness connector. With ignition switch at RUN/START, the meter should indicate continuity.
6. Remove and replace switch if it does not perform as specified.

V150, V175, V200 and V225 models (serial No. 5464486 and up)

1. Disconnect the negative battery lead, then the positive lead.
2. Disconnect remote control wiring harness and instrument panel connector.
3. Connect an ohmmeter between terminals M and m. With ignition switch at OFF, meter should indicate continuity.
4. Connect the ohmmeter between terminals B and A. With ignition switch at RUN, meter should indicate continuity.
5. Place the switch at START. Connect the ohmmeter between terminals B and S; A and S; B and A; and B and M. The meter should indicate continuity in each case.

3

6. Place the switch at CHOKE. Connect the ohmmeter between terminals B and M; B and A; and M and A. The meter should indicate continuity in each case.

7. Remove and replace switch if it does not perform as specified.

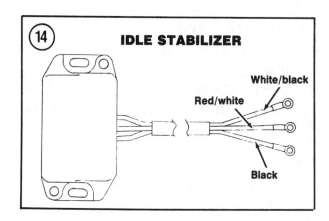

SPARK ADVANCE/IDLE STABILIZER MODULE TROUBLESHOOTING

Electronic Spark Advance Modules

Late-model V6 engines may be equipped with an idle stabilizer or spark advance module. These solid-state modules are non-serviceable and should be replaced if they do not function as described.

Idle Stabilizer Test

When ever engine speed drops below approximately 550 rpm, this device electronically advances ignition timing by up to 9°. The amount of timing advance provided will raise the engine speed to 550 rpm, at which time the module returns timing to normal. An idle stabilizer is mounted on the power head and can be identified by shaft and lead color. See **Figure 14**. To test the idle stabilizer:

1. With the engine in a test tank or mounted on a boat in the water, remove the engine cover and connect a timing light to the No. 1 spark plug lead (top, starboard bank).

2. Start the engine and let it idle above 600 rpm.

3. Point the timing light at the timing marks and slowly pull forward on the spark lever arm to retard the timing.

4. If ignition timing advances up to 9° as the engine speed drops approximately to 550 rpm, the idle stabilizer is functioning properly. If it does not, replace the stabilizer.

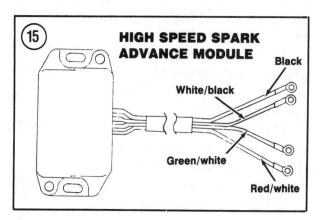

High Speed Spark Advance Module Test

Whenever engine speed increases to approximately 5,600 rpm, the high speed spark advance module electronically advances ignition timing by 6°. The timing will remain advanced until the engine speed drops to 5,400 rpm, at which time the module retards timing by 6°. The module is mounted on the power head and can be identified by shape and lead color. See **Figure 15**. To test the module:

1. With the engine in a test tank or mounted on a boat in the water, remove the engine cover and connect a timing light to the No. 1 spark plug lead (top, starboard bank).

2. Start the engine and gradually increase engine speed to 5,600 rpm while pointing the timing light at the timing marks. The timing should advance 6°.

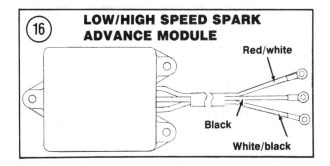

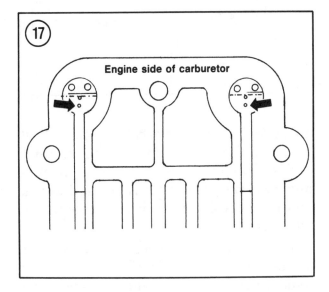

3. Decrease engine speed to 5,400 rpm while pointing the timing light at the timing marks. The timing should retard by 6°.

4. If the timing does not advance and retard as specified in Step 2 and Step 3, replace the module.

Low Speed/High Speed Spark Advance Module Test

The low speed/high speed spark advance module combines the functions of an idle stabilizer and a high speed spark advance module. See **Figure 16**. It can be tested by performing both the *Idle Stabilizer Test* and the *High Speed Spark Advance Module Test* described in this chapter.

FUEL SYSTEM

Many outboard owners automatically assume that the carburetor is at fault when the engine does not run properly. While fuel system problems are not uncommon, carburetor adjustment is seldom the answer. In many cases, adjusting the carburetor only compounds the problem by making the engine run worse.

Fuel system troubleshooting should start at the gas tank and work through the system, reserving the carburetor(s) as the final point. The majority of fuel system problems result from an empty fuel tank, sour fuel, a plugged fuel filter or a malfunctioning fuel pump. **Table 5** provides a series of symptoms and causes that can be useful in localizing fuel system problems.

Troubleshooting

As a first step, check the fuel flow. Remove the fuel tank cap and look into the tank. If there is fuel present, disconnect and ground each spark plug lead as a safety precaution. Disconnect a fuel line at the carburetor and place it in a suitable container to catch any discharged fuel. See if gas flows freely from the line when the primer bulb is squeezed.

If there is no fuel flow from the line, the fuel tap may be shut off, blocked by rust or foreign matter or the fuel line may be stopped up or kinked. If a good fuel flow is present, crank the engine 10-12 times to check fuel pump operation. A pump that is operating satisfactorily will deliver a good, constant flow of fuel from the line. If the amount of flow varies from pulse to pulse, the fuel pump is probably failing.

Carburetor chokes can also present problems. A choke that sticks open will show up as a hard starting problem; one that sticks closed will result in a flooding condition.

During a hot engine shut-down, the fuel bowl temperature can rise above 200°,

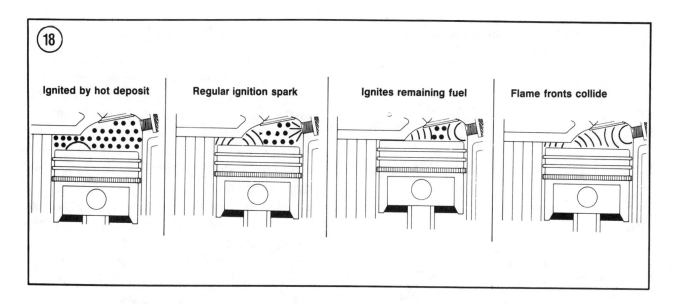

| Ignited by hot deposit | Regular ignition spark | Ignites remaining fuel | Flame fronts collide |

causing the fuel inside to boil. While all Mercury carburetors are vented to atmosphere to prevent this problem, there is a possibility that some fuel will percolate over the high-speed nozzle.

A leaking inlet needle and seat or a defective float will allow an excessive amount of fuel into the intake manifold. Pressure in the fuel line after the engine is shut down forces fuel past the leaking needle/seat. This raises the fuel bowl level and thus allows fuel to overflow into the manifold.

Excessive fuel consumption may not necessarily mean an engine or fuel system problem. Marine growth on the boat's hull, a bent or otherwise damaged propeller or a fuel line leak can cause an increase in fuel consumption. These areas should all be checked before blaming the carburetor.

Idle/Acceleration Problems Resulting in Spark Plug Fouling (V6 Engines)

The following procedure should be used to diagnose and correct this problem.

1. Make sure the boat has no problem coming out of the hole. Install the tilt-thrust bolt in the first pin hole to reduce trim by about 4°. This is necessary with many boat designs which have transoms with excessive angles. This will allow the exhaust to pass into the atmosphere instead of being drawn in under the cowling where it contaminates the intake charge.

2. Remove the air silencer and check the carburetors for debris or other contamination. Locate and eliminate the source of such contamination.

3. On engines below serial No. A157595, remove the fuel pump(s) and replace the gray pump gasket with a new black one (part No. 27-75360A1). The gray gasket can be one source of contamination.

4. Check and reset the carburetor float(s) to specifications. It is a good idea to replace the float(s) with new alcohol-resistant white plastic floats, if this has not already been done.

5. Remove the carburetor(s) from the power head and check that the throttle shutter(s) close properly in the carburetor throat(s). If not, rebuild or replace the carburetor(s).

6. Check and adjust timing and synchronization to specifications as required. Idle speed should be set to 600-700 rpm in FORWARD gear in the water.

7. Install NGK BU10H spark plugs. These are a semi-surface gap plug and run a little hotter that the standard surface gap plug, but not as hot as the coldest of the conventional gap plugs.

NOTE
Step 8 should not be performed on WH-29 (V150) or WH-31 (V200) carburetors. Refer to Step 9 instead.

8. If Steps 1-7 do not solve the problem on V150 models with WH-23 or WH-27 carburetors or V200 models with WH-22 or WH-26 carburetors, remove the carburetor(s) and rework as follows:
   a. Enlarge the second progression holes (arrows, **Figure 17**) to 0.052 in. (V150) or 0.046 in. (V200) with a hand-held pin vise.
   b. Install 0.056 in. idle jets. On WH-23 or WH-27 (V150) carburetors, you may have to install an idle jet as large as 0.062 in.

9. If Steps 1-7 do not solve the problem on V150 models with WH-29 or V200 models with WH-31 carburetors.
   a. Use the primary throttle pickup screw to adjust idle speed to 600-700 rpm in FORWARD gear in the water. Advancing the idle pickup timing slightly will result in a richer air/fuel mixture.
   b. Install 0.056 in. idle jets as required.

ENGINE

Engine problems are generally symptoms of something wrong in another system, such as ignition, fuel or starting. If properly maintained and serviced, the engine should experience no problems other than those caused by age and wear.

Overheating and Lack of Lubrication

Overheating and lack of lubrication cause the majority of engine mechanical problems. Outboard motors are not designed to operate at a standstill for any length of time. Using a spark plug of the wrong heat range can burn a piston. Incorrect ignition timing or an excessively lean fuel mixture can cause the engine to overheat.

Preignition

Preignition is the premature burning of fuel and is caused by hot spots in the combustion chamber (**Figure 18**). The fuel actually ignites before it is supposed to. Glowing deposits in the combustion chamber, inadequate cooling or overheated spark plugs can all cause preignition. This is first noticed in the form of a power loss but will eventually result in extensive damage to the internal parts of the engine because of higher combustion chamber temperatures.

Detonation

Commonly called "spark knock" or "fuel knock," detonation is the violent explosion of fuel in the combustion chamber prior to the proper time of combustion (**Figure 19**). Severe damage can result. Use of low octane gasoline is a common cause of detonation.

Even when high octane gasoline is used, detonation can still occur if the engine is improperly timed. Other causes are over-advanced ignition timing, lean fuel mixture at or near full throttle, inadequate engine cooling, use of a prop that is too large (overpropping), cross-firing of spark plugs, or excessive accumulation of deposits on piston and combustion chamber.

If the knock or detonation occurs only at high speeds, it may go unnoticed due to wind

3

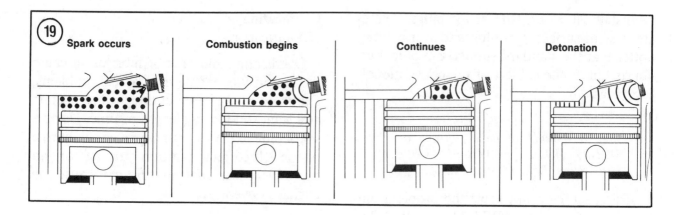

noise. Such inaudible detonation, as it is called, is usually the cause when engine damage occurs for no apparent reason.

Poor Idling

Poor idling can be caused by incorrect carburetor adjustment, incorrect timing or ignition system malfunctions. Check the gas cap vent for an obstruction.

Misfiring

Misfiring can be caused by a weak spark or dirty spark plug. Check for fuel contamination. If misfiring occurs only under heavy load, as when accelerating, it is usually caused by a defective spark plug. Run the motor at night to check for spark leaks along the plug wire and under spark plug cap or use a spark leak tester (**Figure 20**).

> *WARNING*
> *Do not run engine in dark garage to check for spark leak. There is considerable danger of carbon monoxide poisoning.*

Flat Spots

If the engine seems to die momentarily when the throttle is opened and then recovers, check for a dirty main jet in the carburetor, water in the fuel or an excessively lean mixture.

Water Leakage in Cylinder

The fastest and easiest way to check for water leakage in a cylinder is to check the spark plugs. Water will clean a spark plug. If one of the plugs on a multi-cylinder engine is clean and the others are dirty, there is most likely a water leak in the cylinder with the clean plug.

To remove all doubt, install a dirty plug in each cylinder. Run the engine in a test tank or on the boat in water for 5-10 minutes. Shut the engine off and remove the plugs. If one plug is clean and the others are dirty, a water leak in the cylinder(s) is the problem.

Water Damage in Power Head Lower Cylinder

While this problem is generally caused by defective or failed gaskets, manifold plates or covers, water can also enter the lower end of a power head in several ways the casual observer would not consider:

a. When a steep unloading ramp or tilted trailer bed is used to launch the boat from a trailer, the boat enters the water quickly and at a deep angle. This can force water into the drive shaft housing and up through the exhaust chambers into the cylinders if the pistons are not covering the exhaust ports.

b. Sudden deceleration in the water can cause a wave to swamp the engine,

entering the exhaust ports and passing into the cylinder through the lower carburetor(s). This is most prevalent with engines on outboard transom brackets or twin engine installations. Since engine weight is considerably aft of the boat, the stern tends to sink lower into the water. Running the boat in REVERSE at high speed will cause a similar condition.

In either case, water entering the power head can result in a bent connecting rod, a broken piston/piston pin, a cracked cylinder head/piston dome or any combination of these conditions. Even if no immediate physical damage is done to the power head, the entry of water will result in rusting and corrosion of the lower main ball bearing, crankshaft and/or connecting rods.

The solution to this problem lies in changing the mounting of the engine on the transom or the use of an engine with an XL (extra-length) shaft.

Power Loss

Several factors can cause a lack of power and speed. Look for air leaks in the fuel line or fuel pump, a clogged fuel filter or a choke/throttle valve that does not operate properly. Check ignition timing.

A piston or cylinder that is galling, incorrect piston clearance or a worn/sticky piston ring may be responsible. Look for loose bolts, defective gaskets or leaking machined mating surfaces on the cylinder head, cylinder or crankcase. Also check the crankcase oil seal; if worn, it can allow gas to leak between cylinders.

Piston Seizure

This is caused by one or more pistons with incorrect bore clearance, piston rings with an improper end cap, the use of an oil-fuel mixture containing less than 1 part oil to 50 parts of gasoline or an oil of poor quality, a spark plug of the wrong heat range or incorrect ignition timing. Overheating from any cause may result in piston seizure.

Excessive Vibrations

Excessive vibrations may be caused by loose motor mounts, worn bearings or a generally poor running motor.

Engine Noises

Experience is needed to diagnose accurately in this area. Noises are difficult to differentiate and harder yet to describe. Deep knocking noises usually mean main bearing failure. A slapping noise generally comes from a loose piston. A light knocking noise during acceleration may be a bad connecting rod bearing. Pinging should be corrected immediately or damage to the piston will result. A compression leak at the head-cylinder joint will sound like a rapid on-and-off squeal.

3

Tables are on the following pages.

Table 1 MERCURY OUTBOARD DESIGNATIONS

HP	CYL.	Designation
45	I4	Merc 45 or Classic 50
50	I4	Merc 500 or Merc 50
50	I3	Merc 50
60	I3	Merc 60
65	I3	Merc 650
70	I3	Merc 700 or Merc 70
75	I4	Merc 75
80	I4	Merc 800 or Merc 80
80	I3	Merc 80
85	I4	Merc 850
90	I6	Merc 900 or Merc 90
90	I3	Merc 90
100	I4	Merc 100
115	I4	Merc 115
115	I6	Merc 1150 or Merc 115
135	V6	Merc 135
140	I6	Merc 1400
150	I6	Merc 1500
150	V6	Merc 1500 or V150
175	V6	Merc 1750 or V175
200	V6	Merc 2000 or V200
200	V6	200 XRi
220	V6	Laser XRi
225	V6	Merc V225

Table 2 STARTER MOTOR DRAW (AMPERES)

Starter motor part No.	No-load draw	Normal draw
A-50-55601	40	100
A-50-57465	55	190
A-50-64975	55	190
A-50-65436	40	145
A-50-66015	40	120
A-50-67341	40	120
A-50-72467	40	180
A-50-73521	40	100
A-50-77141	40	175
A-50-79472	40	175
A-50-86976	20	190

Table 3 STARTER TROUBLESHOOTING

Trouble	Cause	Remedy
Starter motor has low no-load speed and high current draw	Armature may be dragging on pole shoes from bent shaft, worn bearings or loose pole shoes. Tight or dirty bearings.	Replace shaft or bearings and/or tighten pole shoes. Loosen or clean bearings.

(continued)

Table 3 STARTER TROUBLESHOOTING (continued)

Trouble	Cause	Remedy
High current draw with no armature rotation	A direct ground switch, at terminal or @ brushes or field connections.	Replace defective parts.
	Frozen shaft bearings which prevent armature from rotating.	Loosen, clean or replace bearings.
Starter motor has grounded armature or field winding	Field and/or armature is burned or lead is thrown out of commutator due to excess leakage.	Raise grounded brushes from commutator and insulate them with cardboard. Use Magneto Analyzer (part No. C-91-25213) (Selector No. 3) and test points to check between insulated terminal or starter motor and starter motor frame (remove ground connection of shunt coils on motors with this feature). If analyzer shows resistance (meter needle moves to right), there is a ground. Raise other brushes from armature and check armature and fields separately to locate ground.
Starter motor has grounded armature or field winding abnormal	Current passes through armature first, then to ground field windings.	Disconnect grounded leads, then locate any grounds in motor.
Starter motor fails to operate and draws no current and/or high resistance	Open circuit in fields or armature, @ connections or brushes or between brushes and commutator.	Repair or adjust broken or weak brush springs, worn brushes, high insulation between commutator bars or a dirty, gummy or oily commutator.
High resistance in starter motor	Low no-load speed and a low-current draw and low developed torque.	Close "open" field winding on unit which has 2 or 3 circuits in starter motor (unit in which current divides as it enters, taking 2 or 3 parallel paths).
High free speed and high current draw	Shorted fields in starter motor.	Install new fields and check for improved performance. (Fields normally have very low resistance, thus it is difficult to detect shorted fields, since difference in current draw between normal starter motor field windings would not be very great.)
Excessive voltage drop	Cables too small.	Install larger cables to accomodate high current draw.

(continued)

Table 3 STARTER TROUBLESHOOTING (continued)

Trouble	Cause	Remedy
High circuit resistance	Dirty connections.	Clean connections.
Starter does not operate	Run-down battery.	Check battery with hydrometer. If reading is below 1.230, recharge or replace battery.
	Poor contact @ terminals.	Remove terminal clamps. Scrape terminals and clamps clean and tighten bolts securely.
	Wiring or key switch	Coat with sealer to protect against further corrosion.
Starter does not operate (continued)	Starter solenoid.	Check for resistance between: (a) positive (+) terminal of battery and large input terminal of starter solenoid, (b) large wire @ top of starter motor and negative (-) terminal of battery, and (c) small terminal of starter solenoid and positive battery terminal. Key switch must be in START position. Repair all defective parts.
	Starter motor.	With a fully charged battery, connect a negative (-) jumper wire to upper terminal on side of starter motor and a positive jumper to large lower terminal of starter motor. If motor still does not operate, remove for overhaul or replacement.
Starter turns over too slowly	Low battery or poor contact @ battery terminal.	See "Starter does not operate."
	Poor contact @ starter solenoid or starter motor.	Check all terminals for looseness and tighten all nuts securely.
	Starter mechanism.	Disconnect positive (+) battery terminal. Rotate pinion gear in disengaged position. Pinion gear and motor should run freely by hand. If motor does not turn over easily, clean starter and replace all defective parts.
	Starter motor.	See "Starter does not operate."
Starter spins freely but does not engage engine.	Low battery or poor contact @ battery terminal; poor contact @ starter solenoid or starter motor.	See "Starter does not operate."
	Dirty or corroded pinion drive.	Clean thoroughly and lubricate the spline underneath the pinion with multipurpose lubricant (part No. C-92-63250).

(continued)

Table 3 **STARTER TROUBLESHOOTING (continued)**

Trouble	Cause	Remedy
Starter does not engage freely	Pinion or flywheel gear.	Inspect mating gears for excessive wear. Replace all defective parts.
	Small anti-drift spring.	If drive pinion interferes with flywheel gear after engine has started, inspect anti-drift spring located under pinion gear. Replace all defective parts. NOTE: If drive pinion tends to stay engaged in flywheel gear when starter motor is in idle position, start motor @ 1/4 throttle to allow starter pinion gear to release flywheel ring gear instantly.
Starter keeps on spinning after key is turned ON	Key not fully returned.	Check that key has returned to normal ON position from START position. Replace switch if key constantly stays in START position.
	Starter solenoid.	Inspect starter solenoid to see if contacts have become stuck in closed position. If starter does not stop running with small yellow lead disconnected from starter solenoid, replace starter solenoid.
	Wiring or key switch.	Inspect all wires for defects. Open remote control box and inspect wiring @ switches. Repair or replace all defective parts.
Wires overheat	Battery terminals improperly connected.	Check that negative marking on harness matches that of battery. If battery is connected improperly, red wire to rectifier will overheat.
	Short circuit in wiring system.	Inspect all connections and wires for looseness or defects. Open remote control box and inspect wiring @ switches.
	Short circuit in choke solenoid.	Repair or replace all defective parts. Check for high resistance. If blue choke wire heats rapidly when choke is used, choke solenoid may have internal short. Replace if defective.
	Short circuit in starter solenoid.	If yellow starter solenoid lead overheats, there may be internal short (resistance) in starter solenoid. Replace if defective.
	Battery voltage low.	Battery voltage is checked with an ampere-volt tester only when battery is under a starting load. Battery must be recharged if it registers under 9.5 volts. If battery is below specified hydrometer reading of 1.230, it will not turn engine fast enough to start it.

3

Table 4 IGNITION TROUBLESHOOTING

Symptom	Probable Cause
Engine won't start, but fuel and spark are okay	Defective spark plugs. Spark plug gap set too wide. Improper spark timing.
Engine misfires @ idle	Incorrect spark plug gap. Defective or loose spark plugs. Spark plugs of incorrect heat range. Cracked distributor cap. Leaking or broken high tension wires. Weak armature magnets. Defective coil or condenser. Defective ignition switch. Spark timing out of adjustment.
Engine misfires @ high speed	See "Engine misfires @ idle." Coil breaks down. Coil shorts through insulation. Spark plug gap too wide. Wrong type spark plugs. Too much spark advance.
Engine backfires: Through exhaust	Cracked spark plug insulator. Carbon path in distributor cap. Improper timing. Crossed spark plug wires.
Through carburetor	Improper ignition timing.
Engine preignition	Spark advanced too far. Incorrect type spark plug. Burned spark plug electrodes.
Engine noises (knocking at power head)	Spark advanced too far.
Ignition coil fails	Extremely high voltage. Moisture formation. Excessive heat from engine.
Spark plugs burn and foul	Incorrect type plug. Fuel mixture too rich. Inferior grade of gasoline. Overheated engine. Excessive carbon in combustion chambers.
Ignition causing high fuel consumption	Incorrect spark timing. Leaking high tension wires. Incorrect spark plug gap. Fouled spark plugs. Incorrect spark advance. Weak ignition coil. Preignition.

Table 5 FUEL SYSTEM TROUBLESHOOTING

Symption	Probable cause
No fuel @ carburetor	No gas in tank. Air vent in gas cap not open. Air vent in gas cap clogged. Fuel tank sitting on fuel line. Fuel line fittings not properly connected to engine or fuel tank. Air leak @ fuel connection. Fuel pickup clogged. Defective fuel pump.
Flooding @ carburetor	Choke out of adjustment. High float level. Float stuck. Excessive fuel pump pressure. Float saturated beyond buoyancy.
Rough operation	Dirt or water in fuel. Reed valve open or broken. Incorrect fuel level in carburetor bowl. Carburetor loose @ mounting flange. Throttle shutter not closing completely. Throttle shutter valve installed incorrectly.
Engine misfires @ high speed	Dirty carburetor. Lean carburetor adjustment. Restriction in fuel system. Low fuel pump pressure.
Engine backfires	Poor quality fuel. Air/fuel mixture too rich or too lean. Improperly adjusted carburetor.
Engine preignition	Excessive oil in fuel. Inferior grade of gasoline. Lean carburetor mixture.
Spark plugs burn and foul	Fuel mixture too rich. Inferior grade of gasoline.
High gas consumption: **Flooding or leaking**	Cracked carburetor casting. Leaks @ line connections. Defective carburetor bowl gasket. High float level. Plugged vent hole in cover. Loose needle and seat. Defective needle valve seat gasket. Worn needle valve and seat. Foreign matter clogging needle valve. Worn float pin or bracket. Float binding in bowl. High fuel pump pressure.

3

(continued)

Table 5 FUEL SYSTEM TROUBLESHOOTING (continued)

Symption	Probable cause
Overrich mixture	Choke lever stuck. High float level. High fuel pump pressure.
Abnormal speeds	Carburetor out of adjustment. Too much oil in fuel.

Table 6 OUTBOARD POWER TRIM TROUBLESHOOTING

Malfunction	Causes	Remedy
MECHANICAL Outboard hydraulic system operates normally, but:		
1. Will only trim part way up.	a. Internal resistance in cylinder. b. Tilt pin installed through safety strap.	a. Replace cylinder. b. Remove tilt pin and reinstall after tilting full up.
2. Will not pivot freely within clamp bracket flanges.	Clamp bracket flanges too close together.	Check for proper installation of spacer.
3. Will not trail out easily when going slowly over obstructions.	NOTE: Engine is held in position by reverse lock control @ all times. Release by turning control knob fully in or trim unit out to clear obstructions.	
ELECTRICAL Outboard hydraulic system operates normally, but:		
1. Will only trim part way.	a. Low battery charge. b. Defective key, push button or rocker switch.	a. Charge battery. b. Test, replace defective parts.
2. Trims out beyond bracket flanges.	a. Limit switch not adjusted properly. b. Defective key, push button or rocker switch.	a. Refer to installation or service manual for adjustment procedure. b. Test, replace defective parts.
3. Pump motor runs only in "down" direction.	a. Improper wiring. b. Proper switch not operated. c. Limit switch open or disconnected. d. Solenoid inoperative. e. High resistance in wiring, grounds or solenoid. f. Defective pump motor. g. Defective key, push button or rocker switch.	a. Trace wire and correct connections. b. Use correct switch c. Replace switch or reconnect leads. d. Test, replace defective parts. e. Test, replace defective parts. f. Test, replace defective parts. g. Test, replace defective parts.

(continued)

Table 6 OUTBOARD POWER TRIM TROUBLESHOOTING

Malfunction	Causes	Remedy
ELECTRICAL (continued) **Outboard hydraulic system operates normally, but:**		
4. Pump motor runs only in "up" direction.	a. Improper wiring. b. Proper switch not operated. c. High resistance in wiring, grounds or solenoid d. Defective pump motor. e. Defective key, push button or rocker switch.	a. Trace wire and correct connections. b. Use correct switch c. Test, replace defective parts. d. Test, replace defective parts. e. Test, replace defective parts.
5. Pump motor does not run.	a. Low battery charge. b. Improper wiring. c. High resistance in wiring, grounds or solenoid. d. Defective pump motor. e. Defective key, push button or rocker switch.	a. Charge battery. b. Trace wire and correct connections. c. Test, replace defective parts. d. Test, replace defective parts. e. Test, replace defective parts.
6. Unit tilts up while unattended.	Moisture in key switch.	Test, replace defective parts.
HYDRAULIC **Outboard hydraulic system operates normally, but:**		
1. Will not hold trimmed position in FORWARD gear.	a. External leaks (fittings and parts leak). b. Internal cylinder leaks. c. Pump check valve leak (high pressure).* d. Dirt in system.*	a. Tighten fittings or replace if defective. b. Replace or repair cylinder. c. Replace pump base assembly. d. Flush system with clean oil, fill and bleed system.
2. Will not hold trimmed position in reverse gear.	a. External leaks (fittings and parts leak). b. Internal cylinder leaks. c. Control valve assembly inoperative. d. Reverse lock control turned full in.	a. Tighten fittings or replace if defective. b. Replace or repair cylinder. c. Replace assembly. d. Turn full out to engage reverse locks.
3. Will only trim part way up.	a. Oil level low. b. Too low or no pump pressure.	a. Add oil. b. Replace pump body assembly.
4. Will not tilt up manually.	a. Control valve assembly inoperative. b. Reverse control not turned fully in.	a. Replace assembly. b. Turn full in to disengage reverse locks.
5. Engine swings in and out when shifting from FORWARD to REVERSE to FORWARD.	Air in system.	Check for leaks and bleed system properly.

(continued)

3

Table 6 OUTBOARD POWER TRIM TROUBLESHOOTING (continued)

Malfunction	Causes	Remedy
HYDRAULIC (continued) **Outboard hydraulic system operates normally, but:**		
6. Will not release from power tilted "full up" position.	Too low or no "down" pump pressure.	Replace pump body assembly.
7. Trails out when backing off throttle from high speed.	a. Control valve assembly inoperative.	a. Replace assembly.
	b. Air in system.	b. Check for leaks and bleed system properly.
	c. Reverse lock control knob turned full in.	c. Turn full out to activate reverse locks.
8. Oil foams out of pump vent.	a. Oil level low.	a. Add oil.
9. Will not remain tilted full up.	a. External leaks (fittings and parts leak).	a. Tighten fittings or replace if defective.
	b. Internal cylinder leaks.	b. Replace or repair cylinder.
	c. Pump check valve leak (high pressure).*	c. Replace or repair cylinder.
	d. Dirt in system.*	d. Flush system with clean oil, fill and bleed system.

* Pump check valve may contain entrapped foreign particles which can be cleared by operating system up and down several times when flushing system. If flushing system fails to correct the problem, the check valve is defective.

Chapter Four

Lubrication, Maintenance and Tune-Up

The modern outboard motor delivers more power and performance than ever before, with higher compression ratios, improved electrical systems and other design advances. Proper lubrication, maintenance and tune-ups have thus become increasingly important as ways in which you can maintain a high level of performance, extend engine life and extract the maximum economy of operation.

You can do your own lubrication, maintenance and tune-ups if you follow the correct procedures and use common sense. The following information is based on recommendations from Mercury Marine that will help you keep your outboard motor operating at its peak performance level.

Tables 1-4 are at the end of the chapter.

MODEL REDESIGNATION

A change in the method of rating engine output from crankshaft (power head) to propeller shaft horsepower resulted in a change of designation for the Merc 50 to the Merc 45 in 1986. The engine is also designated as the "Classic 50."

A detuned Merc 60 is designated as the Merc 50 for 1986-on. A detuned Merc V150 is designated as the Merc V135 for 1986-on. The 1987-1988 Laser 220 XRi is designated as the 200 XRi for 1989. Maintenance and service procedures for the 45 (Classic 50), Merc 50, Merc V135 and 200 XRi remain essentially the same as for the previous Merc 50, Merc 60, Merc V150 and Laser 220 XRi.

LUBRICATION

Proper Fuel Selection

Two-stroke engines are lubricated by mixing oil with the fuel. The various components of the engine are thus lubricated as the fuel-oil mixture passes through the crankcase and cylinders. Since two-stroke fuel serves the dual function of producing ignition and distributing the lubrication, the use of marine white gasolines should be avoided due to their low octane rating and tendency to cause ring sticking and port plugging.

All Mercury inline outboards require the use of regular leaded, premium, low-lead or lead-free gasolines with a minimum posted pump octane rating of 86 (research octane number 90).

All Mercury V6 outboards require the use of regular leaded and premium gasolines with a minimum posted pump octane of 89 (research octane number 94).

Sour Fuel

Fuel should not be stored for more than 60 days (under ideal conditions). Gasoline forms gum and varnish deposits as it ages. Such fuel will cause starting problems. A fuel additive such as Sta-Bil may be used to prevent gum and varnish formation during storage or prolonged periods of non-use but it is always better to drain the tank in such cases. Always use fresh gasoline when mixing fuel for your outboard.

Fuel Quality

Gasoline blended with alcohol is widely available, although it is not legally required to be labeled as such in many states. A mixture of 10 percent ethyl alcohol and 90 percent unleaded gasoline is called gasohol.

Fuels with an alcohol content tend to absorb moisture from the air. When the moisture content of the fuel reaches approximately one percent, it combines with the alcohol and separates from the fuel. This separation does not normally occur when gasohol is used in an automobile, as the tank is generally emptied within a few days after filling it.

The problem does occur in marine use, however, because boats often remain idle between start-ups for days or even weeks. This length of time permits separation to take place. The water-alcohol mixture settles at the bottom of the fuel tank where the fuel pickup carries it into the fuel line to the carburetor(s). Since outboard motors will not run on this mixture, it is necessary to drain

the fuel tank, flush out the fuel system with clean gasoline and then remove, clean and reinstall the spark plugs before the engine can be started.

Some methods of blending alcohol with gasoline now make use of "cold solvents" as a suspension agent to prevent the water-alcohol from separating from the gasoline. Gasoline mixed with alcohol in any manner can cause numerous and serious problems with an automotive fuel system.

The major danger of using gasoline blended with alcohol in a outboard motor is that a shot of the water-alcohol mix may be picked up and sent to one of the carburetors of a multi-cylinder engine. Since this mixture contains no oil, it will wash oil off the bore of any cylinder it enters. The other carburetor(s) receiving good fuel-oil mixture will keep the engine running while the cylinder(s) receiving the water-alcohol mixture can suffer internal damage.

The problem of gasoline blended with alcohol has become so prevalent around the United States that Miller Tools (32615 Park Lane, Garden City, MI 48135) now offers an Alcohol Detection Kit (part no. C-4846) so owners can determine the quality of fuel being used.

The detection procedure is performed with water as a reacting agent. However, if cold solvents have been used as a suspension agent in alcohol blending, the test will not show the presence of alcohol unless ethylene glycol (automotive antifreeze) is used instead of water as a reacting agent. It is suggested that a gasoline sample be tested twice using the detection kit: First with water and then with ethylene glycol (automotive antifreeze).

The procedure cannot differentiate between types of alcohol (ethanol, methanol, etc.) nor is it considered to be absolutely accurate from a scientific standpoint, but it is accurate enough to determine whether or not there is enough alcohol in the fuel to cause the user to take precautions. Maintaining a close watch on the quality of fuel used can save hundreds of dollars in fuel system repairs.

Recommended Fuel Mixture

Recent changes in gasoline have made it very important to use only 2-cycle oils or additives that do *not* contain calcium sulfonate. Calcuim sulfonate has the potential of causing the fuel to gel and plug oil injection filter screens. Mercury Marine recommends only the use of Quicksilver 2-cycle oil with a blue, gray and black label. If you have a supply of the older Quicksilver 2-cycle oil with the red, black and white label, it should be used only in engines *without* oil injection.

Use the specified gasoline for your Mercury outboard and mix with Mercury Formula 50-D Quicksilver 2-Cycle Outboard Motor Oil in the following ratios:

CAUTION
Do not, under any circumstances, use multigrade or other high detergent automotive oils or oils which contain metallic additives. This type of oil is harmful to 2-stroke engines and may result in piston scoring, bearing failure or both.

a. During engine break-in, thoroughly mix two 12-ounce cans of Mercury Formula 50-D Quicksilver 2-Cycle Outboard Motor Oil with each 5 gallons (16 ounces with each 3 gallons) of gasoline in your remote fuel tank. This provides a 25:1 mixture.

NOTE
Operation in Canada requires mixing 15 U.S. ounces of Mercury Formula 50-D Quicksilver 2-Cycle Outboard Motor Oil to each 5 Imperial gallons of gasoline in the remote fuel tank.

b. After engine break-in, thoroughly mix one 12-ounce can of Mercury Formula

50-D Quicksilver 2-Cycle Outboard Motor Oil with each 5 gallons (8 ounces with each 3 gallons) of gasoline in your remote fuel tank. This provides a 50:1 mixture.

CAUTION
*There are a number of oil products on the market which specify use at 100:1. They are **not** BIA-TC-W approved and should **not** be used.*

If Formula 50-D is not available, any high-quality 2-cycle oil intended for outboard use may be substituted, as long as the oil meets BIA rating TC-W and specifies so on the container. Follow the manufacturer's mixing instructions on the container but do not exceed a 50:1 ratio, (25:1 during break-in).

Correct Fuel Mixing

Mix the fuel and oil outdoors or in a well-ventilated indoor location. Mix the fuel directly in the remote tank.

WARNING
Gasoline is an extreme fire hazard. Never use gasoline near heat, sparks or flame. Do not smoke while mixing fuel.

Measure the required amounts of gasoline and oil accurately. Pour a small amount of oil into the remote tank and add a small amount of gasoline. Mix it thoroughly by shaking or stirring vigorously; then add the balance of the gasoline and oil and mix again.

Mix gasoline and oil at a 25:1 ratio during the 10-hour break-in period. Operate a new motor at half-throttle (2,500-3,500 rpm) for 2 hours, then avoid sustained full-throttle operation for another 8 hours. After the break-in period, mix gasoline and oil at a 50:1 ratio.

Using less than the specified amount of oil can result in insufficient lubrication and serious engine damage. Using more oil than specified causes spark plug fouling, erratic carburetion, excessive smoking and rapid

4

carbon accumulation. Cleanliness is of prime importance. Even a very small particle of dirt can cause carburetion problems. Always use fresh gasoline. Gum and varnish deposits tend to form in gasoline stored in a tank for any length of time. Use of sour fuel can result in carburetor problems and spark plug fouling.

Oil Injection

Merc V6 models

An oil injection system was introduced on 1984 Merc V6 engines as an option and made standard on 1985 and later V6 models. This system automatically supplies pre-mixed gas and oil to the crankcase according to engine demand. The mixture varies from 100:1 at idle to 50:1 at wide open throttle.

A 3 gallon remote oil tank supplies oil to the reservoir mounted under the cowl (**Figure 1**). An oil injection pump is mounted on the engine block (**Figure 2**) and driven by a gear on the crankshaft. This pump is connected to the throttle linkage to meter the oil flow according to engine rpm. The pump injects oil at the fuel pump on the Merc 200 and just before the fuel pump on the Merc 150. **Figure 3** is a schematic of the injection flow system.

The engine-mounted reservoir provides sufficient oil for 30 minutes of operation if the remote oil tank is empty. In addition, a built-in warning horn will sound if the reservoir cap sensor indicates that the oil level is low or if the injection pump drive system malfunctions. The horn sounds briefly each time the ignition is turned ON to indicate that the warning system is functioning properly. If the horn does not sound or if it remains on when the key is turned ON, do not start the engine. If the horn sounds intermittently when the engine is running, shut the engine off immediately.

If an electric fuel pump is used with oil-injected Merc 150 or 200 models, Mercury Marine specifies that a fuel pressure

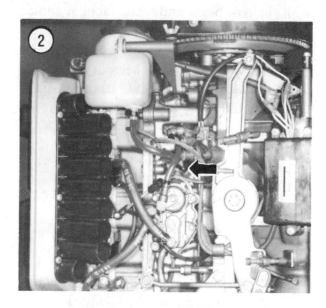

regulator be installed to regulate the pump to 2 psi. See your Mercury dealer for recommended pressure regulators.

AutoBlend Oil Injection

A one-piece optional oil injection system (AutoBlendI) is available for 1986 and later 45-115 hp electric start models. A similar system (AutoBlend II) is offered with 1987 and later 45 hp manual start models. The two systems differ in that AutoBlend I is powered directly by the battery used for starting.

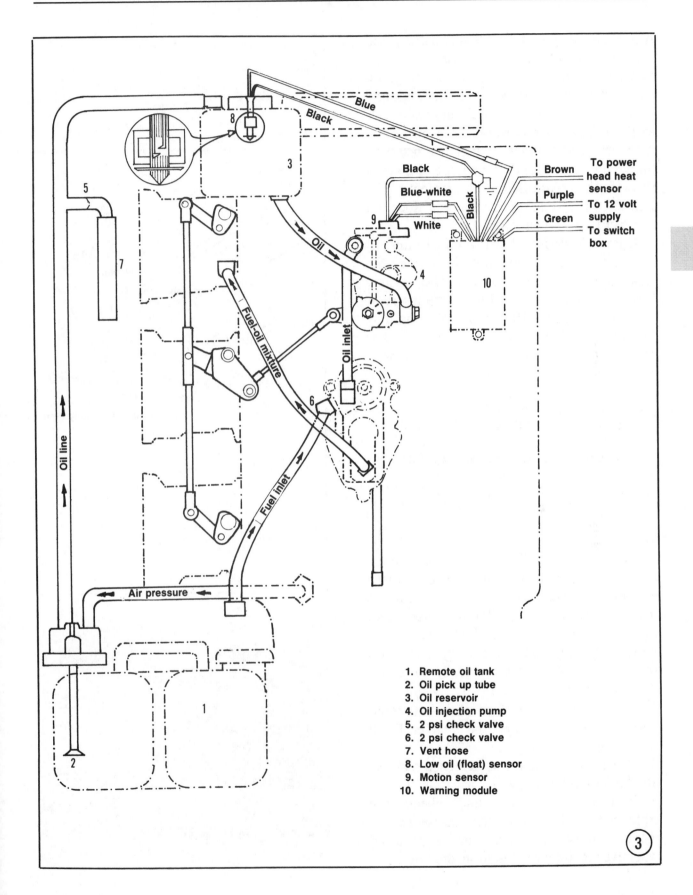

1. Remote oil tank
2. Oil pick up tube
3. Oil reservoir
4. Oil injection pump
5. 2 psi check valve
6. 2 psi check valve
7. Vent hose
8. Low oil (float) sensor
9. Motion sensor
10. Warning module

4

③

AutoBlend II has its own 9-volt battery and can be used with manual models.

A bracket-mounted tank with 3 1/2 qt. oil reservoir connects between the fuel tank and engine fuel inlet. The integral pump connects to the battery to mix the oil at a 50:1 ratio with up to 45 gallons of fuel per reservoir filling under vacuum or pressure. **Figure 4** shows the AutoBlend I system; the AutoBlend II system is similar but does not connect to a 12-volt battery.

A low oil warning horn (A), fuel filter (B) and drain plug (C) are installed under the removable cover. See **Figure 5**. The warning horn is designed to sound when the reservoir level falls to about 30 minutes of remaining operation. The filter screen traps contamination before the fuel is mixed with the oil.

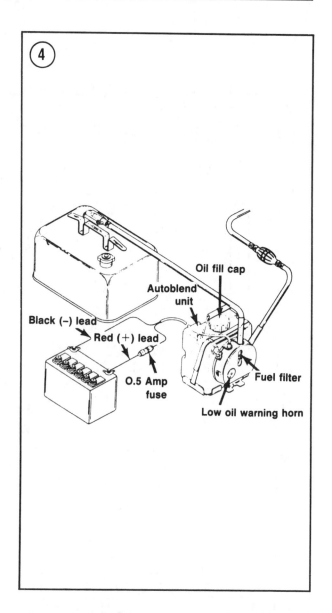

> *CAUTION*
> *Certain BIA TC-W approved oils have a tendency to gel due to the use of additives containing calcium sulfonate and can plug AutoBlend filter screens. A strainer kit, part No. 15387A1, should be installed on units sold without it.*

The drain plug allows fuel to be drained from the unit before storage or during extended periods of non-use. Complete instructions on installation, use and maintenance are furnished with the AutoBlend unit. The following inspection should be performed periodically to assure that the unit functions properly.

1. Check the oil level in the Autoblend reservoir prior to using the engine. Refill reservoir as required.
2. Make sure the fill cap is tightened securely after refilling the reservoir.
3. Remove the cover and check the translucent filter monthly for sediment. Replace once per season or as required whenever sediment is found in the filter.

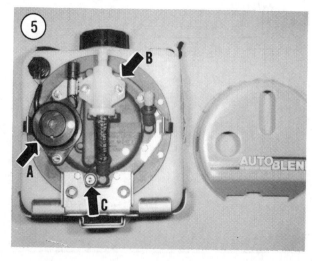

4. Check low oil warning horn after refilling reservoir by removing the AutoBlend from its mounting bracket and inverting it. If the horn does not sound, check the in-line fuse (**Figure 4**). If the fuse is good, return the unit to your Mercury dealer for further diagnosis and troubleshooting.

5. Make sure the AutoBlend is securely mounted in its bracket.

6. Check the fuel lines for stress or kinks and make sure their clamps are tight.

7. Have the AutoBlend diaphragm checked by a Mercury dealer at the beginning of each season. If you drain and store your outboard, be sure to drain the AutoBlend system.

879 Oil Injection System

The newly-designed 1987 and later Merc 70, 80 and 90 hp models, the 1988-on Merc 100 and 1989 Merc 115 models incorporate a different oil injection system than the one used on V6 models since 1984. A large-mouth oil tank mounted on the side of the power head under the cowling holds one gallon, enough to provide 18 hours of operation at wide open throttle. The tank has a sight gauge (**Figure 6**) that is visible through a window in the cowling. A tank-mounted sensor provides a low oil warning signal when the level drops to a 40-50 minute supply at wide open throttle.

The single outlet mechanically-driven oil injection pump couples to the crankshaft to provide uniform lubrication of all cylinders. **Figures 7-9** illustrate the installation on Merc 70, 80 and 90 hp models. **Figure 7** shows the injection flow circuit. **Figure 8** shows the pump connection to the crankshaft and **Figure 9** is an exploded view of the pump.

The pump delivers oil relative to crankshaft speed and throttle position, using engine vacuum to assure that correct oil delivery is provided as the pump components wear. The oil system does not require priming for start-up.

Consistent Fuel Mixtures

The carburetor idle adjustment is sensitive to fuel mixture variations which result from the use of different oils and gasolines or from inaccurate measuring and mixing. This may require readjustment of the idle needle. To prevent the necessity for constant readjustment of the carburetor from one batch of fuel to the next, always be consistent. Prepare each batch of fuel exactly the same as previous ones.

Lower Drive Unit Lubrication

Lubricate the lower drive unit every 25 hours or once every 30 days with Quicksilver Super-Duty Outboard Gear Lubricant (part No. C-92-68617).

> *CAUTION*
> *Do not use regular automotive grease in the lower drive unit. Its expansion and foam characteristics are not suitable for marine use.*

4

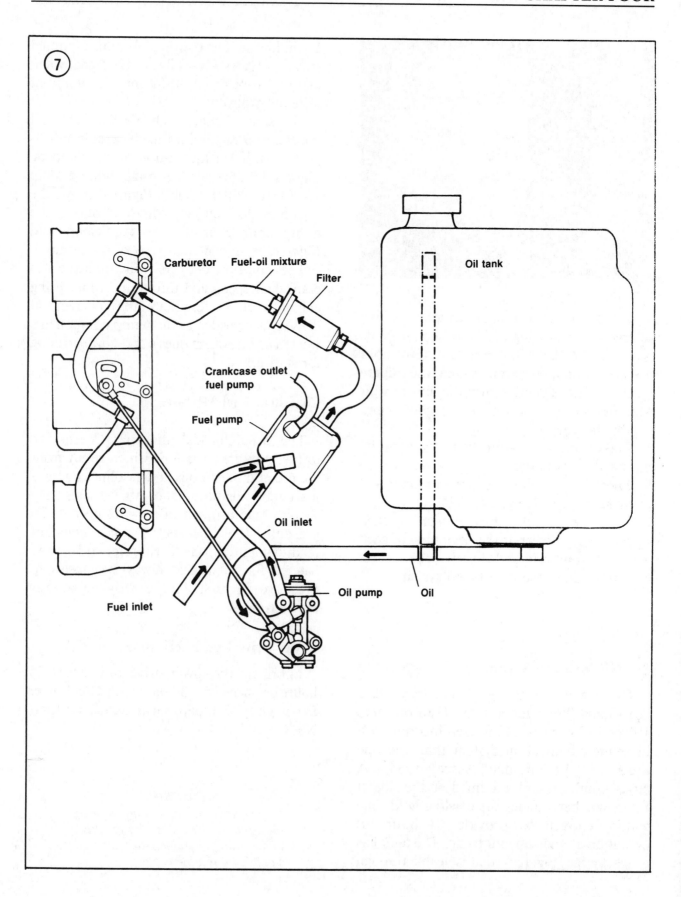

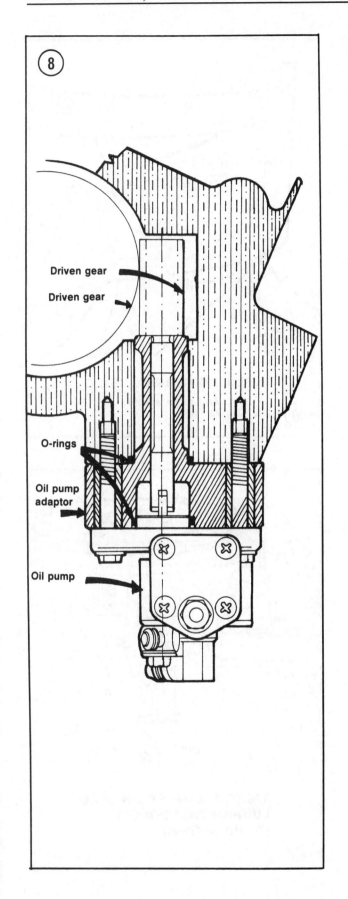

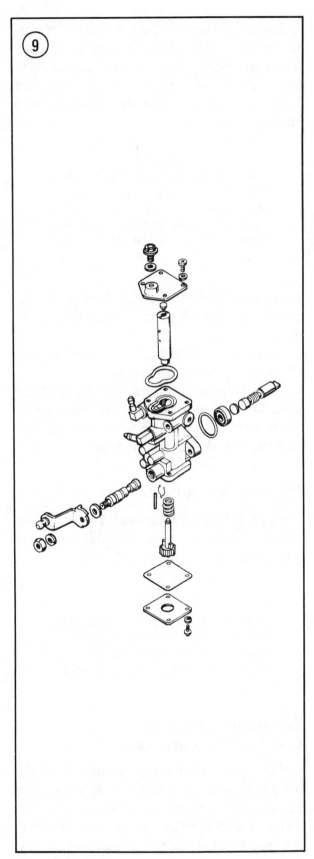

1. Locate and remove the lubricant filler plug on the right side of the gear housing (just above the skeg). Then remove the air vent screw above the anti-cavitation plate. See **Figure 10**. Do not lose the accompanying washers.

> *CAUTION*
> *Never lubricate the lower unit without first removing the air vent screw, as the injected lubricant displaces air which must be allowed to escape. The gear housing cannot be completely filled otherwise.*

2. Inject lubricant into the filler plug hole until excess fluid flows out the air vent screw hole.

3. Drain about one fluid ounce of fluid to allow for lubricant expansion.

4. Install the air vent screw, then the filler plug. Be sure the washers are in place under the head of each, so that water will not leak past the threads into the housing.

Other Lubrication Points

Refer to **Figures 10-25** and **Tables 1-4** for other lubricant points, frequency of lubrication and lubricant to be used.

> *CAUTION*
> *When lubricating steering cable, make sure its core is fully retracted into the cable housing. Lubricating the cable while extended can cause a hydraulic lock to occur.*

Salt Water Corrosion of Gear Housing Bearing Carrier/Nut

Salt water corrosion that is allowed to build up unchecked can eventually split the gear housing and destroy the lower unit. If your motor is used in salt water, remove the cover nut and bearing carrier at least once a year

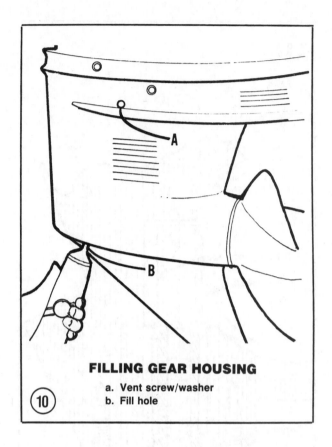

FILLING GEAR HOUSING

  a. Vent screw/washer
  b. Fill hole

⑩

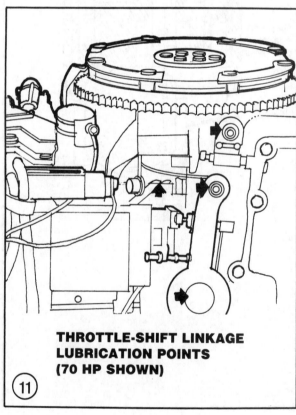

**THROTTLE-SHIFT LINKAGE
LUBRICATION POINTS
(70 HP SHOWN)**

⑪

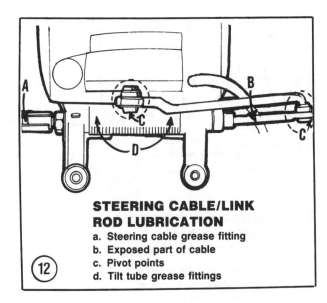

STEERING CABLE/LINK ROD LUBRICATION

a. Steering cable grease fitting
b. Exposed part of cable
c. Pivot points
d. Tilt tube grease fittings

(12)

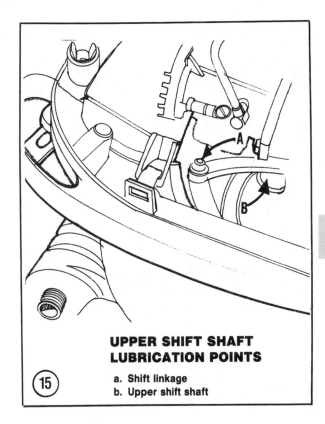

UPPER SHIFT SHAFT LUBRICATION POINTS

a. Shift linkage
b. Upper shift shaft

(15)

4

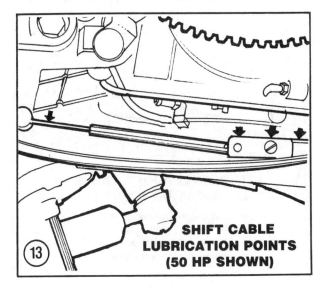

SHIFT CABLE LUBRICATION POINTS (50 HP SHOWN)

(13)

(16)

STARTER PINION GEAR LUBRICATION POINT

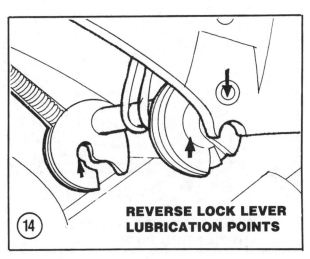

REVERSE LOCK LEVER LUBRICATION POINTS

(14)

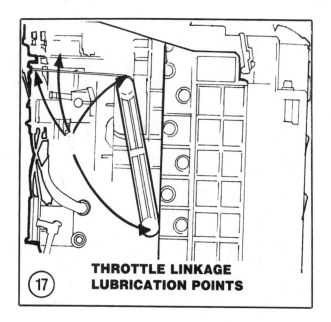

THROTTLE LINKAGE LUBRICATION POINTS

⑰

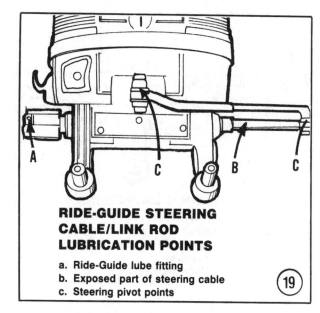

RIDE-GUIDE STEERING CABLE/LINK ROD LUBRICATION POINTS

a. Ride-Guide lube fitting
b. Exposed part of steering cable
c. Steering pivot points

⑲

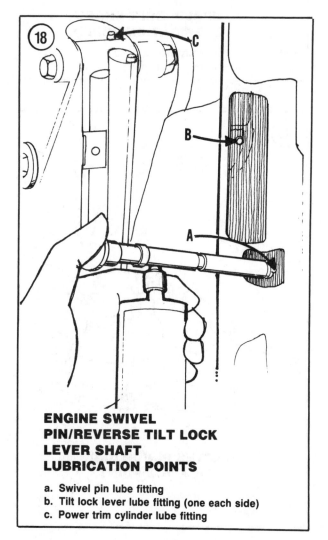

ENGINE SWIVEL PIN/REVERSE TILT LOCK LEVER SHAFT LUBRICATION POINTS

a. Swivel pin lube fitting
b. Tilt lock lever lube fitting (one each side)
c. Power trim cylinder lube fitting

⑱

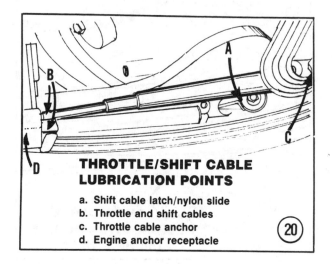

THROTTLE/SHIFT CABLE LUBRICATION POINTS

a. Shift cable latch/nylon slide
b. Throttle and shift cables
c. Throttle cable anchor
d. Engine anchor receptacle

⑳

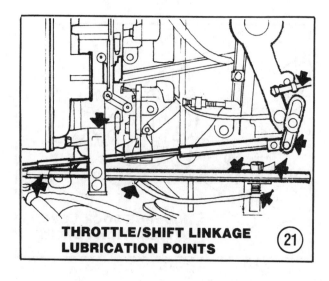

THROTTLE/SHIFT LINKAGE LUBRICATION POINTS

㉑

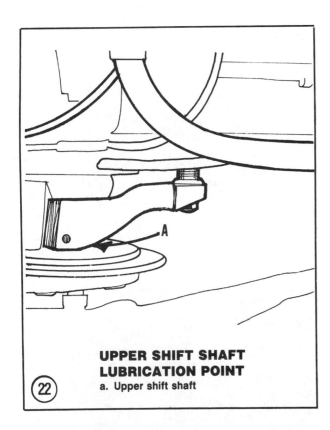

**UPPER SHIFT SHAFT
LUBRICATION POINT**

a. Upper shift shaft

㉒

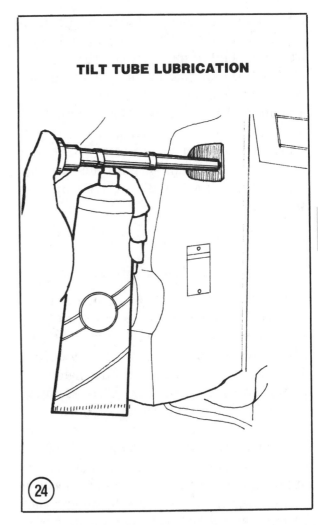

TILT TUBE LUBRICATION

㉔

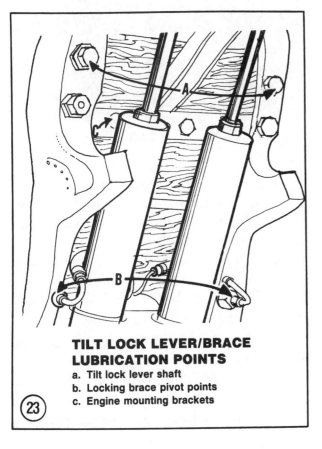

**TILT LOCK LEVER/BRACE
LUBRICATION POINTS**

a. Tilt lock lever shaft
b. Locking brace pivot points
c. Engine mounting brackets

㉓

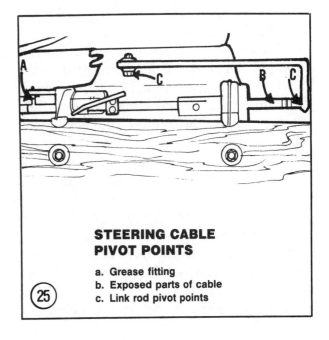

**STEERING CABLE
PIVOT POINTS**

a. Grease fitting
b. Exposed parts of cable
c. Link rod pivot points

㉕

after the initial 20-hour inspection. Clean all corrosive deposits and dried-up lubricant from each end of the carrier (**Figure 26**).

Clean the gear housing internal threads and cover nut external threads. Apply a liberal amount of Perfect Seal (part No. C-92-34277) to each end of the carrier and to the gear housing and cover nut threads. Make sure Perfect Seal does not get into the bearings. Reinstall carrier and tighten nut to specifications.

STORAGE

The major consideration in preparing an outboard motor for storage is to protect it from rust, corrosion and dirt. Mercury Marine recommends the following procedure.
1. Remove the cowling from the engine.
2. Remove the sound box, if so equipped. **Figure 27** shows a typical installation.
3. Operate the motor in a test tank or on the boat. Start the engine and let it warm up.
4. Disconnect the fuel line and let engine run at low rpm while pouring 2 oz. of Quicksilver Storage Seal (part No. C-92-78380) into each carburetor throat. Let engine stall out, indicating that the carburetors have run completely dry.
5. Remove spark plugs as described in this chapter. Spray about one ounce of Storage Seal into each spark plug hole. Turn engine over by hand several times to distribute Storage Seal throughout the cylinders. Reinstall spark plugs.
6. Service the fuel tank filter as follows:
   a. Detach the fuel line from the tank and remove the fuel pickup tube by removing the screws in the top connector housing.
   b. Clean the fine wire mesh filter by rinsing it in clean solvent. Blow dry with compressed air.
7. Service the engine fuel filter as follows:

a. Remove the front bracket (if so equipped) by taking off the cap screws holding it to the front of the bottom cowl and top plate.
b. Remove the screw and flat plastic washer holding filter cover to fuel pump (**Figure 28**). Remove fuel filter cover.
c. Remove and discard O-ring.
d. Clean filter by rinsing it in clean solvent. Blow dry with compressed air.
e. Install filter cover with a new O-ring and tighten screw securely.
f. Install front bracket, if so equipped.

8. Drain and refill lower unit as described in this chapter. Check condition of vent and fill plug gaskets. Replace as required.

9. Refer to **Figures 10-25** and **Tables 1-4** as appropriate and lubricate motor at all specified points.

10. Clean the motor, including all accessible power head parts. Spray with Corrosion and Rust Preventive (part No. C-92-78379). Install the cowling and wipe a thin film of clean engine oil on all painted surfaces.

11. Remove the propeller and lubricate propeller shaft with Perfect Seal. Reinstall propeller.

12. Clean the water pickup with a piece of wire. Disconnect tubing from speedometer (if so equipped) and blow pickup out with low-pressure compressed air.

> *CAUTION*
> *Make certain that all water drain holes in the gear housing are free and open to allow water to drain out. Water expands as it freezes and can crack the gear housing or water pump.*

13. Drain the system completely to prevent damage from freezing. With tubing removed from speedometer fitting, blow through tubing with compressed air to remove water.

14. Service the battery as follows:
   a. Disconnect the negative battery cable, then the positive battery cable.
   b. Remove all grease, sulphate and dirt from the battery surface.
   c. Check the electrolyte level in each battery cell and top up with distilled water, if necessary. Fluid level in each cell should not be higher than 3/16 in. above the perforated baffles.
   d. Lubricate the terminal bolts with grease or petroleum jelly.

> *CAUTION*
> *A discharged battery can be damaged by freezing.*

   e. With the battery in a fully-charged condition (specific gravity 1.260-1.275), store in a dry place where the temperature will not drop below freezing.
   f. Recharge the battery every 45 days or whenever the specific gravity drops below 1.230. Before charging, cover the plates with distilled water, but not more than 3/16 in. above the perforated baffles. The charge rate should not exceed 6 amps. Discontinue charging when the specific gravity reaches 1.260 at 80° F (27° C).
   g. Before placing the battery back into service after winter storage, remove the excess grease from the terminals, leaving a small amount on. Install battery in a fully-charged state.

COMPLETE SUBMERSION

An outboard motor which has been lost overboard should be recovered as quickly as possible. Disassemble and clean it immediately—any delay will result in rust and corrosion of internal components. The following emergency steps should be accomplished immediately if the motor is submerged in fresh water.

1. Remove the cowling.

2. Remove the spark plugs as described in this chapter.

3. Remove the carburetor float bowl covers. See Chapter Six.

4. Wash the outside of the motor with clean water to remove weeds, mud and other debris.

CAUTION
If there is a possibility that sand may have entered the powerhead, do not try to start the motor or severe internal damage may occur.

5. Drain as much water as possible from the power head by placing the motor in a horizontal position. Manually rotate the flywheel with the spark plug holes facing downward.

CAUTION
Do not force the motor if it does not turn over freely when the rewind starter is operated in step 6. This may be an indication of internal damage such as a bent connecting rod or broken piston.

6. Pour alcohol into the carburetor throats to displace water. Operate rewind starter. Position the motor so you can pour alcohol into the spark plug holes. Operate rewind starter again.

7. Repeat Step 6 with Mercury Quicksilver Engine Cleaner (part No. C-92-78382).

8. Reinstall spark plugs and carburetor float bowl covers.

9. Try starting the motor with a fresh fuel source. If motor will start, let it run at least one hour to eliminate any water remaining inside.

CAUTION
If it is not possible to disassemble and clean the motor immediately, resubmerge it in water to prevent rust and corrosion formation until such time as it can be properly serviced.

10. If motor will not start in Step 9, try to diagnose the cause as fuel, electrical or mechanical and correct. If the engine cannot be started within 2 hours, disassemble, clean and oil all parts thoroughly as soon as possible.

ENGINE FLUSHING

Periodic engine flushing will prevent salt or silt deposits from accumulating in the water passageways. This procedure should also be performed whenever an outboard motor is operated in salt water or polluted water.

Keep the motor in an upright position during and after flushing. This prevents water from passing into the power head through the drive shaft housing and exhaust ports during the flushing procedure. It also eliminates the possibility of residual water being trapped in the drive shaft housing or other passageways.

1. Remove the flushing plug (**Figure 29**) and washer from the "FLUSH" hole.

2. Attach the flushing device from the front of the lower unit according to manufacturer's instructions. See **Figure 30**.

3. Connect a garden hose between a water tap and the flushing device.

4. Open the water tap partially—do not use full pressure.

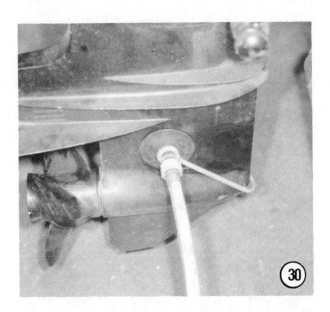

5. Shift into NEUTRAL gear, then start motor. Keep engine speed below 1,200 rpm.

6. Adjust water flow so that there is a slight loss of water around the rubber cups of the flushing device.

7. Check the motor to make sure that water is being discharged from the "tell-tale" nozzle. If it is not, stop the motor immediately and determine the cause of the problem.

CAUTION
Flush the motor for at least 5 minutes if used in salt water.

8. Flush motor until discharged water is clear. Stop motor.

9. Close water tap and remove flushing device from lower unit.

TUNE-UP

A tune-up consists of a series of inspections, adjustments and parts replacements to compensate for normal wear and deterioration of outboard motor components. Regular tune-ups are important for power, performance and economy. Mercury Marine recommends that its outboards be serviced every 6 months or 100

hours of operation. If subjected to limited use, the engine should be tuned at least once a year.

Since proper outboard motor operation depends upon a number of interrelated system functions, a tune-up consisting of only one or two corrections will seldom give lasting results. For best results, a thorough and systematic procedure of analysis and correction is necessary.

Prior to performing a tune-up, it is a good idea to flush the motor as described in this chapter and check for satisfactory water pump operation.

The tune-up sequence recommended by Mercury Marine includes the following:

    a. Compression check.
    b. Spark plug service.
    c. Lower unit and water pump check.
    d. Fuel system service.
    e. Battery, starter motor and solenoid check.
    f. Alternator and rectifier check.
    g. Internal wiring harness check.
    h. Timing, synchronization and adjustment.
    i. Performance test (on boat).

Anytime the fuel or ignition systems are adjusted or defective parts replaced, the engine timing, synchronization and adjustment *must* be checked. These procedures are described in Chapter Five. Perform the timing, synchronization and adjustment procedure for your engine *before* running the performance test.

Compression Check

An accurate cylinder compression check gives a good idea of the condition of the basic working parts of the engine. It is also an important first step in any tune-up, as a motor with low or unequal compression between cylinders *cannot* be satisfactorily tuned. Any compression problem discovered during this check must be corrected before continuing with the tune-up procedure.

1. With the engine warm, disconnect the spark plug wires and remove the plugs as described in this chapter.

2. Ground the spark plug wires to the engine to disable the ignition system.

3. Connect the compression tester to the top spark plug hole according to manufacturer's instructions (**Figure 31**).

4. Make sure the throttle is held wide open and crank the engine through at least 4 compression strokes. Record the gauge reading.

5. Repeat Step 3 and Step 4 for each remaining cylinder.

While minimum compression per cylinder should be no less than 100 psi, actual readings are not as important as the differences in readings when interpreting the results. A variation of more than 10 percent between 2 cylinders indicates a problem with the lower reading cylinder, such as worn or sticking piston rings and/or scored pistons or cylinders. In such cases, pour a tablespoon of engine oil into the suspect cylinder and repeat Step 3 and Step 4. If the compression is raised significantly (by 10 psi in an old engine) the rings are worn and should be replaced.

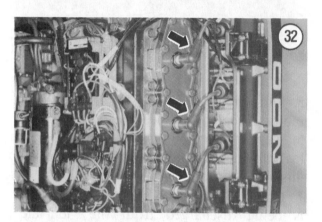

Many outboard owners are plagued by hard starting and generally poor running for which there seems to be no good cause. Carburetion and ignition check out as good and a compression test may show that everything is well in the engine's upper end. What a compression test does not show is lack of primary compression. In a 2-stroke engine, the crankcase must be alternately under high pressure and low pressure. After the piston closes the intake port, further downward movement of the piston causes the entrapped mixture to be pressurized so that it can rush quickly into the cylinder when the scavenging ports are opened. Upward piston movement cre-

ates a lower pressure in the crankcase, enabling fuel/air mixture to pass in from the carburetor.

When the crankshaft seals or case gaskets leak, the crankcase cannot hold pressure and proper engine operation becomes impossible. Any other source of leakage, such as defective cylinder base gaskets or a porous or cracked crankcase casting, will result in the same conditions.

If the power head shows signs of overheating (discolored or scorched paint) but the compression test turns up nothing abnormal, check the cylinders visually through the transfer ports for possible scoring. A cylinder can be slightly scored and still deliver a relatively good compression reading. In such a case, it is also a good idea to double-check the water pump operation as a possible cause for overheating.

4

Spark Plug Replacement

Improper installation of spark plugs is one of the most common causes of poor spark plug performance in outboard motors. The gasket on the plug must be fully compressed against a clean plug seat in order for heat transfer to take place effectively. This requires close attention to proper torquing during installation.

> *CAUTION*
> *Whenever the spark plugs are removed, dirt around them can fall into the plug holes. This can cause engine damage that is expensive to repair.*

1. Blow out any foreign matter from around the spark plugs with compressed air. Use a compressor if you have one. If you do not, use a can of compressed inert gas, available from photo stores.
2. Disconnect the spark plug wires (**Figure 32**, typical) by twisting the wire boot back and forth on the plug insulator while pulling outward. Pulling on the wire instead of the boot may cause internal damage to the wire.
3. Remove the plugs with an appropriate size spark plug socket. Keep the plugs in order so you know which cylinder they came from.
4. Examine each spark plug (**Figure 33**). Compare its condition with **Figure 34**. Spark plug condition indicates engine condition and can warn of developing trouble.

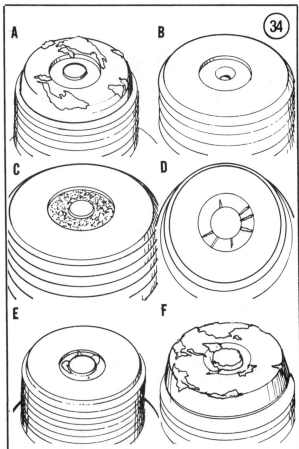

SURFACE GAP SPARK PLUG ANALYSIS

A. Normal—Light tan or gray colored deposits indicate that the engine/ignition system condition is good. Electrode wear indicates normal spark rotation.

B. Worn out—Excessive electrode wear can cause hard starting or a misfire during acceleration.

C. Cold fouled—Wet oil-fuel deposits are caused by "drowning" the plug with raw fuel mix during cranking, overrich carburetion or an improper fuel-oil ratio. Weak ignition will also contribute to this condition.

D. Carbon tracking—Electrically conductive deposits on the firing end provide a low—resistance path for the voltage. Carbon tracks form and can cause misfires.

E. Concentrated arc—Multi-colored appearance is normal. It is caused by electricity consistently following the same firing path. Arc path changes with deposit conductivity and gap erosion.

F. Aluminum throw-off—Caused by preignition. This is not a plug problem but the result of engine damage. Check engine to determine cause and extent of damage.

5. Check each plug for make and heat range. All should be of the same make and number or heat range.

6. Discard the plugs. Although they could be cleaned and reused if in good condition, they seldom last very long. New plugs are inexpensive and far more reliable.

7. Inspect the spark plug hole threads and clean them with a thread chaser (**Figure 35**). Wipe cylinder head seats clean before installing the new plugs.

8. Install new plugs with new gaskets and tighten to 20 ft.-lb. If a torque wrench is not available, seat plug finger-tight on gasket, then tighten an additional 1/4 turn with a wrench.

9. Inspect each spark plug wire before reconnecting it to its cylinder. If insulation is damaged or deteriorated, install a new plug wire. Push wire boot onto plug terminal and make sure it seats fully.

Lower Unit and Water Pump Check

A faulty water pump or one that performs below specifications can result in extensive engine damage. Thus, it is a good idea to replace the water pump impeller, seals and gaskets once a year or whenever the lower unit is removed for service. See Chapter Nine.

While many outboard owners depend upon the visual sign provided by the operation of the "tell-tale" hole, installation of a water pressure kit (available from your Mercury dealer) is a far more effective check of water pump operation. The kit contains a fitting and hose that attaches to the block. It is permanently installed and provided with a gauge for use in the boat.

After installing a pressure kit, note the gauge reading the first time the engine is run. It should be at least 5 psi under full throttle operating conditions. If the pressure reading falls off during subsequent engine use, service the water pump at the first available opportunity. See Chapter Nine.

Fuel Lines

1. Visually check all fuel lines for kinks, leaks, deterioration or other damage.

2. Disconnect fuel lines and blow out with compressed air to dislodge any contamination or foreign material.

NOTE
Liquid Neoprene is not recommended for sealing fuel line fittings. Use only Permatex.

3. Coat fuel line fittings sparingly with Permatex and reconnect the lines.

Fuel Pump Fuel Filter

1. Remove the front bracket (if so equipped) by taking off the cap screws holding it to the front of the bottom cowl and top plate.

2. Remove the screw and flat plastic washer holding filter cover to fuel pump (**Figure 28**). Remove fuel filter cover.

3. Remove and discard O-ring.

4. Clean filter by rinsing it in clean solvent. Blow dry with compressed air.

5. Install filter cover with a new O-ring and tighten screw securely.

6. Install front bracket, if so equipped.

Inline Canister Fuel Filter

A translucent filter canister (**Figure 36**) is installed between the fuel pump and carburetors on all 1986 and later 75-200 engines. This provides additional filtering

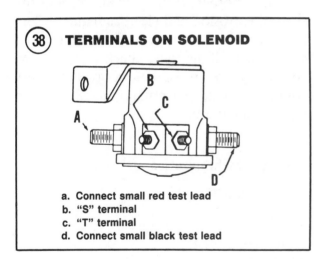

TERMINALS ON SOLENOID

a. Connect small red test lead
b. "S" terminal
c. "T" terminal
d. Connect small black test lead

protection and permits a visual inspection to determine if there is water in fuel.

Mercury Marine recommends the removal of this filter on V200 models with carburetors WH-28 or WH-31 between serial numbers 6537933 and A927074. It has been found that the extremely volatile gas currently sold causes vapor lock and/or fuel starvation with

these engines when pulling fuel through the water-separating filter assembly during hot weather. See your Mercury dealer for a satisfactory replacement filter.

To change the canister-type filter:
1. Unclamp and disconnect the inlet and outlet lines from the filter canister. Remove the canister from the engine.
2. Grasp the cover tightly and unscrew from the filter canister.
3. Remove the filter element.
4. Clean the element and canister in clean kerosene.
5. Check for correct positioning of the canister sealing ring.
6. Reconnect the inlet and outlet lines to the canister. Install new clamps.
7. Check the filter assembly for leakage by priming the fuel system with the fuel line primer bulb.

Fuel Pump

The fuel pump does not generally require service during a tune-up. However, if the engine has 100 hours on it since the fuel pump was last serviced, it is a good idea to remove and disassemble the pump, inspect each part carefully for wear or damage and reassemble it with a new diaphragm.

Fuel pump diaphragms are fragile and one that is defective often produces symptoms that are diagnosed as an ignition system problem. A common malfunction results from a tiny pinhole in the diaphragm. This pinhole allows gasoline to enter the crankcase and wet-foul the spark plug at idle speed. The problem disappears at higher speeds, as fuel quantity is limited. Since the plug is not fouled, it fires normally.

Fuel Pump Pressure Test

NOTE
Fuel pump pressure cannot be tested on integral fuel pump carburetors.

1. Install a pressure gauge (part No. C-91-30692) at the end of the fuel line leading to the upper carburetor.

2. Run the engine at idle. The fuel pump pressure must be:
   a. 50-70 hp—at least 2 psi.
   b. 80-85 hp—2.5-3.5 psi.
   c. Inline 6-cylinder and V6—3-4 psi.

3. Run the engine at wide-open throttle. The pressure must be:
   a. 50-70 hp—at least 2 psi.
   b. 80-85 hp—4.25-5.25 psi.
   c. 1987-on 70-115 hp—4-6 psi.
   d. V6—4.0-5.5 psi.
   e. Inline 6-cylinder—5.0-6.0 psi.

4. If the fuel pump does not perform within specifications, repair or replace as required.

Battery and Starter Motor Check

1. Check the battery's state of charge. See Chapter Seven.

2. Connect a voltmeter between the starter motor positive terminal (**Figure 37**) and ground.

3. Turn ignition switch to START and check voltmeter scale.

4A. If voltage exceeds 9.5 volts and the starter motor does not operate, replace the motor.

4B. If voltage is less than 9.5 volts, recheck the battery and connections. Recharge battery, if necessary, and repeat the procedure.

Solenoid Check

Any good volt/ohm/ammeter (VOA) can be used for this test.

1. Disconnect all leads from the starter solenoid. See **Figure 38**.

2. Connect the VOA meter leads to large solenoid terminals (A and D, **Figure 38**).

3. Set the meter to the R×1 scale.

4. Connect a 12-volt battery between small solenoid terminals (B and C, **Figure 38**).

5. If the solenoid does not click and the VOA meter reads zero ohms, replace the solenoid.

Alternator and Rectifier Check

Test the stator and rectifier with an ohmmeter. See Chapter Three.

Internal Wiring Harness Check

1. Check the wiring harness for signs of frayed or chafed insulation.

2. Check for loose connections between the wires and terminal ends.

3. Check harness connector for bent electrical prongs.

4. Check harness connector and prongs for signs of corrosion and clean as required.

5. If harness is suspected of contributing to electrical malfunctions, check all wires for continuity and resistance between harness connection and terminal end. Repair or replace as required.

Timing, Synchronization and Adjustment

See Chapter Five.

Performance Test (On Boat)

Before performance testing the engine, make sure that the boat bottom is cleaned of all marine growth and that there is no evidence of a "rocker" or "hooker" in the bottom. Any of these conditions will reduce performance considerably.

The boat should be performance tested with an average load and with the motor tilted at an angle that will allow the boat to ride on an even keel. If equipped with an adjustable trim tab, it should be properly adjusted to allow the boat to steer in either direction with equal ease.

Check engine rpm at full throttle. If not within the range for the motor as specified in Chapter Five, check the propeller pitch. A high pitch propeller will reduce rpm while a lower pitch prop will increase it.

Readjust the idle mixture and speed under actual operating conditions as required to obtain the best low-speed engine performance.

Table 1 45-70 HP LUBRICATION POINTS

Frequency	Item	Figure No.	Lubricant type
Every 60 days (fresh water); every 30 days (salt water)	Steering cable	12	Multipurpose lubricant (part No. C-92-63250)
	Throttle cable/linkage	11	
	Upper shift shaft	15	
	Reverse lock lever	14	
	Shift linkage/shift cable	11/13	
	Steering link rod pivot points	12	SAE 30W engine oil
	Clamp screws	—	Anti-corrosion grease (part No. C-9263290)
Once in season (fresh water); every 60 days (salt water)	Starter pinion	16	SAE 10W engine oil
	Propeller shaft	—	Perfect Seal (part No. C-92-34277)
After 1st 10 days of season, then each 30 days	Gear housing	10	Super-Duty Lubricant (part No. C-92-68617)

Table 2 80-150 HP INLINE ENGINE LUBRICATION POINTS

Frequency	Item	Figure No.	Lubricant type
Every 60 days (fresh water); every 30 days (salt water)	Steering cable/ tilt tube	12/19	Multipurpose lubricant (part No. C-92-63250)
	Throttle/shift linkage	15/17	
	Upper shift shaft	15	
	Reverse lock lever	14	
	Throttle/shift shift cable	20	
	Power trim cylinder	18	
	Tilt lock lever	18	
	Steering link rod pivot points	19	SAE 30W engine oil
	Clamp screws	—	Anti-corrosion Grease (part No. C-9263290)
Once in season (fresh water); every 60 days (salt water)	Starter pinion	16	SAE 10W engine oil
	Propeller shaft	—	Perfect Seal (part No. C-92-34277)

(continued)

4

Table 2 80-150 HP INLINE ENGINE LUBRICATION POINTS (cont.)

Frequency	Item	Figure No.	Lubricant type
After 1st 10 days of season, then each 30 days	Gear housing	10	Super-Duty Lubricant (part No. C-92-68617)

Table 3 1500/2000 V6 LUBRICATION POINTS

Frequency	Item	Figure No.	Lubricant type
Every 60 days (fresh water); every 30 days (salt water)	Throttle/shift linkage Upper shift shaft Steering cable Tilt tube and swivel pin Steering link rod pivot points Tilt lock lever, shaft and locking brace pivot points	21 22 25 24 25 23	Multipurpose Lubricant (part No. C-92-63250) SAE 30W engine oil
Once in season (fresh water); every 60 days (salt water)	Propeller shaft	—	Perfect Seal (part No. C-92-34277)
After 1st 10 days of season, then each 30 days	Gear housing	10	Super-Duty Lubricant (Part No. C-92-68617)

Table 4 V150, V175, V200 AND V225 LUBRICATION POINTS

Frequency	Item	Figure No.	Lubricant type
Every 60 days (fresh water); every 30 days (salt water)	Throttle/shift linkage Upper shift shaft Steering cable, tilt tube and swivel pin Steering link rod pivot points Tilt lock lever, shaft and locking brace pivot points	21 22 24, 25 25 23	Multipurpose Lubricant (Part No. C-92-63250) SAE 30W engine oil
Once in season (fresh water); every 60 days (salt water)	Propeller shaft	—	Quicksilver Special Lubricant (part No. C-92-79214A1)
After 1st 10 days of season, then each 30 days	Gear housing	10	Super-Duty Lubricant (Part No. C-92-68617)

Chapter Five

Timing, Synchronizing and Adjusting

If a multi-cylinder engine is to deliver its maximum efficiency and peak performance, the ignition must be timed and carburetor operation synchronized with the ignition. The engine must be timed and synchronized as the final step of a tune-up or whenever the fuel or ignition systems are serviced or adjusted.

Procedures for timing, synchronizing and adjusting Mercury outboard engines differ according to model and ignition system. This chapter is divided into self-contained sections dealing with particular models/ignition systems for fast and easy reference. Each section specifies the appropriate procedure and sequence to be followed and it provides

the necessary tune-up data. Read the general information at the beginning of the chapter and then select the section pertaining to your outboard.

> *NOTE*
> *Factory timing specifications provided by Mercury Marine are given in **Tables 1-17**. Due to the poor quality of available fuels, however, Mercury Marine has occasionally found it necessary to modify their specifications during production of late-model engines. If your engine has a decal attached to the power head or air box, always follow the specifications provided on the decal instead of the specifications in **Tables 1-18**.*

Engine Timing

As engine rpm increases, the ignition system must fire the spark plugs more rapidly. Proper ignition timing synchronizes spark plug firing with engine speed.

Some early model engines do not have timing marks on the flywheel. A dial indicator is required to properly time such engines. See **Figure 1**.

All late model engines have some form of timing mark and can be timed with a timing light. See **Figure 2**.

This method is not always practical, as the engine must be run at full throttle in forward gear. This requires the use of a test tank, as timing an engine while speeding across open water is neither easy nor safe.

Some late model engines can be timed with a timing light while the engine is cranked. A test tank is not required in this procedure, but a flushing device (**Figure 3**) must be used to supply water to the cooling system and specific engine speed limits must be strictly observed to avoid engine damage.

Synchronizing

As engine speed increases, the carburetor must provide an increased amount of fuel for combustion. Synchronizing is the process of timing the carburetor operation to the ignition (and thereby to engine speed).

Required Equipment

Static timing of an engine requires the use of an accurate dial indicator to determine top dead center (TDC) of the No. 1 piston before making any timing adjustment. TDC is determined by removing the No. 1 spark plug and installing the dial indicator in the plug opening. See **Figure 1**.

Dynamic engine timing uses a stroboscopic timing light connected to the No. 1 spark plug wire. As the engine is cranked or operated, the light flashes each time the spark plug fires. When the light is pointed at the moving flywheel, the mark on the flywheel appears to stand still. The flywheel mark should align with the stationary timing pointer on the engine. See **Figure 2**.

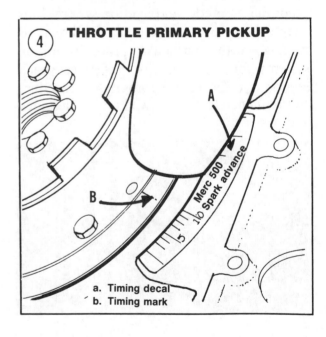

THROTTLE PRIMARY PICKUP

a. Timing decal
b. Timing mark

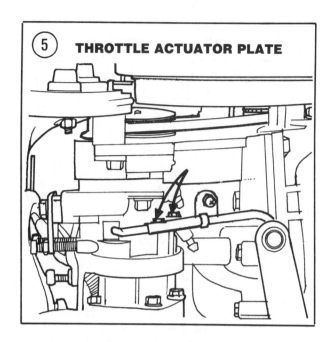

THROTTLE ACTUATOR PLATE

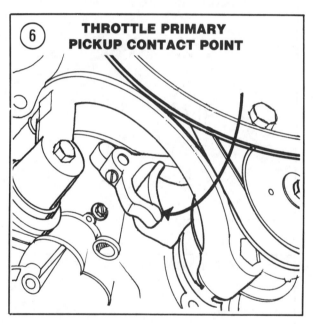

**THROTTLE PRIMARY
PICKUP CONTACT POINT**

A tachometer connected to the engine is used to determine engine speed during idle and high-speed adjustments.

CAUTION
Never operate the engine without water circulating through the lower unit to the engine. This will damage the water pump and the lower unit and can cause engine damage.

Some form of water supply is required whenever the engine is operated during the procedure. Using a test tank is the most convenient method, although the procedures may be carried out with the boat in the water or with the aid of a flushing device, if necessary.

MERCURY 500 WITH LIGHTNING ENERGIZER IGNITION

Timing Adjustments

Refer to **Table 1** and **Table 2** for tune-up data.

1. Install the engine in a test tank. Connect the fuel line and electrical harness.
2. Remove the cowling.
3. Lightly seat the carburetor idle mixture screws, then back out 1 1/4 turn.
4. Connect a timing light and tachometer to the engine according to manufacturer's instructions.
5. Start engine and run in forward gear. Point the timing light at the flywheel and open the throttle until the straight line on the flywheel rim aligns with the throttle primary pickup specification (**Table 1**) on the timing decal (**Figure 4**).
6. Hold the throttle in that position and loosen the 2 actuator plate screws (**Figure 5**).
7. Rotate the plate as required until the primary cam just contacts the primary pickup lever on the carburetor cluster (**Figure 6**), then tighten the actuator plate screws.
8. Run the engine at wide-open throttle and note the engine speed indicated by the tachometer. Refer to **Table 2** and determine the correct maximum spark advance required.
9. With the engine at wide-open throttle in forward gear, adjust the maximum spark stop

screw (**Figure 7**) until the flywheel timing mark aligns with the specified degree mark on the timing decal, then tighten the locknut.

10. Bring the engine back to idle and shut it off. Disconnect the timing light.

11. Holding the distributor adaptor against the maximum spark stop screw, turn the throttle secondary pickup screw (**Figure 5**) until it just contacts the secondary pickup arm on the carburetor cluster. See **Figure 8**. Tighten the locknut.

12. Rotate the throttle to its wide-open position. Adjust the throttle stop screw (**Figure 7**) to permit full carburetor opening without allowing the carburetor shutters to act as a stop or allowing the carburetor cluster to hit the carburetor filter cover.

Carburetor Adjustments

1. Start the engine and run in forward gear. Adjust the idle mixture screw for the best idle. See Chapter Six.

2. Set idle rpm to specifications (**Table 1**) in forward gear.

**MERCURY 500 WITH
DISTRIBUTOR-LESS IGNITION
(TO SERIAL NO. 4576236)**

Timing Adjustments

Refer to **Table 3** for tune-up data.

1. Install the engine in a test tank. Connect the fuel line and electrical harness.

2. Remove the cowling.

3. Lightly seat the carburetor idle mixture screw, then back out one full turn.

4. Connect a timing light and tachometer to the engine according to manufacturer's instructions.

5. Start the engine and run in forward gear. Move the throttle arm to bring engine speed to the specified idle rpm (**Table 3**). Adjust idle stop screw against throttle arm and tighten the locknut.

6. Point the timing light at the flywheel and move the throttle arm until timing pointer on

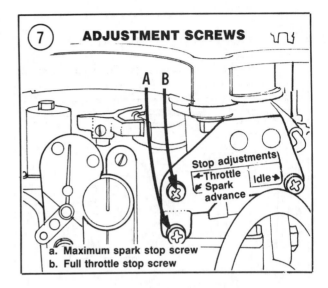

7 ADJUSTMENT SCREWS

a. Maximum spark stop screw
b. Full throttle stop screw

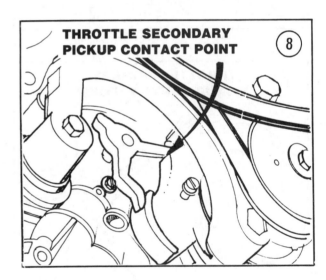

THROTTLE SECONDARY
PICKUP CONTACT POINT 8

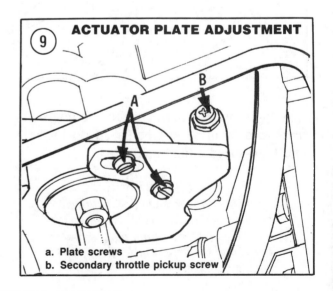

9 ACTUATOR PLATE ADJUSTMENT

a. Plate screws
b. Secondary throttle pickup screw

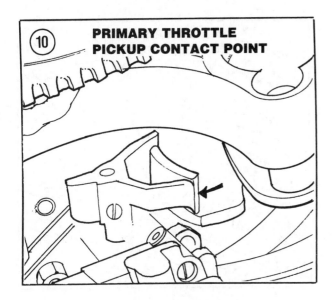

PRIMARY THROTTLE PICKUP CONTACT POINT

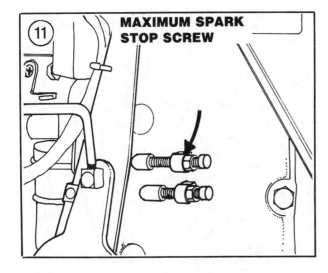

MAXIMUM SPARK STOP SCREW

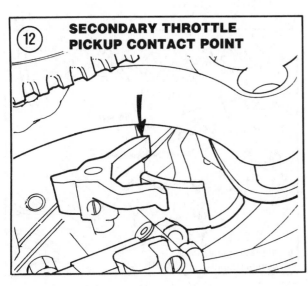

SECONDARY THROTTLE PICKUP CONTACT POINT

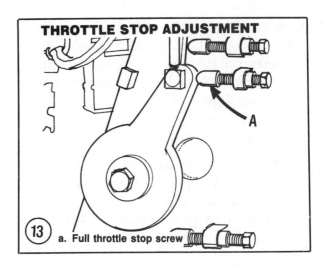

THROTTLE STOP ADJUSTMENT

a. Full throttle stop screw

the engine aligns with the throttle primary pickup specification (**Table 3**) on the timing decal.

7. Hold the throttle in that position and loosen the 2 actuator plate screws (**Figure 9**).

8. Rotate the plate as required until the primary cam just contacts the primary pickup lever on the carburetor cluster (**Figure 10**), then tighten the actuator plate screws.

NOTE
This ignition system requires that the maximum spark advance be set at 32° BTDC in Step 9 to obtain the specified 30° BTDC advance at 5,000 rpm.

9. Open the throttle as required to align the 32° BTDC mark on the flywheel decal with the timing pointer. Adjust the maximum spark stop screw (**Figure 11**) until it contacts the spark arm, then tighten the locknut.

10. Bring the engine back to idle and shut it off. Disconnect the timing light.

11. Move the throttle until spark arm contacts the spark stop screw. Turn the actuator plate secondary pickup screw (**Figure 9**) until it just contacts the secondary lever on the carburetor cluster. See **Figure 12**. Tighten the locknut.

12. Rotate the throttle to its wide-open position. Adjust the throttle stop screw (**Figure 13**) to permit full carburetor opening

5

without allowing the carburetor shutters to act as a stop. There should be a 0.010-0.015 in. clearance between the carburetor cluster secondary lever and the secondary pickup screw. See **Figure 14**.

Carburetor Adjustments

1. Start the engine and run in forward gear. Adjust the idle mixture screw for the best idle. See Chapter Five.
2. Set idle rpm to specifications (**Table 3**) in forward gear.

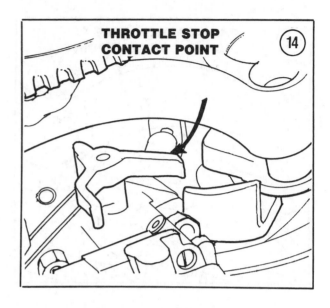

MERCURY 500, 45 AND 50 (4-CYL.) WITH DISTRIBUTOR-LESS IGNITION (SERIAL NO. 4576236 AND ABOVE)

Timing Adjustments

Refer to **Table 4** for tune-up data.
1. Install the engine in a test tank. Connect the fuel line and electrical harness.
2. Remove the cowling.
3. Lightly seat the carburetor idle mixture screw, then back out one full turn.
4. Connect a timing light and tachometer to the engine according to manufacturer's instructions.
5. Start the engine and run in forward gear. Point the timing light at the flywheel and move the throttle arm until timing pointer on the engine aligns with the throttle primary pickup specification (**Table 4**) on the timing decal.
6. Hold the throttle in that position and loosen the 2 actuator plate screws (**Figure 15**).
7. Rotate the plate as required until the primary cam just contacts the primary pickup lever on the carburetor cluster (**Figure 16**), then tighten the actuator plate screws.

NOTE
This ignition system requires that the maximum spark advance be set at 32° BTDC in Step 8 to obtain the specified 30° BTDC advance at 5,000 rpm.

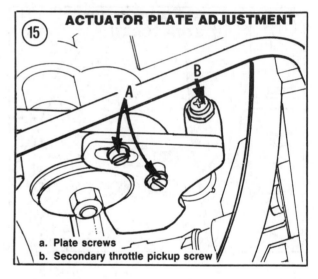

a. Plate screws
b. Secondary throttle pickup screw

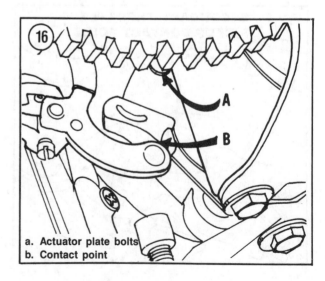

a. Actuator plate bolts
b. Contact point

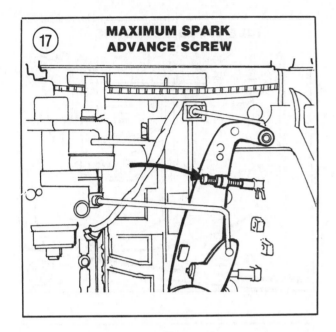

MAXIMUM SPARK ADVANCE SCREW

(17)

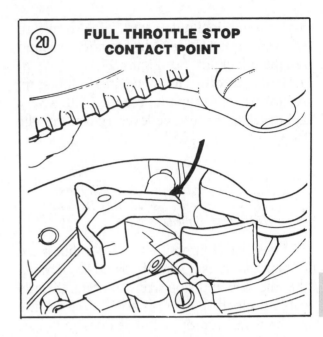

FULL THROTTLE STOP CONTACT POINT

(20)

5

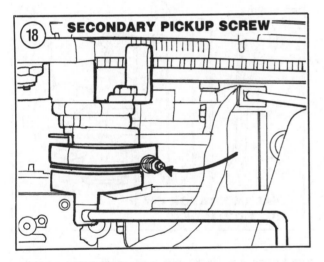

SECONDARY PICKUP SCREW

(18)

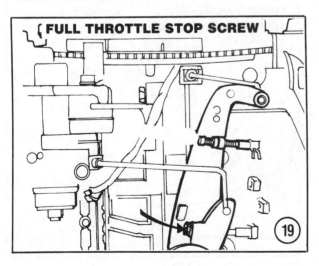

FULL THROTTLE STOP SCREW

(19)

8. Open the throttle as required to align the 32° BTDC mark on the flywheel decal with the timing pointer. Adjust the maximum spark stop screw (**Figure 17**) until it contacts the spark arm, then tighten the locknut.

9. Bring the engine back to idle and shut it off. Disconnect the timing light.

10. Move the throttle lever until the maximum spark advance screw contacts the stop. Turn the secondary pickup screw (**Figure 18**) until it just contacts the secondary lever.

11. Rotate the throttle to its wide-open position. Adjust the throttle stop screw (**Figure 19**) to permit full carburetor opening without allowing the carburetor shutters to act as a stop. There should be a 0.010-0.015 in. clearance between the carburetor cluster secondary lever and the secondary pickup screw. See **Figure 20**.

Carburetor Adjustments

1. Start the engine and run in forward gear. Adjust the idle mixture screw for the best idle. See Chapter Six.

2. Remove throttle cable barrel from barrel retainer on cable anchor bracket.

3. Loosen locknut, set idle rpm to specifications (**Table 4**) in forward gear and retighten locknut. See **Figure 21**.

4. Hold throttle lever against idle stop. Adjust barrel to slip into retainer with a very light preload of throttle lever against the idle stop.

> *NOTE*
> *Excessive preload in Step 5 will make shifting from FORWARD to NEUTRAL difficult.*

5. Lock barrel in position. Place a thin piece of paper such as a matchbook cover between the idle stop and stop screw to check throttle cable preload. If there is some drag on the paper when removed but it does not tear, preload is correct. If not, readjust cable barrel.

MERCURY 650
DISTRIBUTOR-LESS IGNITION

Timing Pointer Adjustment

If the engine has an adjustable timing pointer, it must be properly adjusted before the engine can be timed.

1. Remove the cowling.

2. Disconnect all spark plug leads. Remove the spark plugs from the engine.

3. Install a dial indicator in the No. 1 (top) cylinder (**Figure 22**).

4. Rotate flywheel clockwise until the No. 1 piston is at TDC. Zero the dial indicator and tighten its set screw.

5. Rotate the flywheel counterclockwise until the dial indicator needle is about 1/4 turn beyond the 0.464 in. mark on the flywheel timing decal.

6. Rotate the flywheel clockwise until the dial indicator needle reads exactly 0.464 in.

7. Check the timing pointer alignment. The pointer groove should align with the 0.464 in. mark on the flywheel timing decal. If not, loosen pointer attachment screw, position

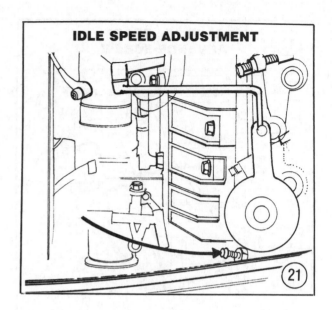

IDLE SPEED ADJUSTMENT

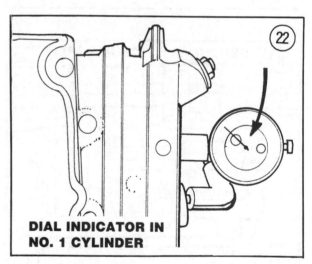

DIAL INDICATOR IN NO. 1 CYLINDER

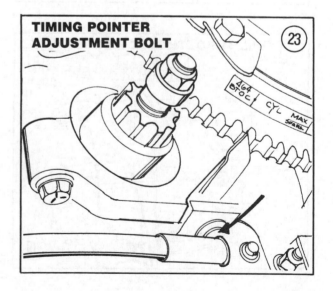

TIMING POINTER ADJUSTMENT BOLT

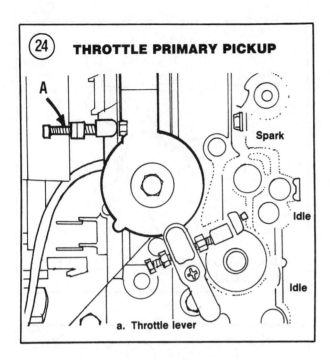

THROTTLE PRIMARY PICKUP

A

Spark

Idle

Idle

a. Throttle lever

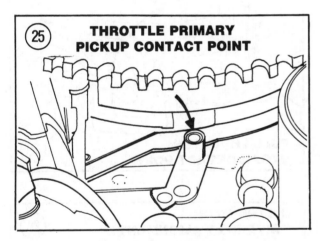

THROTTLE PRIMARY PICKUP CONTACT POINT

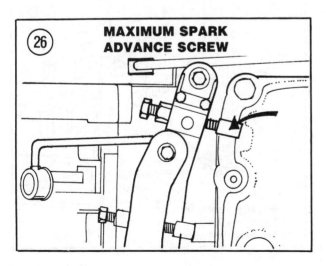

MAXIMUM SPARK ADVANCE SCREW

pointer correctly and retighten the screw. See **Figure 23**.

8. Remove dial indicator. Reinstall spark plugs and connect spark plug leads.

Timing Adjustments

Refer to **Table 5** for this procedure.

1. Install the engine in a test tank. Connect the electrical harness. Disconnect the spark plug leads.

2. Lightly seat the carburetor idle mixture screws, then back out 1 1/2-1 3/4 turn.

3. Connect a timing light according to manufacturer's specifications.

4. Point the timing light at the flywheel while cranking the engine. With the engine cranking, align the timing pointer with the throttle primary pickup specification (**Table 5**) on the timing decal.

5. Hold the throttle lever in that position and adjust the primary pickup adjusting screw (**Figure 24**) until the throttle actuator cam just contacts the throttle cluster pin (**Figure 25**). Tighten the locknut.

NOTE
This ignition system requires that the maximum spark advance be set at 28° BTDC at cranking rpm in Step 6 to obtain the specified 23° BTDC advance at 5,300 rpm.

6. Point the timing light at the flywheel while cranking the engine. With the engine cranking, move the throttle lever to align the timing pointer and the 28° BTDC mark on the timing decal.

7. Holding the throttle in this position, adjust maximum spark stop screw until it just contacts the spark stop and tighten the locknut. See **Figure 26**.

8. Rotate the throttle to its wide-open position. Adjust the throttle stop screw

5

(Figure 27) to permit full carburetor opening without allowing the carburetor shutter to act as a stop. There should be a 0.010-0.015 in. clearance between the throttle actuator cam and carburetor cluster pin when the throttle lever contacts the throttle stop screw. See **Figure 28**.

9. Return the throttle lever to the idle position. Disconnect the timing light.

Carburetor Adjustments

1. Install the engine in a test tank. Connect the fuel line and electrical harness.
2. Start the engine and run in forward gear. Adjust the idle mixture screws for the best idle. See Chapter Six.
3. Remove throttle cable barrel from barrel retainer on cable anchor bracket.
4. Loosen locknut, set idle rpm to specifications (**Table 5**) in forward gear and retighten locknut.
5. Hold throttle lever against idle stop. Adjust barrel to slip into retainer with a very light preload of throttle lever against idle stop.

> *NOTE*
> *Excessive preload in Step 6 will make shifting from FORWARD to NEUTRAL difficult.*

6. Lock barrel in position. Place a thin piece of paper such as a matchbook cover between the idle stop and stop screw to check throttle cable preload. If there is some drag on the paper when removed but it does not tear, preload is correct. If not, readjust cable barrel.

MERCURY 650 WITH DISTRIBUTOR CD IGNITION

Distributor Pulley Alignment

Refer to **Figure 29** for this procedure.
1. Remove the engine cowling.

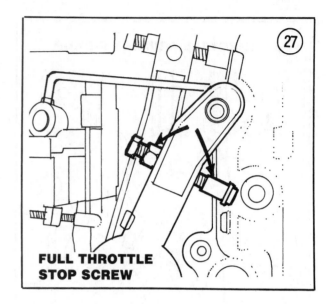

FULL THROTTLE STOP SCREW

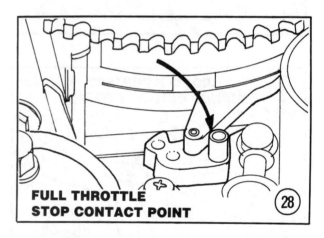

FULL THROTTLE STOP CONTACT POINT

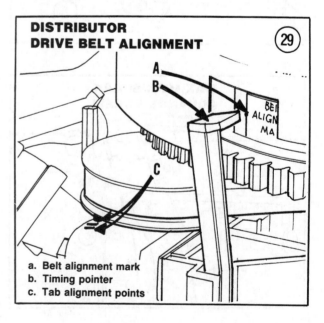

DISTRIBUTOR DRIVE BELT ALIGNMENT

a. Belt alignment mark
b. Timing pointer
c. Tab alignment points

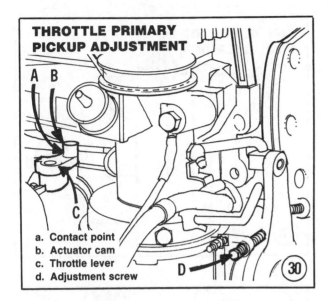

THROTTLE PRIMARY PICKUP ADJUSTMENT

a. Contact point
b. Actuator cam
c. Throttle lever
d. Adjustment screw

30

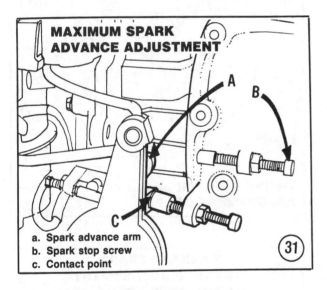

MAXIMUM SPARK ADVANCE ADJUSTMENT

a. Spark advance arm
b. Spark stop screw
c. Contact point

31

FULL THROTTLE STOP SCREW

32

2. Remove timing pointer from emergency start rope pouch and install in cylinder block notch.

3. Remove distributor pulley cover and slip cogged belt off pulley.

4. Rotate flywheel as required to align timing pointer and belt alignment mark on the flywheel.

5. Align the distributor pulley tab with the raised area on the distributor adaptor.

6. Install distributor drive belt over pulley. Install pulley cover and tighten screw to 60 in.-lb.

Timing Adjustments

Refer to **Table 6** for tune-up data.

1. Install the engine in a test tank. Connect the fuel line and electrical harness.

2. Lightly seat the carburetor idle mixture screws, then back out one full turn.

3. Connect a timing light and tachometer to the engine according to manufacturer's instructions.

4. Start engine and run in forward gear. Point the timing light at the flywheel and open the throttle until the timing pointer on the block aligns with the throttle primary pickup specification (**Table 6**) on the flywheel timing decal.

5. Adjust screw between throttle and spark arm until the throttle actuator cam just contacts the throttle lever pin. See **Figure 30**.

6. Loosen locknut on maximum spark stop screw. Open the throttle until the 23° BTDC mark on the flywheel decal is aligned with the timing point. Adjust maximum spark stop screw until it just contacts the spark arm and tighten locknut. See **Figure 31**.

7. Rotate the throttle to its wide-open position. Adjust the throttle stop screw (**Figure 32**) to permit full carburetor opening without allowing the carburetor shutters to act as a stop. There should be a 0.010-0.015 in. clearance between the throttle lever actuator cam and pin.

5

MERC 700, 70 (PRIOR TO 1984), 60 AND 50 (3-CYL.) WITH FLYWHEEL CD IGNITION

Timing Pointer Adjustment

If the engine has an adjustable timing pointer, it must be properly adjusted before the engine can be timed.

1. Remove the cowling.

2. Disconnect all spark plug leads. Remove the spark plugs from the engine.

3. Install a dial indicator in the No. 1 (top) cylinder (**Figure 33**).

4. Rotate flywheel clockwise until the No. 1 piston is at TDC. Zero the dial indicator and tighten its set screw.

5. Rotate the flywheel counterclockwise until the dial indicator needle is about 1/4 turn beyond the 0.464 in. mark on the flywheel timing decal.

6. Rotate the flywheel clockwise until the dial indicator needle reads exactly 0.464 in.

7. Check the timing pointer alignment. The pointer groove should align with the 0.464 in. mark on the flywheel timing decal. If not, loosen pointer attachment screw, position pointer correctly and retighten the screw. See **Figure 34**.

8. Remove dial indicator. Reinstall spark plugs and connect spark plug leads.

Timing Adjustments

Refer to **Table 7** for this procedure.

1. Install the engine in a test tank. Connect the electrical harness.

2. Lightly seat the carburetor idle mixture screws, then back out 1 1/2-1 3/4 turns.

3. Connect a timing light according to manufacturer's specifications.

4. Start engine and run in forward gear at 5,000-5,500 rpm. Loosen maximum spark advance screw locknut. Point the timing light at the flywheel and adjust the maximum spark advance screw (**Figure 35**) until the 23° BTDC mark on the flywheel decal aligns with the timing pointer on the block.

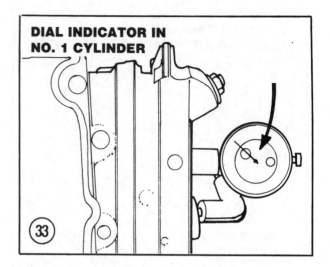

DIAL INDICATOR IN NO. 1 CYLINDER

(33)

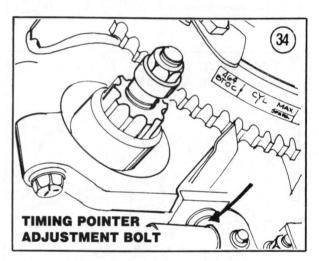

(34)

TIMING POINTER ADJUSTMENT BOLT

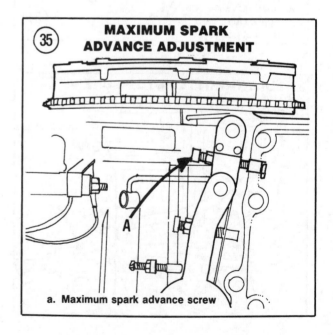

(35) **MAXIMUM SPARK ADVANCE ADJUSTMENT**

A

a. Maximum spark advance screw

FULL THROTTLE STOP SCREW

(36)

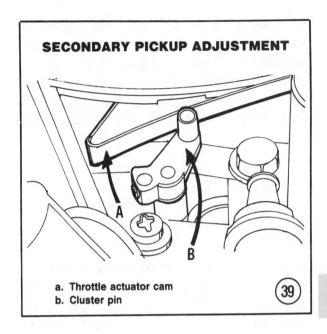

SECONDARY PICKUP ADJUSTMENT

a. Throttle actuator cam
b. Cluster pin

(39)

5

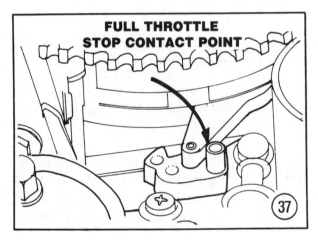

FULL THROTTLE
STOP CONTACT POINT

(37)

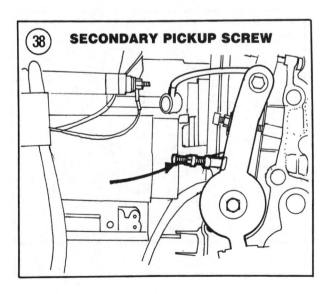

(38) SECONDARY PICKUP SCREW

5. Tighten spark advance locknut. Return throttle to idle and shut engine off. Disconnect timing light.

6. With engine off, rotate the throttle to its wide-open position. Adjust the throttle stop screw (**Figure 36**) to permit full carburetor opening without allowing the carburetor shutter to act as a stop. There should be a 0.010-0.015 in. clearance between the carburetor cluster pin and the throttle actuator cam. See **Figure 37**.

7. Now move the spark lever to obtain maximum spark and hold in that position. Loosen secondary pickup screw locknut and adjust screw (**Figure 38**) until carburetor cluster pin rides on secondary pickup point on the actuator cam. See **Figure 39**.

8. Tighten spark screw locknut and return throttle lever to its idle position.

Carburetor Adjustments

1. Start the engine and run in forward gear. Adjust the idle mixture screws for the best idle. See Chapter Six.

2. Remove throttle cable barrel from barrel retainer on cable anchor bracket.

3. Loosen locknut, set idle rpm to specifications (**Table 7**) in forward gear and retighten locknut. See **Figure 40A**.

4. Hold throttle lever against idle stop. Adjust barrel to slip into retainer with a very light preload of throttle lever against idle stop.

> *NOTE*
> *Excessive preload in Step 5 will make shifting from FORWARD to NEUTRAL difficult.*

5. Lock barrel in position. Place a thin piece of paper such as a matchbook cover between the idle stop and stop screw to check throttle cable preload. If there is some drag on the paper when removed but it does not tear, preload is correct. If not, readjust cable barrel.

1987-ON MERCURY 70, 80 AND 90

Timing Pointer Adjustment

1. Remove the cowling and the aft cowl support bracket.

2. Disconnect all spark plug leads. Remove the spark plugs from the engine.

3. Install a dial indicator into the No. 1 (top cylinder) spark plug hole.

4. Rotate the flywheel clockwise until the No. 1 piston is at TDC. Set the dial indicator to zero and tighten its set screw.

5. Rotate the flywheel counterclockwise until the dial indicator needle is about 1/4 turn beyond the 0.491 BTDC reading.

6. Rotate the flywheel clockwise until the dial indicator needle reads exactly 0.491 BTDC.

7. Check the timing pointer alignment. The pointer groove should align with the 0.491 BTDC mark on the flywheel. If not, loosen the 2 flywheel cover timing pointer attaching screws. Position the timing pointer to correctly align with

the flywheel mark, then tighten the 2 flywheel cover attaching screws to secure adjustment.

8. Remove the dial indicator. Reinstall the spark plugs and connect the spark plug leads. Reinstall the aft cowl support bracket.

Timing Adjustments

Refer to **Table 8** for this procedure.

1. Connect a timing light according to manufacturer's instructions.

2. Place engine in NEUTRAL and hold the throttle arm with the idle timing screw (1, **Figure 40B**) against its stop. Pointing the timing light at the flywheel, crank the engine and adjust the idle screw until the timing pointer aligns with the 2 degree BTDC mark on the flywheel. Tighten the locknut.

> *NOTE*
> *The cranking speed adjustment made in Step 3 will automatically retard 2 degrees when engine is operated at wide open throttle due to the design of the ignition system.*

3. Loosen the maximum spark advance screw (2, **Figure 40B**) locknut. Hold the control arm with the maximum spark advance screw against its stop. Pointing the

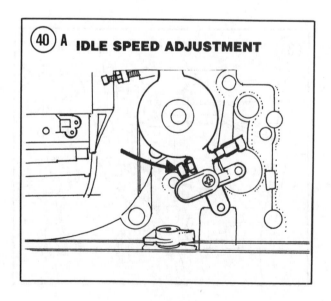

40 A **IDLE SPEED ADJUSTMENT**

timing light at the flywheel, crank the engine and adjust the spark advance screw to align the 24 degree BTDC mark (Models 70 and 80 prior to serial No. B23942) or the 28 degree BTDC mark (all other models) on the flywheel with the timing pointer. Tighten locknut and disconnect timing light.

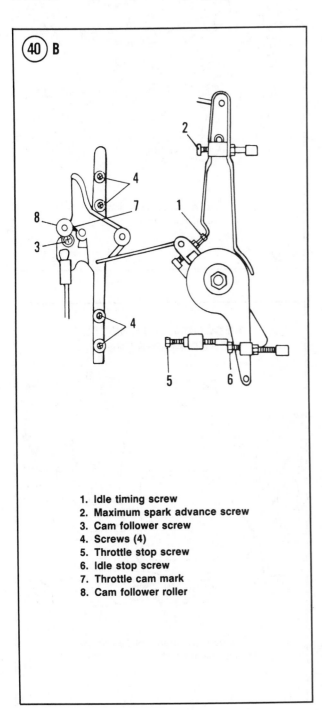

40 B

1. Idle timing screw
2. Maximum spark advance screw
3. Cam follower screw
4. Screws (4)
5. Throttle stop screw
6. Idle stop screw
7. Throttle cam mark
8. Cam follower roller

4. With the engine in water or in a test tank and the timing light connected, start the engine. Make final timing checks with the engine running at both idle speed and 5,000 rpm to check idle and maximum spark advance settings. If not correct, repeat this procedure.

Synchronization

1. Remove the sound box cover.
2. Loosen the cam follower screw (3, **Figure 40B**) 1/4-1/2 turn.
3. Loosen the 4 carbauretor linkage synchronization screws (4, **Figure 40B**) and let the throttle shutters close freely.
4. Make sure all carburetor throttle shutters are completely closed. Tighten the 4 carburetor linkage synchronization screws.
5. Recheck the carburetors to make sure that the throttle shutters are completely closed. If not, repeat Step 3 and Step 4.
6. Loosen the idle stop screw (6, **Figure 40B**) locknut. Hold the throttle arm with the idle stop screw against its stop.
7. Move the cam follower roller against the throttle cam and hold in that position. Adjust the idle stop screw until the raised mark (7, **Figure 40B**) on the throttle cam aligns with the center of the cam follower roller (8, **Figure 40B**). Tighten the idle stop screw locknut.
8. Holding the throttle cam at idle position, adjust the cam follower to provide a clearance of 0.025-0.050 in. between the throttle cam and cam follower roller, then tighten the cam follower screw loosened in Step 2.
9. Loosen the throttle stop screw (5, **Figure 40B**) locknut and move the throttle arm to its wide open throttle position. Adjust the stop screw to permit the carburetor butterflies to completely open. Carburetor butterflies should still be able to move an additional 0.015 in., with throttle arm in wide open

5

position, to prevent butterflies from being used as throttle stop. Tighten the locknut.

10. Reinstall the sound box cover.

Carburetor/Oil Pump Synchronization

On some models, the oil pump body may contain 2 stamped marks. If so, disregard the right-hand mark (looking straight at pump) and use only the left-hand mark for this procedure.

1. Move the throttle arm to the idle position. The left-hand stamped mark on the oil pump body should align with the stamped mark on the pump lever.

2. If the marks do not align in Step 1, disconnect the oil pump link rod and turn the end of the rod to adjust its length until the 2 marks will align when the link rod is reconnected.

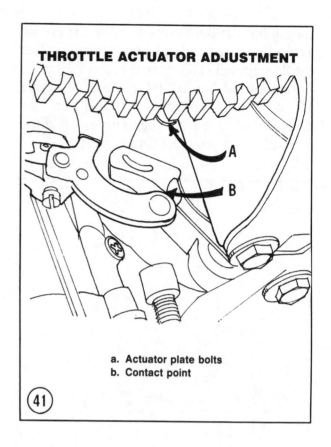

THROTTLE ACTUATOR ADJUSTMENT

a. Actuator plate bolts
b. Contact point

④1

MERCURY 850 WITH DISTRIBUTOR CD IGNITION

Distributor Pulley Alignment

1. Remove the engine cowling.

2. Remove distributor pulley cover and slip cogged belt off pulley.

3. Rotate flywheel to align 3 vertical dots on timing decal with center of distributor shaft.

4. Rotate distributor pulley to align arrow on pulley with decal dots.

> *NOTE*
> *If Step 5 has to be performed, alignment will appear to be about 1/2 tooth off. This is normal.*

5. If the arrow and dot(s) do not align properly, align the arrow slightly to the *right* of the dots.

6. Install distributor drive belt over pulley. Install pulley cover and tighten screw to 60 in.-lb.

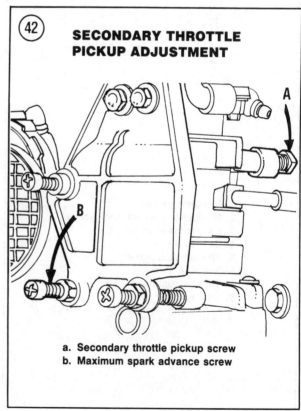

④2   **SECONDARY THROTTLE PICKUP ADJUSTMENT**

a. Secondary throttle pickup screw
b. Maximum spark advance screw

Timing Adjustments

Refer to **Table 9** for tune-up data.

1. Install the engine in a test tank. Connect the fuel line and electrical harness.

2. Lightly seat the carburetor idle mixture screws, then back out 1 3/4 turn.

3. Connect a timing light and tachometer to the engine according to manufacturer's instructions.

4. Start engine and run in forward gear. Point the timing light at the flywheel and open the throttle until the timing pointer aligns with the timing mark specification (**Table 9**) on the flywheel timing decal.

5. Hold the throttle in that position and loosen the 2 actuator plate screws (**Figure 41**).

6. Rotate the plate as required until the primary cam just contacts the primary pickup lever on the carburetor cluster (**Figure 41**), then tighten the actuator plate screws.

7. Open the throttle as required to align the 27° BTDC mark on the flywheel decal with the timing pointer. Loosen the maximum spark advance screw (**Figure 42**) and adjust screw until it contacts the distributor adaptor, then tighten the locknut.

8. Bring the engine back to idle and shut it off. Disconnect the timing light.

9. Move the throttle to its maximum spark advance position without activating the economizer collar spring. Loosen secondary throttle pickup screw locknut and adjust screw until the secondary pickup just contacts the secondary lever on the carburetor cluster. See **Figure 41**. Tighten the locknut.

10. Rotate the throttle to its wide-open position. Adjust the throttle stop screw to permit full carburetor opening without allowing the carburetor shutters to act as a stop. There should be about 1/32 in. clearance between the carburetor cluster secondary lever and the secondary pickup screw. See **Figure 43**.

Carburetor Adjustments

1. Start the engine and run in forward gear. Adjust the idle mixture screws for the best idle. See Chapter Six.

2. Set idle rpm to specifications (**Table 9**) in forward gear.

MERCURY 75, 80 (PRIOR TO 1984), 800 AND 850 WITH DISTRIBUTOR-LESS IGNITION

Timing Pointer Adjustment

1. Remove the cowling.

2. Disconnect all spark plug leads. Remove the spark plugs from the engine.

3. Install a dial indicator in the No. 1 (top) cylinder.

4. Rotate flywheel clockwise until the No. 1 piston is at TDC. Zero the dial indicator and tighten its set screw.

5. Rotate the flywheel counterclockwise until the dial indicator needle is about 1/4 turn beyond the 0.464 in. mark on the flywheel timing decal.

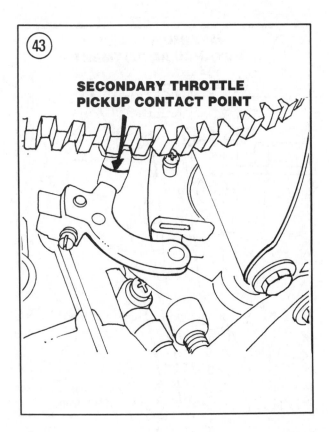

SECONDARY THROTTLE PICKUP CONTACT POINT

5

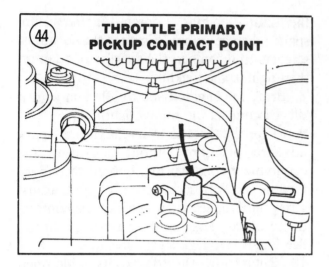

44 THROTTLE PRIMARY
PICKUP CONTACT POINT

6. Rotate the flywheel clockwise until the dial indicator needle reads exactly 0.464 in.

7. Check the timing pointer alignment. The pointer groove should align with the 0.464 in. mark on the flywheel timing decal. If not, loosen pointer attachment screw, position pointer correctly and retighten the screw.

8. Remove dial indicator. Reinstall spark plugs and connect spark plug leads.

Timing Adjustments

Refer to **Table 10** for this procedure.

1. Install the engine in a test tank. Connect the fuel line and electrical harness.

2. Lightly seat the carburetor idle mixture screws, then back out 1 1/2 turn.

3. Connect a timing light according to manufacturer's specifications.

4. Start the engine and run in forward gear. Loosen primary pickup screw locknut. Move throttle lever until throttle pickup cam just contacts carburetor cluster pin (**Figure 44**).

5. Hold throttle lever in that position, point the timing light at the flywheel and adjust primary pickup screw (**Figure 45**) until the timing pointer aligns with the throttle primary pickup specification (**Table 10**) on the timing decal. Tighten locknut.

6. Loosen maximum spark advance screw locknut. Point the timing light at the flywheel

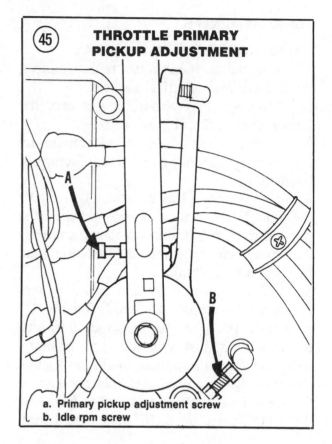

45 THROTTLE PRIMARY
PICKUP ADJUSTMENT

A

B

a. Primary pickup adjustment screw
b. Idle rpm screw

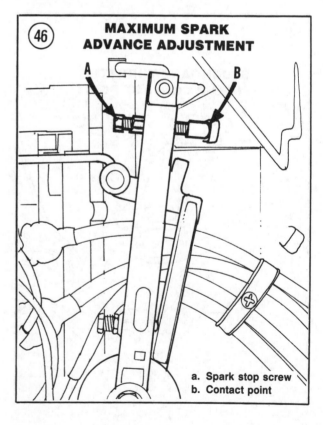

46 MAXIMUM SPARK
ADVANCE ADJUSTMENT

A   B

a. Spark stop screw
b. Contact point

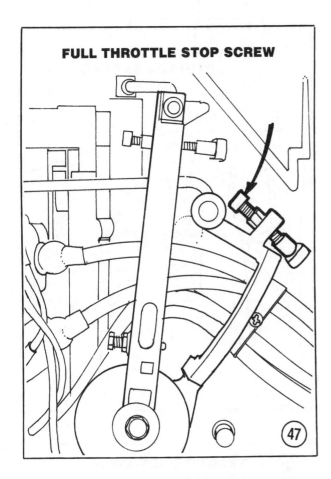

FULL THROTTLE STOP SCREW

(47)

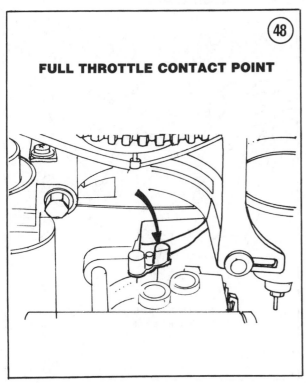

(48)

FULL THROTTLE CONTACT POINT

and open the throttle until the timing pointer aligns with the maximum spark advance specification (**Table 10**) on the timing decal.

7. Hold throttle lever in that position and adjust the maximum spark advance screw until it just contacts the screw stop (**Figure 46**). Tighten locknut.

8. Return the throttle to idle. Shut the engine off. Disconnect the timing light.

9. Rotate the throttle to its wide-open position. Loosen the throttle stop screw locknut and adjust stop screw (**Figure 47**) to permit full carburetor opening without allowing the carburetor shutters to act as a stop. There should be a 0.010-0.015 in. clearance between the carburetor cluster pin and the throttle cam. See **Figure 48**.

Carburetor Adjustments

1. Start the engine and run in forward gear. Adjust the idle mixture screws for the best idle. See Chapter Six.

2. Remove throttle cable barrel from barrel retainer on cable anchor bracket.

3. Loosen idle rpm screw locknut and adjust screw (**Figure 45**) to set idle rpm to specifications (**Table 10**) in forward gear. Tighten locknut.

4. Hold throttle lever against idle stop. Adjust barrel to slip into retainer with a very light preload of throttle lever against idle stop.

> *NOTE*
> *Excessive preload in Step 5 will make shifting from FORWARD to NEUTRAL difficult.*

5. Lock barrel in position. Place a thin piece of paper such as a matchbook cover between the idle stop and stop screw to check throttle cable preload. If there is some drag on the paper when removed but it does not tear, preload is correct. If not, readjust cable barrel.

MERCURY 900, 1150, 1400, 1500 AND 1500XS WITH DISTRIBUTOR CD IGNITION

Distributor Pulley Alignment

1. Remove the engine cowling.
2. Remove distributor pulley cover and slip cogged belt off pulley.

> *NOTE*
> *Mercury 1150/1500 models prior to 1978 have 3 vertical dots instead of the single dot described in Step 3.*

3. Rotate flywheel to align the single dot on timing decal with center of distributor shaft.
4. Rotate distributor pulley to align pulley arrow with dot(s).

> *NOTE*
> *If Step 5 has to be performed, alignment will appear to be about 1/2 tooth off. This is normal.*

5. If the arrow and dots do not align properly, align the arrow slightly *counterclockwise* of the dot(s).
6. Install distributor drive belt over pulley. Install pulley cover and tighten screw to 60 in.-lb.

Timing Pointer Adjustment

1. Disconnect all spark plug leads. Remove the spark plugs from the engine.
2. Install a dial indicator in the No. 1 (top) cylinder.
3. Rotate flywheel clockwise until the No. 1 piston is at TDC. Zero the dial indicator and tighten its set screw.
4. Rotate the flywheel counterclockwise until the dial indicator needle is about 1/4 turn beyond the 0.464 in. mark on the flywheel timing decal.
5. Rotate the flywheel clockwise until the dial indicator needle reads exactly 0.464 in.

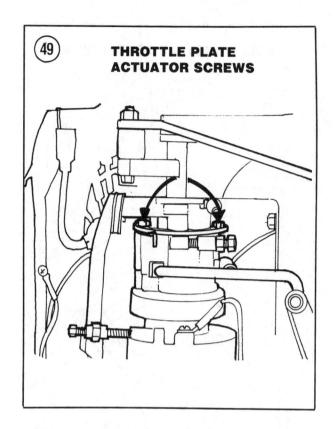

(49) THROTTLE PLATE ACTUATOR SCREWS

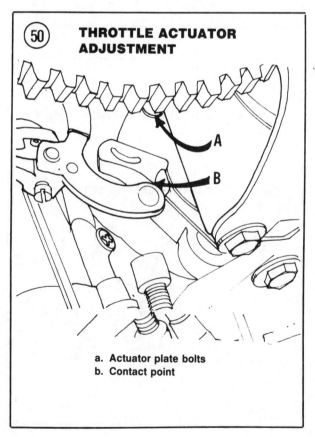

(50) THROTTLE ACTUATOR ADJUSTMENT

a. Actuator plate bolts
b. Contact point

MAXIMUM SPARK ADVANCE STOP SCREW

(51)

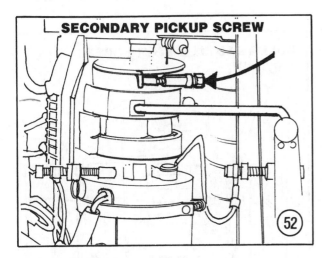

SECONDARY PICKUP SCREW

(52)

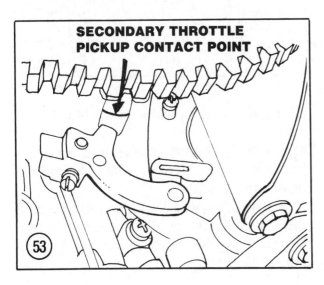

SECONDARY THROTTLE PICKUP CONTACT POINT

(53)

6. Check the timing pointer alignment. The pointer groove should align with the 0.464 in. mark on the flywheel timing decal. If not, loosen pointer attachment screw, position pointer correctly and retighten the screw.

7. Remove dial indicator. Reinstall spark plugs and connect spark plug leads.

Timing Adjustments

Refer to **Table 11** for this procedure.

1. Install the engine in a test tank. Connect the fuel line and electrical harness.

2. Lightly seat the carburetor idle mixture screws, then back out 1 1/4 turn.

3. Connect a timing light according to manufacturer's specifications.

4. Start the engine and run in forward gear. Point the timing light at the flywheel and open the throttle until the timing pointer aligns with the throttle primary pickup specification (**Table 11**) on the timing decal.

5. Hold the throttle in that position and loosen the 2 actuator plate bolts (**Figure 49**).

6. Rotate the plate as required until the throttle cam just contacts the primary pickup lever on the carburetor cluster (**Figure 50**), then tighten the actuator plate bolts.

7. Open the throttle as required to align the timing pointer with the specified maximum spark advance (**Table 11**). Loosen the maximum spark stop screw (**Figure 51**) and adjust screw until it contact the distributor adaptor, then tighten the locknut.

8. Bring the engine back to idle and shut it off. Disconnect the timing light.

9. Move the throttle to its maximum spark advance position without activating the economizer collar spring. Loosen secondary throttle pickup screw locknut and adjust screw (**Figure 52**) until the secondary pickup just contacts the secondary lever on the carburetor cluster. See **Figure 53**. Tighten the locknut.

5

10. Rotate the throttle to its wide-open position. Adjust the throttle stop screw to permit full carburetor opening without allowing the carburetor shutters to act as a stop. See **Figure 54** or **Figure 55**. There should be about 0.010-0.015 in. clearance between the carburetor secondary lever and the secondary pickup.

Carburetor Adjustments

1. Start the engine and run in forward gear. Adjust the idle mixture screws for the best idle. See Chapter Six.
2. Remove throttle cable barrel from barrel retainer on cable anchor bracket.
3. Loosen idle rpm screw locknut and adjust screw to set idle rpm to specifications (**Table 11**) in forward gear. Tighten locknut.
4. Hold throttle lever against idle stop. Adjust barrel to slip into retainer with a very light preload of throttle lever against idle stop.

> *NOTE*
> *Excessive preload in Step 5 will make shifting from FORWARD to NEUTRAL difficult.*

5. Lock barrel in position. Place a thin piece of paper such as a matchbook cover between the idle stop and stop screw to check throttle cable preload. If there is some drag on the paper when removed but it does not tear, preload is correct. If not, readjust cable barrel.

MERCURY 90, 115 AND 140 HP (6-CYLINDER) WITH DISTRIBUTOR-LESS IGNITION

Timing Pointer Adjustment

1. Remove the cowling.
2. Disconnect all spark plug leads. Remove the spark plugs from the engine.

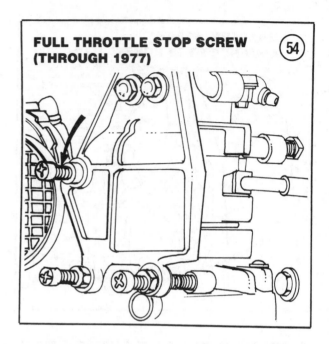

FULL THROTTLE STOP SCREW (THROUGH 1977) (54)

FULL THROTTLE STOP SCREW (1978-ON) (55)

3. Install a dial indicator in the No. 1 (top) cylinder.
4. Rotate flywheel clockwise until the No. 1 piston is at TDC. Zero the dial indicator and tighten its set screw.
5. Rotate the flywheel counterclockwise until the dial indicator needle is about 1/4 turn beyond the 0.464 in. mark on the flywheel timing decal.

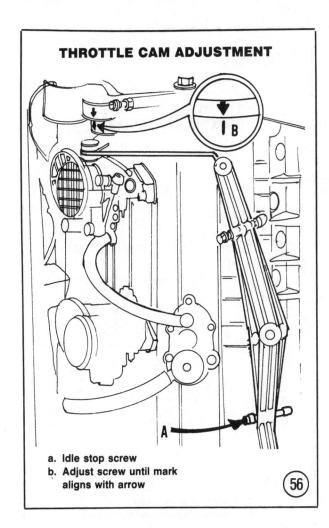

THROTTLE CAM ADJUSTMENT

a. Idle stop screw
b. Adjust screw until mark aligns with arrow

(56)

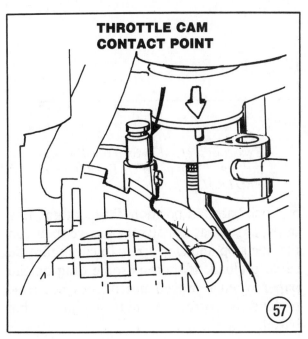

THROTTLE CAM CONTACT POINT

(57)

6. Rotate the flywheel clockwise until the dial indicator needle reads exactly 0.464 in.

7. Check the timing pointer alignment. The pointer groove should align with the 0.464 in. mark on the flywheel timing decal. If not, loosen pointer attachment screw, position pointer correctly and retighten the screw.

8. Remove dial indicator. Reinstall spark plugs and connect spark plug leads.

Timing Adjustments

Refer to **Table 12** for this procedure.
1. If equipped with an idle stabilizer (located on rear of front cowl support), disconnect the white/black leads at the upper switchbox terminal. Cover the terminal end of the wire leading to the stabilizer with tape to prevent it from shorting. Reinstall the other white/black to the switchbox terminal.

2. Remove spark plugs from all cylinders except the No. 1 (top).

3. Disconnect the remote fuel line at the engine.

4. Connect the engine electrical harness.

5. Remove the throttle cable barrel from its retainer on the cable anchor bracket.

6. Loosen idle stop screw locknut (A, **Figure 56**) and turn screw until throttle cam marks aligns with crankcase bracket arrow. See B, **Figure 56**. Tighten locknut.

7. Loosen carburetor lever screw. Holding idle stop screw against the stop, move carburetor lever until the shutters are completely closed. The roller should just contact the throttle cam. See **Figure 57**.

8. Connect a timing light to the engine according to manufacturer's instructions.

9. Place engine in NEUTRAL and position throttle lever with idle stop screw against its stop. Pointing the timing light at the flywheel, crank the engine and adjust primary pickup

5

screw (A, **Figure 58**) until timing pointer aligns with the throttle primary pickup specification (**Table 12**).

NOTE
This ignition system requires that the maximum spark advance be set at 20° BTDC at cranking rpm in Step 10 to obtain the specified 18° BTDC advance at maximum rpm.

10. Loosen the maximum spark advance screw locknut and position the throttle lever with the screw against its stop. Pointing the timing light at the flywheel, crank the engine and adjust screw (B, **Figure 58**) until timing pointer aligns with the 20° mark on the flywheel timing decal. Tighten locknut.

11. Rotate the throttle to its wide-open position. Adjust the throttle stop screw (**Figure 59**) to permit full carburetor opening without allowing the carburetor shutters to act as a stop. There should be a 0.010-0.015 in. clearance between the carburetor lever roller and throttle cam. See **Figure 60**.

12. Reinstall spark plugs and connect plug wires.

13. Untape and reconnect idle stabilizer lead to switchbox, if so equipped.

Carburetor Adjustments

1. Install the engine in a test tank. Connect the electrical harness and fuel line.

2. Start the engine and run in forward gear. Adjust the idle mixture screws for the best idle. See Chapter Six.

3. Remove throttle cable barrel from barrel retainer on cable anchor bracket.

4. Loosen locknut, set idle rpm to specifications (**Table 12**) in forward gear and retighten locknut.

5. Hold throttle lever against idle stop. Adjust barrel to slip into retainer with a very light preload of throttle lever against the idle stop.

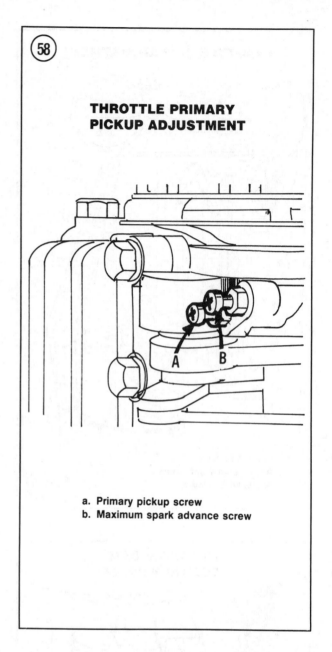

THROTTLE PRIMARY PICKUP ADJUSTMENT

a. Primary pickup screw
b. Maximum spark advance screw

NOTE
Excessive preload in Step 6 will make shifting from FORWARD to NEUTRAL difficult.

6. Lock barrel in position. Place a thin piece of paper such as a matchbook cover between the idle stop and stop screw to check throttle cable preload. If there is some drag on the paper when removed but it does not tear, preload is correct. If not, readjust cable barrel.

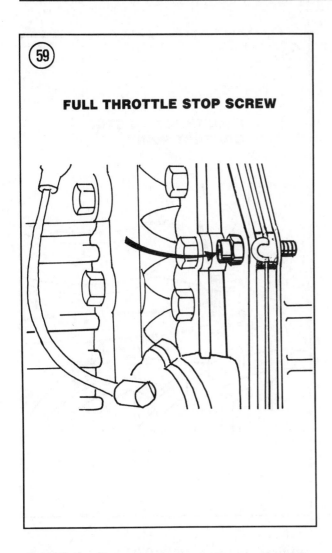

FULL THROTTLE STOP SCREW

MERCURY 100 (1988-ON) AND 115 (1989) WITH FLYWHEEL CD IGNITION

Timing Pointer Adjustment

1. Remove the cowling and the aft cowl support bracket.

2. Disconnect all spark plug leads. Remove the spark plugs from the engine.

3. Install a dial indicator into the No. 1 (top cylinder) spark plug hole.

4. Rotate the flywheel clockwise until the No. 1 piston is at TDC. Set the dial indicator to zero and tighten its set screw.

5. Rotate the flywheel counterclockwise until the dial indicator needle is about 1/4 turn beyond the 0.554 BTDC mark on the flywheel timing decal.

6. Rotate the flywheel clockwise until the dial indicator needle reads exactly 0.554 BTDC.

7. Check the timing pointer alignment. The pointer groove should align with the 0.554 BTDC mark on the flywheel timing decal. If not, loosen the pointer attachment screw, position the pointer correctly and retighten the screw.

8. Remove the dial indicator. Reinstall the spark plugs and connect the spark plug leads. Reinstall the aft cowl support bracket.

Timing Adjustments

Refer to **Table 13** for this procedure.

1. Connect a timing light according to manufacturer's instructions.

2. Place engine in NEUTRAL and hold the throttle arm with the idle stop screw against its stop. Pointing the timing light at the flywheel, crank the engine and adjust the idle screw until the timing pointer aligns with the timing decal mark specification (**Table 13**). Tighten the locknut.

NOTE
The cranking speed adjustment made in Step 3 will automatically retard to 23° BTDC at an engine speed of 5,000 rpm due to the design of the ignition system.

3. Loosen the maximum spark advance screw locknut. Hold the control arm with the maximum spark advance screw against its stop. Pointing the timing light at the flywheel, crank the engine and adjust the spark advance screw to align the 27° BTDC mark (Model 100) or 25° BTDC mark (Model 115) on the timing decal with the timing pointer. Tighten locknut and disconnect timing light.

4. With the engine in water or in a test tank and the timing light connected, start the

5

engine. Make final timing checks with the engine running at both idle speed and 3,000 rpm to check idle and maximum spark advance settings. If not correct, repeat this procedure.

Synchronization

1. Remove the sound box cover.
2. Loosen the cam follower screw 1/4-1/2 turn.
3. Loosen each carburetor synchronizing screw and let the throttle shutter close freely.
4. Make sure all carburetor throttle shutters are completely closed. Lightly depress the carburetor synchronizing shaft and tighten each carburetor synchronizing screw, starting from the top and working to the bottom carburetor.
5. Recheck the carburetors to make sure that the throttle shutters are completely closed. If not, repeat Step 3 and Step 4.
6. Loosen the idle stop screw locknut. Hold the throttle arm with the idle stop screw against its stop.
7. Move the cam follower roller against the throttle cam and hold in that position. Adjust the idle stop screw until the raised mark on the throttle cam aligns with the center of the cam follower roller. Tighten the idle stop screw locknut.
8. Holding the throttle cam at idle position, adjust the cam follower to provide a clearance of 0.005-0.020 in. between the throttle cam and cam follower roller, then tighten the cam follower screw loosened in Step 2.
9. Loosen the throttle stop screw locknut and move the throttle arm to its wide open throttle position. Adjust the stop screw to permit the carburetor butterfly to open fully. Tighten the locknut.
10. Loosen the accelerator pump mounting fasteners. Holding the throttle arm in its wide open position, move the accelerator pump as

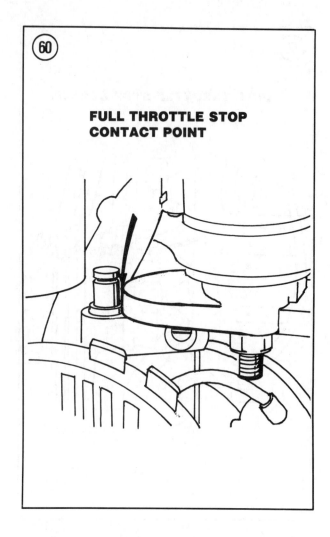

required to provide a 0.030 in. clearance, then tighten the mounting fasteners.

Carburetor/Oil Pump Synchronization

On early models, the oil pump lever may contain 2 stamped marks. If so, disregard the right-hand mark and use only the left mark for this procedure.

1. Move the throttle arm to the idle position. The stamped mark on the oil pump body should align with the stamped mark on the pump lever.
2. If the marks do not align in step 1, disconnect the oil pump link rod and turn the end of the rod to adjust its length until the 2 marks will align when the link rod is reconnected.

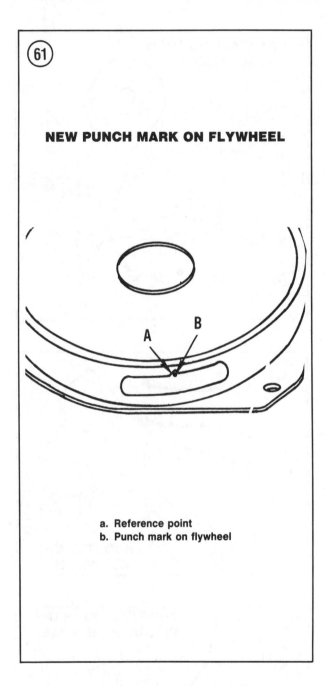

NEW PUNCH MARK ON FLYWHEEL

a. Reference point
b. Punch mark on flywheel

MERCURY 1750 V6
(1976-1977)

All Merc 1750 V6 models should have a revised timing mark on the flywheel. If the timing mark has not been modified, make the change as described in Step 6 and Step 7 before attempting to time the engine. If timing mark has already been revised, proceed with *Timing Adjustments*.

Timing Mark Change

1. Remove the cowling.
2. Disconnect the spark plug leads and remove all spark plugs.
3. Install a dial indicator in the No. 1 (top) spark plug hole.
4. Rotate flywheel clockwise until the No. 1 piston is at TDC. Zero the dial indicator and tighten its set screw.

NOTE
Do not rotate flywheel counterclockwise to locate 0.069 in. BTDC position in Step 5. If you rotate the flywheel too much and miss the mark, start the step over again.

5. Rotate the flywheel counterclockwise until the dial indicator reads approximately 0.100 in. *before* TDC. Rotate the flywheel clockwise until the dial indicator reads 0.069 in. BTDC.
6. Use the existing timing mark on the cover as a guide and make a new punch mark on the flywheel in the center of the timing mark as shown in **Figure 61**.
7. Remove or deface the timing decal on the front air box cover.

NOTE
If the engine is to be timed, install only the No. 1 spark plug in Step 8.

8. Reinstall spark plugs and connect spark plug wires.

Timing Adjustments

Refer to **Table 14** for this procedure.
1. Disconnect the remote fuel line at the engine and install engine in a test tank.
2. Remove all spark plugs except the No. 1 (top cylinder, starboard bank) plug.
3. Connect the electrical harness to the engine.
4A. If reed block housing boss has no edge, remove the throttle cable barrel from its

retainer on the cable anchor bracket. Adjust idle rpm stop screw to provide 1/8 in. clearance at dimension A in **Figure 62**. Leave cable disconnected.

4B. If reed block housing boss has an edge, remove the throttle cable barrel from its retainer on the cable anchor bracket. Adjust idle rpm stop screw until top of throttle cam aligns with edge on reed block housing boss. See **Figure 63**.

5. Connect a timing light according to manufacturer's instructions.

6. Place engine in NEUTRAL and hold throttle lever with idle stop screw against its stop (A, **Figure 64**). Loosen the primary pickup screw locknut (B, **Figure 64**). Pointing the timing light at the flywheel, crank the engine and adjust the primary pickup screw until the 3 flywheel punch marks align with the flywheel cover window notch. Tighten locknut.

7. Loosen the synchronizing screw on each carburetor. Holding the throttle lever against the idle stop, move the roller arm until the roller just contacts the throttle cam. Hold roller arm in that position and tighten all carburetor synchronizing screws.

NOTE
The revised timing mark is not used in Step 8. The maximum spark timing will be set properly by using the original single flywheel mark.

8. Loosen maximum spark advance screw locknut (C, **Figure 64**). Hold throttle lever with screw against its stop. Pointing the timing light at the flywheel, crank the engine and adjust the spark advance screw to align the single flywheel punch mark with the flywheel cover window notch. Tighten locknut and disconnect timing light.

9. Rotate the throttle to its wide-open position. Adjust the throttle stop screw (A,

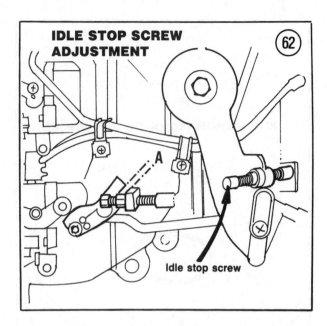

IDLE STOP SCREW ADJUSTMENT

Idle stop screw

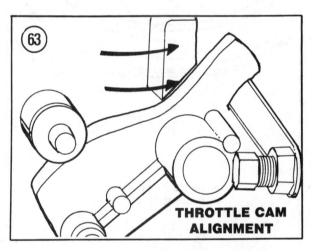

THROTTLE CAM ALIGNMENT

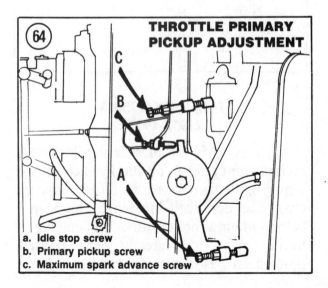

THROTTLE PRIMARY PICKUP ADJUSTMENT

a. Idle stop screw
b. Primary pickup screw
c. Maximum spark advance screw

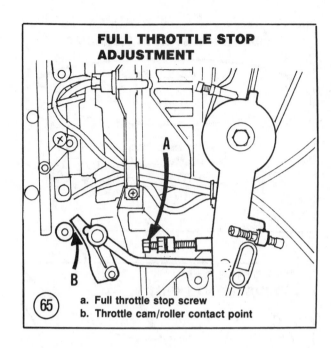

FULL THROTTLE STOP ADJUSTMENT

a. Full throttle stop screw
b. Throttle cam/roller contact point

(65)

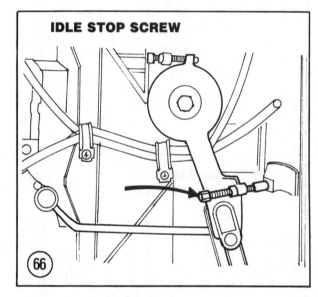

IDLE STOP SCREW

(66)

Figure 65) to permit full carburetor opening without allowing the carburetor shutters to act as a stop. There should be a 0.010-0.015 in. clearance between the roller and throttle cam. See B, **Figure 65**.

Carburetor Adjustments

There is no idle mixture adjustment screw on V6 carburetors. Mixture adjustment requires a change in jet size. See Chapter Six.

1. Install the engine in a test tank. Connect the fuel line and electrical harness to the engine.
2. Start the engine and run in forward gear.
3. Throttle cable barrel should have been removed from barrel retainer on cable anchor bracket during *Timing Adjustments*. If not, remove now.
4. Loosen idle adjustment screw locknut, set idle rpm to specifications (**Table 14**) in forward gear and retighten locknut. See **Figure 66**.
5. Hold throttle lever against idle stop. Adjust barrel to slip into retainer with a very light preload of throttle lever against the idle stop.

NOTE
Excessive preload in Step 6 will make shifting from FORWARD to NEUTRAL difficult.

6. Lock barrel in position. Place a thin piece of paper such as a matchbook cover between the idle stop and stop screw to check throttle cable preload. If there is some drag on the paper when removed but it does not tear, preload is correct. If not, readjust cable barrel.

MERCURY 1750 AND 175 V6 (1978-ON)

Timing Pointer Adjustment

1. Remove the cowling.
2. Disconnect all spark plug leads. Remove the spark plugs from the engine.
3. Install a dial indicator in the No. 1 cylinder, starboard bank) spark plug hole.
4. Rotate flywheel clockwise until the No. 1 piston is at TDC. Zero the dial indicator and tighten its set screw.
5. Rotate the flywheel counterclockwise until the dial indicator needle is about 1/4 turn beyond the 0.462 in. mark on the flywheel timing decal.

5

6. Rotate the flywheel clockwise until the dial indicator needle reads exactly 0.462 in.

7. Check the timing pointer alignment. The pointer groove should align with the 0.462 in. mark on the flywheel timing decal. If not, loosen pointer attachment screw, position pointer correctly and retighten the screw. See **Figure 67**.

8. Remove dial indicator. Reinstall spark plugs and connect spark plug leads.

Timing Adjustments

Refer to **Table 15** for this procedure.

1. Disconnect the remote fuel line and electrical harness at the engine.

2. Remove all spark plugs except the No. 1 (top cylinder, starboard bank) plug.

3. Remove throttle cable barrel from its retainer on the cable anchor bracket.

4. Remove sound box.

5. Loosen each carburetor synchronizing screw and let throttle shutter close freely.

6. Press cam follower roller against cam with light pressure and lift up on the bottom carburetor throttle shaft to remove any slack in the linkage. Hold in this position during Step 7 and Step 8.

7. Loosen idle stop screw locknut. Adjust screw until the short slash mark on the throttle cam contacts the roller (**Figure 68**). Tighten locknut.

8. Tighten all carburetor synchronizing screws. Make sure that the shutters are completely closed when the throttle cam contacts the roller and that there is no slack in the throttle linkage.

9. Operate the throttle and spark levers several times, then recheck shutter position and throttle linkage slack. If not correct, repeat Steps 5-8.

10. Install sound box.

11. Connect a timing light according to manufacturer's instructions.

TIMING POINTER ALIGNMENT

67

THROTTLE CAM ADJUSTMENT POINT

68

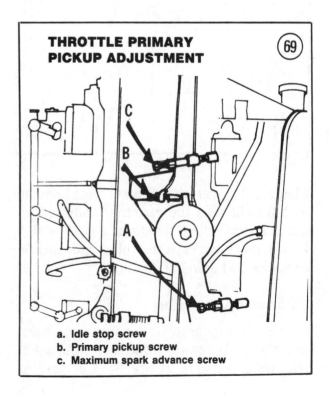

THROTTLE PRIMARY PICKUP ADJUSTMENT

69

a. Idle stop screw
b. Primary pickup screw
c. Maximum spark advance screw

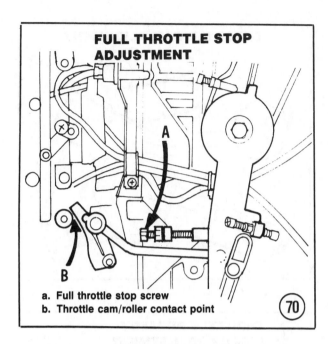

FULL THROTTLE STOP ADJUSTMENT

a. Full throttle stop screw
b. Throttle cam/roller contact point

⑦⓪

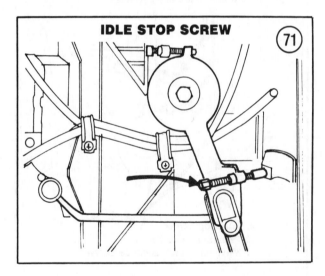

IDLE STOP SCREW ⑦①

12. Place engine in NEUTRAL and hold throttle lever with idle stop screw against its stop (A, **Figure 69**). Loosen the primary pickup screw locknut (B, **Figure 69**). Pointing the timing light at the flywheel, crank the engine and adjust the primary pickup screw until the timing pointer aligns with the timing decal mark specification (**Table 15**). Tighten locknut.

13. Loosen maximum spark advance screw locknut (C, **Figure 69**). Hold throttle lever with screw against its stop. Pointing the

timing light at the flywheel, crank the engine and adjust the spark advance screw to align the 20° BTDC mark on the timing decal with the timing pointer. Tighten locknut and disconnect timing light.

14. Rotate the throttle to its wide-open position. Adjust the throttle stop screw (A, **Figure 70**) to permit full carburetor opening without allowing the carburetor shutters to act as a stop. There should be a 0.010-0.015 in. clearance between the roller and throttle cam. See B, **Figure 70**.

Carburetor Adjustments

There is no idle mixture adjustment screw on V6 carburetors. Mixture adjustment requires a change in jet size. See Chapter Six.

1. Install the engine in a test tank. Connect the fuel line and electrical harness to the engine.

2. Start the engine and run in forward gear.

3. Throttle cable barrel should have been removed from barrel retainer on cable anchor bracket during *Timing Adjustments*. If not, remove now.

4. Loosen idle adjustment screw locknut, set idle rpm to specifications (**Table 15**) in forward gear and retighten locknut. See **Figure 71**.

5. Hold throttle lever against idle stop. Adjust barrel to slip into retainer with a very light preload of throttle lever against the idle stop.

NOTE
Excessive preload in Step 6 will make shifting from FORWARD to NEUTRAL difficult.

6. Lock barrel in position. Place a thin piece of paper such as a matchbook cover between the idle stop and stop screw to check throttle cable preload. If there is some drag on the paper when removed but it does not tear, preload is correct. If not, readjust cable barrel.

5

MERCURY 135, 1500, 150
150 XR2, 150 XR4, 2000 AND 200 V6
(BELOW SERIAL NO. 6073192)

Timing Pointer Adjustment

See *Merc 1750 and 175 V6 (1978-on)* in this chapter.

Timing Adjustments

Refer to **Table 16** or **Table 17** for this procedure.

1. On engine equipped with an idle stabilizer, disconnect the white/black wires at the outer switchbox terminal. Tape the terminal end of the wire leading to the stabilizer to prevent it from grounding. Reinstall other white/black wire to switchbox.

2. Disconnect the remote fuel line and electrical harness at the engine.

3. Remove all spark plugs except the No. 1 (top cylinder, starboard bank) plug.

4. Remove throttle cable barrel from its retainer on the cable anchor bracket.

5A. Merc 1500 and 150 (below serial No. 5203429); Merc 2000 and 200 (below serial No. 5363918)—Loosen idle stop screw locknut. Adjust screw until top of throttle cam aligns with the edge of the reed block housing boss. See **Figure 72**.

5B. Merc 1500 and 150 (above serial No. 5203428); Merc 2000 and 200 (above serial No. 5363917)—Loosen idle stop screw locknut. Adjust screw until bottom edge of throttle cam is 1/8 in. from the front corner of the throttle stop screw boss.

6. Connect a timing light according to manufacturer's instructions.

7. Place engine in NEUTRAL and hold throttle arm with idle stop screw against its stop (A, **Figure 73**). Loosen the primary pickup screw locknut (B, **Figure 73**). Pointing the timing light at the flywheel, crank the engine and adjust the primary pickup screw until the timing pointer aligns with the timing

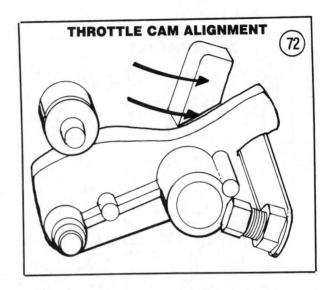

THROTTLE CAM ALIGNMENT ⑦²

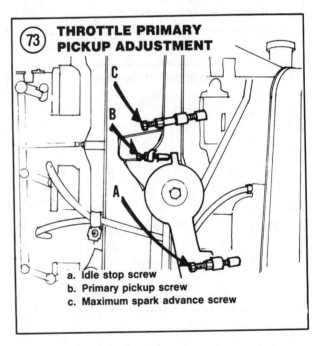

⑦³ THROTTLE PRIMARY
PICKUP ADJUSTMENT

C
B
A

a. Idle stop screw
b. Primary pickup screw
c. Maximum spark advance screw

decal mark specification (**Table 16** or **Table 17**). Tighten locknut.

8. Remove the sound box.

9. Loosen each carburetor synchronizing screw and let throttle shutter close freely.

10. Move throttle lever to place idle stop screw against its stop. Move roller arm until roller just contacts throttle cam. Hold in this position during Step 11.

11. Tighten all carburetor synchronizing screws. Make sure that the shutters are

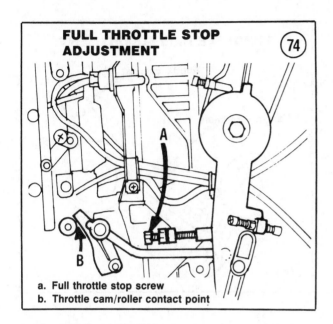

FULL THROTTLE STOP ADJUSTMENT (74)

a. Full throttle stop screw
b. Throttle cam/roller contact point

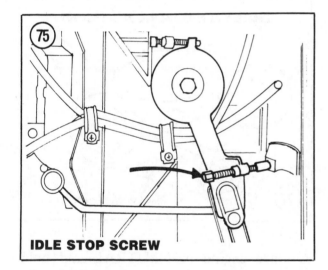

(75)

IDLE STOP SCREW

completely closed when the throttle cam contacts the roller and that there is no slack in the throttle linkage.

12. Operate the throttle and spark levers several times, then recheck shutter position and throttle linkage slack. If not correct, repeat Steps 9-11.

13. Install sound box.

14. Loosen maximum spark advance screw locknut (C, **Figure 73**). Hold throttle lever with screw against its stop. Pointing the timing light at the flywheel, crank the engine and adjust the spark advance screw to align the specified mark on the timing decal with the timing pointer. See. **Table 16** or **Table 17**. Tighten locknut and disconnect timing light.

15. Rotate the throttle to its wide-open position. Adjust the throttle stop screw (A, **Figure 74**) to permit full carburetor opening without allowing the carburetor shutters to act as a stop. There should be a 0.010-0.015 in. clearance between the roller and throttle cam. See B, **Figure 74**.

16. Reconnect idle stabilizer lead to outer switchbox, if so equipped.

Carburetor Adjustments

There is no idle mixture adjustment screw on V6 carburetors. Mixture adjustment requires a change in jet size. See Chapter Six.

1. Install the engine in a test tank. Connect the fuel line and electrical harness to the engine.

2. Start the engine and run in forward gear.

3. Throttle cable barrel should have been removed from barrel retainer on cable anchor bracket during *Timing Adjustments*. If not, remove now.

> *NOTE*
> *Do not allow idle speed to exceed 800 rpm in gear.*

4. Loosen idle adjustment screw locknut, set idle rpm to specifications (**Table 16** or **Table 17**) in forward gear and retighten locknut. See **Figure 75**.

5. Hold throttle lever against idle stop. Adjust barrel to slip into retainer with a very light preload of throttle lever against the idle stop.

> *NOTE*
> *Excessive preload in Step 6 will make shifting from FORWARD to NEUTRAL difficult.*

6. Lock barrel in position. Place a thin piece of paper such as a matchbook cover between the idle stop and stop screw to check throttle cable preload. If there is some drag on the

5

paper when removed but it does not tear, preload is correct. If not, readjust cable barrel.

MERCURY 200 V6 (ABOVE SERIAL NO. 6073191) AND 225 V6

Timing Pointer Adjustment

See *Merc 1750 and 175 V6 (1978-on)* in this chapter.

Timing Adjustments

Refer to **Table 18** for this procedure.

1. On engines equipped with an idle stabilizer or 3-wire spark advance module, disconnect the white/black wires at the outer switchbox terminal. Tape the terminal end of the wire leading to the stabilizer to prevent it from grounding. Reinstall other white/black wire to switchbox. This step is not required if engine is equipped with a 4-wire spark advance module.

2. Disconnect the remote fuel line and electrical harness at the engine.

3. Remove all spark plugs except the No. 1 (top cylinder, starboard bank) plug.

4. Remove throttle cable barrel from its retainer on the cable anchor bracket.

5. Unbolt sound attenuator, remove from carburetors and place to one side out of the way.

6. Loosen idle stop screw locknut. Insert a 1/8 in. rod or drill into the throttle cam hole. On 1981 V225 and 1982 V200 engines equipped with a cam stamped 95790 and carburetors marked WH20-1, WH20-2 and WH20-3, see **Figure 76** for correct cam hole location. On other models, see **Figure 77**. Hold the rod or drill perpendicular to the throttle cam and adjust idle stop screw until rod or drill is against the edge of the carburetor flange. Tighten locknut and remove rod or drill.

7. Connect a timing light according to manufacturer's instructions.

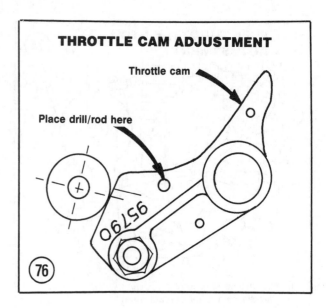

THROTTLE CAM ADJUSTMENT

Throttle cam

Place drill/rod here

95790

(76)

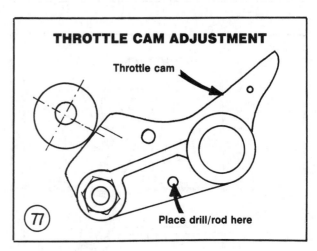

THROTTLE CAM ADJUSTMENT

Throttle cam

(77)

Place drill/rod here

8. Place engine in NEUTRAL and hold throttle arm with idle stop screw against its stop (A, **Figure 78**). Loosen the primary pickup screw locknut (B, **Figure 78**). Pointing the timing light at the flywheel, crank the engine and adjust the primary pickup screw until the timing pointer aligns with the timing decal mark specification (**Table 18**). Tighten locknut.

9. Loosen each carburetor synchronizing screw and let throttle shutter close freely.

10. Move throttle lever to place idle stop screw against its stop. Move roller arm until roller just contacts throttle cam. Hold in this position during Step 11.

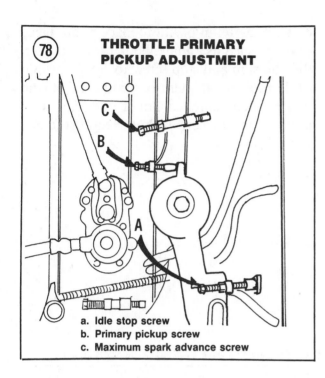

THROTTLE PRIMARY PICKUP ADJUSTMENT

a. Idle stop screw
b. Primary pickup screw
c. Maximum spark advance screw

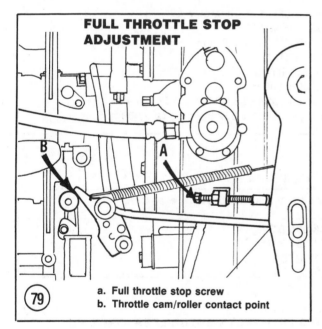

FULL THROTTLE STOP ADJUSTMENT

a. Full throttle stop screw
b. Throttle cam/roller contact point

11. Tighten all carburetor synchronizing screws. Make sure that the shutters are completely closed when the throttle cam contacts the roller and that there is no slack in the throttle linkage.

12. Operate the throttle and spark levers several times, then recheck shutter position and throttle linkage slack. If not correct, repeat Steps 9-11.

13. Install sound attenuator on carburetors and tighten attaching bolts securely.

14. Loosen maximum spark advance screw locknut (C, **Figure 78**). Hold throttle lever with screw against its stop. Pointing the timing light at the flywheel, crank the engine and adjust the spark advance screw to align the specified mark on the timing decal with the timing pointer. See **Table 18**. Tighten locknut and disconnect timing light.

15. Rotate the throttle to its wide-open position. Adjust the throttle stop screw (A, **Figure 79**) to permit full carburetor opening without allowing the carburetor shutters to act as a stop. There should be a 0.010-0.015 in. clearance between the roller and throttle cam. See B, **Figure 79**.

16. Reconnect idle stabilizer lead to outer switchbox, if so equipped.

Carburetor Adjustments

There is no idle mixture adjustment screw on V6 carburetors. Mixture adjustment requires a change in jet size. See Chapter Six.

1. Install the engine in a test tank. Connect the fuel line and electrical harness to the engine.

2. Start the engine and run in forward gear.

3. Throttle cable barrel should have been removed from barrel retainer on cable anchor bracket during *Timing Adjustments*. If not, remove now.

CAUTION
Do not allow idle speed to exceed 750 rpm in gear.

4. Loosen idle adjustment screw locknut, set idle rpm to specifications (**Table 18**) in forward gear and retighten locknut.

5

5. Hold the throttle lever against idle stop. Adjust barrel to slip into retainer with a very light preload of throttle lever against the idle stop.

NOTE
Excessive preload in Step 6 will make shifting from FORWARD to NEUTRAL difficult.

6. Lock barrel in position. Place a thin piece of paper such as a matchbook cover between the idle stop and stop screw to check throttle cable preload. If there is some drag on the paper when removed but it does not tear, preload is correct. If not, readjust cable barrel.

Table 1 TUNE-UP SPECIFICATIONS (MERC 500 WITH LIGHTNING ENERGIZER SYSTEM)

Firing order	1-3-2-4
Spark plug	AC-V40FFM or Champion L77V
Spark plug gap	Not adjustable
Maximum advance	35° BTDC @ 5,200 rpm
Throttle primary pickup	7-9° BTDC
Throttle secondary pickup	@ 35° BTDC stop
Full throttle rpm	4,800-5,500 rpm
Idle rpm	550-600 rpm (3-5° ATDC) in FORWARD gear
Water pressure (at cylinder block)	3-5 psi (0.211-0.352 kg/cm²) @ 2,000 rpm

Table 2 MERC 500 MAXIMUM SPARK ADVANCE

Engine rpm @ wide-open throttle	Maximum spark advance setting
2,000-4,000	38-39° BTDC
4,000-4,800	37-38° BTDC
5,200-5,500	35° BTDC

Table 3 TUNE-UP SPECIFICATIONS (MERC 500 WITH DISTRIBUTOR-LESS IGNITION)

Firing order	1-3-2-4
Spark plug	AC-V40FFM or Champion L77V
Spark plug gap	Not adjustable
Maximum advance	30° BTDC @ 5,000 rpm
Throttle primary pickup	7-9° BTDC
Throttle secondary pickup	@ maximum stop (30° BTDC)
Full throttle rpm	4,800-5,500 rpm
Idle rpm	550-600 rpm (5° ATDC) in FORWARD gear
Water pressure (at cylinder block)	3-5 psi (0.211-0.352 kg/cm²) @ 2,000 rpm

Table 4 TUNE-UP SPECIFICATIONS (MERC 500, 45 AND 50 [4-CYL.] ABOVE SERIAL NO. 4576236)

Firing order	1-3-2-4
Firing sequence	90° consecutive
Spark plug	AC-V40FFK or Champion L78V
Spark plug gap	Not adjustable
Maximum advance	30° BTDC @ 5,000 rpm
Throttle primary pickup	7-9° BTDC*
Throttle secondary pickup	@ maximum stop (30° BTDC)
Full throttle rpm	5,000-5,500 rpm
Idle rpm	550-600 rpm (5° ATDC) in FORWARD gear
Water pressure (at cylinder block)	3-5 psi (0.211-0.352 kg/cm²) @ 2,000 rpm

* With serial No. above 5632037 (U.S.), 7150562 (Canada), 8066280 (Australia) and 9265180 (Belgium): 0-2° ATDC.

5

Table 5 TUNE-UP SPECIFICATIONS (MERC 650 DISTRIBUTOR-LESS IGNITION)

Firing order	1-2-3
Spark plug	AC-V40FFM or Champion L76V
Spark plug gap	Not adjustable
Maximum advance	23° BTDC @ 5,300 rpm
Throttle primary pickup	6-8° BTDC
Throttle secondary pickup	Not adjustable
Full throttle rpm	4,800-5,300 rpm
Idle rpm	550-600 rpm (6-8° ATDC) in FORWARD gear
Water pressure (at cylinder block)	3 or more psi (0.211 or more kg/cm²) @ 2,000 rpm

Table 6 TUNE-UP SPECIFICATIONS (MERC 650 WITH DISTRIBUTOR CD IGNITION)

Firing order	1-2-3[1]
Spark plug	AC-V40FFM or Champion L77V
Spark plug gap	Not adjustable
Maximum advance	23° BTDC
Throttle primary pickup	3-5° BTDC[2]
Throttle secondary pickup	Not adjustable
Full throttle rpm	4,800-5,300 rpm
Idle rpm	550-600 rpm
Water pressure (at cylinder block)	3-5 psi (0.211-0.352 kg/cm²) @ 2,000 rpm

1. Firing order changed to 1-3-2 above serial No. 5467466 (U.S.), 7135987 (Canada), 8063334 (Australia) and 9238105 (Belgium).
2. Below serial No. 3552906, 0-2° BTDC.

**Table 7 TUNE-UP SPECIFICATIONS
(MERC 700/70/60/50 [3-CYLINDER] WITH FLYWHEEL CD IGNITION)**

Firing order	1-2-3*
Spark plug	AC-V40FFM or Champion L76V
Spark plug gap	Not adjustable
Maximum advance	23° BTDC @ 5,500 rpm
Throttle primary pickup	Not adjustable
Throttle secondary pickup	Maximum spark (static setting)
Full throttle rpm	5,000-5,500 rpm
Idle rpm	650-750 rpm (6-8° ATDC) in FORWARD gear
Water pressure (at cylinder block)	3 or more psi (0.211 or more kg/cm²) @ 2,000 rpm

* Firing order changed to 1-3-2 above serial No. 5467466 (U.S.), 7135987 (Canada), 8063334 (Australia) and 9238105 (Belgium).

Table 8 TUNE-UP SPECIFICATIONS (1987-ON MERC 70, 80 AND 90)

Firing order	1-3-2
Spark plug	NGK-BUHW-2, Champion L78V or AC-V40FFK
Spark plug gap	Not Adjustable
Maximum advance	
Cranking	
Models 70 and 80 (Prior to serial No. B239242)	24° BTDC
Models 70 and 80 (After serial No. B239241)	28° BTDC
Model 90	28° BTDC
Running	
Models 70 and 80 (Prior to serial No. B239243)	22° BTDC
Models 70 and 80 (After serial No. B239241)	26° BTDC
Model 90	26° BTDC
Idle timing	0-4° BTDC
Idle rpm in forward gear	650-700 rpm
Full throttle rpm	
Models 70 and 80	4750-5250 rpm
Model 90	5000-5500 rpm

Table 9 TUNE-UP SPECIFICATIONS (MERC 850 WITH DISTRIBUTOR CD IGNITION)

Firing order	1-3-2-4
Spark plug	AC-V40FFM or Champion L76V
Spark plug gap	Not adjustable
Maximum advance	27° BTDC
Throttle primary pickup	3-5° BTDC
Throttle secondary pickup	27° BTDC
Full throttle rpm	4,800-5,500 rpm
Idle rpm	550-650 rpm
Water pressure (at cylinder block)	2-5 psi (0.141-0.352 kg/cm²) @ 2,000 rpm

Table 10 TUNE-UP SPECIFICATIONS
(MERC 70/80 [PRIOR TO 1984]/800/850 WITH DISTRIBUTOR-LESS IGNITION)

Firing order	1-3-2-4
Spark plug	AC-V40FFK or Champion L78V
Spark plug gap	Not adjustable
Maximum advance	27° BTDC
Throttle primary pickup	2° BTDC-2° ATDC*
Throttle secondary pickup	Not adjustable
Full throttle rpm	5,000-5,500 rpm
Idle rpm	550-650 rpm (5-8° ATDC) in FORWARD gear
Water pressure (at cylinder block)	2-5 psi (0.141-0.352 kg/cm^2) @ 2,000 rpm

* Below serial No. 4423112, 2-4°

Table 11 TUNE-UP SPECIFICATIONS
(MERC 900, 1150, 1400, 1500 AND 1500XS WITH DISTRIBUTOR CD IGNITION)

Firing order	1-4-5-2-3-6
Spark plug	AC-V40FFM or Champion L76V
Spark plug gap	Not adjustable
Maximum advance	21° BTDC
Throttle primary pickup	4-6° BTDC
Throttle secondary pickup	Not adjustable
Full throttle rpm	
Merc 900	4,500-5,000 rpm
Merc 1150	5,000-5,500 rpm
Merc 1400, 1500	5,300-5,800 rpm
Merc 1500 XS	5,800-6,300 rpm
Idle rpm	550-650 rpm in FORWARD gear
Water pressure (at cylinder block)	2-5 psi (0.141-0.352 kg/cm^2) @ 2,000 rpm

5

Table 12 TUNE-UP SPECIFICATIONS
(MERC 90-140 HP [6-CYLINDER] WITH DISTRIBUTOR-LESS IGNITION)

Firing order	1-4-5-2-3-6
Spark plug	AC-V40FFM or Champion L76V
Spark plug gap	Not adjustable
Maximum advance	18° BTDC*
Throttle primary pickup	4-6° BTDC
Throttle secondary pickup	
Merc 90	1-3° BTDC
Merc 115	5-7° ATDC
Merc 140	4-6° ATDC
Full throttle rpm	
Merc 90	4,500-5,000 rpm
Merc 115	5,000-5,500 rpm
Merc 140	5,300-5,800 rpm
Idle rpm	550-650 prm in FORWARD gear
Water pressure (at cylinder block)	2-5 psi (0.141-0.352 kg/cm^2) @ 2,000 rpm

* 20° @ cranking speed.

Table 13 TUNE-UP SPECIFICATIONS (1988-ON MERC 100 AND 1989 MERC 115)

Firing order	1-3-2-4
Spark plug	NGK BUHW, Champion L76V or AC-V40FFM
Spark plug gap	Not adjustable
Maximum advance	
Cranking	
Model 100	27° BTDC
Model 115	25° BTDC
Running	23° BTDC
Idle timing	2-4° BTDC
Idle rpm in forward gear	
Model 100	600-700 rpm
Model 115	650-700 rpm
Full throttle rpm	4,750-5,250 rpm
Water pressure (at cylinder block)	1-5 psi @ 5,000 rpm

Table 14 TUNE-UP SPECIFICATIONS (MERC 1750 V6, 1976-1977)

Firing order	1-2-3-4-5-6
Spark plug	AC-V40FFM or Champion L76V
Spark plug gap	Not adjustable
Maximum advance	15° BTDC[1]
Throttle primary pickup	8-10° ATDC[2]
Throttle secondary pickup	Not adjustable
Full throttle rpm	4,800-5,800 rpm
Idle rpm	550-650 rpm in FORWARD gear
Water pressure (at cylinder block)	8-11 psi (0.56-0.77 kg/cm²) @ 3,000 rpm

1. One punch mark.
2. Three punch marks.

Table 15 TUNE-UP SPECIFICATIONS (MERC 1750 AND 175 V6, 1978-ON)

Firing order	1-2-3-4-5-6
Spark plug	AC-V40FFM or Champion L76V
Spark plug gap	Not adjustable
Maximum advance	18° BTDC[1]
Throttle primary pickup	14° ATDC[2]
Throttle secondary pickup	Not adjustable
Full throttle rpm	5,300-5,800 rpm
Idle rpm	600-700 rpm in FORWARD gear
Water pressure (at cylinder block)	18-25 psi (1.27-1.76 kg/cm²) @ 5,000 rpm

1. 20° BTDC @ cranking speed.
2. Serial no. 6618751 and above; 7° ATDC.

Table 16 TUNE-UP SPECIFICATIONS
(MERC 1500 AND 150 HP V6 BELOW SERIAL NO. 5203429
MERC 2000 AND 200 HP V6 BELOW SERIAL NO. 5363918)

1500 AND 150	
Firing order	1-2-3-4-5-6
Spark plug	AC-V40FFM or Champion L76V
Spark plug gap	Not adjustable
Maximum advance	16° BTDC[1]
Throttle primary pickup	7.5-8.5° ATDC
Throttle secondary pickup	Not adjustable
Full throttle rpm	5,000-5,500 rpm
Idle rpm	600-700 rpm (7.5-8.5° ATDC) in FORWARD gear
Water pressure (at cylinder block)	18-25 psi (1.27-1.76 kg/cm²) @ 5,000 rpm

2000 AND 200 HP	
Firing order	1-2-3-4-5-6
Spark plug	AC-V40FFM or Champion L76V
Spark plug gap	Not adjustable
Maximum advance	18° BTDC[2]
Throttle primary pickup	8-10° ATDC
Throttle secondary pickup	Not adjustable
Full throttle rpm	5,300-5,800 rpm
Idle rpm	550-650 rpm (12-15° ATDC) in FORWARD gear[3]
Water pressure (at cylinder block)	18-25 psi (1.27-1.76 kg/cm²) @ 5,000 rpm

1. 18° @ cranking.
2. 20° @ cranking.
3. Never exceed 800 rpm idle in gear.

5

Table 17 TUNE-UP SPECIFICATIONS
(MERC 135 HP)
(MERC 150 HP AND V150 XR2 V6 SERIAL NO. 5203429 AND ABOVE)
(MERC 200 HP V6 SERIAL NO. 5363918 AND ABOVE)

135 HP AND 150 HP	
Firing order	1-2-3-4-5-6
Spark plug	AC-V40FFM or Champion L76V
Spark plug gap	Not adjustable
Maximum advance	16° BTDC[1]
Throttle primary pickup	11° ATDC
Throttle secondary pickup	Not adjustable
Full throttle rpm	5,000-5,500 rpm
Idle rpm	600-700 rpm
Water pressure (at cylinder block)	18-25 psi (1.27-1.76 kg/cm²) @ 5,000 rpm

MERC V150 XR2	
Firing order	1-2-3-4-5-6
Spark plug	NGK-BUHW, AC-V40FFM or Champion L76V
Spark plug gap	Not adjustable
Maximum timing	20° BTDC (22° BTDC @ cranking speed)
Throttle primary pickup	11° ATDC
Full throttle rpm	5,500-6,000 rpm
Idle rpm	600-700 in FORWARD gear

200 HP	
Firing order	1-2-3-4-5-6
Spark plug	AC-V40FFM or Champion L76V
Spark plug gap	Not adjustable
Maximum advance	18° BTDC[2]
Throttle primary pickup	10° ATDC
Throttle secondary pickup	Not adjustable
Full throttle rpm	5,300-5,800 rpm
Idle rpm	600-700 rpm (12-15° ATDC) in FORWARD gear[3]
Water pressure (at cylinder block)	18-25 psi (1.27-1.76 kg/cm²) @ 5,000 rpm

1. 18° @ cranking.
2. 20° @ cranking.
3. Never exceed 800 rpm idle in gear.

Table 18 TUNE-UP SPECIFICATIONS (MERC 150 XR4, V200¹ AND V225)

Firing order	1-2-3-4-5-6
Spark plug	NGK-BUHW, AC-V40FFM or Champion L76V
Spark plug gap	Not adjustable
Maximum timing	22° BTDC @ cranking speed
	20° BTDC @ 5,400 rpm
	26° BTDC over 5,600 rpm
Throttle primary pickup	
Below serial No. 657932	12° ATDC
Above serial No. 657933	
or WH-28 carburetor	7° ATDC
Full throttle rpm	5,300-5,800 rpm
Idle rpm	600-700 in FORWARD gear

1. Serial No. 6073192 and above.
2. High speed spark advance module automatically advances maximum timing to 26° @ engine speed of 5,500 ±100 rpm.

5

Chapter Six

Fuel System

This chapter contains removal, overhaul, installation and adjustment procedures for fuel pumps, carburetors, enrichener valves/choke solenoids, fuel tanks and connecting lines used with the Mercury outboards covered in this book. Carburetor jet size recommendations are provided in **Tables 1-6** at the end of this chapter.

FUEL PUMP

The diaphragm-type fuel pump used on Mercury outboards is operated by crankcase pressure. Since this type of fuel pump cannot create sufficient pressure to draw fuel from the tank during cranking, fuel is transferred to the carburetor for starting by hand-operating the primer bulb installed in the fuel line.

Pressure pulsations created by movement of the pistons reaches the fuel pump through a passageway between the crankcase and the pump.

Upward piston motion creates a low pressure on the pump diaphragm. This low pressure opens the inlet check valve in the pump, drawing fuel from the line into the pump. At the same time, the low pressure draws the air-fuel mixture from the carburetor into the crankcase.

Downward piston motion creates a high pressure on the pump diaphragm. This pressure closes the inlet check valve and opens the outlet check valve, forcing the fuel into the carburetor and drawing the air-fuel mixture from the crankcase into the cylinder for combustion. **Figure 1** shows the operational sequence of a typical Mercury outboard fuel pump.

Mercury fuel pumps are extremely simple in design and reliable in operation. Diaphragm failures are the most common problem, although the use of dirty or improper fuel-oil mixtures can cause check valve problems.

NOTE
A black fuel pump diaphragm gasket (part No. 27-75360A1) is available as a replacement for earlier gray gaskets which have shown a tendency to decompose and contaminate the fuel system. Avoid the use of gray-colored gaskets when rebuilding a fuel pump.

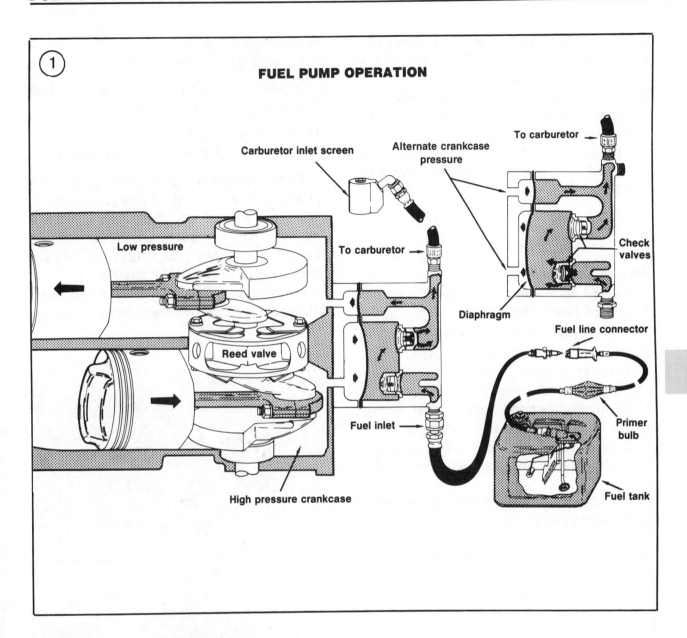

FUEL PUMP OPERATION

Carburetor inlet screen

Alternate crankcase pressure

To carburetor

Low pressure

To carburetor

Check valves

Reed valve

Diaphragm

Fuel line connector

High pressure crankcase

Fuel inlet

Primer bulb

Fuel tank

6

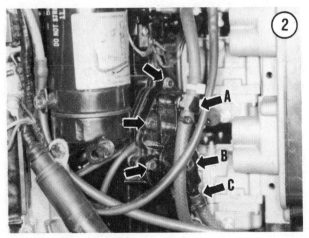

Removal/Installation
All Engines
(Except Integral Fuel Pump Carburetor)

Figure 2 shows the V6 and inline 6-cylinder pump; others are similar.

1. Remove and discard any straps holding the carburetor fuel line to the fuel pump. Disconnect the line at the pump (A, **Figure 2**).

2. Remove the screw and flat washer holding the fuel filter cover to the pump (B, **Figure 2**). Remove cover from pump.

3. Remove and discard fuel filter O-ring (A, **Figure 3**). Remove filter (B, **Figure 3**) for cleaning or replacement.

4. Remove screws holding pump assembly to engine (C, **Figure 2** shows 3 of the 5 screws). Remove pump from engine.

5. Installation is the reverse of removal. Coat fuel line fittings with Aviation Permatex and install new straps.

Removal/Installation
(Integral Fuel Pump Carburetor, Except 45 and 50 [4-cyl.] hp Models)

Refer to **Figure 4** for this procedure.

1. Disconnect fuel line at inlet cover.
2. Remove strainer cover screw. Remove cover, gasket and strainer. Discard gasket.
3. Remove 4 screws holding fuel pump components to the side of the carburetor.
4. Remove the fuel strainer body, fuel pump body diaphragms and gaskets. Discard the gaskets.
5. Installation is the reverse of removal. Install new gaskets.

Removal/Installation
(45 and 50 [4-cyl.] hp Models)

See *Integral Fuel Pump Carburetor (With Primer System)* in this chapter.

Disassembly/Assembly
(Except Integral Fuel Pump Carburetor)

Refer to **Figure 5** (V6 and inline 6-cylinder) or **Figure 6** (all others) for this procedure.

1A. V6 and inline 6-cylinder pump—separate the fuel pump assembly into the base, pulse chamber, diaphragm and housing components. Discard all 4 gaskets.

1B. All others—separate the 2 gaskets and diaphragm from the fuel pump housing. Discard both gaskets.

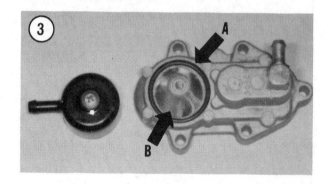

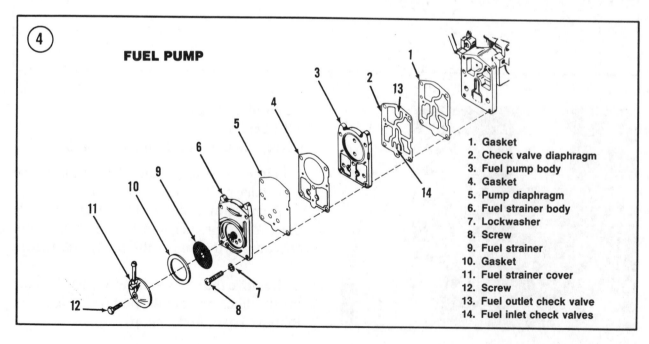

FUEL PUMP

1. Gasket
2. Check valve diaphragm
3. Fuel pump body
4. Gasket
5. Pump diaphragm
6. Fuel strainer body
7. Lockwasher
8. Screw
9. Fuel strainer
10. Gasket
11. Fuel strainer cover
12. Screw
13. Fuel outlet check valve
14. Fuel inlet check valves

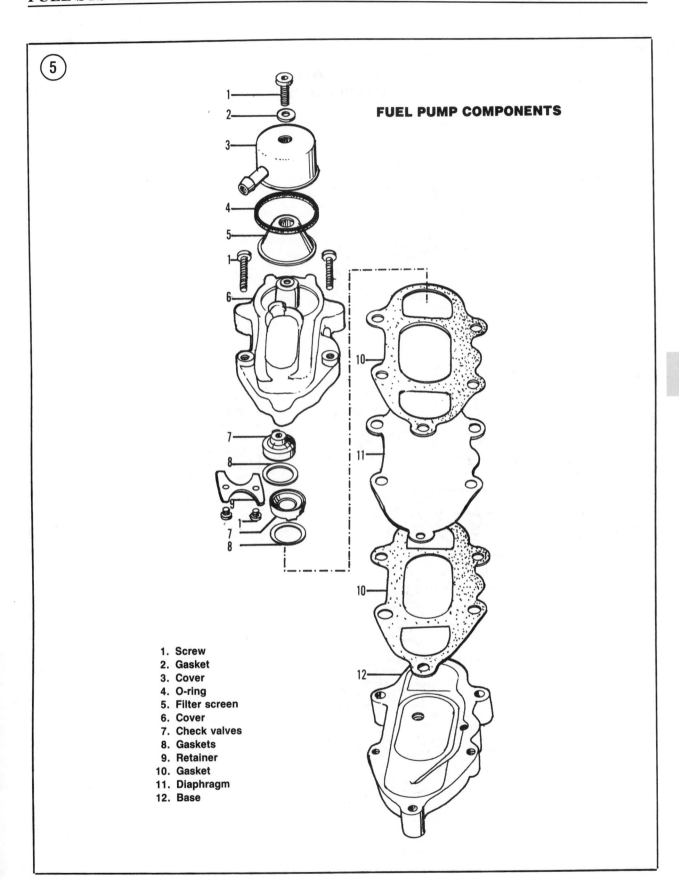

FUEL PUMP COMPONENTS

1. Screw
2. Gasket
3. Cover
4. O-ring
5. Filter screen
6. Cover
7. Check valves
8. Gaskets
9. Retainer
10. Gasket
11. Diaphragm
12. Base

6

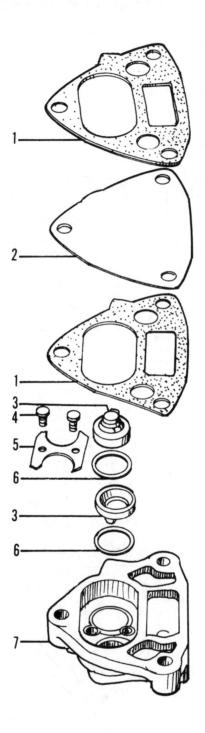

⑥

**FUEL PUMP
COMPONENTS**

1. Gasket
2. Diaphragm
3. Check valves
4. Screws
5. Retainer
6. Gaskets
7. Housing

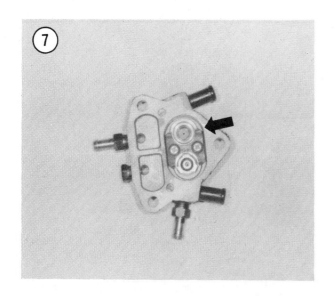

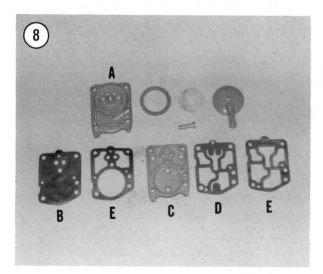

2. Remove the screws holding the check valve retainer to the pump housing (**Figure 7**).
3. Remove retainer and inlet and outlet check valves. Remove and discard check valve gaskets.
4. Install new check valve gaskets in pump housing.

NOTE
Merc 70 outboards that suffer vapor lock during extremely hot weather can be cured by installing new check valves (part No. C-21-92346A3) or by drilling a 0.031 in. hole in the center of both original check valves in the fuel pump.

5. Install check valves in pump housing.

6. Install check valve retainer with ends facing upward. Tighten retainer screws securely.

7. Check outlet valve after installation by sucking through the outlet hole. You should be able to draw air through the valve but not blow air through it.

8. Check inlet valve by reversing the procedure in Step 7. You should be able to blow through the valve but not draw air through it.

NOTE
Do not use any form of gasket sealer with fuel pump gaskets.

6

9A. V6 and inline 6-cylinder pump—assemble the pump components with new gaskets in the following order:

   a. Pump housing.
   b. Diaphragm-to-housing gasket.
   c. Diaphragm.
   d. Pulse chamber-to-diaphragm gasket.
   e. Pulse chamber.
   f. Base-to-pulse chamber gasket.
   g. Base.
   h. Base-to-engine gasket.
9B. All others—sandwich the diaphragm between new gaskets and position on rear of pump housing.

10. Install fuel pump assembly to engine as described in this chapter.

**Disassembly/Assembly
(Integral Fuel Pump Carburetor, Except 45 and 50 [4-cyl.] hp Models)**

Refer to **Figure 8** for this procedure.

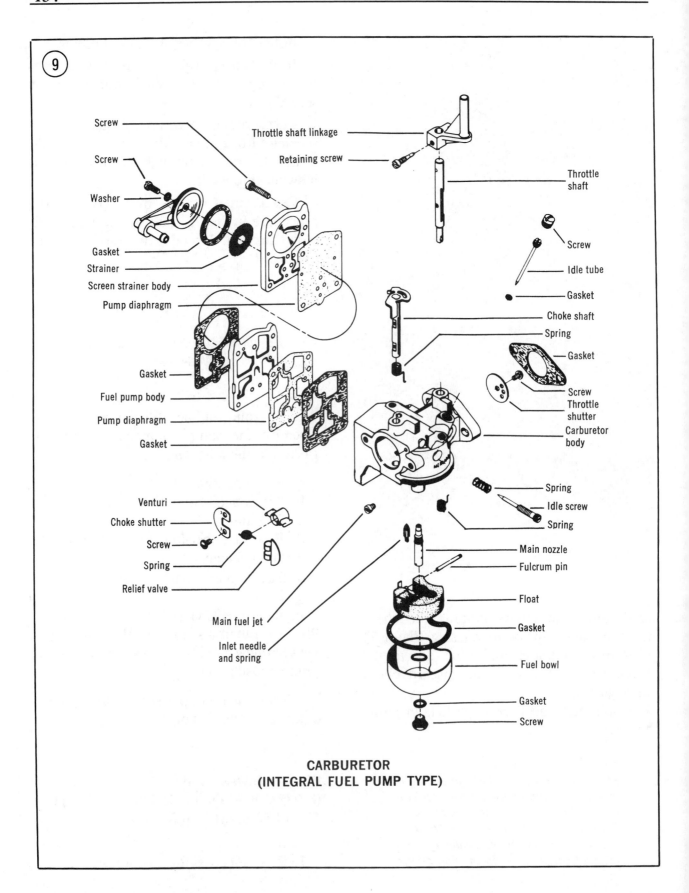

**CARBURETOR
(INTEGRAL FUEL PUMP TYPE)**

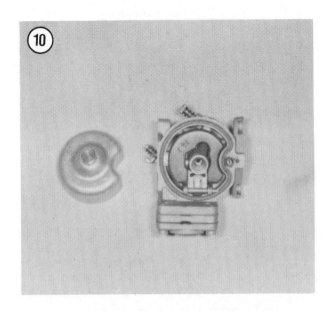

1. Separate strainer body (A), diaphragm (B), fuel pump body (C), check valve diaphragm (D) and gaskets (E) as shown in **Figure 8**. Discard gaskets.

2. Assemble components with new gaskets in reverse of order given in Step 1.

Cleaning/Inspection
(Except 1977-on Merc 500, 45 and 50 [4-cyl.])

1. Clean housing and check valves in solvent. Dry housing with compressed air. Let check valves air dry.

2. Inspect check valves for warpage and spring tension. Replace any valve that is slightly warped, has weak tension or broken springs.

3. Check housing condition. Make sure the valve seats provide a flat contact area for the valve disc. Replace housing if cracks or rough gasket mating surfaces are found.

4. Check housing fitting. If loose or damaged, tighten or replace as required.

Cleaning/Inspection
1977-on Merc 500, 45 and 50 (4-cyl.)
With Integral Fuel Pump Carburetor

1. Clean strainer and fuel pump bodies in solvent. Blow dry with compressed air.
2. Inspect check valve diaphragm for damage. Replace as required.

INTEGRAL FUEL PUMP CARBURETOR (EXCEPT 45 AND 50 [4-CYL.] HP MODELS)

Carburetor Float

A redesigned alcohol-resistant float of hollow plastic is installed in many late-model carburetors. The floats are also available as service replacements for earlier models. Read the instructions accompanying the plactic float carefully, as float settings are changed on some models when the plastic float is installed.

Removal/Installation

1. Disconnect the choke cable from the choke lever. Remove the cap screw and spacer holding the choke cable to the carburetor.
2. Remove the 2 carburetor-to-power head nuts.
3. Remove the cap screw, then remove the fuel line and fuel connector with the carburetor.

Disassembly

Refer to **Figure 9** for this procedure.

1. Remove the fuel bowl and gasket (**Figure 10**).
2. Remove the float fulcrum pin and float assembly (**Figure 11**).
3. Invert carburetor and catch inlet needle and spring assembly as it falls out.

6

4. Lightly seat the idle mixture needle (**Figure 12**), counting the number of turns required. Back the needle out and remove with spring.

5. Remove the idle restrictor tube plug screw (A, **Figure 13**).

6. Unscrew the idle restrictor tube from inside the main discharge nozzle on top of the carburetor (B, **Figure 13**). Do not lose the metal washer(s) on the tube.

7. Remove the fixed high-speed jet from the side of the main discharge nozzle housing, then remove the main nozzle with a jet remover tool or appropriate size screwdriver blade. See **Figure 14**.

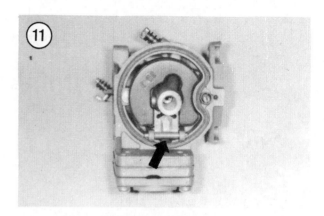

> *NOTE*
> *When the main nozzle is removed, the plastic venturi will drop from the carburetor throat.*

8. Remove the strainer cover screw, cover, gasket and screen (**Figure 15**).

9. Remove the screws holding the fuel pump to the side of the carburetor.

10. Remove the strainer body, pump diaphragm, gasket, pump body, diaphragm and gasket (**Figure 16**). Discard the gaskets.

> *NOTE*
> *This completes carburetor disassembly for routine cleaning. Perform Steps 11-16 only if the throttle or choke shutters require replacement.*

11. Remove the screw and washer holding the throttle shutter to the throttle shaft. Remove the throttle shutter return spring from the throttle shaft.

12. Pull the throttle shaft from the top of the carburetor.

13. Remove the cap screws holding trash screen.

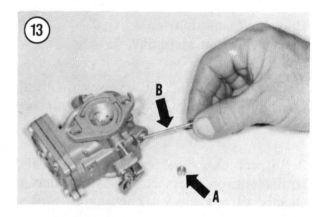

14. Remove the screws and washers from the choke shutter. Remove one-half of the choke shutter.

15. Pull the choke spring and shutter from the top of the carburetor.

16. Remove the other half of the choke shutter and shutter spring from the carburetor throat.

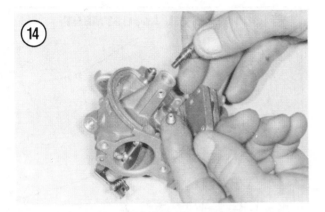

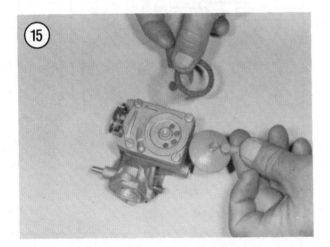

Cleaning and Inspection

1. Clean the carburetor body and metal parts in a carburetor cleaning solution to remove gum, dirt and varnish. Carburetor cleaners are available through local automotive supply stores. Follow the instructions provided with the cleaner.

2. Rinse the carburetor components thoroughly in clean solvent after removing them from the cleaning solution.

3. Blow carburetor body dry with compressed air. Be sure to blow through all orifices, nozzles and passages.

CAUTION
Do not use wire or drill bits to clean carburetor passages as this can ruin the carburetor.

4. Check the float for saturation or deterioration. Replace as required.

Reassembly

Refer to **Figure 8** for this procedure.

1. Insert the tapered end of the venturi inside the carburetor throat toward the choke.

2. Install and tighten the main nozzle, using a jet installer tool or a screwdriver of the proper size.

3. Insert the inlet needle and spring assembly into the seat, making sure that the needle does not stick.

4. Install the float and float fulcrum pin.

5. Install the high-speed jet in the side of the nozzle housing.

6. Check the float level and drop adjustment as described in this chapter.

7. Install a new float bowl gasket. Install the bowl with 2 fiber washers and the screw. Tighten screw securely.

8. Install the idle restrictor tube and washer(s).

9. Install the idle restrictor tube plug screw.

10. Slide the spring onto the idle mixture screw. Install the screw in the carburetor body until it lightly seats, then back out the number of turns noted during disassembly.

11. Assemble new gasket, diaphragm, pump body, new gasket, pump diaphragm and strainer body to carburetor. Secure with 4 screws and washers.

6

12. Assemble the strainer screen, new gasket and cover. Install to fuel pump and secure with washer and screw.

NOTE
If the throttle or choke shutters were removed, perform Steps 13-20.

13. Insert throttle shaft into carburetor body.
14. Install throttle shaft return spring on throttle shaft with approximately 1/4 turn windup, holding tension on the spring.
15. Center throttle shutter in throttle shaft slot, then install washer and screw.
16. Press cam lever tightly against carburetor body and tighten shutter screw.
17. Fit choke shaft return spring on choke shaft.
18. Assemble choke shaft, relief valve and relief valve spring into carburetor with approximately 1/4 turn windup.
19. Center choke shutter in choke shaft and install screws with washers.
20. Install trash screen with cap screws.

Float Level and Drop Adjustment

1. Check float level as shown in **Figure 17**. It should be 1/4 in. ±1/64 in. from float bottom to casting. Adjust if necessary by bending float tab in.
2. Invert carburetor and check float drop as shown in **Figure 18**. It should be 1/16-1/32 in. between bottom of float and fixed jet. Adjust if necessary by bending float tang.

Carburetor Adjustment

1. Jet size recommendations (**Table 1**) are made only as a guide. When in doubt, try a size smaller to lean mixture or a size larger to richen mixture.
2. A change in spark advance is not recommended for operation at high elevation. Use a propeller with lower pitch at high elevation to allow proper engine rpm.

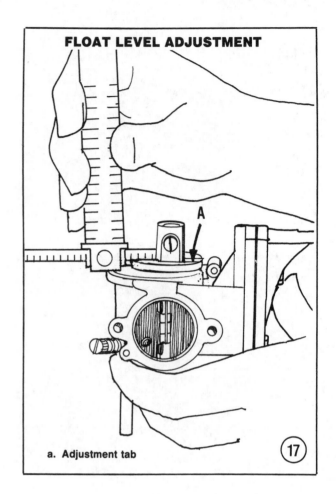

FLOAT LEVEL ADJUSTMENT

a. Adjustment tab

(17)

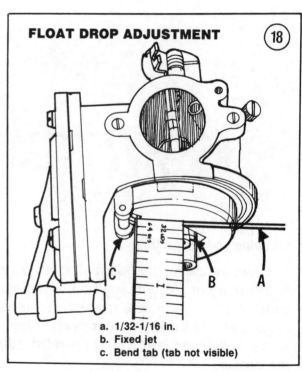

FLOAT DROP ADJUSTMENT   (18)

a. 1/32-1/16 in.
b. Fixed jet
c. Bend tab (tab not visible)

3. The carburetor uses a fixed main jet. Adjustments are not possible, but poor running at high speed may indicate the need for replacement.

Idle Mixture Adjustment

The idle mixture and idle speed are both factory-set but can be adjusted to suit local conditions. Do not adjust mixture leaner than necessary for a smooth idle or hard starting and engine damage may result. It is always better to set the idle mixture too rich than too lean.

1. With carburetor installed on engine and engine in the water or a test tank, set the idle mixture screw 1 1/2 turns open from a lightly seated condition.

2. Start the engine and let it warm to normal operating temperature in forward gear.

3. Slowly turn idle mixture screw counterclockwise until the affected cylinders begin to load up or fire unevenly from the over-rich mixture.

4. Now slowly turn idle mixture screw clockwise until the cylinder firing smooths out and the engine gains rpm. Continue turning screw clockwise until the engine slows down and misfires, indicating a too-lean mixture.

5. Set idle mixture screw 1-1 1/4 turns counterclockwise from lean-out position in Step 4.

6. Accelerate engine. If engine hesitates, idle mixture is too lean and should be richened until engine acceleration is smooth.

7. Idle engine and adjust idle stop screw on bracket so the engine will idle at the recommended rpm in forward gear. See Chapter Five.

8. Run in forward gear at 4,000-5,000 rpm to clear engine of any excess fuel. Recheck idle speed.

INTEGRAL FUEL PUMP CARBURETOR (45 AND 50 [4-CYL.] HP MODELS)

This carburetor is installed on 1986 and later Classic 50 (45 hp) and 50 (4-cylinder) hp models. It contains a simplified integral fuel pump and a diaphragm-operated primer system.

Removal/Installation

1. Remove the engine cover.

2. Disconnect the fuel line at the carburetor. Plug the line to prevent leakage and entry of contamination.

3. Remove the carburetor mounting nuts. Remove the carburetor and discard the gasket.

4. Disconnect the idle wire from the primer ratchet.

5. Installation is the reverse of removal. Use a new gasket.

Disassembly/Assembly

Refer to **Figure 19** for this procedure.

1. Remove the fasteners holding the primer assembly to the carburetor. Remove the primer assembly.

2. Remove the low speed mixture screw and spring (**Figure 20**).

3. Remove the fuel bowl retainer. The high speed jet is located inside the retainer. See **Figure 21**.

4. Remove the fuel bowl from the carburetor. Remove the float from the carburetor. See **Figure 22**.

5. Remove the primer cover screws. Remove the cover, diaphragm, gasket and spring. See **Figure 23**.

6. Remove the plug from the bottom of the primer housing. Remove the gasket, spring and check ball (**Figure 24**).

6

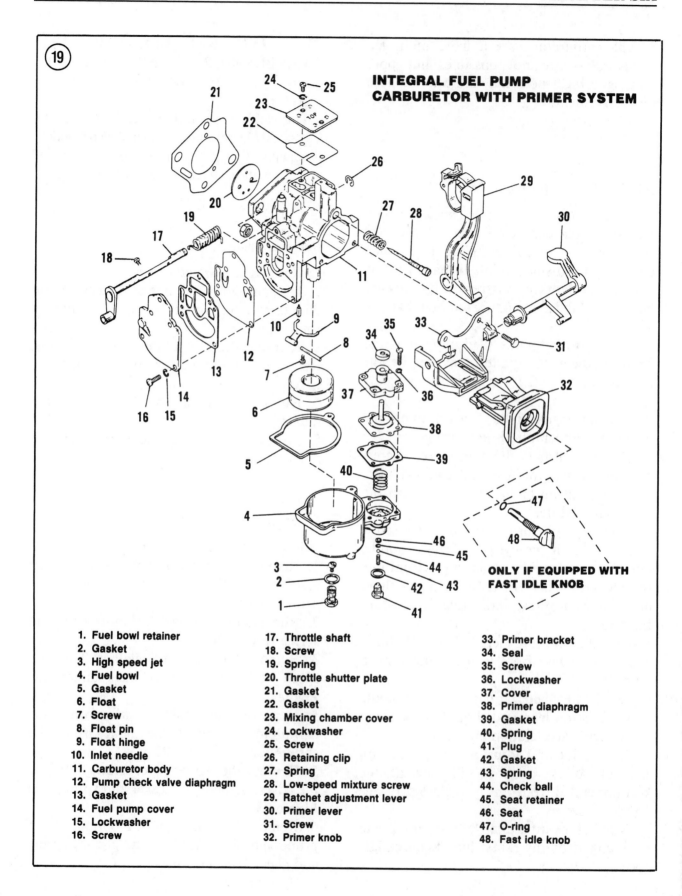

⑲

**INTEGRAL FUEL PUMP
CARBURETOR WITH PRIMER SYSTEM**

**ONLY IF EQUIPPED WITH
FAST IDLE KNOB**

1. Fuel bowl retainer
2. Gasket
3. High speed jet
4. Fuel bowl
5. Gasket
6. Float
7. Screw
8. Float pin
9. Float hinge
10. Inlet needle
11. Carburetor body
12. Pump check valve diaphragm
13. Gasket
14. Fuel pump cover
15. Lockwasher
16. Screw

17. Throttle shaft
18. Screw
19. Spring
20. Throttle shutter plate
21. Gasket
22. Gasket
23. Mixing chamber cover
24. Lockwasher
25. Screw
26. Retaining clip
27. Spring
28. Low-speed mixture screw
29. Ratchet adjustment lever
30. Primer lever
31. Screw
32. Primer knob

33. Primer bracket
34. Seal
35. Screw
36. Lockwasher
37. Cover
38. Primer diaphragm
39. Gasket
40. Spring
41. Plug
42. Gasket
43. Spring
44. Check ball
45. Seat retainer
46. Seat
47. O-ring
48. Fast idle knob

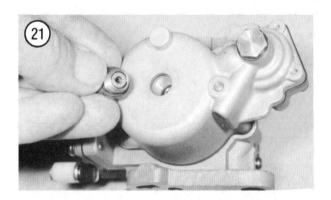

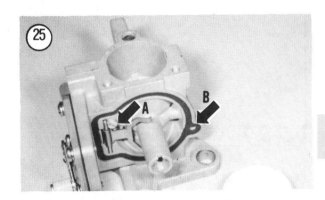

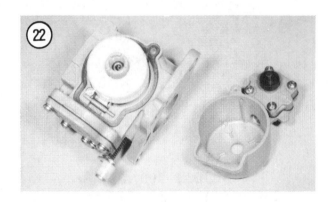

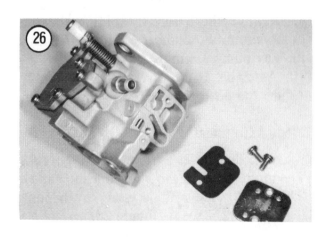

7. Remove the screw holding the float hinge in place (A, **Figure 25**). Remove the float hinge and the inlet needle under it. Remove the fuel bowl gasket (B, **Figure 25**).

8. Remove the mixing chamber cover and gasket. See **Figure 26**.

NOTE
If fuel pump is desassembled in Step 9,
*do **not** reuse the check valve diaphragm*

6

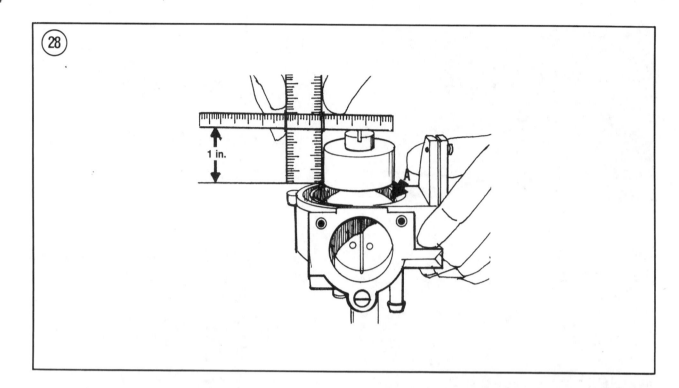

1 in.

and gasket shown in Figure 27. If pump does not require cleaning, it is not necessary to disassemble it.

9. Remove the 5 screws holding the fuel pump assembly to the carburetor. Remove the fuel pump assembly (**Figure 27**).

10. Assembly is the reverse of disassembly. Adjust the float as described in this chapter.

Float Adjustment

Check float level as shown in **Figure 28**. The top of the float should be one inch above the casting. Adjust if necessary by bending the float hinge. See A, **Figure 28**.

Carburetor Adjustment

1. Jet size recommendations (**Table 1** or **Table 2**) are made only as a guide. When in doubt, try a size smaller to lean the mixture or a size larger to enrich the mixture.

2. A change in spark advance is not recommended for operation at high elevation. Use a propeller with a lower pitch at high elevation to allow proper engine rpm.

MODEL 100 AND MODEL 115 CONCEPT 2 + 2

The 1988-on Mercury 100 and 1989 Mercury 115 4-cylinder engines utilize a variation in carburetion design called Concept 2 + 2. This is the first multiple-cylinder, multiple-carburetor outboard engine that operates on 2 carburetors at idle, with the remaining 2 carburetors coming on-stream only after engine speed accelerates beyond a specified rpm.

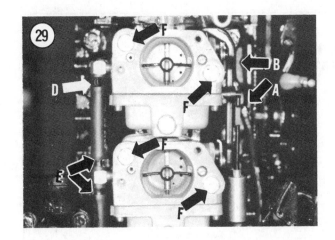

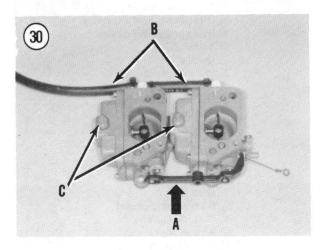

carburetors from coming into play until engine speed reaches approximately 1,800 rpm. At the point where these 2 carburetors come on-stream, there is some roughness in engine firing, but in most applications, it will not be noticed.

A linkage-operated accelerator pump, attached to the side of the power head, provides required additional fuel to the No. 3 and No. 4 carburetors during rapid acceleration, such as during water skiing.

The Model 100 and Model 115 use the same Mercury WME carburetors found on 1987-on 70-90 hp models and described in this chapter. The primary difference is in the location of the off-idle discharge points in the No. 3 and No. 4 carburetors (which has no bearing on service procedures for the carburetors).

CENTER BOWL CARBURETOR

Removal/Installation

1. Remove air silencer cover and support frame, if so equipped. Remove carburetor plate from carburetor(s).
2. If removing both carburetors, disconnect linkage at A, **Figure 29**. To remove only one carburetor, disconnect linkage at B (top carburetor) or C (bottom carburetor).
3. To remove both carburetors, disconnect fuel line at fuel pump. To remove only one carburetor, disconnect fuel line at D, **Figure 29** (top carburetor) or E, **Figure 29** (both carburetors).
4. Remove 2 bolts holding each carburetor to engine (F, **Figure 29**). Remove carburetor(s) from engine.
5. If both carburetors were removed, disconnect choke linkage (A, **Figure 30**) and remove fuel lines from carburetor inlets (B, **Figure 30**).
6. Installation is the reverse of removal. Use new flange gaskets.

These engines are designed to provide 4-stroke-like smoothness at idle and low speeds while practically eliminating smoke and reducing hydrocarbon emissions. If the engine is used considerably at idle and trolling speeds, there is also a significant savings in fuel.

Here's how the system works in brief. At idle speeds, the flow of fuel to the No. 3 and No. 4 cylinders is reduced to a point where the air/fuel mixture is too lean to burn yet enough is provided to adequately lubricate the cylinders and provide corrosion protection. This small amount of fuel is recirculated for burning in the cylinders that are firing. Relocation of the off-idle progression holes or discharge ports in the No. 3 and No. 4 carburetor bores prevent the

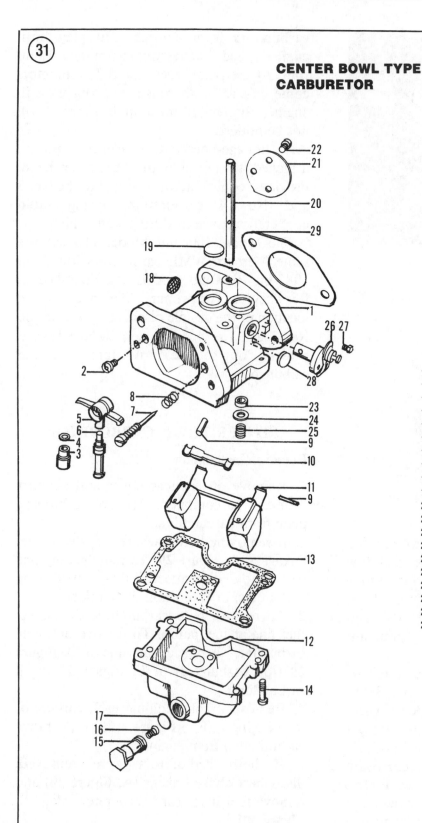

③

**CENTER BOWL TYPE
CARBURETOR**

1. Carburetor body
2. Fuel bowl vent jet
3. Inlet needle/seat assembly
4. Inlet needle seat gasket
5. Venturi
6. Nozzle
7. Idle mixture screw
8. Idle mixture screw spring
9. Hinge pin
10. Float lever
11. Float
12. Fuel bowl
13. Fuel bowl gasket
14. Screw with lockwasher
15. Main jet plug
16. Main jet
17. Main jet plug gasket
18. Fuel inlet screen
19. 9/16 in. welch plug
20. Throttle shaft
21. Throttle shutter plate
22. Screw with lockwasher
23. Rubber seal
24. Flat washer
25. Throttle return spring
26. Enrichment valve assembly
27. Screw with lockwasher
28. 7/16 in. welch plug
29. Flange gasket

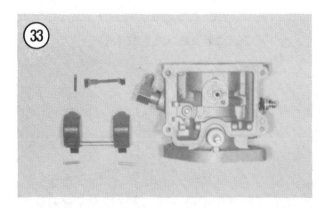

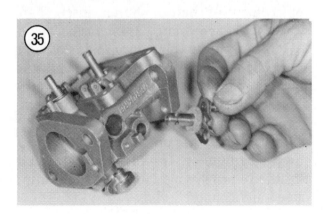

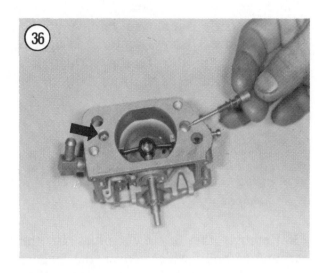

Disassembly

Refer to **Figure 31** for this procedure.

1. Remove main jet plug and gasket (C, **Figure 30**) from carburetor fuel bowl.

2. Remove screws and lockwashers holding fuel bowl to carburetor body. Separate fuel bowl from carburetor (**Figure 32**).

3. Remove and discard fuel bowl gasket.

4. Push float hinge pins toward outer side of carburetor with a small punch. Remove hinge pins and float assembly. Remove hinge pin and float lever. See **Figure 33**.

5. Remove inlet needle from seat (A, **Figure 34**). Remove seat with a wide-blade screwdriver. Remove metal gasket under seat.

6. Remove fuel inlet fitting (B, **Figure 34**). Check inlet screen in carburetor body. If loose, torn or damaged, remove screen.

7. Remove screw and lockwasher holding enrichment valve assembly to carburetor body. Remove valve assembly (**Figure 35**).

8. Turn idle mixture screw clockwise counting number of turns until it lightly seats. Back screw out and remove from carburetor with spring (**Figure 36**).

9. Remove fuel bowl vent jet (arrow, **Figure 36**) from carburetor with a jet remover or screwdriver blade.

10. Remove nozzle from carburetor body (C, **Figure 34**).

6

11. After nozzle is removed, remove plastic venturi. **Figure 37** shows venturi and nozzle.

12. Remove throttle return spring, flat washer and rubber seal from bottom of throttle shaft.

> *CAUTION*
> *When removing welch plugs in Step 13, do not let drill bit pass into carburetor casting or the discharge ports may be damaged.*

13. Remove the 3 welch plugs in the carburetor body which cover the bypass holes. Drill a 1/8 in. hole in each plug and pry plug from body with a pointed punch. This completes disassembly required for cleaning.

14. If throttle shutter or shaft requires replacement, remove the 2 screws holding the shutter to the shaft. Remove shutter from shaft, then pull shaft from carburetor.

Cleaning and Inspection

1. Clean the carburetor body, fuel bowl and metal parts in a carburetor cleaning solution to remove gum, dirt and varnish. Carburetor cleaners are available through local automotive supply stores. Follow the instructions provided with the cleaner.

2. After removal from the cleaning solution, rinse the carburetor components thoroughly with water, then with clean solvent.

3. Blow components dry with compressed air. Be sure to blow through all orifices, nozzles and passages.

> *CAUTION*
> *Do not use wire or drill bits to clean carburetor passages, as this can ruin the carburetor.*

4. Check the float for saturation or deterioration. Replace as required.

5. Check inlet needle and seat for wear or damage. Replace as required.

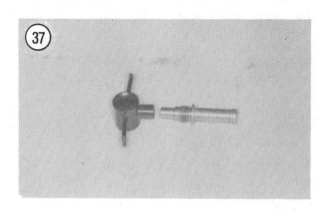

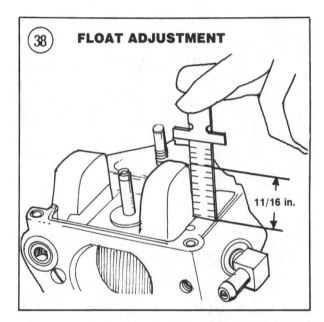

FLOAT ADJUSTMENT

11/16 in.

Reassembly

Refer to **Figure 31** for this procedure.

1. Install new welch plugs (convex side up) in casting counterbore. Flatten to a tight fit.

2. If throttle shaft was removed for replacement of shaft or shutter, insert shaft with lever attached into carburetor body.

3. Position shutter plate into shaft slot with stamped numbers on plate facing outward toward rear of carburetor. Install new shutter-to-shaft screws and lockwashers. Tighten screws securely.

4. Install rubber seal on throttle shaft with lip toward carburetor. Install flat washer and throttle return spring. Hold throttle shutter closed and connect spring.

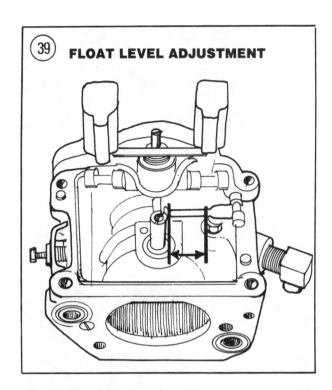

FLOAT LEVEL ADJUSTMENT

5. Install idle mixture screw and spring. Lightly seat, then back screw out the number of turns noted during disassembly.

6. Install fuel bowl vent jet in carburetor body and tighten securely.

7. Install enrichment valve assembly and tighten screw securely.

8. Install venturi in carburetor bore slots. Install nozzle through top of carburetor and into venturi. Tighten nozzle securely.

NOTE
Ridged side of rubber insert must face out when installed in needle seat assembly in Step 9.

9. Install rubber insert in inlet needle seat. Install seat with new metal gasket. Tighten seat securely with wide-blade screwdriver and install needle in seat.

10. Install float lever in carburetor body with hinge pin.

11. Install float assembly in carburetor body with hinge pins.

12. Check float adjustment as described in this chapter.

13. Install fuel bowl to carburetor body with a new gasket. Tighten screws securely.

14. Install main jet plug in fuel bowl with main jet and a new gasket. Tighten plug securely.

15. Install new filter screen in carburetor body inlet, if necessary.

16. Install fuel inlet fitting to carburetor body and tighten securely.

Float Adjustment

1. Check float level as shown in **Figure 38**. It should be 11/16 in. from bottom of float to carburetor body. Adjust if necessary by bending float tab lever within the dimensions shown in **Figure 39**.

Carburetor Adjustment

1. Jet size recommendations (**Table 3**) are made only as a guide. When in doubt, try a size smaller to lean mixture or a size larger to richen mixture.

2. A change in spark advance is not recommended for operation at high elevation. Use a propeller with lower pitch at high elevation to allow proper engine rpm.

3. The carburetor uses a fixed main jet. Adjustments are not possible, but poor running at high speed may indicate the need for replacement.

Idle Mixture Adjustment

The idle mixture and idle speed are both factory-set but can be adjusted to suit local conditions. Do not adjust mixture leaner than necessary for a smooth idle or hard starting and engine damage may result. It is always better to set the idle mixture too rich than too lean.

1. With carburetor installed on engine and engine in the water or a test tank, set the idle mixture screw one turn open from a lightly seated condition.

6

2. Start the engine and let it warm to normal operating temperature in forward gear.

3. Slowly turn idle mixture screw counterclockwise until the affected cylinder begins to load up or fires unevenly from the over-rich mixture.

4. Now slowly turn idle mixture screw clockwise until the cylinder firing smooths out and the engine gains rpm.

5. Accelerate engine. If engine hesitates, idle mixture is too lean and should be richened until engine acceleration is smooth.

6. Idle engine and adjust idle speed screw so that the engine will idle at the recommended rpm in forward gear. See Chapter Five.

7. Run in forward gear at 4,000-5,000 rpm to clear engine of any excess fuel. Recheck idle speed.

DUAL-FLOAT CENTER BOWL CARBURETOR

Removal/Installation

1. Remove the idle stabilizer module (**Figure 40**) at the top of the silencer/sound box cover, if so equipped.

2. Disconnect the rubber hose from the rear of the silencer box, if so equipped.

3. On 1979 and later V6 models, remove electrical harness and fuel bayonet from silencer box bracket.

4. Remove screw holding choke knob and remove knob, if so equipped.

5. Remove the silencer/sound box cover. Remove silencer box from carburetors, if so equipped.

6. On 1976-1978 V6 models, remove electrical harness and fuel line from choke plate bracket. Remove choke plate.

7. Disconnect throttle linkage (A, **Figure 41**) by removing synchronization screws (B, **Figure 41**).

8. Disconnect fuel lines from enrichener valve (C, **Figure 41**), if so equipped.

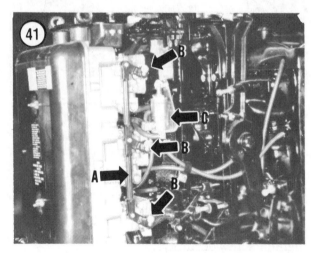

9. Disconnect fuel lines at the carburetors.

10. Remove 4 nuts holding each carburetor to be removed. Lift carburetor(s) from engine.

11. Clean all gasket residue from engine mounting surfaces and carburetor(s). Work carefully to avoid damaging gasket surfaces.

12. Installation is the reverse of removal. Connect enrichener valve lines (if so equipped) as described in this chapter. If equipped with choke solenoid, insert solenoid plunger into solenoid and attach choke plate to carburetors. Tighten all fasteners securely. Synchronize carburetors. See Chapter Five.

Disassembly

Refer to **Figure 42** for this procedure.

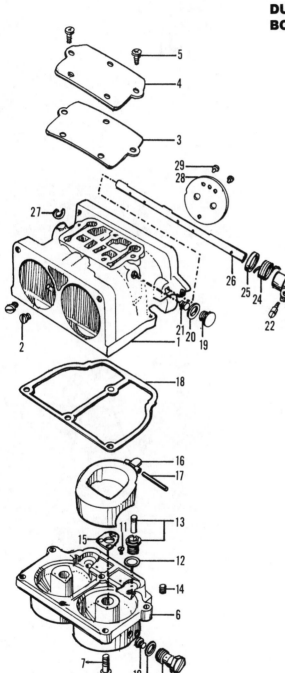

DUAL FLOAT CENTER BOWL CARBURETOR

1. Carburetor body
2. Fuel bowl vent jet
3. Cover plate gasket
4. Cover plate
5. Cover plate screw
6. Fuel bowl
7. Fuel bowl screw
8. High speed jet plug
9. High speed jet gasket
10. High speed jet
11. Float pin screw
12. Inlet needle seat gasket
13. Inlet needle/seat assembly
14. Fuel inlet screen
15. Nozzle gasket
16. Float
17. Float pin
18. Fuel bowl gasket
19. Idle jet plug
20. Idle jet gasket
21. Idle jet
22. Throttle lever screw
23. Throttle lever
24. Throttle return spring
25. Plastic spacer
26. Throttle shaft
27. Retainer ring
28. Throttle shutter
29. Throttle shutter screw and lockwasher

6

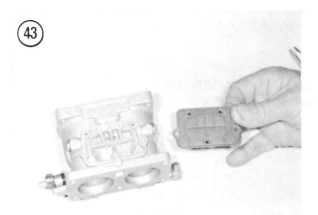

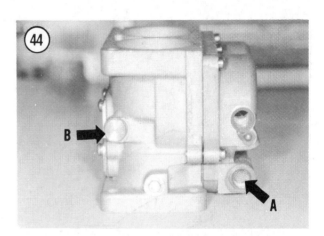

1. Remove cover plate and gasket from carburetor body (**Figure 43**).

2. Remove fuel line fitting from carburetor body. Check for loose torn or plugged fuel screen (A, **Figure 44**) in carburetor body. Remove screen if defective.

3. Remove idle jet plug and gasket from each side of carburetor (B, **Figure 44**). Remove idle jet with a jet remover or appropriate size screwdriver.

4. Remove 6 screws holding carburetor float bowl to body. Separate body and float bowl (**Figure 45**).

5. Remove and discard the float bowl and nozzle gaskets (A and B, **Figure 46**).

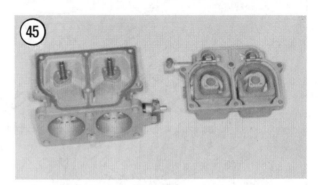

NOTE
Early carburetors use the circular float shown on the left in **Figure 47**; *late model carburetors use the floats shown on the right.*

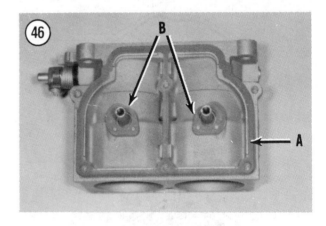

6. Remove the screw holding the float pin to the fuel bowl. Remove the float, float pin and inlet needle from the fuel bowl. See **Figure 48**. Remove the other float in the same manner.

7. Remove the main jet plug/gasket assembly from each side of the fuel bowl (**Figure 49** shows one side removed).

8. Remove the jet from the plug. See **Figure 50**. Discard the plug gasket.

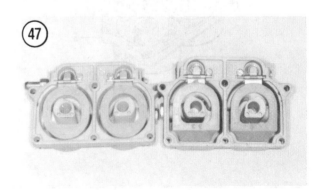

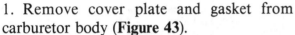

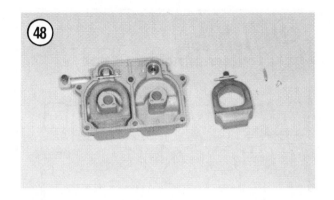

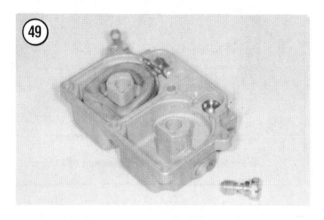

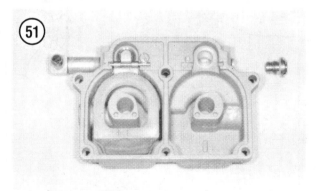

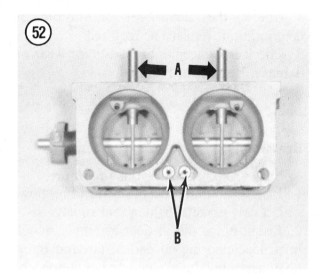

9. Remove the inlet needle seats and gaskets with a wide-blade screwdriver. If the gaskets do not come out with the seats, remove them from the fuel bowl. Discard the gaskets. **Figure 51** shows one needle seat/float assembly removed.

10. This completes disassembly of the carburetor for cleaning. It is not necessary to remove the main discharge/idle tubes (A, **Figure 52**) or fuel bowl vent jets (B, **Figure 52**) for cleaning.

Cleaning and Inspection

1. Clean the carburetor body, fuel body and metal parts in a carburetor cleaning solution to remove gum, dirt and varnish. Carburetor cleaners are available through local automotive supply stores. Follow the instructions provided with the cleaner.

2. After removal from the cleaning solution, rinse the carburetor components thoroughly in water, then in clean solvent.

3. Blow carburetor parts dry with compressed air. Be sure to blow through all orifices, nozzles and passages.

CAUTION
Do not use wire or drill bits to clean carburetor passages, as this can ruin the carburetor.

6

4. Check the floats for saturation or deterioration. Replace as required.

5. Check inlet needles and seats for wear or damage. Replace as required.

Reassembly

Refer to **Figure 42** for this procedure.

1. Install each inlet needle seat in fuel bowl with a new gasket. Tighten seat snugly.

2. Install hinge pin in float assembly. Hook inlet needle spring on end of tab and insert float assembly into fuel bowl, guiding the inlet needle into the seat. Install hinge pin screw snugly. Repeat step to install second float assembly.

3. Check float adjustment as described in this chapter.

4. Install new fuel bowl and nozzle gaskets on carburetor body. Install fuel bowl to carburetor body. Tighten fuel bowl screws securely in sequence shown in **Figure 53**. Retighten screw No. 1 after completing sequence.

5. Install main jets to main jet plugs. Install new plug gaskets. Install main jet plugs to fuel bowl and tighten securely.

6. Install idle jets in carburetor body. Tighten jets securely, then install idle jet plugs with new gaskets. Tighten plugs securely.

7. Install cover plate with new gasket. Tighten screws securely.

8. If fuel screen was removed from carburetor body, install a new screen, then install the fuel inlet fitting and tighten securely.

Float Adjustment

Invert fuel bowl and check float drop as shown in **Figure 54**. It should be 1/16 in. from top of float to carburetor body. Adjust if necessary by bending float tab.

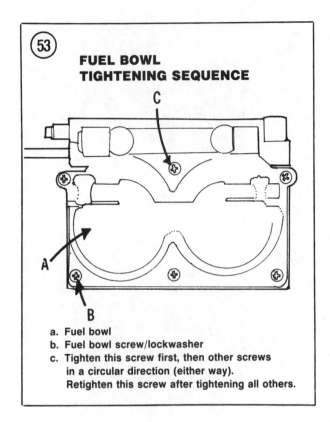

(53)

FUEL BOWL TIGHTENING SEQUENCE

a. Fuel bowl
b. Fuel bowl screw/lockwasher
c. Tighten this screw first, then other screws in a circular direction (either way).
   Retighten this screw after tightening all others.

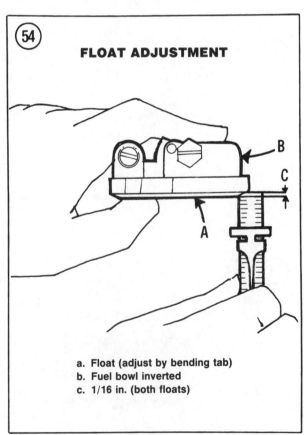

(54)

FLOAT ADJUSTMENT

a. Float (adjust by bending tab)
b. Fuel bowl inverted
c. 1/16 in. (both floats)

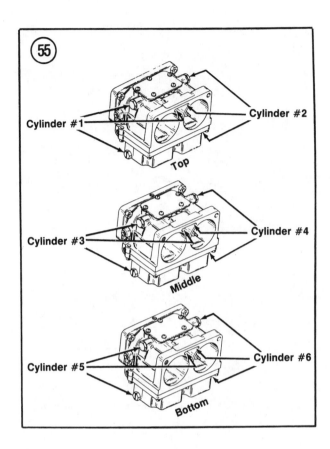

Figure 55

Cylinder #1
Cylinder #2
Top

Cylinder #3
Cylinder #4
Middle

Cylinder #5
Cylinder #6
Bottom

Carburetor Adjustment

1. Carburetors are not equipped with adjustment screws. All adjustments are made by changing the size of the fixed jets.

2. Jet locations depend upon reed block mounting. See **Figure 55** and **Figure 56** to determine correct jet locations for each cylinder according to model and serial number.

3. The fuel-air mixture demands are not the same for all cylinders on V6 outboards, therefore the jets are not identical in all carburetors. Jet size recommendations (**Table 5**) are made only as a guide. When in doubt, try a size smaller to lean mixture or a size larger to richen mixture.

4. A change in spark advance is not recommended for operation at high elevation. Use a propeller with lower pitch at high elevation to allow proper engine rpm.

6

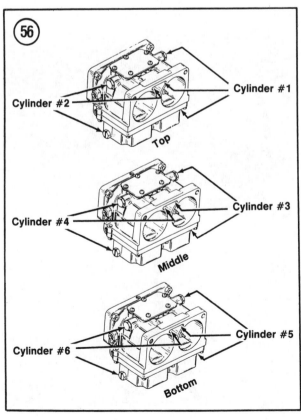

Figure 56

Cylinder #2
Cylinder #1
Top

Cylinder #4
Cylinder #3
Middle

Cylinder #6
Cylinder #5
Bottom

SIDEBOWL AND BACK DRAG CARBURETOR

Removal/Installation

1. Disconnect manual choke cable from carburetor choke linkage.

2. Remove front cowl support bracket from engine.

3. Disconnect fuel line(s) at the carburetor(s).

4. Remove the nut holding the choke linkage return spring to the top carburetor.

5. Remove nuts holding choke linkage to top and center carburetors. Remove linkage.

6. Remove 2 nuts holding each carburetor to the engine. Remove the carburetors with coupling assemblies (**Figure 57**).

7. Clean all gasket residue from carburetor mounting surfaces on engine and carburetors.

8. Installation is the reverse of removal. Use new gaskets *without* gasket sealer. Tighten carburetor mounting nuts to 150 in.-lb.

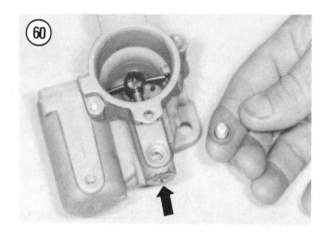

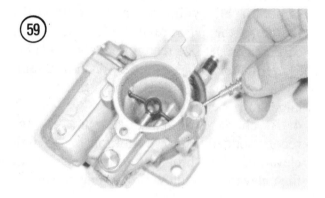

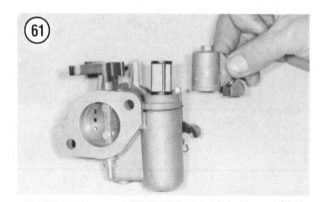

Disassembly

Refer to **Figure 58** for this procedure.

1. Lightly seat idle adjustment screw, counting number of turns required. Back screw out and remove with spring (**Figure 59**).

2. Remove plug and idle restriction tube from top of carburetor. Do not lose the small restriction tube gasket.

3. Remove brass hex plug and gasket from carburetor (**Figure 60**). Remove main jet from inside plug hole with an appropriate size screwdriver.

4. Remove plug (arrow, **Figure 60**) and unscrew main fuel nozzle with a wide-blade screwdriver.

5. Loosen fuel inlet cover screw. Remove cover and strainer (**Figure 61**). Discard strainer gaskets.

6. Remove float bowl cover. Invert housing and remove float from carburetor (**Figure 62**).

7. Remove lower float lever pin and lever (A, **Figure 63**). Remove upper lever pin and lever (B, **Figure 63**).

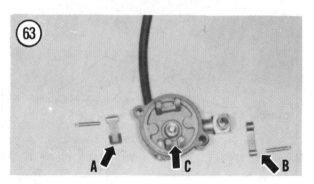

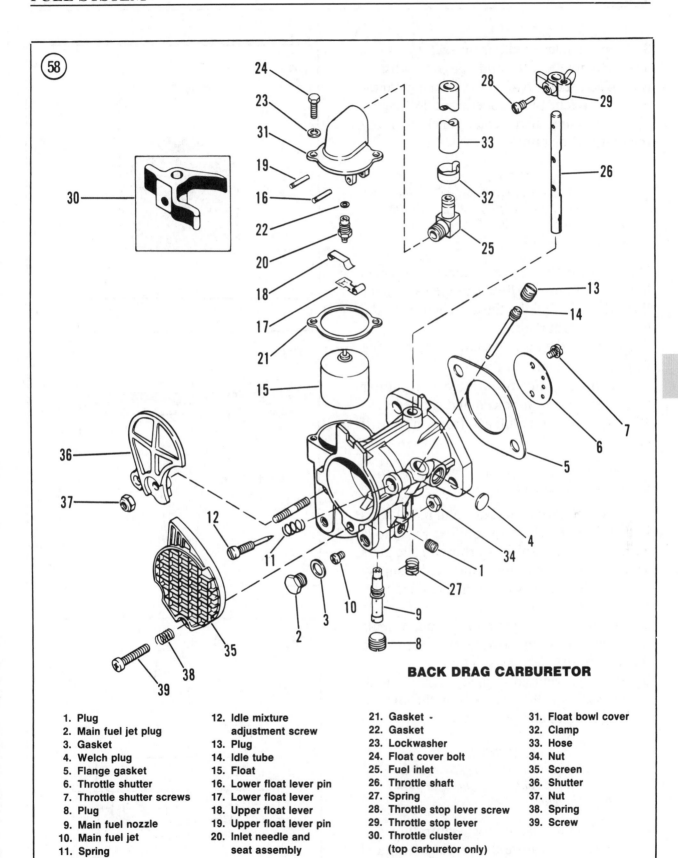

BACK DRAG CARBURETOR

1. Plug
2. Main fuel jet plug
3. Gasket
4. Welch plug
5. Flange gasket
6. Throttle shutter
7. Throttle shutter screws
8. Plug
9. Main fuel nozzle
10. Main fuel jet
11. Spring
12. Idle mixture adjustment screw
13. Plug
14. Idle tube
15. Float
16. Lower float lever pin
17. Lower float lever
18. Upper float lever
19. Upper float lever pin
20. Inlet needle and seat assembly
21. Gasket -
22. Gasket
23. Lockwasher
24. Float cover bolt
25. Fuel inlet
26. Throttle shaft
27. Spring
28. Throttle stop lever screw
29. Throttle stop lever
30. Throttle cluster (top carburetor only)
31. Float bowl cover
32. Clamp
33. Hose
34. Nut
35. Screen
36. Shutter
37. Nut
38. Spring
39. Screw

6

8. Remove inlet needle from seat (C, **Figure 63**). Remove seat and gasket with a wide-blade screwdriver. Discard the gasket.

9. Tap welch plug covering idle bypass chamber with a sharp center punch, then pry plug off and discard.

> *NOTE*
> *Steps 10-13 are not required for routine cleaning. Perform these steps only if throttle or choke shutter require replacement.*

10. Remove the 2 screws and lockwashers holding the throttle shutter to the carburetor throttle shaft. Pull the throttle shaft from the top of the carburetor.

11. Remove the throttle shutter return spring from the carburetor body.

12. Remove 2 nuts from the choke shutter and screen. Remove screen and shutter.

13. Remove choke linkage from shutter, if applicable.

Cleaning and Inspection

1. Clean the carburetor body and metal parts in a carburetor cleaning solution to remove gum, dirt and varnish. Carburetor cleaners are available through local automotive supply stores. Follow the instructions provided with the cleaner.

2. Rinse the carburetor components thoroughly in clean solvent after removing them from the cleaning solution.

3. Blow carburetor body dry with compressed air. Be sure to blow through all orifices, nozzles and passages.

> *CAUTION*
> *Do not use wire or drill bits to clean carburetor passages, as this can ruin the carburetor.*

4. Check the float for saturation or deterioration. Measure float spring. It should be approximately 3/32 in. from top of float

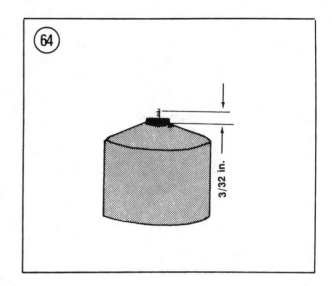

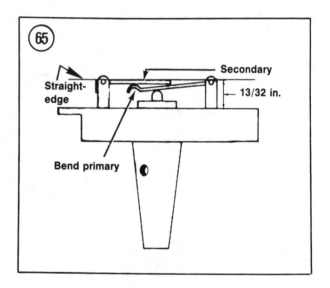

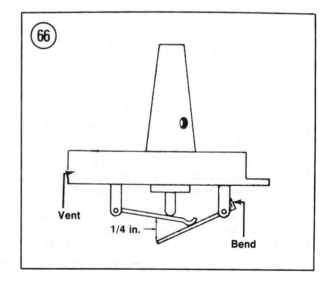

(not from the insert) to the end of the exposed spring (**Figure 64**). Replace as required.

5. Check fuel strainer for chips or cracks. Replace as required.

Reassembly

Refer to **Figure 58** for this procedure.

1. Install new inlet seat gasket in float bowl cover. Install seat and tighten to 60 in.-lb. Install inlet needle in seat.

2. Install upper float lever and pin. Install lower float lever and pin.

3. Adjust float as described in this chapter.

4. Install a new float bowl cover gasket. Install cover to float bowl with vent hole facing carburetor mounting flange and tighten screws securely.

5. Install fuel strainer gasket, strainer, another gasket and strainer bowl cover. Tighten bowl cover cap screw securely.

NOTE
Steps 6-9 apply only if the throttle or choke shutters were removed for replacement.

6. Reassemble choke shutter and screen on the carburetor throat studs. Secure with 2 nuts.

7. Reassemble choke linkage to shutter, if removed.

NOTE
Each carburetor repair kit has 2 throttle shutter return springs. The higher tension spring is for single carburetor installations (or the upper carburetor on multi-carb installations). The lighter tension spring is for carburetors which are operated by the carburetor above them (3-, 4- and 6-cylinder motors).

8. Install throttle shaft in top of carburetor. Insert throttle shutter in carburetor throat and attach to throttle shaft with 2 screws and lockwashers.

9. Install throttle shaft return spring in recess at lower end of carburetor. Spring must engage throttle shaft slot. Wind spring one turn to provide enough tension to return throttle to closed position.

10. Align plastic boost venturi (if removed) in carburetor throat. Install main nozzle and thread into place with an appropriate size screwdriver. Thread plug into place and tighten securely.

11. Install main jet with new gasket (if used) and tighten snugly in place. Install brass plug with new gasket.

12. Install idle restriction tube with gasket and tighten snugly.

13. Install a new welch plug over the idle bypass chamber and seal with Liquid Neoprene.

14. Install idle adjustment screw with spring. Light seat and back out the number of turns counted during disassembly.

Float Adjustment

1. With float bowl cover held as shown in **Figure 65**, measure the distance from the face of the shoulder to the secondary lever; it should be 13/32 in. $\pm 1/64$ in. Bend primary lever as necessary to bring adjustment into specifications.

2. Turn cover upright and make sure inlet needle moves freely on primary lever.

3. With float bowl cover held upright, the distance between the levers should be 1/4 in. (**Figure 66**). If adjustment is required, bend tab on secondary lever.

Carburetor Adjustment

1. Jet size recommendations (**Table 6**) are made only as a guide. When in doubt, try a size smaller to lean mixture or a size larger to richen mixture.

6

2. A change in spark advance is not recommended for operation at high elevation. Use a propeller with lower pitch at high elevation to allow proper engine rpm.

3. The carburetor uses a fixed main jet. Adjustments are not possible, but poor running at high speed may indicate the need for replacement.

Idle Mixture Adjustment

The idle speed is factory-set but can be adjusted to suit local conditions. Do not adjust mixture leaner than necessary for a smooth idle or hard starting and engine damage may result. It is always better to set the idle mixture too rich than too lean.

1. With carburetors installed on engine and engine in the water or a test tank, set all idle needles one turn open from a lightly seated condition.

2. Start the engine and let it warm to normal operating temperature in forward gear.

3. Slowly turn idle mixture needle counterclockwise until the affected cylinders begin to load up or fire unevenly from the over-rich mixture.

4. Now slowly turn idle mixture needle clockwise until the cylinder firing smooths out and the engine gains rpm. Continue turning needle clockwise until the mixture is too lean. The engine will slow down and misfire.

5. Turn needle counterclockwise 1/2-3/4 turn from lean-out position.

6. Accelerate engine. If engine hesitates, idle mixture is too lean and should be richened until engine acceleration is smooth.

7. Idle engine and adjust idle stop screw so that the engine will idle at the recommended rpm in forward gear. See Chapter Five.

8. Run in forward gear at 4,000-5,000 rpm to clear engine of any excess fuel. Recheck idle speed.

WME CARBURETOR

WME type carburetors (**Figure 67**) are used on 1987-on Merc 70, 80 and 90 models and 1988-on Merc 100 and 115 models. One carburetor is used per cylinder. On Merc 100 and 115 models, the No. 3 and No. 4 cylinder carburetors differ from the No. 1 and No. 2 cylinder carburetors. An idle discharge restriction is used in the No. 3 and No. 4 cylinder carburetors to allow only enough fuel mixture to be discharged through the idle discharge port to lubricate the internal engine components. When the engine is at idle (approximately 700 rpm), the idle fuel mixture is too lean to fire. The off-idle discharge ports on the No. 3 and No. 4 cylinder carburetors are located farther toward the front of the carburetor than the No. 1 and No. 2 cylinder carburetors to delay off-idle fuel flow until the engine reaches approximately 1800 rpm. Thus the fuel mixture provided to the No. 3 and No. 4 cylinders, when the engine is operated below 1800 rpm, is only used to lubricate the internal engine components as the fuel mixture is too lean to fire.

On Merc 100 and 115 models, the four carburetors are numbered. Make sure carburetor number 11-1 is positioned for the No. 1 (top) cylinder, carburetor number 11-2 is positioned for the No. 2 cylinder, carburetor number 11-3 is positioned for the No. 3 cylinder and carburetor number 11-4 is positioned for the No. 4 cylinder.

Removal/Installation
1987-on Merc 70, 80 and 90

1. Remove engine cowling.
2. Disconnect the battery and spark plug leads.
3. Remove front cowl bracket.
4. Remove 8 screws retaining air box cover then withdraw cover.

WME CARBURETOR

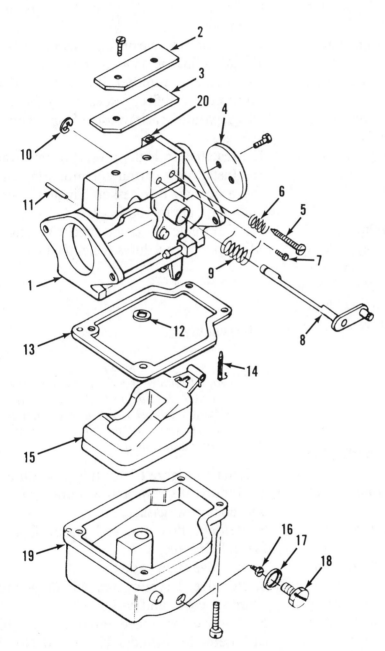

1. Body
2. Mixing chamber cover
3. Mixing chamber gasket
4. Throttle plate
5. Low speed mixture screw
6. Spring
7. Back drag jet (3-cyl. models)
8. Throttle shaft
9. Spring
10. "E" clip
11. Float pin
12. Stem gasket
13. Float bowl gasket
14. Fuel inlet needle
15. Float
16. Main jet
17. Washer
18. Plug
19. Float bowl
20. Air correction screw
   (Factory preset)

6

5. Remove lower oil tank support bolt (10 mm) and the two upper oil tank neck brace bolts (8 mm)

6. Remove 6 nuts retaining air box then withdraw air box.

7. Disconnect oil lines from oil tank and plug then withdraw tank.

8. Disconnect throttle linkage from center carburetor ball socket.

9. Disconnect fuel supply hose and fuel primer hose from top carburetor.

10. Withdraw carburetor assemblies and actuating linkage as a complete unit.

11. Scribe a number on casting of each carburetor to reflect respective cylinder.

12. Separate carburetors from actuating linkage.

13. Installation is the reverse of removal.

14. Install new carburetor mounting gaskets and a new air box gasket. Tighten 6 air box retaining nuts to 100 in.-lb.

15. Complete timing, synchronizing and adjustment procedures (Chapter Five).

1988-on Merc 100 and 115

1. Remove engine cowling.

2. Disconnect the battery and spark plug leads.

3. Disconnect fuel supply hose from engine bayonet fitting.

4. Remove the 2 upper oil tank neck brace bolts.

5. Remove the 2 bottom cowl support bracket bolts.

6. Remove vapor return hose from tee fitting located between fuel supply bayonet fitting and fuel pump.

7. Remove bayonet fitting retaining bolt at bottom cowl support bracket, then withdraw support bracket.

8. Remove 10 screws retaining air box cover, then withdraw cover.

9. Remove oil tank bottom front support bracket bolt.

10. Remove 8 nuts retaining air box then withdraw air box.

11. Disconnect hoses from carburetor fittings to allow removal of carburetors as an assembly.

12. Withdraw carburetor assemblies and actuating linkage as a complete unit.

13. Scribe a number on casting of each carburetor to reflect respective cylinder.

14. Separate carburetors from actuating linkage.

15. Installation is the reverse of removal.

16. Install new carburetor mounting gaskets and a new air box gasket. Tighten 8 air box retaining nuts to 100 in.-lb.

17. Complete timing, synchronizing and adjustment procedures (Chapter Five).

Disassembly

NOTE
Do not remove the air correction screw (located on the port aft side of the mixing chamber cover) as the screw is factory set and should not require further adjustment.

Refer to **Figure 67** for this procedure.

1. Remove 4 screws and withdraw float bowl and float bowl gasket.

2. Remove float pin and plastic float with fuel inlet needle.

3. Remove stem gasket.

4. Remove 2 screws and withdraw mixing chamber cover and gasket.

5. Remove low speed mixture screw (Only carburetor for cylinder No. 1 and No. 2 on 1988-on Merc 100 and 115).

6. 1987-on Merc 70, 80 and 90—Remove back drag (bowl vent) jet.

7. Remove fuel bowl plug and washer, then remove main jet.

Cleaning and Inspection

1. Clean the carburetor body, float bowl and metal parts in a carburetor cleaning solution to remove gum, dirt and varnish. Carburetor cleaners are available through local automotive supply stores. Follow the instructions provided with the cleaner.

2. After removal from the cleaning solution, rinse the carburetor components thoroughly in water, then in clean solvent.

3. Blow carburetor parts dry with compressed air. Be sure to blow through all orifices, nozzles and passages.

CAUTION
Do not use wire or drill bits to clean carburetor passages, as it can ruin the carburetor.

4. Check the plastic float for saturation or deterioration. Replace as required.

5. Check inlet needle for wear or damage. Replace as required.

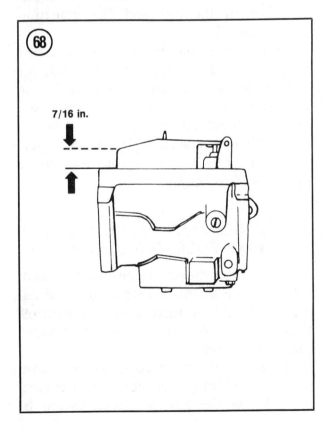

Reassembly

Refer to **Figure 67** for this procedure.

1. Install main jet and fuel bowl plug with a new gasket.

2. 1987-on Merc 70, 80 and 90—Install back drag (bowl vent) jet.

3. Install low speed mixture screw (Only carburetor for cylinders No. 1 and No. 2 on 1988-on Merc 100 and 115).

4. Install mixing chamber cover with a new gasket and securely tighten 2 retaining screws.

5. Install a new stem gasket.

6. Hook clip on fuel inlet needle over float tab and install needle in seat.

7. Install float pin.

8. Install float bowl with a new gasket and securely tighten 4 retaining screws.

Float Adjustment

Invert carburetor body without float bowl gasket and check float height as shown in **Figure 68**. Front bottom of float should be 7/16 in. from float bowl mating surface on carburetor body. Adjust if necessary by bending float tab.

Carburetor Adjustment

Initial adjustment of low speed mixture screws is 1-1/4 turns out from a lightly seated position. This setting will allow engine to start and run. During final adjustment procedure, do not adjust mixture leaner than necessary for a smooth idle as hard starting, a flat spot during acceleration and engine damage could result. It is always better to set the idle mixture too rich than too lean.

1. With carburetors installed on engine and lower unit submerged in water or a test tank, set all low speed mixture screws at 1-1/4 turns out from a lightly seated position.

2. Start the engine and let it warm up to normal operating temperature in FORWARD gear.

6

3. Slowly turn each low speed mixture screw in (clockwise) until affected cylinder begins to slow down and misfire.

4. Turn low speed mixture screw out (counterclockwise) 1/4 turn or more from lean-out position.

5. Accelerate engine. If engine hesitates, low speed mixture screws are adjusted too lean and should be richened until engine acceleration is smooth. On 1988-on Merc 100 and 115 models, during quick accelerations make sure accelerator pump assembly operates properly.

6. Idle engine and adjust idle stop screw so that the engine will idle at the recommended rpm in FORWARD gear. See Chapter Five.

7. Run engine in forward gear at wide open throttle to clear engine of any excess fuel. Recheck idle speed.

ELECTRONIC FUEL INJECTION (EFI)

The 1987-1988 Laser XRi is a V200 model equipped with sequential multi-point electronic fuel injection. The Laser XRi delivers 220 hp at the propeller and has a full throttle rpm range of 5,600-6,000 rpm. For 1989, this model is redesignated as the 200 XRi and delivers 200 hp with a full throttle rpm range of 5,400-5,900 rpm.

A fuel rail containing 6 injectors is installed on the injection manifold instead of carburetors and reed blocks. Each cylinder receives a fuel charge at the precise moment when air is being inducted. Fuel is delivered relative to the mass of air inducted into the engine.

An electronic control unit (ECU) installed on the rear of the power head receives input from various power head sensors which tell the ECU engine speed, throttle angle, altitude and barometric pressure and air/engine temperature. Based on this data, the ECU controls the fuel injection and spark timing.

A piezoelectric sensor mounted in the cylinder head monitors engine vibrations. When an engine knock condition is sensed, the ECU first retards spark timing, then enriches the mixture while continuing to retard the spark until the knock condition is eliminated.

Other features include:

a. A two-pump system containing a high-pressure electric fuel pump controlled by the ECU and a pulse-type pump to draw fuel from the tank and send it to the electric pump.

b. A sensor in the water-separating fuel filter which monitors fuel content for excessive moisture. When water is detected in the fuel, a warning horn sounds.

c. A pressure regulator to maintain a constant pressure differential between fuel in the rail and the induction manifold.

No attempt should be made by the owner to adjust the EFI system operation. Diagnosis and troubleshooting requires the use of an expensive Quicksilver fuel injection tester part No. 91-11001A2. If the system does not seem to be operating correctly, take the engine to a Mercury dealer for diagnosis and service by a trained technician.

ENRICHENER VALVE AND CHOKE SOLENOID SYSTEMS

Early multi-cylinder engines are equipped with a choke solenoid. Late-model engines use an enrichener valve system. **Figure 69** shows the V6 and inline 6-cylinder enrichener circuit.

The electrically operated enrichener valve provides additional fuel for a cold engine start. When the key or choke button is

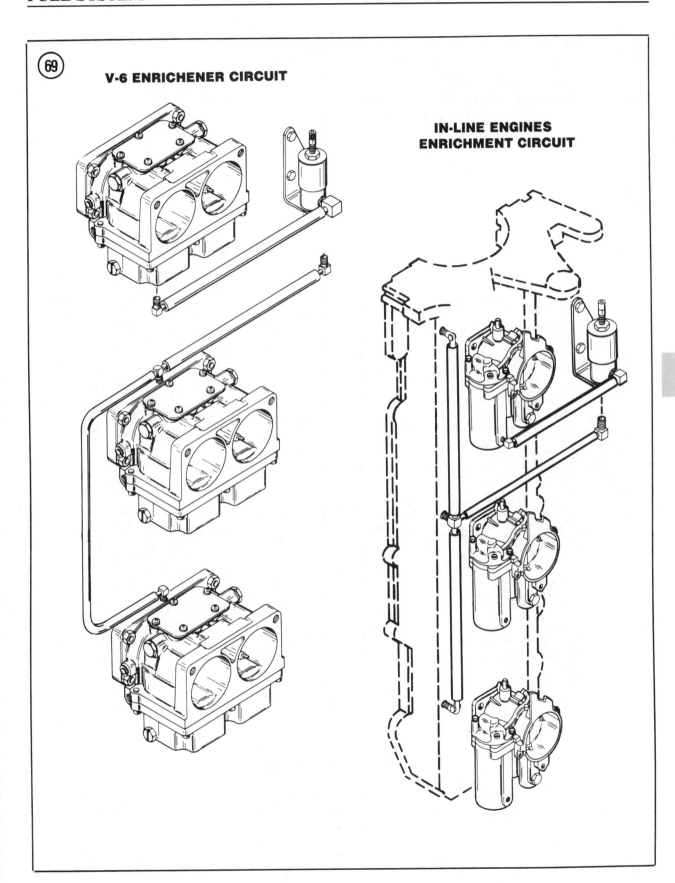

V-6 ENRICHENER CIRCUIT

**IN-LINE ENGINES
ENRICHMENT CIRCUIT**

6

depressed and held, the valve sends extra fuel from the fuel bowl of the top carburetor to the middle and bottom carburetors. Hose routing is shown in **Figure 70** (starboard mounted valve) and **Figure 71** (port mounted valve).

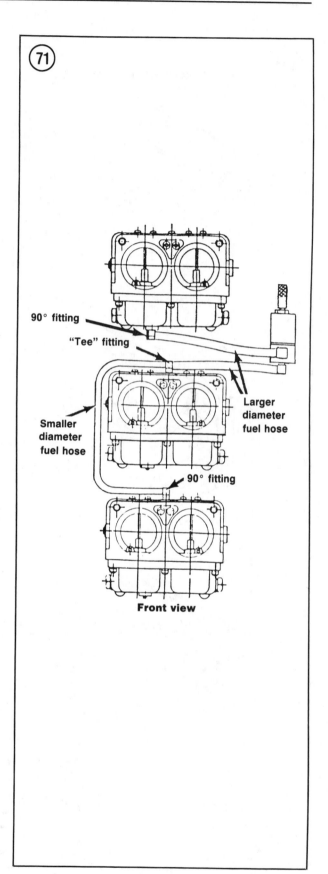

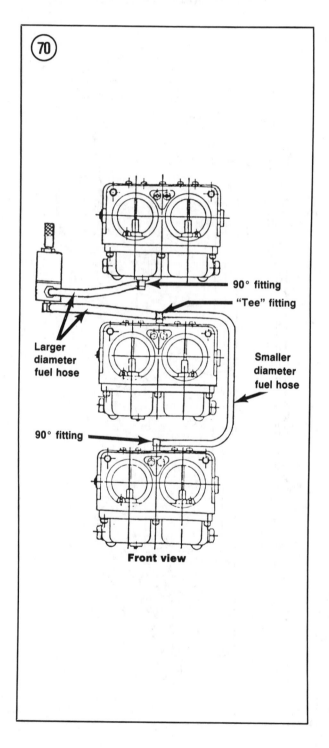

Enrichener Valve Test

1. Depress key or choke button and listen for the valve to click. If valve clicks, squeeze primer bulb until it is firm, then remove line at bottom of valve. Hold a suitable container under the valve fitting. Depress and hold key or choke button and check fuel flow from fitting:

  a. If fuel flows, valve is good.
  b. If fuel does not flow, disconnect top carburetor line at valve.
  c. If fuel flows from this line, replace valve; if not, check all lines and fittings for restrictions.

2. If valve does not click in Step 1, connect a voltmeter between the valve yellow/black wire at the terminal block and a good engine ground. Depress key or choke button and note voltmeter reading:

  a. If no voltage is shown, look for an open in the yellow/black wire.
  b. If voltage is shown, clean and tighten engine harness yellow/black and enrichener valve black wire connection at terminal block. Make sure that other enrichener valve black wire at terminal block is properly grounded.
  c. After repairing connections as required, depress key or choke button again. Replace valve if it still does not click.

Enrichener Valve Replacement

1. Disconnect enrichener valve leads at the terminal block.
2. Disconnect all lines at the valve.
3. Remove the bolts holding the valve mounting bracket to the engine (**Figure 72**). Remove bracket and valve assembly.
4. Separate valve from bracket. Wipe bracket screw threads with a drop of Loctite A (part No. C-92-32609-1) and install new valve to bracket with screw.
5. Remove fittings from old valve. Wipe fitting threads with Quicksilver Gasket Sealer (part No. C-92-72592-1) and reinstall fittings in new valve. Tighten and locate fittings in same position as old valve to accept fuel lines.
6. Install fuel lines to new valve. See **Figure 70** or **Figure 71**.
7. Wipe threads of bracket bolts with a drop of Loctite A and install bracket to engine.
8. Reconnect valve leads to terminal block.

Choke Solenoid Replacement

1. Remove top and rear cowl frame supports.
2. Disconnect manual choke linkage at choke rod.
3. Remove lead at choke solenoid terminal.
4. Disconnect plunger linkage from choke rod.
5. Remove screws and wire harness clamp holding solenoid to front support frame.
6. Installation is the reverse of removal. If installing a new solenoid, apply Quicksilver Multipurpose Lubricant (part No. C-92-63250) to the plunger hole and choke linkage grommets.

ANTI-SIPHON DEVICES

In accordance with industry safety standards, late-model boats equipped with a built-in fuel tank will have some form of anti-siphon device installed between the fuel tank outlet and the outboard fuel inlet. This device is designed to shut the fuel supply off

6

in case the boat capsizes or is involved in an accident. Quite often, the malfunction of such devices leads the owner to replace a fuel pump in the belief that it is defective.

Anti-siphon devices can malfunction in one of the following ways:

a. Anti-siphon valve: orifice in valve is too small or clogs easily; valve sticks in closed or partially closed position; valve fluctuates between open and closed position; thread sealer, metal filings or dirt/debris clogs orifice or lodges in the relief spring.

b. Solenoid-operated fuel shut-off valve: solenoid fails with valve in closed position; solenoid malfunctions, leaving valve in partially closed position.

c. Manually-operated fuel shut-off valve: valve is left in completely closed position; valve is not fully opened.

The easiest way to determine if an anti-siphon valve is defective is to bypass it by operating the engine with a remote fuel supply. If a fuel system problem is suspected, check the fuel filter first. See Chapter Four. If the filter is not clogged or dirty, bypass the anti-siphon device. If the engine runs properly with the anti-siphon device bypassed, contact the boat manufacturer for replacement of the anti-siphon device.

FUEL TANK

Figure 73 shows the components of the remote fuel tank. To remove any dirt or water that may have entered the tank during refilling, clean the inside of the tank once each season by flushing with clean lead-free gasoline or kerosene.

To check fuel tank filter for possible restrictions, remove cover and withdraw outlet tube from tank. The filter on the end of the outlet tube can be cleaned by rinsing in clean lead-free gasoline or kerosene.

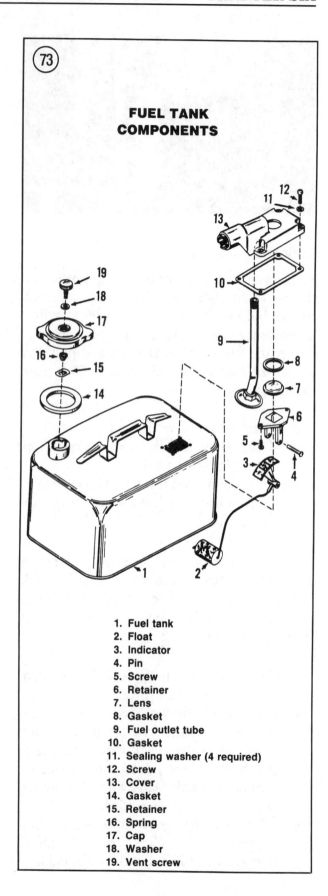

(73)

FUEL TANK COMPONENTS

1. Fuel tank
2. Float
3. Indicator
4. Pin
5. Screw
6. Retainer
7. Lens
8. Gasket
9. Fuel outlet tube
10. Gasket
11. Sealing washer (4 required)
12. Screw
13. Cover
14. Gasket
15. Retainer
16. Spring
17. Cap
18. Washer
19. Vent screw

FUEL LINE AND PRIMER BULB

Figure 74 shows the fuel line and primer bulb components. The line and bulb should be checked periodically for cracks, breaks, restrictions and chafing. Make sure all fuel line connections are tight and securely clamped.

A loss of power and/or top end rpm can be caused by insufficient travel of the check valves in the primer bulb, resulting in a pressure drop that reduces the flow of fuel. When replacing check valves or fuel lines, order the following components:

a. Inlet check valve part No. 21-13883A1 (red).

b. Outlet check valve part No. 21-13883A2 (gray).

c. Fuel line assembly part No. 89396A19 or part No. 89396A20.

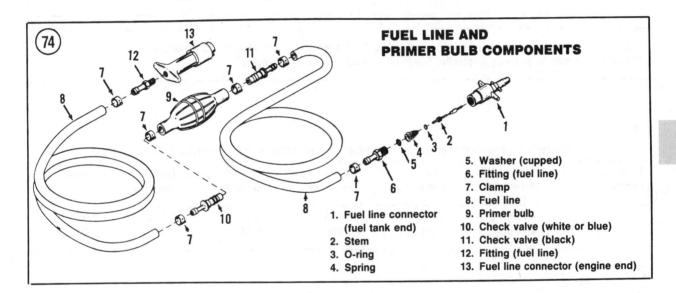

FUEL LINE AND PRIMER BULB COMPONENTS

1. Fuel line connector (fuel tank end)
2. Stem
3. O-ring
4. Spring
5. Washer (cupped)
6. Fitting (fuel line)
7. Clamp
8. Fuel line
9. Primer bulb
10. Check valve (white or blue)
11. Check valve (black)
12. Fitting (fuel line)
13. Fuel line connector (engine end)

Tables are on the following pages.

Table 1 CARBURETOR JET SIZE FOR ELEVATIONS (45-50 [4-cyl.] HP MODELS)

Engine model	Serial No. range	Jet type	Sea level to 2,500'	2,500-5,000'	5,000-7,500'	7,500' and up
500	4280269 and below	Main	0.063	0.061	0.059	0.057
500	4280270 to 4357639	Main	0.065	0.063	0.061	0.059
		Vent	0.086	0.084	0.082	0.080
500 and 50	4357640 to 4576236*	Main	0.055	0.053	0.051	0.049
		Vent	0.096	0.094	0.092	0.090
45 and 50	4576237 and up**	Main	0.057	0.055	0.053	0.051
		Vent	0.098	0.096	0.094	0.092

* Canada, 7068998 to 708857; Australia, 8030090 to 8042649; Europe 9107214 to 9136249.
**Canada, 7088598 and up; Australia, 8042650 and up; Europe, 9136250.

Table 2 CARBURETOR JET SIZE FOR ELEVATIONS (50 [3-cyl.] HP MODELS)

Engine model	Serial No. range	Jet type	Sea level to 2,500'	2,500-5,000'	5000-and up	7,500'
50	A912478 and up	Main	0.058	0.054	0.052	0.050
		Vent	0.096	0.094	0.092	0.090

Table 3 CARBURETOR JET SIZE FOR ELEVATIONS (60-70 [Prior to 1984] HP MODELS)

Engine model	Serial No. range	Jet type	Sea level to 2,500'	2,500-5,000'	5,000-7,500'	7,500' and up
60	4571652 to 4576236	Main	0.086	0.084	0.082	0.080
		Vent	0.066	0.064	0.062	0.060
60	4576237 and up*	Main				
		Top	0.0785	0.076	0.074	0.072
		Bottom	0.072	0.070	0.068	0.066
		Vent	0.096	0.094	0.092	0.090
650	4382056 and below	Main	0.074	0.072	0.070	0.068
		Vent	0.086	0.084	0.082	0.080
650XS	4304235	Main	0.086	0.084	0.082	0.080
650 (long shaft)	4382057 and up	Main	0.088	0.086	0.084	0.082
		Vent	0.052	0.050	0.048	0.046
650 (short shaft)	4382057 and up	Main	0.080	0.078	0.076	0.074
		Vent	0.072	0.070	0.068	0.066
700 and 70	4571652 to 6428681**	Main	0.086	0.084	0.082	0.080
		Vent	0.066	0.064	0.062	0.060

*Canada, 7088598 and up; Australia, 8042650 and up; Europe, 9136250 and up.
**Canada, 7067823 to 7208333; Australia, 8042350 to 8074512; Europe, 9135825 and up.

6

Table 4 CARBURETOR JET SIZE FOR ELEVATIONS (1987-ON MERC 70-100 HP)

Engine model	Serial No. range	Jet type	Sea level to 2,500'	2,500-5,000'	5,000-7,500'	7,500' and up
70	B110054 and up	Main	0.072	0.070	0.068	0.066
		Vent	0.094	0.092	0.090	0.088
80	A966142 and up	Main	0.064	0.062	0.060	0.058
		Vent	0.094	0.092	0.090	0.088
90	B110054 and up	Main	0.072	0.070	0.068	0.066
		Vent	0.094	0.092	0.090	0.088
100	B209468 and up	Main	0.054	0.052	0.050	0.048
		Vent	N.A.	N.A.	N.A.	N.A.

Table 5 STANDARD JET CHART

NOTE: Jets listed are for engine operation from 0-2500 feet (0-762m) of elevation.

CARBURETOR NO. (STAMPED ON TOP OF CARBURETOR MOUNTING FLANGE)		MAIN JET						IDLE JET						VENT JET					
		CYL 1	CYL 2	CYL 3	CYL 4	CYL 5	CYL 6	CYL 1	CYL 2	CYL 3	CYL 4	CYL 5	CYL 6	CYL 1	CYL 2	CYL 3	CYL 4	CYL 5	CYL 6
Top	WH1-1	.074	.074					.048	.048					.090	.090				
Center	WH1-2			.074	.074					.048	.048					.082	.082		
Bottom	WH1-3					.074	.074					.048	.048					.082	.082
Top	WH2-1	.056	.056					.060	.060					.098	.098				
Center	WH2-2			.056	.056					.060	.060					.098	.098		
Bottom	WH2-1					.056	.056					.060	.060					.098	.098
Top	WH3-1	.078	.078					.046	.046					.084	.084				
Center	WH3-2			.078	.078					.046	.046					None	.084		
Bottom	WH3-3					.078	.078					.046	.046					None	.084
Top	WH3-1A	.078	.078					.044	.044					.084	.084				
Center	WH3-2A			.078	.078					.044	.044					None	.084		
Bottom	WH3-3A					.078	.078					.044	.044					None	.084
Top	WH3M11	.082	.082					.044	.044					.084	.084				
Center	WH3M12			.082	.082					.044	.044					None	.084		
Bottom	WH3M13					.082	.082					.044	.044					None	.084
Top	WH4-1	.074	.074					.048	.048					.094	.094				
Center	WH4-2			.074	.074					.048	.048					.094	.094		
Bottom	WH4-3					.078	.074					.048	.048					.094	.094
Top	WH5-1	.078	.078					.048	.048					.094	.094				
Center	WH5-2			.078	.078					.048	.048					.094	.094		
Bottom	WH5-3					.078	.078					.048	.048					.094	.094
Top	WH6-1	.074	.074					.046	.046					.090	.090				
Center	WH6-2			.074	.074					.046	.046					None	.082		
Bottom	WH6-3					.078	.074					.046	.046					None	None
Top	WH7-1	.074	.074					.044	.044					.090	.090				
Center	WH7-2			.074	.074					.044	.044					None	.082		
Bottom	WH7-3					.078	.074					.044	.044					None	None
Top	WH7-1A	.074	.074					.044	.044					.090	.090				
Center	WH7-2A			.074	.074					.044	.044					None	.082		
Bottom	WH7-3A					.078	.074					.044	.044					None	None
Top	WH8-1	.082	.082					.044	.044					.084	.084				
Center	WH8-2			.082	.082					.044	.044					None	.084		
Bottom	WH8-3					.082	.082					.044	.044					None	.084
Top	WH9-1	.048	.048					.060	.060					.098	.098				
Center	WH9-2			.048	.048					.060	.060					.098	.098		
Bottom	WH9-1					.048	.048					.060	.060					.098	.098
Top	WH11-1	.062	.062					.052	.052					.096	.096				
Center	WH11-2			.062	.062					.052	.052					.096	.096		
Bottom	WH11-1					.062	.062					.052	.052					.096	.096
Top	WH11-1	.062	.062					.052	.052					.096	.096				
Center	WH11-2			.062	.062					.052	.052					.096	.096		
Bottom	WH11-3					.068	.068					.052	.052					None	None
Top	WH12-1	.048	.048					.060	.060					.098	.098				
Center	WH12-2			.048	.048					.060	.060					.098	.098		
Bottom	WH12-3					.048	.048					.060	.060					.098	.098
Top	WH13-1	.074	.074					.044	.044					.090	.090				
Center	WH13-2			.074	.074					.044	.044					None	.082		
Bottom	WH13-3					.078	.074					.044	.044					None	None
Top	WH14-1	.062	.062					.052	.052					.096	.096				
Center	WH14-2			.062	.062					.052	.052					.096	.096		
Bottom	WH14-3					.068	.062					.052	.052					None	None
Top	WH15-1	.072	.072					.042	.042					None	None				
Center	WH15-2			.072	.072					.042	.042					None	None		
Bottom	WH15-3					.072	.072					.042	.042					None	None
Top	WH17-1	.074	.074					.044	.044					.090	.090				
Center	WH17-2			.074	.074					.044	.044					None	.082		
Bottom	WH17-3					.078	.074					.044	.044					None	None
Top	WH17-1R	.074	.074					.048	.048					.090	.090				
Center	WH17-2R			.074	.074					.048	.048					None	.082		
Bottom	WH17-3R					.078	.074					.048	.048					None	None
Top	WH18-1	.062	.062					.052	.052					.096	.096				
Center	WH18-2			.062	.062					.052	.052					None	.096		
Bottom	WH18-3					.068	.062					.052	.052					None	None
Top	WH20-1	.072	.074					.046	.046					None	None				
Center	WH20-2			.072	.072					.046	.046					None	None		
Bottom	WH20-3					.072	.072					.046	.046					None	None
Top	WH21-1	.076	.076					.050	.050					.092	.092				
Center	WH21-2			.076	.076					.050	.050					None	.092		
Bottom	WH21-3					.076	.076					.050	.050					None	.092
Top	WH22-1	.074	.076					.046	.046					.096	None				
Center	WH22-2			.074	.074					.046	.046					.096	.096		
Bottom	WH22-3					.076	.074					.046	.046					None	.096
Top	WH23-1	.064	.064					.052	.052					.096	None				
Center	WH23-2			.064	.064					.052	.052					.096	.096		
Bottom	WH23-3					.064	.064					.052	.052					None	.096
Top	WH1-1	.074	.074					.048	.048					.090	.090				
Center	WH4-2			.074	.074					.048	.048					.094	.094		
Bottom	WH4-3					.078	.074					.048	.048					.094	.094

Table 5 STANDARD JET CHART (continued)

NOTE: Jets listed are for engine operation from 0-2500 feet (0-762m) of elevation.

CARBURETOR NO. (STAMPED ON TOP OF CARBURETOR MOUNTING FLANGE)		MAIN JET						IDLE JET						VENT JET					
		CYL 1	CYL 2	CYL 3	CYL 4	CYL 5	CYL 6	CYL 1	CYL 2	CYL 3	CYL 4	CYL 5	CYL 6	CYL 1	CYL 2	CYL 3	CYL 4	CYL 5	CYL 6
Top	WH26-1	.074	.076					048	048					096	None				
Center	WH26-2			.074	.074					048	048					096	096		
Bottom	WH26-3					.076	.074					048	048					None	.096
Top	WH27-1	.064	.064					054	054					None	None				
Center	WH27-2			.064	.064					054	054					None	None		
Bottom	WH27-3					.064	.064					054	054					None	None
Top	WH28-1	.074	.076					056	056					096	None				
Center	WH28-2			.074	.074					056	056					.096	.096		
Bottom	WH28-3					.076	.074					056	056					None	.096
Top	WH29-1	.064	.064					056	056					None	None				
Center	WH29-2			.064	.064					056	056					None	None		
Bottom	WH29-3					.064	.064					056	056					None	None

Table 6 is on the next page.

6

Table 6 CARBURETOR JET SIZES FOR ELEVATION (80-150 HP MODELS)

Engine model	Serial No. range	Jet type	Sea level 2,500'	2,500-5,000'	5,000-7,500'	7,500' and up
800	All 1978	Main	0.090	0.088	0.086	0.084
		Vent	0.072	0.070	0.068	0.066
850	All 1983	Main	0.080	0.078	0.076	–
850	4366801 and below	Main	0.076	0.074	0.072	0.070
		Vent	0.092	0.090	0.088	0.086
850	4366802-4423111	Main	0.088	0.086	0.084	0.082
		Vent	0.080	0.078	0.076	0.074
850 and 85	4423112 and up	Main	0.090	0.088	0.086	0.084
		Vent	0.072	0.070	0.068	0.066
900 and 90	–	Main	0.070	0.068	0.066	0.064
		Vent	0.092	0.090	0.088	0.086
1150 and 115	5050762 and below	Main	0.072	0.070	0.068	0.066
		Vent	0.092	0.090	0.088	0.086
1150 and 115	5050763 and up	Main	0.074	0.072	0.070	0.068
		Vent	0.096	0.096	0.096	0.096
1250SS	–	Main	0.082	0.080	0.0785	–
1350	–	Main	0.078	0.076	0.074	–
1400 and 140	1978-on*	Main	0.080	0.078	0.076	0.074
		Vent	0.092	0.090	0.088	0.086
1500 (long shaft)	4121435** and up	Main	0.080	0.0875	0.076	0.074
1500XS (short shaft)	4121435 and up	Main	0.082	0.080	0.078	0.076
		Vent	0.092	0.090	0.088	0.086
150	–	Main	0.080	0.078	0.076	0.074
		Vent	0.092	0.090	0.088	0.086

* Some models may have 0.082 or 0.084 as standard jet.
** Some models may have 0.080 or 0.082 as standard jet.

Chapter Seven

Ignition and Electrical Systems

This chapter provides service procedures for the battery, starter motor and each of the 4 ignition systems used on Mercury outboard motors during the years covered by this manual. Wiring diagrams are included at the end of the book. **Tables 1-3** are at the end of the chapter.

BATTERY

Since batteries used in marine applications endure far more rigorous treatment than those used in an automotive charging system, they are constructed differently. Marine batteries have a thicker exterior case to cushion the plates inside during tight turns and rough weather. Thicker plates are also used, with each one individually fastened within the case to prevent premature failure. Spill-proof caps on the battery cells prevent electrolyte from spilling into the bilges. Automotive batteries are not designed to be run down and recharged repeatedly. For this

reason, they should *only* be used in an emergency situation when a suitable marine battery is not available.

Mercury Marine recommends that any battery used to crank an outboard motor have a cold cranking amperage of 350 amps and a reserve capacity of at least 100 minutes.

CAUTION
*Sealed or maintenance-free batteries are **not** recommended for use with the unregulated charging systems on Mercury outboards. Excessive charging during continued high-speed operation will cause the electrolyte to boil, resulting in its loss. Since water cannot be added to such batteries, the battery will be ruined.*

Separate batteries may be used to provide power for any accessories such as lighting, fish finders, depth finder, etc. To determine the required capacity of such batteries, calculate the average discharge rate of the accessories and refer to **Table 1**. Batteries may be wired in parallel to double the ampere hour capacity while maintaining a 12-volt system. See **Figure 1**. For accessories which require 24 volts, batteries may be wired in series (**Figure 2**) but only accessories specifically requiring 24 volts should be connected into the system. Whether wired in parallel or in series, batteries should be individually charged.

Care and Inspection

1. Remove the battery tray or container cover. See **Figure 3** for a typical installation.
2. Disconnect the negative battery cable. Disconnect the positive battery cable. See **Figure 4**.

> *NOTE*
> *Some batteries have a built-in carry strap (**Figure 5**) for use in Step 3.*

3. Attach a battery carry strap to the terminal posts. Remove the battery from the battery tray or container.
4. Check the entire battery case for cracks.
5. Inspect the battery tray or container for corrosion and clean if necessary with a solution of baking soda and water.

> *NOTE*
> *Keep cleaning solution out of the battery cells in Step 6 or the electrolyte will be seriously weakened.*

6. Clean the top of the battery with a stiff bristle brush using the baking soda and water

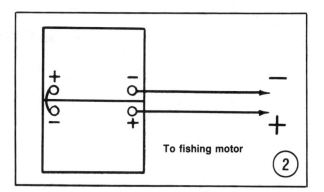

To fishing motor

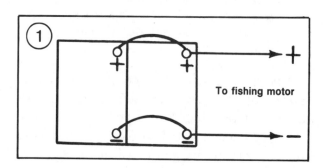

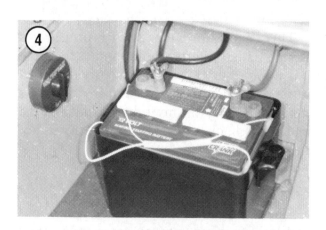

To fishing motor

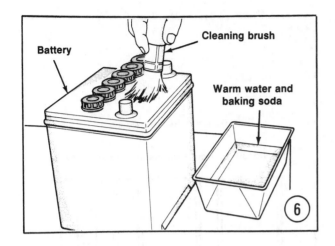

Battery

Cleaning brush

Warm water and baking soda

6

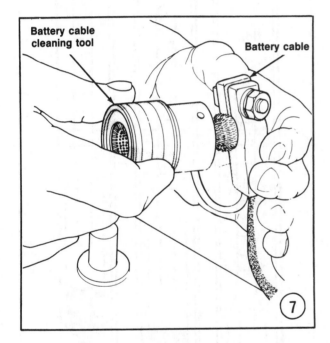

Battery cable cleaning tool

Battery cable

7

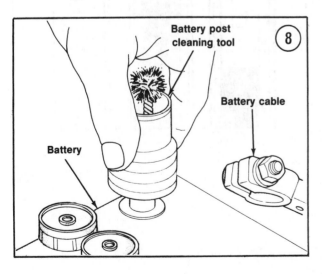

8 **Battery post cleaning tool**

Battery cable

Battery

solution (**Figure 6**). Rinse the battery case with clear water and wipe dry with a clean cloth or paper towel.

7. Position the battery in the battery tray or container.

8. Clean the battery cable clamps with a stiff wire brush or one of the many tools made for this purpose (**Figure 7**). The same tool is used for cleaning the battery posts. See **Figure 8**.

9. Reconnect the positive battery cable, then the negative cable.

> *CAUTION*
> *Be sure the battery cables are connected to their proper terminals. Connecting the battery backwards will reverse the polarity and damage the rectifier(s).*

10. Tighten the battery connections and coat with a petroleum jelly such as Vaseline or a light mineral grease.

> *NOTE*
> *Do not overfill the battery cells in Step 11. The electrolyte expands due to heat from charging and will overflow if the level is more than 3/16 in. above the battery plates.*

11. Remove the filler caps and check the electrolyte level. Add distilled water, if necessary, to bring the level up to 3/16 in. above the plates in the battery case. See **Figure 9**.

7

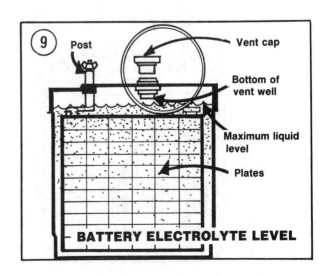

9 **Post**

Vent cap

Bottom of vent well

Maximum liquid level

Plates

BATTERY ELECTROLYTE LEVEL

Testing

Hydrometer testing is the best way to check battery condition. Use a hydrometer with numbered graduations from 1.100-1.300 rather than one with just color-coded bands. To use the hydrometer, squeeze the rubber ball, insert the tip in a cell and release the ball (**Figure 10**).

NOTE
Do not attempt to test a battery with a hydrometer immediately after adding water to the cells. Charge the battery for 15-20 minutes at a rate high enough to cause vigorous gassing and allow the

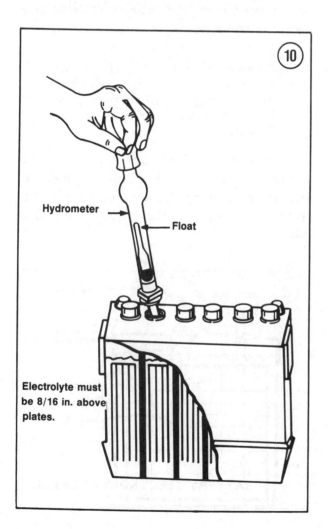

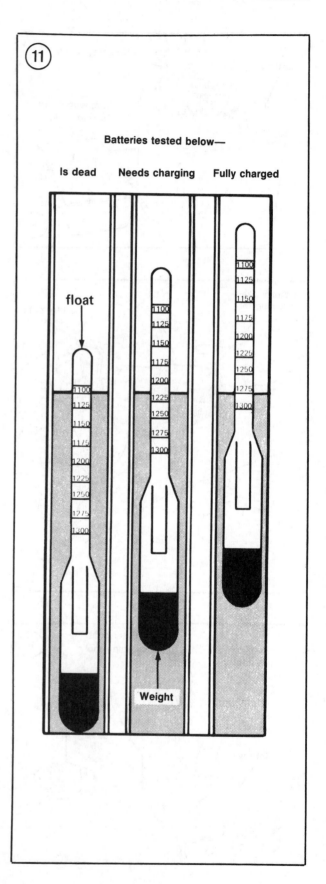

water and electrolyte to mix thoroughly.

Draw enough electrolyte to float the weighted float inside the hydrometer. When using a temperature-compensated hydrometer, release the electrolyte and repeat this process several times to make sure the thermometer has adjusted to the electrolyte temperature before taking the reading.

Hold the hydrometer vertically and note the number in line with the surface of the electrolyte (**Figure 11**). This is the specific gravity for the cell. Return the electrolyte to the cell from which it came.

The specific gravity of the electrolyte in each battery cell is an excellent indicator of that cell's condition. A fully charged cell will read 1.260 or more at 68° F (20° C). A cell that is 75 percent charged will read from 1.220-1.230 while one with a 50 percent charge reads from 1.170-1.180. If the cell tests below 1.120, the battery must be recharged and one that reads 1.100 or below is dead. Charging is also necessary if the specific gravity varies more than 0.050 from cell to cell.

NOTE
If a temperature-compensated hydrometer is not used, add 0.004 to the specific gravity reading for every 10° above 80° F (25° C). For every 10° below 80° F (25° C), subtract 0.004.

Charging

A good state of charge should be maintained in batteries used for starting. Check the battery with a voltmeter as shown in **Figure 12**. Any battery that cannot deliver at least 9.6 volts under a starting load should be recharged. If recharging does not bring it up to strength or if it does not hold the charge, replace the battery.

The battery does not have to be removed from the boat for charging, but it is a recommended safety procedure since a charging battery gives off highly explosive hydrogen gas. In many boats, the area around the battery is not well ventilated and the gas may remain in the area for hours after the charging process has been completed. Sparks or flames occuring near the battery can cause it to explode, spraying battery acid over a wide area.

7

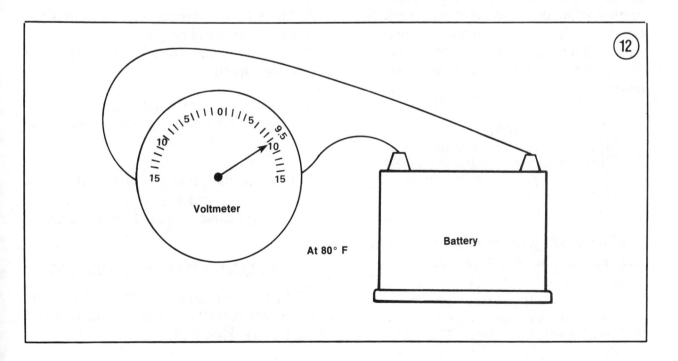

For this reason, it is important that you:

a. Do not smoke around batteries that are charging or have been recently charged.

b. Do not break a live circuit at the battery terminals and cause an electrical arc that can ignite the hydrogen gas.

Disconnect the negative battery cable first, then the positive cable. Make sure the electrolyte is fully topped up.

Connect the charger to the battery—negative to negative, positive to positive. If the charger output is variable, select a 4 amp setting. Set the voltage regulator to 12 volts and plug the charger in. If the battery is severely discharged, allow it to charge for at least 8 hours. Batteries that are not as badly discharged require less charging time. **Table 2** gives approximate charge rates for batteries used primarily for starting. Check the charging progress with the hydrometer.

Jump Starting

If the battery becomes severely discharged, it is possible to start and run an engine by jump starting it from another battery. If the proper procedure is not followed, however, jump starting can be dangerous. Check the electrolyte level before jump starting any battery. If it is not visible or if it appears to be frozen, do not attempt to jump start the battery.

> *WARNING*
> *Use extreme caution when connecting a booster battery to one that is discharged to avoid personal injury or damage to the system.*

1. Connect the jumper cables in the order and sequence shown in **Figure 13**.

> *WARNING*
> *An electrical arc may occur when the final connection is made. This could*

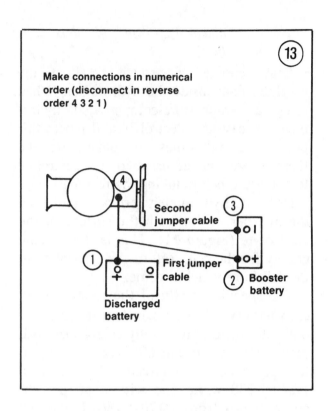

Make connections in numerical order (disconnect in reverse order 4 3 2 1)

Second jumper cable

First jumper cable

Discharged battery

Booster battery

cause an explosion if it occurs near the battery. For this reason, the final connection should be made to a good ground away from the battery and not to the battery itself.

2. Check that all jumper cables are out of the way of moving engine parts.

3. Start the engine. Once it starts, run it at a moderate speed.

> *CAUTION*
> *Racing the engine may cause damage to the electrical system.*

4. Remove the jumper cables in the exact reverse of the order shown in **Figure 13**. Remove the cable at point 4, then 3, 2 and 1.

BATTERY CHARGING SYSTEM

The battery charging system used on Merc outboards consists of a stator, rectifier and the battery (**Figure 14**).

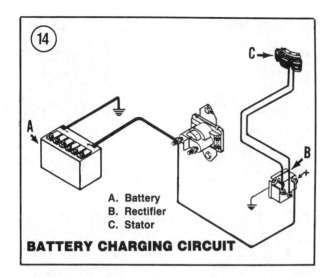

BATTERY CHARGING CIRCUIT

A. Battery
B. Rectifier
C. Stator

Alternating current created by the alternator stator coils is sent to the rectifier where it is converted into direct current to charge the battery.

A malfunction in the battery charging system will result in an undercharged battery. Perform the following visual inspection to determine the cause of the problem. If the visual inspection proves satisfactory, test the stator and rectifier. See Chapter Three.

1. Make sure that the battery cables are connected properly. The red cable must be connected to the positive battery terminal. If polarity is reversed, check for a damaged rectifier.

2. Inspect the battery terminals for loose or corroded connections. Tighten or clean as required.

3. Inspect the physical condition of the battery. Look for bulges or cracks in the case, leaking electrolyte and corrosion build-up.

4. Carefully check the wiring between the stator and battery for signs of chafing, deterioration or other damage.

5. Check the circuit wiring for corroded, loose or disconnected connections. Clean, tighten or connect as required.

6. Determine if the electrical load on the battery from accessories is greater than the battery capacity.

STARTING SYSTEM

The outboard starting system is a mechanical means of cranking the engine. The system consists of the battery, starter solenoid, starter motor, neutral start switch, ignition switch and connecting wiring.

When the ignition switch is turned to START with the shift control lever in NEUTRAL, current from the battery passes through the solenoid coil. The solenoid contacts close, allowing battery current to flow to the starter motor. As the starter motor cranks, its drive assembly is thrust upward to engage the flywheel teeth and turn the engine over.

If the shift control lever is not in NEUTRAL, the neutral start switch opens to prevent current flow through the solenoid coil.

STARTER MOTOR

Marine starter motors are very similar in design and operation to those found on automotive engines. Mercury has used starters manufactured by American Bosch, Delco-Remy and Prestolite. All have an inertia-type drive in which external spiral splines on the armature shaft mate with internal splines on the drive assembly.

The starter motor produces a very high torque but only for a brief period of time, due to heat buildup. Never operate the starter motor continuously for more than 30 seconds. Let the motor cool for at least 2 minutes before operating it again. If the starter motor does not turn over, check the battery and all connecting wiring for loose or corroded connections. If this does not solve the problem, refer to Chapter Three. Except for brush replacement, service to the starter motor in the field is limited to replacement with a new or rebuilt unit.

7

Removal

1. Disconnect the positive battery cable.
2. Remove the cowling.
3. Remove the sound box (**Figure 15**, typical), if so equipped.
4. Remove the carburetor plate (**Figure 16**, typical), if so equipped.
5. Disconnect yellow cable at starter (A, **Figure 17**, typical).
6. Disconnect the black ground cable at the starter (B, **Figure 17**, typical).
7. Remove the 4 bolts holding the upper and lower starter mounting clamps (C, **Figure 17**).
8. Remove the starter. If it will not clear the upper carburetor hose fitting, loosen the carburetor mounting nuts or bolts and tilt the carburetor(s) away from the starter.
9. If the mounting clamps did not break free from the starter, remove with the rubber collars and spacer (if so equipped). See **Figure 18**.
10. Installation is the reverse of removal. Tighten mounting bolts to specifications (**Table 3**).

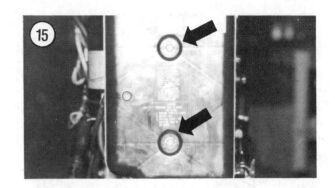

Brush Replacement
(Bosch)

Always replace brushes in complete sets. A brush retainer tool should be fabricated from 18-gauge sheet metal to the dimensions shown in **Figure 19**. This tool is necessary to position the brushes properly and prevent damaging them when reassembling the starter end cap to the housing.

1. Remove the starter as described in this chapter.
2. Remove the 2 through bolts and commutator end cap from the starter. Do not lose brush springs from end cap.
3. Inspect the brushes in the end cap. Replace all brushes if any are oil-soaked or worn to 1/4 in. or less.

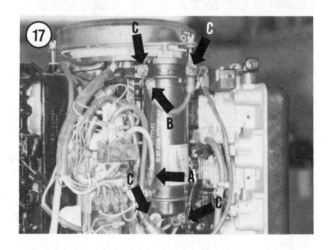

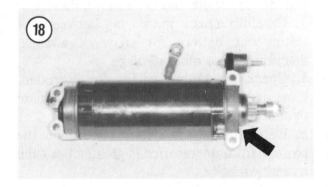

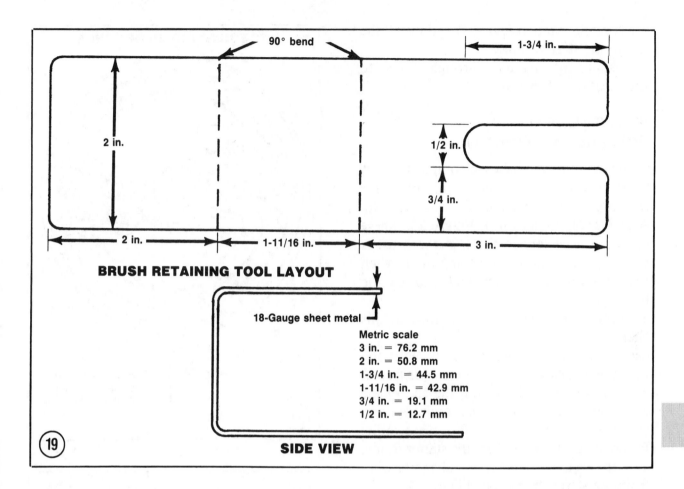

BRUSH RETAINING TOOL LAYOUT

18-Gauge sheet metal

Metric scale
3 in. = 76.2 mm
2 in. = 50.8 mm
1-3/4 in. = 44.5 mm
1-11/16 in. = 42.9 mm
3/4 in. = 19.1 mm
1/2 in. = 12.7 mm

SIDE VIEW

7

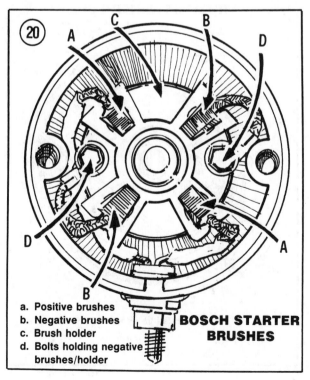

a. Positive brushes
b. Negative brushes
c. Brush holder
d. Bolts holding negative brushes/holder

BOSCH STARTER BRUSHES

4. Remove brush holder from end cap. See **Figure 20**.
Unbolt and remove negative brushes from brush holder.

5. Remove hex nut and washers from positive terminal. Remove positive terminal and positive brushes from the end cap as an assembly.

6. Install new positive brushes and terminal assembly in the commutator end cap. The longest brush lead should be at the left side of the positive terminal. See **Figure 21**.

7. Install the negative brushes to the brush holder. Tighten cap screws securely.

8. Fit springs and brushes into the holder as shown in **Figure 20**. Hold in place with the

brush retainer tool (**Figure 22**) and install the cap to the starter frame.

9. Install and tighten through bolts to specifications (**Table 3**).

Brush Replacement
(Delco-Remy and Prestolite)

Always replace brushes in complete sets. A brush retainer tool should be fabricated for each brush from a coil retaining clip (part No. A-398-2321) as shown in **Figure 23**. These tools are necessary to position the brushes properly and prevent damaging them when reassembling the starter end cap to the housing.

1. Remove the starter as described in this chapter.

2. Remove the 2 through bolts. Pull the commutator end cap from the starter frame.

3. Remove the washers from the end of the armature shaft, noting the quantity and sequence of installation for reassembly. Remove the armature from the starter frame.

4. Remove the positive terminal and brushes from the starter frame. See **Figure 24**.

5. Cut the negative brush leads at the point where they are attached to the field coils.

6. File or grind off solder from ends of field coil leads where old brushes were connected.

7. Use rosin soldering flux and solder the leads of new negative brushes to the field coils, making sure that they are in the right position to reach the brush holders. See **Figure 24**.

> *NOTE*
> *The leads should be soldered to the back sides of the coils so that excessive solder will not rub the armature. Do not overheat the leads, as the solder will run onto the lead and it will no longer be flexible.*

8. Install new positive brushes and positive terminal assembly (**Figure 24**).

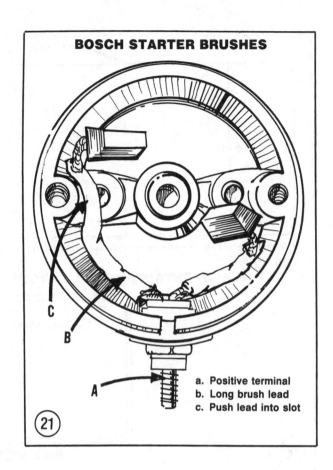

BOSCH STARTER BRUSHES

a. Positive terminal
b. Long brush lead
c. Push lead into slot

(21)

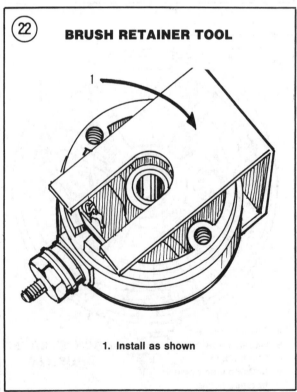

(22) **BRUSH RETAINER TOOL**

1. Install as shown

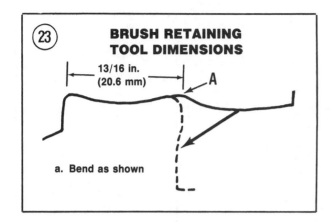

(23) BRUSH RETAINING TOOL DIMENSIONS

13/16 in.
(20.6 mm)

A

a. Bend as shown

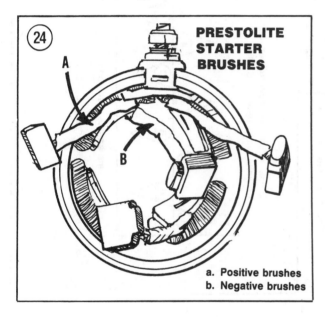

(24) PRESTOLITE STARTER BRUSHES

A

B

a. Positive brushes
b. Negative brushes

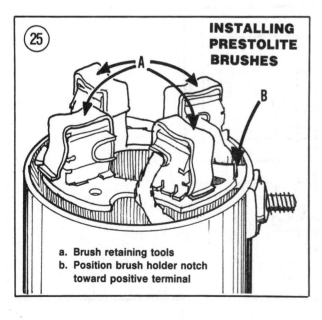

(25) INSTALLING PRESTOLITE BRUSHES

A

B

a. Brush retaining tools
b. Position brush holder notch toward positive terminal

9. Install the brush plate with the notch facing the positive terminal. Route brush leads over plate as shown in **Figure 25**.

10. Install one brush spring and brush in its holder. Secure in place with a brush retaining tool. Repeat this step for each remaining brush. See **Figure 25**.

11. Install armature in starter frame, aligning tab on drive end plate with starter frame slot.

12. Remove brush retaining tools from the brushes.

13. Reinstall washers on armature shaft in the same order as removed.

14. Install end cap with raised lines facing positive terminal.

15. Install through bolts and tighten to specifications (**Table 3**).

IGNITION SYSTEM

Four different ignition systems have been used on Mercury outboards covered by this manual. Refer to Chapter Three for troubleshooting and testing procedures.

LIGHTNING ENERGIZER IGNITION (MODEL 500 THROUGH 1975)

The alternator driver or charging part of the distributor contains a 4-pole permanent magnet rotor, stationary poles and high- and low-speed voltage generating coils. The rotor is driven at crankshaft speed by the timing belt. As the rotor poles pass the stationary and generating coils, 4 AC voltage cycles are created per engine revolution.

One side of the AC cycle charges a capacitor. The other side of the cycle discharges the capacitor into the ignition coil. The high voltage induced in the coil secondary winding is sent to the spark plugs by the ignition rotor, distributor cap and spark plug wires. Since each engine revolution produces 4 AC voltage cycles, this charge/discharge sequence occurs 4 times per engine revolution.

7

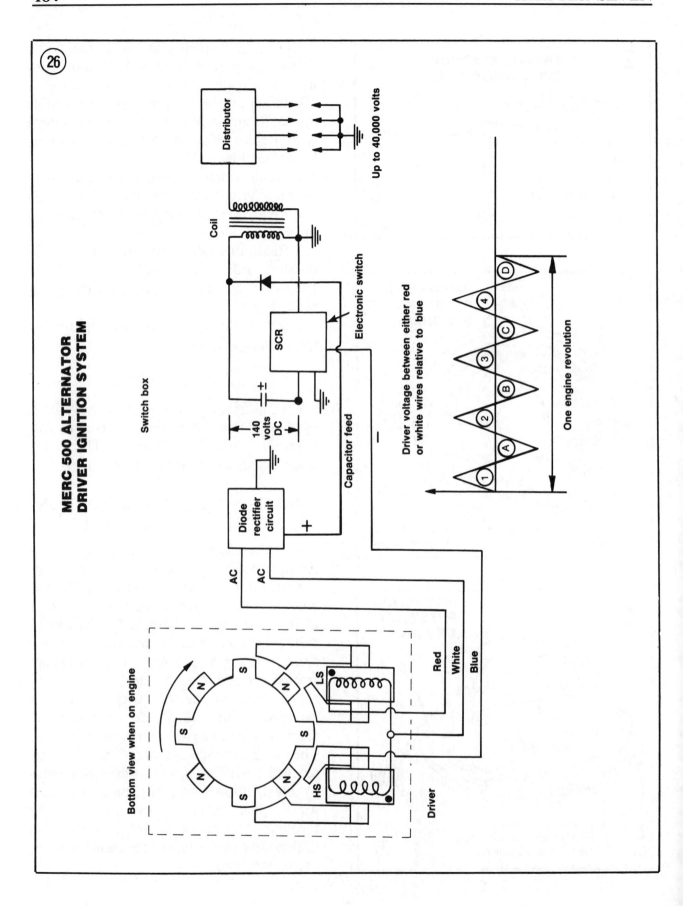

MERC 500 ALTERNATOR DRIVER IGNITION SYSTEM

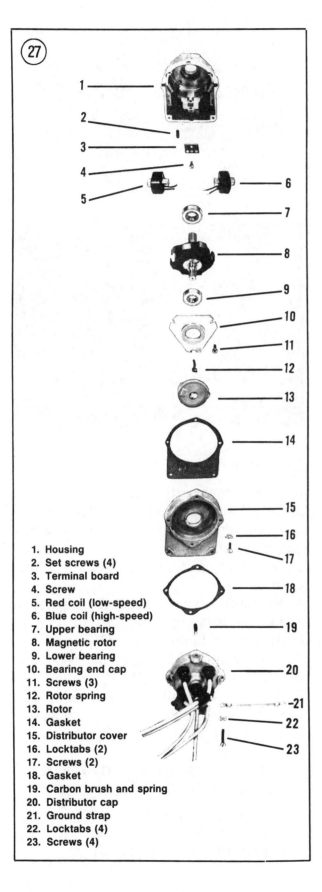

1. Housing
2. Set screws (4)
3. Terminal board
4. Screw
5. Red coil (low-speed)
6. Blue coil (high-speed)
7. Upper bearing
8. Magnetic rotor
9. Lower bearing
10. Bearing end cap
11. Screws (3)
12. Rotor spring
13. Rotor
14. Gasket
15. Distributor cover
16. Locktabs (2)
17. Screws (2)
18. Gasket
19. Carbon brush and spring
20. Distributor cap
21. Ground strap
22. Locktabs (4)
23. Screws (4)

Figure 26 is a schematic of the Lightning Energizer system.

The spark is advanced or retarded by changing the position of the charging and stationary coils relative to the permanent magnet rotor poles.

Removal

1. Disconnect the positive battery terminal.
2. Remove the cowling.
3. Disconnect the red, white and blue wires at the switchbox.
4. Remove the 4 bolts holding the ignition driver to the distributor adaptor.
5. Slide the ignition driver assembly downward and out of the adaptor/drive shaft.
6. Tilt the driver assembly enough to disconnect the ground strap. Disconnect any vent hoses from the ignition driver.
7. Remove the distributor cap retaining screws. Separate the driver assembly from the cap and remove from the engine.

Disassembly

Refer to **Figure 27** for this procedure.
1. Remove the ignition rotor.
2. Remove the distributor cover screws and cover.
3. Remove magnetic rotor bearing end cap screws.
4. Tap magnetic rotor from housing with a soft mallet.
5. If charging coil replacement is necessary, remove screw at terminal board and unsolder coil leads.
6. Break charging coil setscrews loose by heating to approximately 200° F (93° C). Remove setscrews and lift charging coil from housing.
7. If magnetic rotor shaft bearings require replacement, press them off rotor shaft.

7

Cleaning and Inspection

1. Check ignition driver housing for rust or corrosion. If present, remove with No. 320 grit carborundum cloth.

2. Check magnetic rotor and stationary poles. If rusted or corroded, clean up with No. 320 grit carborundum cloth or No. 00 sandpaper *only*.

3. Wash rotor and housing in clean solvent to remove grit.

> *NOTE*
> *Do not clean bearings in Step 4 by washing in solvent. This will destroy the bearing lubrication and result in premature failure.*

4. Check magnetic rotor shaft bearings. If any defects are found, replace bearings. If bearings are satisfactory, wipe with a clean dry cloth.

5. Inspect ignition rotor and distributor cap for cracks or corrosion. Look for signs of burning or arcing. Replace if any defects are found.

Assembly

Refer to **Figure 27** for this procedure.

1. Press bearings on magnetic rotor shaft, if removed.

2. If one or both charging coils were removed, position new coil in housing. Wipe coil setscrew threads with Loctite. Attach coil to stationary poles with setscrews.

3. Solder coil leads to terminal board. Green coil lead goes to the white distributor wire; red coil lead to the red distributor wire; and blue coil lead to the blue distributor wire.

4. Cover solder connections with Liquid Neoprene. Install terminal board with screw.

5. Position magnetic rotor in housing. Install end cap and tighten screws snugly.

6. Install distributor cover with new gasket.

7. Make sure the ignition rotor spring is properly installed in the rotor hole. Put 3 drops of Loctite in rotor hole and install rotor to rotor shaft.

Installation

1. Make sure the carbon brush and spring are properly installed in the distributor cap.

2. Install cap to distributor cover with a new gasket and align index marks.

3. Install distributor cap screws and ground strap.

4. Rotate distributor rotor shaft to align shaft blank with blank in drive shaft, then install ignition driver to distributor adaptor.

5. Install ignition driver to adaptor bolts and tighten securely.

6. Connect red, white and blue distributor wires to the respective switchbox terminals.

7. Set ignition timing. See Chapter Five.

THUNDERBOLT CD IGNITION SYSTEM WITH DISTRIBUTOR

This system is used on:

a. 1975 Mercury 650-850.

b. 1975-1976 Mercury 1150-1500.

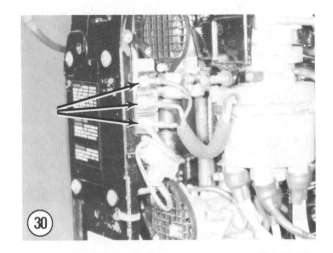

winding. When the SCR turns off, the magnetic field collapses and induces a high voltage in the secondary winding which is sent to the spark plugs through the distributor rotor, cap and spark plug wires.

NOTE
A defective trigger assembly can cause erratic engine operation, such as a misfire or engine shutdown for no apparent reason. Even with the use of an ignition analyzer, this may be a difficult problem to pinpoint. A poor solder connection is generally the cause of the problem. If all solder joints are satisfactory and the problem persists, replace the distributor housing (trigger assembly).

The spark is advanced or retarded by changing the position of the trigger coils relative to the rotor disc windows.

Removal
(4- and 6-cylinder Models)

1. Disconnect the positive battery cable.
2. Remove the wrap-around and top cowl assemblies.
3. Remove the top cowl support frame and rear support bracket by removing 3 nuts from the top cowl frame rubber mounts; 2 bolts and lockwashers at the forward top of the cowl support frame; and 4 bolts and lockwashers at the bottom of the rear support. Disconnect the manual choke or choke solenoid wire. Lift the top cowl support frame and rear support bracket from the power head.
4. Remove distributor cap retaining clamp screw and nut (**Figure 29**). Remove distributor cap and clamp.
5. Disconnect 3 trigger leads at switchbox (**Figure 30**).
6. Remove bolt and cover from distributor pulley (**Figure 31**).

Turning the ignition key switch ON sends battery (DC) voltage to the switchbox where it is inverted and stepped up to a high AC voltage. The high AC voltage is then rectified and stored in the switchbox capacitor. Turning the ignition key switch ON also sends a reduced voltage to the trigger in the distributor housing. The trigger is composed of 2 coils which face each other but are separated by a rotor disc containing one slot or window for each engine cylinder. **Figure 28** shows a 6-cylinder and 4-cylinder rotor disc.

The sender coil produces a magnetic field. When a rotor disc window passes between the 2 coils, the receiver coil produces a trigger signal. The trigger signal activates an SCR (solid state switch) which causes the switchbox capacitor to discharge the AC voltage into the ignition coil primary

7

7. Slip timing belt off pulley (**Figure 32**). Remove pulley from distributor shaft.

8. Remove the pulley drive key. Remove the spacer from under the keyway.

9. Remove drag link rod nut, flat washer and wave washer at vertical throttle lever (A, **Figure 33**). Disconnect drag link from throttle lever.

10. Disconnect ground lead (B, **Figure 33**).

11. Remove the 3 nuts, washers and bolts holding distributor housing to cylinder block. Remove the distributor assembly (**Figure 34**).

Installation
(4- and 6-cylinder Models)

1. Position spacer over distributor shaft. Install drive key into shaft keyway.

2. Install distributor assembly to cylinder block and align bolt holes. Make sure the throttle primary and secondary pickup cams are behind the carburetor primary and secondary levers respectively.

3. Install distributor assembly bolts, washers and nuts.

4. Install distributor cap with retainer clamp. Tighten clamp screw securely.

5. Connect drag link to throttle lever and install wave washer, flat washer and nut.

6. Install timing belt. See Chapter Five.

7. Reconnect 3 trigger leads according to color coding at switchbox terminals. Coat connections with Liquid Neoprene.

8. Install cowl support brackets.

9. Connect manual choke or choke solenoid wire. Coat choke solenoid wire connection with Liquid Neoprene.

10. Connect positive battery cable.

11. Set ignition timing. See Chapter Five.

12. Install top and wrap-around cowl assemblies.

Removal
(3-cylinder Models Through 1974)

1. Disconnect the positive battery cable.

2. Remove the wrap-around cowl.

3. Remove the 4 cap screws from the front and rear center support. Remove the center support assembly.

4. Remove the flywheel nut and washer.

5. Hold flywheel with tool part No. C-91-52344 and remove flywheel with puller part No. C-91-48501A1.

6. Remove stator attaching screws. Remove stator.

7. Disconnect the distributor ground strap.

8. Disconnect the spark plug leads at the spark plugs.

9. Remove the retainer from the exhaust cover, the distributor actuating arm linkage from the distributor and the secondary coil lead and coil lead clamp.

10. Remove 2 capscrew mounting bolts under the pulley. Pry the pulley free with 2 screwdrivers and remove the pulley key and spacer.

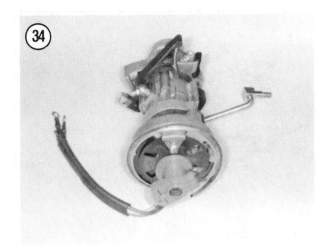

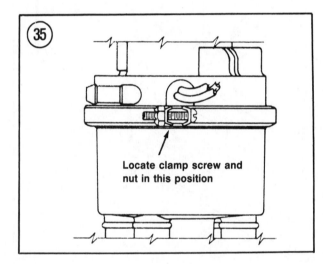

Locate clamp screw and nut in this position

11. Remove 3 screws, washers and nuts holding distributor assembly to cylinder block. Remove the distributor assembly.

Installation
(3-cylinder Models Through 1974)

1. Position the distributor cap assembly on the distributor housing. Be careful not to damage the brush and spring. Install the distributor cap clamp and retainer with the screw and nut. Locate the clamp screw and nut as shown in **Figure 35**.

2. Position the distributor and adaptor assembly on the cylinder block mounting flange. Distributor pulley spacer and drive key should be in place.

3. Install distributor adaptor to cylinder block with 3 screws, washers and nuts. Tighten fasteners securely.

4. Install capscrew mounting bolts under the pulley.

5. Install the secondary coil lead and clamp screw, the distributor actuating arm linkage and the exhaust cover retainer.

6. Connect the spark plug leads and distributor ground strap.

7. Install the stator and tighten attaching screws securely.

8. Install the flywheel and hold with tool part No. C-91-52344. Install washer and nut on flywheel shaft, then tighten nut to specifications (**Table 3**) with tool part No. C-91-48501A1.

9. Install center support assembly.

10. Connect the positive battery cable.

11. Set ignition timing. See Chapter Five.

12. Install wrap-around cowl.

Removal
(1975 3-cylinder Model)

1. Disconnect the positive battery cable.

2. Remove the cowling.

3. Remove distributor cap clamp screw, nut and clamp. Remove distributor cap.

4. Remove distributor pulley cover bolt. Remove cover and slip timing belt off pulley.

5. Remove pulley, drive key and spacer from distributor shaft.

6. Disconnect 3 trigger leads at switchbox.

7. Disconnect ground wire at distributor trigger housing.

8. Remove rubber mount nuts. Pull front support forward and remove rubber mount.

9. Remove 2 bolts holding distributor adaptor to cylinder block.

10. Disconnect drag link at distributor trigger housing.

7

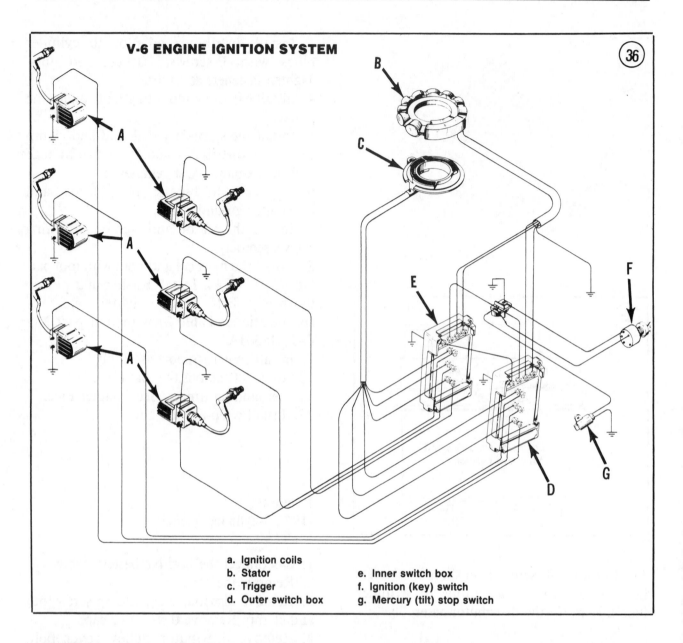

V-6 ENGINE IGNITION SYSTEM (36)

a. Ignition coils
b. Stator
c. Trigger
d. Outer switch box
e. Inner switch box
f. Ignition (key) switch
g. Mercury (tilt) stop switch

Installation
(1975 3-cylinder Model)

1. Fit spacer over distributor shaft. Install drive key in shaft keyway, then install pulley.

2. Connect drag link to distributor trigger housing.

3. Position distributor assembly on cylinder block with adaptor locating pins in cylinder block holes. Install attaching bolts/nuts and tighten securely.

4. Install and align timing belt. See Chapter Five.

5. Reconnect 3 trigger leads according to color coding at switchbox terminals. Coat connections with Liquid Neoprene.

6. Install rubber mount and tighten nuts securely.

7. Index and install distributor cap. Tighten clamp screw securely.

8. Connect the positive battery cable.

9. Set ignition timing. See Chapter Five.

10. Install cowling.

THUNDERBOLT CD IGNITION SYSTEM (WITHOUT DISTRIBUTOR)

This system was introduced on 1976 Merc 500, 600, 850 and 1750 models. Variations of the system are used on all late-model Merc outboards. Its major components include the flywheel, stator assembly, trigger assembly, switchbox(es), ignition coils, spark plugs and connecting wiring. See **Figure 36**.

The stator is located under the flywheel and contains 2 coils (45, 50, 60, 70, 80, 90 [4-cyl.], 100 and 115 [4-cyl.] hp) or 4 coils (all others). The flywheel is also fitted with permanent magnets inside the outer rim. As the crankshaft and flywheel rotate, the flywheel magnets pass the stationary stator coils. This creates an AC voltage in the stator coils. The AC voltage is sent to one or more switchboxes where it is rectified and stored in a capacitor.

A trigger assembly also mounted under the flywheel contains 2 coils (4-cylinder) or 3 coils (3- and 6-cylinder). A second set of magnets located around the flywheel hub pass the stationary trigger coils. This creates an AC voltage in the trigger coils. The AC voltage is routed to an SCR (solid state switch) in the switchbox(es). The SCR discharges the capacitor into the ignition coil at the proper time and in the correct firing order sequence. This eliminates the need for a distributor.

Spark timing is changed by rotating the trigger coil position relative to the flywheel hub magnets.

Component Wiring

Modern outboard motor electrical wiring is quite complex, especially on the higher output engines. **Figure 37** shows a typical Merc V6 switchbox assembly, starter, rectifiers and associated wiring. For this reason, electrical wiring is color-coded and the terminal on switchboxes, rectifiers, etc. to which each wire connects is embossed with the correct wire color. When used in conjunction with the electrical wiring diagram for your model found at the end of the book, incorrect wire connections should be held to a minimum.

Wire routing, however, is also very important to prevent possible electrical interference and/or damage to the wiring harnesses from mechanical engine components. Mercury outboards are shipped from the factory with all wiring harnesses and leads properly positioned and secured with J clamps and plastic straps.

When component replacement is necessary, it is highly recommended that you take the time to either carefully draw a picture of the area to be serviced, noting the positioning of all wire harnesses involved, or use an instant camera to take several photographs at close range of the harness routing and location. Either can be invaluable when it comes time to reroute the harnesses for reassembly. Be sure to reinstall J clamps and new straps where necessary to keep the wiring properly routed.

Flywheel Removal/Installation

1. Electric start models—disconnect the positive battery cable.
2. Remove the front, wrap-around and top cowl assemblies as necessary.

7

3. Remove the top and rear cowl support brackets from the engine, if so equipped.

4. Manual start models—remove the rewind starter assembly.

5. Disconnect the electric choke solenoid lead, if so equipped.

6. Remove the timing pointer (**Figure 38**, typical).

7. Remove the plastic cap from the flywheel hub, if so equipped, to expose the flywheel nut (**Figure 39**, typical).

8A. Manual start models—hold flywheel with a strap wrench and remove the flywheel nut and washer. See **Figure 40**.

8B. Electric start models—hold flywheel with tool part No. C-91-52344 and remove the flywheel nut.

> *CAUTION*
> *Flywheel removal without the use of a protector cap on the end of the crankshaft can cause crankshaft damage.*

9. Install a protector cap on the end of the crankshaft.

> *CAUTION*
> *Do not apply heat or hammer while removing the flywheel in Step 10. Heat may cause the flywheel to seize on the crankshaft, while hammering can damage the crankshaft and/or bearings.*

10. Install an appropriate flywheel puller. Hold puller with one wrench and tighten puller screw with a second wrench until flywheel is drawn off the crankshaft end.

11. To reinstall flywheel, position on crankshaft end. Install flat washer and flywheel nut.

12. Hold flywheel with strap wrench (manual) or flywheel holder part No. C-91-52344 (electric) and tighten flywheel nut to specifications (**Table 3**).

13. Install plastic cap in flywheel hub, if so equipped.

14. Install timing pointer.

15. Set ignition timing. See Chapter Five.

16. Reverse Steps 1-5 to complete installation.

Stator Replacement

1. Remove the flywheel as described in this chapter.

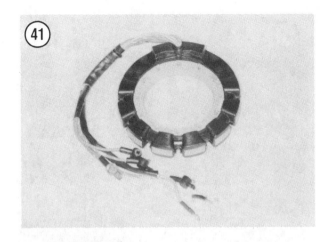

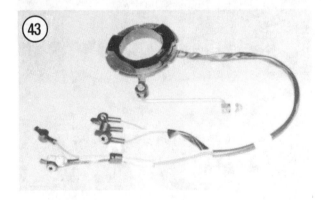

2. Note the stator wire routing in relation to the end cap. Make a drawing or take an instant picture of the wiring for reassembly reference.

3. Remove the screws holding the stator to the end cap.

4A. Inline engines—disconnect all stator leads from their respective terminals.

4B. V6 engines—remove outer switchbox mounting screws. Separate outer and inner switchboxes. Disconnect all stator leads from their respective terminals.

5. Remove stator from engine (**Figure 41**).

6. Position new stator on end cap. Wipe stator attaching screw threads with Loctite Type A. Install screws and tighten to specifications (**Table 3**).

7. Route stator wires according to drawing or photo made before disassembly.

8. Connect stator leads to their respective terminals. On V6 models, install outer switchbox over inner switchbox with spacers and mounting screws. Refer to the appropriate wiring diagram at the end of the book, if necessary.

9. Reinstall flywheel as described in this chapter.

Trigger Coil Replacement

1. Remove the flywheel as described in this chapter.

2. Remove the stator as described in this chapter.

3. Note the trigger coil harness routing. Make a drawing or take an instant picture of the wiring for reassembly reference.

4. Remove the screws holding the trigger assembly to the end cap. Lift assembly from end cap and move to one side.

5. Remove locknut holding link rod swivel to spark advance lever (**Figure 42** shows link rod swivel with flywheel installed). Disconnect link rod from lever.

6A. Inline engines—disconnect all trigger leads from their respective switchbox terminals.

6B. V6 engines—remove outer switchbox mounting screws. Separate outer and inner switchboxes. Disconnect all trigger leads from their respective terminals.

7. Remove trigger coil assembly (**Figure 43**) from engine.

7

8. If installing a new trigger coil assembly, remove link rod from old trigger coil and install to new one.

9. Installation is the reverse of removal. Route trigger coil leads according to drawing or photo made before disassembly. On V6 models, install outer switchbox to inner switchbox with spacers and mounting screws. Refer to the appropriate wiring diagram at the end of the book, if necessary.

Ignition Coil Replacement

Orange-colored coils have a short wire which extends from the back side of the coil. This wire must be positioned across the rubber portion on the back of the coil to ensure proper grounding to the engine when installed.

1. Disconnect the spark plug wire from the coil(s) to be replaced.

2. Disconnect the switchbox wire(s) at the positive coil terminal(s). Disconnect the black ground wire(s) at the negative coil terminal(s).

3. Remove the coil cover bolts with star washers (**Figure 44**, typical). Remove coil cover with coils (and coil plate, if so equipped) from the engine.

4. Remove the defective coil(s) from the coil cover.

5. Installation is the reverse of removal. With orange-colored coils, make sure the short wire extending from the back of each coil is positioned over the rubber portion of the coil.

Switchbox Replacement

Although the wiring is color-coded and the switchbox terminals are embossed with the proper color coding, it is a good idea to make a drawing or take an instant picture of the switchbox wiring on inline 6-cylinder models. The dual switchbox installation (**Figure 45**) is visually confusing and might result in improper wire connection.

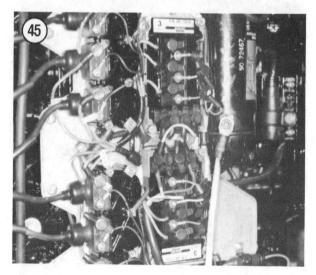

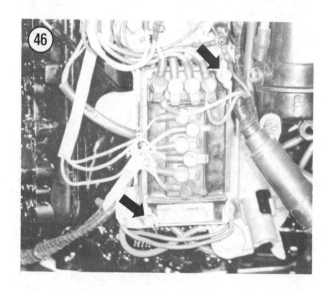

Inline models

1. Unsnap the neoprene cap on each wire connected to the switchbox terminals. Pull caps back and remove nuts holding wires to terminals. Remove wires from terminals.
2A. 4-cylinder models—remove 4 switchbox mounting bolts.
2B. 6-cylinder inline models—remove 2 mounting screws holding switchbox to engine.
3. Remove the switchbox.
4. Installation is the reverse of removal.

V6 models

> *NOTE*
> *The switchboxes are grounded to the engine through the mounting screws and round metal spacers.*

1. Remove the 2 screws holding the outer switchbox to the inner switchbox (**Figure 46**). Separate the switchboxes and remove the round metal spacers.
2. Unsnap the neoprene cap on each wire connected to the terminals of the switchbox(es) to be removed. Pull caps back and remove nuts holding wires to terminals. Remove wires from terminals. Remove the switchbox(es).
3. Installation is the reverse of removal. The wires with yellow identification sleeves connect to the outer switchbox. Refer to the wiring diagram at the end of the book for your particular model if necessary to assure that wires are properly connected. Tighten switchbox mounting screws snugly.

Table 1 BATTERY CAPACITY (HOURS)

Accessory draw	80 Amp-hour battery provides continuous power for:	Approximate recharge time
5 amps	13.5 hours	16 hours
15 amps	3.5 hours	13 hours
25 amps	1.8 hours	12 hours
Accessory draw	105 Amp-hour battery provides continuous power for:	Approximate recharge time
5 amps	15.8 hours	16 hours
15 amps	4.2 hours	13 hours
25 amps	2.4 hours	12 hours

Table 2 STATE OF BATTERY CHARGE

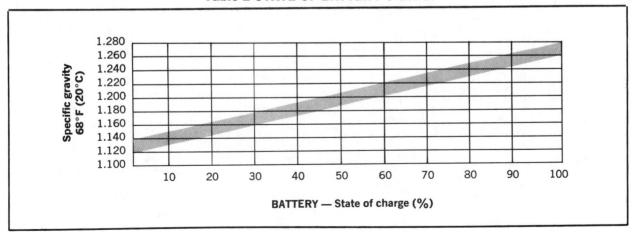

7

Table 3 TIGHTENING TORQUES

Fastener	in.-lb.	ft.-lb.
Coil terminal nuts		
Merc 500, 650, 700	30	
All others	20	
Flywheel nut		
Merc 500, 45, 50 (4-cyl.)		65
Merc 650, 700, 50 (3-cyl.), 60, 70		
(Prior to 1974)		85
Merc 70-115 (1987-on)		120
All others		100
Starter		
Motor-to-crankcase		
Merc 500, 45, 50 (4-cyl.)	160	
Merc 650, 700, 50 (3-cyl.), 60, 70		
(Prior to 1974), V6	180	
Merc 70-90 (1987-on)	165	
Merc 100-115 (1988-on)	180	
All others	150	
Motor-to-bracket nuts	85	
Through bolts	70	
Stator screws		
Merc 70-115 (1987-on)	60[1]	
All others	30	
Trigger coil screws	30	

1. If a Patch screw is not used, apply Loctite grade A on screw threads prior to installation.

Chapter Eight

Power Head

Basic repair of Mercury outboard power heads is similar from model to model, with minor differences. However, this chapter does not cover overhaul of the Laser XRi or 200 XRi power heads due to the nature of the electronic control and fuel injection system. Owner service to this power head should be restricted to removal from the drive shaft housing; take the power head to a dealer for service.

Some procedures require the use of special tools, which can be purchased from a Mercury dealer. Certain tools may be fabricated by a machinist, often at substantial savings. Power head stands are available from specialty shops and marine product distributors. Make sure the engine stand is of sufficient capacity to support the size of engine you are servicing.

Work on the power head requires considerable mechanical ability. You should carefully consider your own capabilities before attempting any operation involving major disassembly of the engine.

Much of the labor charge for dealer repairs involves the removal and disassembly of other parts to reach the defective component. Even if you decide not to tackle the entire power head overhaul after studying the text and illustrations in this chapter, it can be cheaper to perform the preliminary operations yourself and then take the power head to your dealer. Since many marine dealers have lengthy waiting lists for service (especially during the spring and summer season), this practice can reduce the time your unit is in the shop. If you have done much of the preliminary work, your repairs can be scheduled and performed much quicker.

Repairs go much faster and easier if your motor is clean before you begin work. There are special cleaners for washing the motor and related parts. Just spray or brush on the cleaning solution, let it stand, then rinse it away with a garden hose. Clean all oily or greasy parts with fresh solvent as you remove them.

WARNING
Never use gasoline as a cleaning agent. It presents an extreme fire hazard. Be sure to work in a well-ventilated area when using cleaning solvents. Keep a fire extinguisher rated for gasoline and oil fires nearby in case of emergency.

Once you have decided to do the job yourself, read this chapter thoroughly until you have a good idea of what is involved in completing the overhaul satisfactorily. Make arrangements to buy or rent any special tools necessary and obtain replacement parts before you start. It is frustrating and time-consuming to start an overhaul and then be unable to complete it because the necessary tools or parts are not at hand.

Before beginning the job, re-read Chapter Two of this manual. You will do a better job with this information fresh in your mind.

Since this chapter covers a large range of models over a lengthy time period, the procedures are somewhat generalized to accommodate all models. Where individual differences occur, they are specifically pointed out. The power heads shown in the accompanying pictures are current designs. While it is possible that the components shown in the pictures may not be identical with those being serviced, they are representative and the step-by-step procedures may be used with all models covered in this manual.

Tables 1-6 are at the end of the chapter.

ENGINE SERIAL NUMBERS

Mercury outboards are identified by serial number instead of model year. The serial number is stamped on a plate riveted to the transom clamp. It is also stamped on a welch plug installed in the power head (**Figure 1**, typical).

This information identifies the outboard and power head. It indicates if there are unique parts or if internal changes have been made during the model run. It is essential when ordering replacement parts for the engine.

GASKET AND SEALANT

Two types of sealant materials are recommended: Permatex 2C-12 (part No. C-92-72592) and Loctite Master Gasket sealant (part No. 92-12564-1).

Permatex 2C-12 is applied in a thin, even coat covering the entire mating surface when sealing the crankcase cover/cylinder block with a gasket strip. Loctite Master Gasket sealant is applied in a continuous 1/16 in. bead to seal the same surfaces without a gasket strip.

When sealing the crankcase cover/cylinder block, both mating surfaces must be free of all sealant residue, dirt and oil. Locquic Primer T (part No. C-92-59327), lacquer thinner, acetone or similar solvents work well when used with a broad, flat scraper or a somewhat dull putty knife. Solvents with an oil, wax or petroleum base should not be used. Clean the aluminum surfaces carefully to avoid nicking them with the scraper or putty knife.

POWER HEAD

Removal/Installation
(Merc 50 [3 cyl.], 60, 70
[Prior to 1984], 650 and 700)

1. Remove the front cover, clam-shell cowl and top cowl support bracket.

2. Disconnect the battery and spark plug leads.

3. Disconnect the water inlet/outlet and fuel lines at the engine.

4. Disconnect the remote control harness at the engine (**Figure 2**, typical).

5. Clip and remove straps holding hoses and electrical harnesses in place.

6. Disconnect fuel pump lines at the pump.

7. Remove the fasteners holding the rear cowl support bracket to the powerhead. Remove bracket.

NOTE
Insufficient clearance will prevent the removal of all fasteners in Step 8. Those which cannot be removed in this step should be left for removal in Step 12.

8. Loosen and remove the nuts/bolts holding the power head to the drive shaft housing/exhaust plate.

9. Shift motor into NEUTRAL.

10. Remove shift cable latch assembly locknut. Remove latch, flat washer and nylon wear plate from control cable anchor bracket.

11. Remove plastic cap from center of flywheel. Install lifting eye (part No. C-91-75132) in flywheel as far as possible.

12. Attach a hoist to the lifting eye and raise the power head enough to remove the power head fasteners that could not be removed in Step 8.

13. Pull shift linkage slightly from its neutral position while lifting the power head from the drive shaft housing. This prevents the link from pulling out of the drive shaft housing.

14. Secure power head stand (part No. C-91-25821A1) in a vise and install power head on stand. Remove the lifting eye.

15. Remove the flywheel. See Chapter Seven.

16. Remove manual choke cable screw and push cable down through air box opening.

17. Disconnect the throttle lever linkage. Reinstall bushing, flat washer and locknut on end of linkage.

18. Remove stator attaching screws. Lift stator up and place to one side on the power head.

19. Disconnect all switchbox leads (**Figure 2**, typical).

20. Remove trigger assembly. See Chapter Seven.

21. Disconnect starter motor cables at the motor. Reinstall fasteners to motor.

22. Unclamp high tension leads and pull out from behind the fuel line.

23. Remove the fuel pump, filter and carburetors as an assembly.

24. Remove the starter motor. See Chapter Seven.

25. Remove air box, switchbox and coils as an assembly.

26. Remove screw and pull actuator lever from power head.

27. Unbolt and remove throttle lever and actuator as an assembly.

28. Installation is the reverse of removal. Route the wiring harnesses as noted during disassembly. Install new straps as required. Match the switchbox terminals with their appropriate color leads. Coat appropriate connections with Liquid Neoprene. Tighten

8

all fasteners to specifications (**Table 1**). Complete timing, synchronizing and adjustment procedures (Chapter Five).

Removal/Installation
(1987-on Merc 70, 80 and 90)

1. Remove engine cowling.
2. Disconnect the battery and spark plug leads.
3. Remove front cowl bracket.
4. Remove 8 screws retaining air box cover then withdraw cover.
5. Remove lower oil tank support bolt (10 mm) and the two upper oil tank neck brace bolts (8 mm).
6. Remove 6 nuts retaining air box then withdraw air box.
7. Disconnect oil lines from oil tank and plug then withdraw tank.
8. Disconnect throttle linkage from center carburetor ball socket.
9. Disconnect fuel supply hose and fuel primer hose from top carburetor.
10. Withdraw carburetor assemblies and actuating linkage as a complete unit.
11. Remove the flywheel cover.
12. Remove the flywheel. See Chapter Seven.

> *NOTE*
> *It is recommended that you make a series of drawings or take instant pictures prior to starting Step 13 to provide reassembly reference.*

13. Disconnect all electrical and ignition wiring as needed and remove with component mounting plates.
14. Loosen and remove fasteners holding power head to drive shaft housing.
15. Remove shift arm linkage.
16. Temporarily install flywheel with retaining nut.
17. Install lifting eye (part No. 91-90455) onto flywheel end. Eye must thread at least 5 turns onto flywheel end. Attach a hoist to the lifting eye.
18. Remove any component not previously noted that will interfere with power head removal.
19. Lift power head from drive shaft housing and install on a suitable engine stand. Remove the lifting eye.
20. Remove the spark plugs with an appropriate size plug remover socket.
21. Remove the intake manifolds and reed block assemblies.
22. Installation is the reverse of removal.
23. Install a new gasket over drive shaft housing alignment pins. Route the wiring harnesses as noted during disassembly. Tighten all fasteners to specifications (**Table 2**). Complete timing, synchronizing and adjustment procedures (Chapter Five).

Removal/Installation
(1988-on Merc 100 and 115)

1. Remove engine cowling.
2. Disconnect the battery and spark plug leads.
3. Disconnect tell-tale water hose from aft cowl support bracket.
4. Remove 4 bolts retaining aft cowl support bracket then withdraw bracket.
5. Remove 4 screws retaining ignition plate cover then withdraw cover.
6. Disconnect negative battery lead from terminal on starter motor and positive battery lead from terminal on starter solenoid.

> *NOTE*
> *It is recommended that you make a series of drawings or take instant pictures prior to starting Step 7 to provide reassembly reference.*

7. Disconnect power trim/tilt leads from respective solenoid on ignition plate and power trim/tilt fuse located at top of starter motor.

8. Remove 2 screws and clamp retaining supply wiring harness assembly to bottom cowl support bracket at the front of the engine.

9. Disconnect supply wiring harness from engine wiring harness at ignition plate connector, then disconnect any wire connection not previously noted that will interfere with supply wiring harness removal and remove wiring harness.

10. Disconnect fuel supply hose from engine bayonet fitting.

11. Disconnect throttle and shift cables from engine linkage, then remove cables from engine mounting bracket.

12. Remove shift arm linkage.

13. Install lifting eye (part No. 91-90455) onto flywheel end. Eye must thread at least 5 turns onto flywheel end. Attach a hoist to the lifting eye.

14. Loosen and remove fasteners holding power head to drive shaft housing.

15. Remove any component not previously noted that will interfere with power head removal.

16. Lift power head from drive shaft housing and install on a suitable engine stand. Remove the lifting eye.

17. Remove the spark plugs with an appropriate size plug remover socket.

18. Remove the flywheel. See Chapter Seven.

19. Disconnect starter cable, then remove 4 starter motor mounting bolts and withdraw starter.

20. Remove the 2 upper oil tank neck brace bolts.

21. Remove the 2 bottom cowl support bracket bolts.

22. Remove vapor return hose from tee fitting located between fuel supply bayonet fitting and fuel pump.

23. Remove bayonet fitting retaining bolt at bottom cowl support bracket, then withdraw support bracket.

24. Remove 10 screws retaining air box cover, then withdraw cover.

25. Remove oil tank bottom front support bracket bolt.

26. Remove 8 nuts retaining air box then withdraw air box.

27. Disconnect hoses from carburetor fittings to allow removal of carburetors as an assembly.

28. Withdraw carburetor assemblies and actuating linkage as a complete unit.

29. Disconnect oil line from oil tank and plug.

30. Remove oil tank bottom rear support bracket bolt.

31. Disconnect throttle linkage from throttle cam.

32. Remove 2 fuel enrichment hoses from intake manifold fittings.

33. Remove fuel enrichment valve with hoses and lay to the side.

34. Remove the intake manifold and reed block assemblies. Pry points are located on the starboard side of the intake manifolds.

35. Complete disassembly as outlined under *Disassembly* in this chapter.

36. Installation is the reverse of removal.

37. Install a new gasket over drive shaft housing alignment pins. Route the wiring harness as noted during disassembly. Tighten all fasteners to specifications (**Table 2**). Complete timing, synchronizing and adjustment procedures (Chapter Five).

**Removal/Installation
(4-[Except 1988-on Merc 100 and
115] and 6-cylinder Inline Engine)**

1. Remove front, wrap-around and top cowling.

2. Disconnect the battery and spark plug leads.

3. Remove top and rear cowl supports as an assembly.

4. Remove trim cover from bottom cowl (**Figure 3**).

5. Loosen and remove fasteners holding power head to drive shaft housing (**Figure 4**).

NOTE
It is recommended that you make a series of drawings or take instant pictures during completion of Step 6 to provide reassembly reference.

6. Disconnect all electrical and ignition wire terminals on the power head.

7. Remove nut holding shift link to guide block (**Figure 5**).

8. Disconnect fuel inlet line at the fuel pump.

9. Remove manual choke from carburetor linkage.

10. Disconnect and remove water hose from tell-tale outlet on cylinder block cover.

11. Remove plastic cap from center of flywheel. Install lifting eye (part No. C-91-75132) in flywheel as far as possible. Attach a hoist to the lifting eye.

12. Secure power head stand (part No. C-91-30591A1) in a vise. Lift power head from drive shaft housing and install on stand. Remove the lifting eye.

13. Remove the flywheel. See Chapter Seven.

14. Remove the starter. See Chapter Seven.

15. Remove the spark plugs with an appropriate size plug remover socket.

16. Remove throttle arm attaching bolt.

17. Remove the stator and trigger assembly or stator, timing belt and distributor, as appropriate.

18. Remove the carburetor mounting nuts. Remove the carburetors as an assembly (**Figure 6**, typical).

19. Installation is the reverse of removal. Install a new gasket on the power head studs. Make sure throttle plate opening is

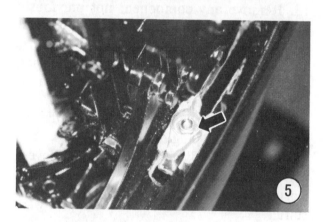

synchronized. Route the wiring harnesses as noted during disassembly. Install new straps as required. Match the switchbox terminals with their appropriate color leads. Coat appropriate connections with Liquid Neoprene. Tighten all fasteners to specifications (**Table 3**). Complete timing, synchronizing and adjustment procedures (Chapter Five).

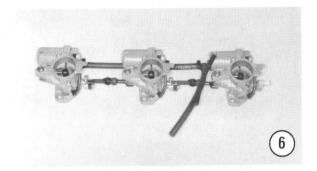

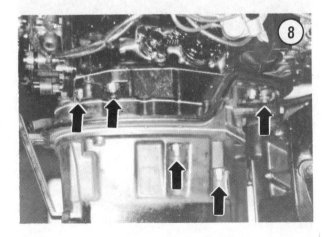

Removal/Installation
(V6 Engine)

1. Remove the front cover. Remove the clam-shell cowling.

2. Disconnect the battery and spark plug leads.

3. Disconnect the fuel tank line at the engine.

4. Drain and remove oil injection reservoir, if so equipped.

5. Remove the remote control harness retainer.

6. Shift the engine into NEUTRAL.

7. Remove locknut holding shift cable latch assembly. Remove latch, washer, nylon wear plate and spring from control cable anchor bracket.

8. Clip and remove all straps.

9. Disconnect tell-tale water hose from exhaust plate elbow fitting.

10. Unbolt and remove rear cowl support bracket from power head (**Figure 7**).

11. Remove 5 locknuts and washers holding power head on each side to drive shaft housing (**Figure 8**).

12. Remove plastic cap from center of flywheel. Install lifting eye (part No. C-91-90455) in flywheel as far as possible.

13. Attach a hoist to the lifting eye. Secure power head stand (part No. C-91-30591A1) in a vise. Lift power head from drive shaft housing and install on stand. Remove the lifting eye.

14. Remove the flywheel. See Chapter Seven.

15. Disconnect all electrical and ignition wire connections on the power head. Make diagrams or take instant pictures of terminal connections and harness routings for reassembly reference.

16. Remove the stator and trigger assemblies. See Chapter Seven.

17. Remove the idle stabilizer (if so equipped) at the top of the air silencer. Remove the air silencer.

18. Remove the carburetors, linkage and fuel pump. See Chapter Six.

19. Remove the starter motor, solenoid, ignition coils and switchboxes. See Chapter Seven.

8

20. Remove the spark plugs with an appropriate size plug wrench.

21. Remove the shift cable latch and control cable anchor bracket assemblies.

22. Remove the oil injection pump (A, **Figure 9**) and drive shaft (B).

23. Installation is the reverse of removal. Install a new gasket on the power head studs. Lubricate drive shaft splines with Quicksilver Multipurpose Lubricant (part No. C-92-63250). Route the wiring harnesses as noted during disassembly. Install new straps as appropriate. Match the switchbox terminals with their appropriate color leads. Coat appropriate connections with Liquid Neoprene. Thread shift link locknut on rod to expose 2-3 threads and do not tighten further. Tighten all other fasteners to specifications (**Table 4**). Complete timing, synchronizing and adjustment procedures (Chapter Five).

Disassembly (Inline Engine [Except 1987-on 70-115 hp])

1. Remove power head from power head stand and vise. Carefully place it on a clean workbench surface.

2. On 4- and 6-cylinder power heads, bend center main bearing lock tabs down (**Figure 10**) and remove main bearing screws.

3. Remove crankcase cover and end cover bolts.

CAUTION
The crankcase cover and cylinder block are a matched, line-bored unit. Take care not to scratch or mar the machined surfaces.

4. Split the crankcase cover gasket seal carefully with a putty knife to avoid damage to the gasket sealing surfaces. See **Figure 11**.

5. Remove crankcase cover (**Figure 12**, typical).

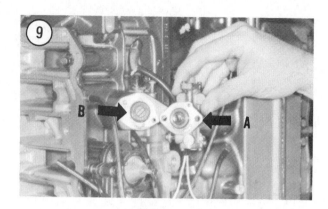

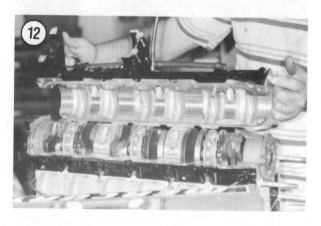

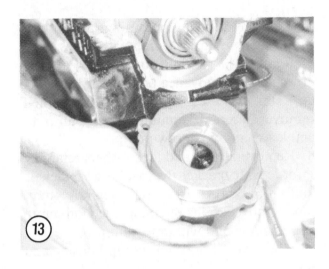

(13)

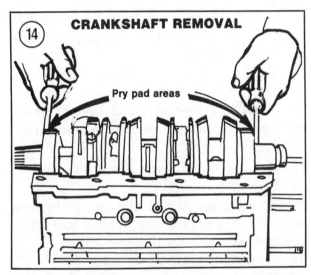

(14) **CRANKSHAFT REMOVAL**

Pry pad areas

(15)

CAUTION
Do not tap on end cover shims in Step 6.

6. Tap end caps off crankcase with a soft mallet. Remove end caps (**Figure 13**, typical).

7. Pad the crankcase mating surfaces near the ends of the crankshaft with clean shop cloths. Loosen main bearing supports/reed blocks from cylinder block locating pins with a pair of pry bars or screwdrivers. See **Figure 14**.

8. Lift the crankshaft straight up and remove it from the cylinder block. Install crankshaft upright on power head stand in vise.

9. Unbolt and remove exhaust cover and gasket from cylinder block (**Figure 15**, typical). Discard the gasket.

10. Carefully pry baffle plate from cylinder block with a putty knife. Remove baffle plate (**Figure 16**, typical). Discard the gasket.

NOTE
Do not remove inner water jacket cover from 4- and 6-cylinder blocks unless absolutely necessary.

11. Unbolt and remove transfer port cover(s) and gasket(s) (**Figure 17**, typical). Discard the gaskets.

12. Unbolt and remove cylinder block cover and gasket (**Figure 18**, typical). Discard the gasket.

Disassembly
(1987-on Merc 70, 80 and 90)

1. Remove power head from engine stand. Carefully place power head assembly on a clean workbench surface.

2. Remove hoses from oil injection pump then remove 2 bolts retaining injection pump to crankcase and withdraw pump.

3. Remove oil injection pump housing and shaft.

8

4. Remove hoses from fuel pump then remove 2 bolts retaining fuel pump to crankcase and withdraw pump.

5. Remove 5 bolts retaining thermostat housing then withdraw housing.

6. Remove thermostat and poppet valve components from cylinder block cover passages.

7. Remove remaining cylinder block cover bolts.

8. Split the cylinder block cover gasket seal carefully. Pry only at the pry-tabs located at the bottom and on each side of the cylinder block cover.

9. Remove exhaust cover bolts.

10. Split the exhaust cover and divider plate gasket seals carefully. Pry only at the pry-tab located at the bottom aft end of the exhaust cover. Discard the gaskets.

11. Remove crankcase bolts and lower end cap bolt which threads into crankcase cover.

12. Split the lower crankcase half gasket seal carefully. Pry only at the pry-tabs located at the bottom and on each side of the lower crankcase half.

13. Remove crankcase cover.

14. Remove 2 remaining lower end cap mounting bolts then remove end cap.

15. Lift the crankshaft assembly straight up and remove it from the cylinder block. Install the crankshaft assembly upright on a crankshaft holding fixture mounted in a vise.

Disassembly
(1988-on Merc 100 and 115)

1. Remove 4 stator mounting screws and trigger actuating linkage from throttle arm.

2. Remove any electrical connection not previously noted that will interfere with ignition plate removal.

3. Remove 4 ignition plate mounting bolts, then withdraw ignition plate with electrical components and associated wiring.

4. Remove 2 accelerator pump hoses from cylinders 3 and 4, check valve fittings.

5. Remove 2 bolts retaining accelerator pump then withdraw pump with hoses.

6. Remove 17 mm nut to withdraw throttle arm and spark advance arm assembly.

7. Remove hoses from fuel pump then remove 2 screws retaining fuel pump to crankcase and withdraw pump.

8. Remove 2 bolts and lockwashers retaining throttle/shift bracket then withdraw bracket.

9. Remove hoses from oil injection pump then remove 2 bolts retaining injection pump to crankcase and withdraw pump.

10. Remove oil injection pump housing and shaft.

11. Remove power head from engine stand. Carefully place power head assembly on a clean work bench surface.

12. Remove 5 bolts retaining thermostat housing then withdraw housing.

13. Remove thermostat and poppet valve components from cylinder block cover passages.

14. Remove remaining cylinder block cover bolts.

15. Split the cylinder block cover gasket seal carefully. Pry only at the pry-tab located at the bottom port side of the cover.

16. Remove exhaust cover bolts.

17. Split the exhaust cover and divider plate gasket seals carefully. Pry only at the pry-tab located at the bottom of the cover and at the pry-tab located at the top fore end of the cover. Discard the gaskets.

18. Remove crankcase end cap.

19. Remove crankcase bolts.

20. Split the lower crankcase half gasket seal carefully. Pry only at the pry-tab located at the middle port side of the lower crankcase half and at the pry-tab located at the bottom starboard side of the lower crankcase half.

21. Lift the crankshaft assembly straight up and remove it from the cylinder block. Install the crankshaft assembly upright on a power head stand mounted in a vise.

22. Remove accelerator pump check valves from cylinders 3 and 4. Check valves should be cleaned with WD-40 and tested using air pressure applied by a hand pump. Check valve should open at a pressure between 11-14 psi and should not drop below 5 psi

within 30 seconds. Replace valve if contamination is noted or does not pass air pressure test.

Disassembly
(V6 Engine)

1. Place power head in a repair stand or on a clean workbench.
2. Unbolt and remove each cylinder head cover. **Figure 19** shows the Type 1 (early model design) with cover off.
3. Unbolt and remove thermostat cover (A, **Figure 20**) and thermostat (B, **Figure 20**) from cylinder head cover.
4. Remove the idle shutoff/water pressure relief valve cover and valve (**Figure 21**).
5. Remove the cylinder heads. See **Figure 22** (Type 1) or **Figure 23** (Type 2).
6. Remove the exhaust manifold cover and divider plate. Remove the divider plate seal from the engine.
7. Remove the reed block housing and gasket from the engine. Place the housing on a flat surface to prevent damage to the reed valve. **Figure 24** shows the horizontal reed block

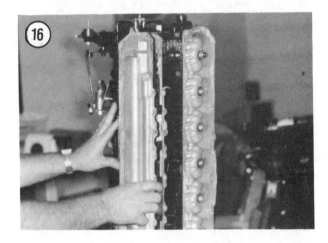

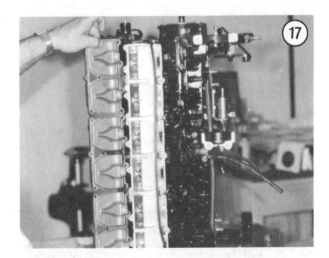

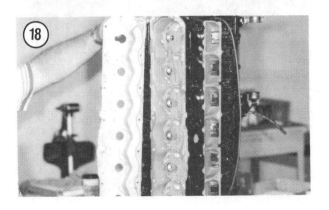

8

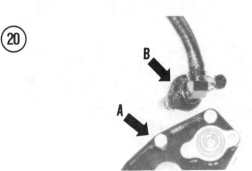

design. **Figure 25** shows the vertical reed block design. Remove and discard the gasket.

8. Remove end cap bolts. See **Figure 26** (upper end cap) and **Figure 27** (lower end cap).

9. Remove bolts holding crankcase cover to cylinder block. Locate the recess provided for prying at each end of cover and carefully pry cover from block with screwdrivers. See **Figure 28**.

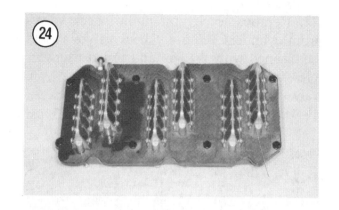

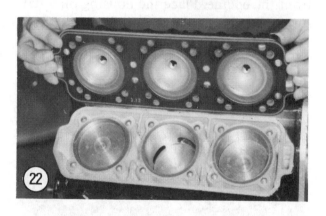

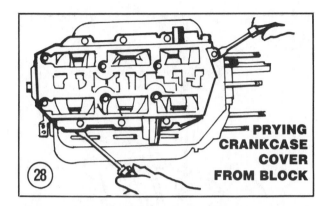

PRYING CRANKCASE COVER FROM BLOCK

28

10. Rotate crankshaft to position one connecting rod cap at the bottom of its throw. Check rod and cap for cylinder identification number. If none are found, scribe your own with an awl or electric pencil.

11. Loosen connecting rod cap bolts (**Figure 29**) and remove cap, bearings and bearing cage from connecting rod.

12. Place one hand under the cylinder block to catch the piston and push it out with the other hand (**Figure 30**).

> *CAUTION*
> *Each connecting rod and rod cap is a matched machined set and should not be mismatched.*

13. Reassemble the rod cap to its piston.

14. Repeat Steps 10-13 to remove each of the remaining pistons.

15. Remove each end cap from the crankshaft. See **Figure 31**.

16. Carefully lift the crankshaft straight up and out of the cylinder block (**Figure 32**). Install crankshaft upright on power head stand in vise.

Crankshaft Disassembly
(Inline Engines Except 1987-on 70-115 hp)

1. Remove the piston rings with expander tool part No. C-91-24697 (**Figure 33**).

2. Remove both piston pin lockrings with lockring remover (part No. C-91-52952A1). See **Figure 34**. Discard lockrings.

8

29

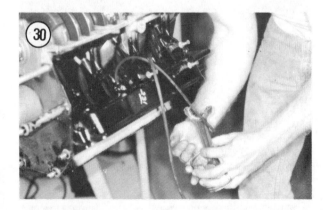

30

31

32

3. Number pistons with an indelible felt marker to match connecting rod position (**Figure 35**).

> *WARNING*
> *The lamp used in Step 4 throws off an intense light. Wear the glasses included with the lamp and do not look directly at the lamp. Wear an asbestos glove to handle the piston or wrap it in several folds of shop cloths.*

4. Use torch lamp (part No. C-91-63209) and heat piston dome to approximately 190° F. See **Figure 36**. This should take 60-90 seconds. Turn lamp off and place it out of the way.

5. Immediately support the piston/connecting rod and drive pin from piston with a hammer and pin tool part No. C-91-76159A1 or equivalent.

> *NOTE*
> *Cleanliness is absolutely essential in Step 6. Do not get dirt or lint on the needle bearings.*

6. Remove the piston from the connecting rod. Remove the locating washers and needle bearings (**Figure 37**). Store bearings in clean

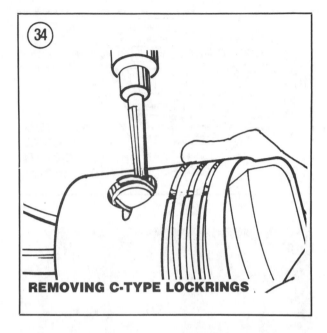

REMOVING C-TYPE LOCKRINGS

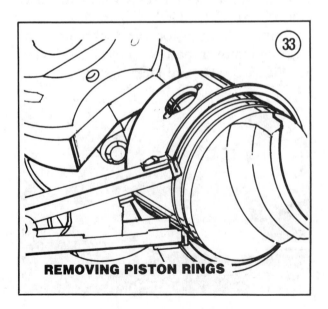

REMOVING PISTON RINGS

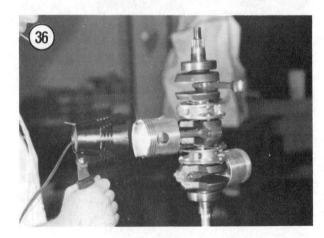

numbered containers corresponding to the piston/rod number for reinstallation.

7. Remove connecting rod nuts/bolts. Carefully remove rod cap, then remove the bearings and cages (**Figure 38**). Store bearings and cages in clean numbered containers corresponding to the rod number for reinstallation.

NOTE
*Two types of connecting rods are used. Early models use a machined cap style of rod. Late models use a cracked cap design in which the rod is frozen during manufacture and the large end broken to produce a unique match between cap and rod (**Figure 39**). The cracked cap style rod supercedes the machined cap style and can be used in its place. Do not, however, use a machined cap rod in a power head normally fitted with the cracked cap rod.*

8. Reinstall cap to rod to prevent any mixup.

NOTE
Steps 9-11 apply only to Merc 500, 45, 50, 60, 650, 700 and 70 models.

9. Remove the Phillips head screw on each side of the reed valve/main bearing assembly (**Figure 40**).

10. Tap the solid section of the reed cage to separate the 2 sections, then remove the assembly carefully to prevent damage to the reed valves. Temporarily reassemble to prevent mismatch during engine reassembly.

8

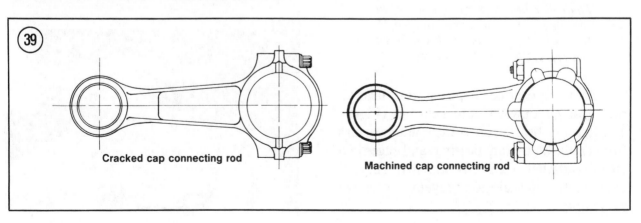

Cracked cap connecting rod

Machined cap connecting rod

NOTE
The roller bearings are free when the bearing races are separated in Step 11. Do not lose any rollers in this step or a new set will have to be installed.

11. Pry main bearing snap ring from bearing race grooves upward onto bearings. Remove bearing outer races and bearings from crankshaft. Store bearings and cages in a clean container. Carefully slip snap ring off crankshaft journal to prevent excessive stretching.

NOTE
Steps 12-16 apply to all other Merc inline engines.

12. Remove the Phillips head screw on each side of the center main bearing supports (**Figure 41**).

13. Separate and remove the center main bearing supports (**Figure 42**). Reassemble to prevent mismatch during reassembly.

14. Remove the Phillips head screw on each side of the reed valve/main bearing assembly.

15. Tap the solid section of the reed cage to separate the 2 sections, then remove the assembly carefully to prevent damage to the reed valves. See **Figure 43**. Temporarily reassemble to prevent mismatch during engine reassembly.

NOTE
The roller bearings are free when the bearing races are separated in Step 16. Do not lose any rollers in this step or a new set will have to be installed.

16. Pry main bearing snap ring from bearing race grooves upward onto bearings (**Figure 44**). Remove bearing outer races and bearings from crankshaft. Store bearings and cages in a clean container. Carefully slip snap ring off crankshaft journal to prevent excessive stretching.

NOTE
Step 17 applies to all engines. Do not remove bearing unless it is defective.

17. If crankshaft end bearing requires replacement, remove it with a universal bearing puller plate and arbor press.

**Crankshaft Disassembly
(1987-on 70-115 hp)**

1. Number pistons with an indelible felt marker to match connecting rod position.

2. Scribe an identification mark on each cylinder's connecting rod and cap so that components will be matched during reassembly and installed on the correct crankcase journal.

3. Remove each connecting rod and piston assembly from crankshaft journals one assembly at a time.

4. Loosen connecting rod cap bolts and remove cap, bearings and bearing cage. Remove connecting rod and piston assembly

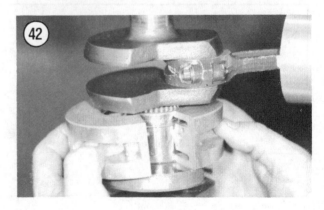

with bearings and bearing cage. Keep all components together.

CAUTION
Each connecting rod and rod cap is a matched machined set and should not be mismatched.

CAUTION
Connecting rod cap bolts should be replaced during reassembly procedure.

5. Remove the piston rings with expander tool part No. C-91-24697.
6. Remove both piston pin lockrings. Discard lockrings.
7. Support the piston/connecting rod assembly and drive pin from piston with a hammer and pin tool part No. 91-74607A2 or equivalent. Note which side of connecting rod faces toward "UP" stamped on piston crown and scribe on connecting rod.

NOTE
Cleanliness is absolutely essential in Step 8. Do not get dirt or lint on the needle bearings.

8. Remove the piston from the connecting rod. Remove the locating washers and needle bearings (29 needle bearings). Store bearings in clean numbered containers corresponding to the piston/rod number for reinstallation.
9. Repeat Steps 5-8 to remove each remaining piston from its connecting rod.

NOTE
The crankshaft center main roller bearings are free when the bearing races are separated in Step 10. Do not lose any rollers in this step or a new set will have to be installed.

10. Remove the retaining ring from one center main bearing race (A, **Figure 45**, typical). Remove bearing races and roller bearings from crankshaft journal. Store bearings and race halves in a clean container for reinstallation on the same journal. Repeat this step to remove the remaining crankshaft center main roller bearings.
11. Check oil injection pump drive gear. Do not remove gear from crankshaft unless it is damaged. If removal is necessary, refer to Step 12 and press lower main ball bearing from crankshaft end for access to drive gear.

NOTE
Do not remove the lower main ball bearing unless bearing or oil injection pump drive gear is defective.

12. To remove lower main ball bearing, remove snap ring and press bearing from shaft with a universal bearing puller and arbor press.

8

Crankshaft Disassembly (V6 Engine)

CAUTION
*Early V6 engines use a 3-ring piston that cannot be reused if removed from the connecting rod. Unless the piston, piston pin or connecting rod must be replaced, **do not** remove a 3-ring piston from its connecting rod.*

1. Number pistons with an indelible felt marker to match connecting rod position.
2. Remove the piston rings with expander tool part No. C-91-24697.
3. Remove both piston pin lockrings with lockring remover (part No. C-91-52952A1). Discard lockrings.

WARNING
The lamp used in Step 4 throws off an intense light. Wear the glasses included with the lamp and do not look directly at the lamp. Wear an asbestos glove to handle the piston or wrap it in several folds of shop cloths.

4. Use torch lamp (part No. C-91-63209) and heat piston dome to approximately 190° F. This should take 60-90 seconds. Turn lamp off and place it out of the way.

NOTE
The pin used with a 3-ring piston is slightly tapered. The pin hole on the piston side marked "UP" on the pin boss is slightly smaller than the other side. The pin must be removed and installed from this side.

5. Immediately support the piston/connecting rod and drive pin from piston with a hammer and pin tool part No. C-91-76159A1 or equivalent.

NOTE
Cleanliness is absolutely essential in Step 6. Do not get dirt or lint on the needle bearings.

6. Remove the piston from the connecting rod. Remove the locating washers and needle

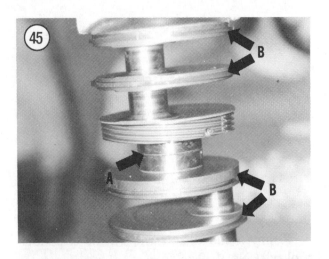

bearings. Store bearings in clean numbered containers corresponding to the piston/rod number for reinstallation.
7. Repeat Steps 3-6 to remove each remaining piston from its connecting rod.

NOTE
The roller bearings are free when the bearing races are separated in Step 8. Do not lose any rollers in this step or a new set will have to be installed.

8. Remove the bearing retaining ring (A, **Figure 45**) from the upper main bearing race. Remove bearing races and roller bearings from crankshaft journal. Store bearings and race in a clean container for reinstallation on

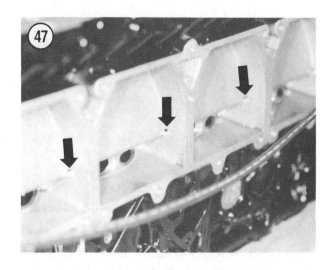

the same journal. Repeat this step to remove the lower main bearing.

9. Check but do not remove crankshaft sealing rings (B, **Figure 45**). Sealing rings do not require replacement unless broken.

10. Check oil injection pump drive gear (if so equipped). Do not remove gear from crankshaft unless it is damaged. If removal is necessary, loosen gear retaining screw (**Figure 46**), spread gear at split and remove from crankshaft. Discard retaining screw.

NOTE
Do not remove the crankshaft end bearing in Step 10 unless it is defective.

11. If crankshaft end bearing requires replacement, remove snap ring and press bearing from shaft with a universal bearing puller and arbor press.

Cleaning and Inspection
(Cylinder Block and Crankcase Cover)

The Merc outboard cylinder block and crankcase cover are a matched, line-bored assembly. For this reason, you should not attempt to assemble an engine with parts salvaged from other blocks. If the following inspection procedure indicates that the block and cover requires replacement, replace as an assembly.

1. Clean cylinder block, heads and crankcase/exhaust cover thoroughly with solvent and a brush.

2. Carefully remove all gasket and sealant residue from mating surfaces.

3. Check exhaust ports and remove any carbon deposits or varnish with a carbon remover solution or a fine wire brush and electric drill.

4. Check block, heads and covers for cracks, fractures, stripped bolt or spark plug holes or other damage.

5. Inspect gasket mating surfaces for nicks, grooves, cracks or distortion. Any of these defects will cause compression leakage.

6. Check all water and oil passages in the block and cover for obstructions. Make sure plugs are properly and tightly installed.

NOTE
Restrictors should be removed from the transfer bleed holes if it is necessary to submerge the cover/block in a strong cleaning solvent. Be sure to install new restrictors after cleaning.

7. Inspect the transfer port bleed holes (except Merc 45, 500 and 50 [prior to 1986]) to make sure the restrictors (**Figure 47**) are in place and in good condition (the bottom cylinder does not use a restrictor). Missing restrictors will cause cylinder flooding and affect idle operation.

NOTE
Merc V200 and V225 engines have chrome cylinder bores which cannot be salvaged by honing or reboring by the amateur mechanic or dealers. Step 8 and Step 9 apply to models other than those with chrome bores.

8. Check the cylinder bores (except Merc 175 [1985-on] V200 and V225) for any signs of aluminum transfer from the pistons to the cylinder walls. If such "scoring" is not excessive, have the bores honed or rebored by a dealer or qualified machine shop.

8

9. Measure cylinder bore diameter with an inside micrometer. Take 4 measurements near the top of bore and 45° from each other. If cylinder bore is tapered, worn or out-of-round more than 0.006 (V6) or 0.003-0.004 (inline), rebore the cylinder to 0.015 in. oversize and install oversize piston/rings during reassembly. If inline engine bore(s) are tapered, worn or out-of-round more than 0.015 in. from the standard cylinder block finish hone diameter (**Table 4**), replace the block and cover.

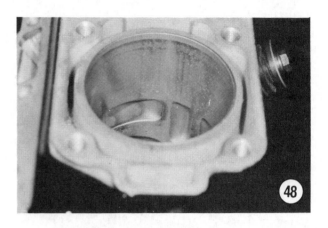

> *NOTE*
> *Steps 10-12 apply to Merc V175 (1985-on), V200 and V225 models, which have chrome cylinder bores. Chrome cylinder bores have a porous appearance (**Figure 48**). Do not mistake this for cylinder damage.*

10. Check Merc V175 (1985-on), V200 and V225 cylinder bores for signs of flaking, grooving, scoring or other damage. Mercury Marine provides a replating surface as long as the damage is no greater than 0.005 in. deep. If bore damage exceeds 0.005 in., a cast iron cylinder sleeve kit containing the sleeve and 2 special piston rings is available for local installation. Contact your Mercury dealer for cost and installation information.

11. If Merc V175 (1985-on), V200 and V225 cylinder bore is scored with aluminum transfer from piston, clean loose deposits from bore with a stiff bristle brush. Apply a small quantity of muriatic acid (or toilet bowl cleaner) on aluminum deposits. A bubbling action indicates that the aluminum is being removed. Wait 1-2 minutes and wash cylinder thoroughly with hot water and detergent. Repeat this procedure until deposits are gone, then lightly oil cylinder walls to prevent rusting.

12. Check cylinder for out-of-round condition with an inside micrometer. Take 4 measurements at top of bore and 45° from

each other. If measurements indicate cylinder is out-of-round by more than 0.006 in., replace the block and cover.

13. On 1987-on 70-115 hp models, inspect check valves located in crankcase cover beneath center main roller bearings. If no ball is noted or ball sticks in brass casing then check valve is defective and must be replaced. Check valve is driven from cover by tapping with a hammer and punch forward inside of cover. When installing valve, the single hole faces toward inside of cover.

Cleaning and Inspection (Pistons)

1. Check pistons for signs of scoring, cracking, cracked or worn piston pin bosses or metal damage. Replace piston and pin if any of these defects are noted.

2. Check piston ring grooves for distortion, loose ring locating pins and excessive wear. If flex action of the rings has not kept the lower surface of the ring grooves carbon-free, clean with a bristle brush and solvent.

> *NOTE*
> *Do not use an automotive ring groove cleaning tool in Step 3 as it can damage the piston ring locating pin. V6 pistons may have tapered or rectangular ring grooves. Determine which type of grooves the piston has and use a piece of the same type ring as a cleaning tool in Step 3.*

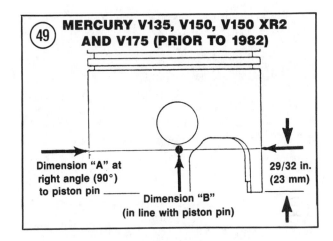

MERCURY V135, V150, V150 XR2 AND V175 (PRIOR TO 1982)

Dimension "A" at right angle (90°) to piston pin

Dimension "B" (in line with piston pin)

29/32 in. (23 mm)

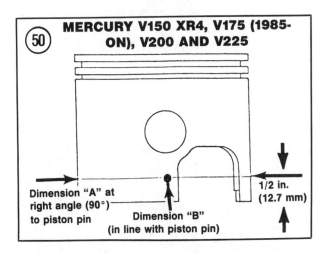

MERCURY V150 XR4, V175 (1985-ON), V200 AND V225

Dimension "A" at right angle (90°) to piston pin

Dimension "B" (in line with piston pin)

1/2 in. (12.7 mm)

3. Clean piston skirt, grooves and dome with the recessed end of a broken ring to remove any carbon deposits.

4. Immerse pistons in a carbon removal solution to remove any carbon deposits. If the solution does not remove all of the carbon, carefully use a fine wire brush and avoid burring or rounding the machined edges. Polish piston skirt with crocus cloth.

5A. Inline pistons—Measure piston skirt and top diameters with a micrometer. Compare to specifications in **Table 5**.

NOTE
V6 pistons have a barrel profile.

5B. Merc V135/V150/V150 XR2/V175 (prior to 1982)—Measure piston diameter at the points shown in **Figure 49**. Dimension "A" should be:

a. Standard piston—3.115 ± 0.002 in.
b. 0.015 in. oversize piston—3.130 ± 0.002 in.
c. 0.030 in. oversize piston—3/145 ± 0.002 in.

Dimension B should be within 0.008 in. of dimension A for all pistons. If not, replace piston/pin assembly.

5C. Merc V150 XR4/V175 (1985-on)/V200 and V225—Measure piston diameter at the points shown in **Figure 50**. Dimension A should be 3.372 ± 0.002 in. Dimension B should be within 0.008 in. of dimension A. If not, replace piston/pin assembly.

Cleaning and Inspection
(Connecting Rods)

1. Check connecting rod straightness. Place each rod/cap assembly on a smooth, flat surface and press downward on rod. The rod should not wobble under pressure. Try inserting a 0.002 in. flat feeler gauge between the machined portion of the rod and the flat surface. If it fits, replace the rod.

2. Check connecting rod bearings for rust or bearing failure.

3. Check the connecting rod big and small end bearing surfaces for rust, water marks, spalling, chatter marks, heat discoloration and excessive/uneven wear.

4. Slight defects noted in Step 3 may be cleaned up as follows:

a. Reassemble connecting rod cap to rod end with etch marks aligned. Tighten cap bolts securely.

b. If connecting rod uses a caged roller bearing, clean bearing surfaces with crocus cloth.

c. If connecting rod uses uncaged bearings, clean bearing surfaces with 320 grit carborundum cloth.

d. Clean piston pin bearing surfaces with 320 grit carborundum cloth.

e. Wash connecting rod thoroughly in solvent to remove any abrasive grit,

8

then recheck the bearing surface condition.

f. Replace any rod/cap assembly that does not clean up properly.

g. Lightly oil bearing surfaces of rod/cap assemblies that will be reused.

Cleaning and Inspection (Crankshaft)

1. Check splines on drive shaft end of crankshaft for damage or wear. Replace as required.

2. Check crankshaft oil seal surfaces for grooving, pitting or scratches.

3. Check crankshaft bearing surfaces for rust, water marks, chatter marks and excessive or uneven wear. Minor rust and water or chatter marks may be cleaned up with 320 grit carborundum cloth (Merc 45, 500 and 50 [prior to 1986]) or crocus cloth (all others).

4. If 320 grit or crocus cloth is used, clean crankshaft and bearing in solvent and recheck surfaces. If they did not clean up properly, replace the crankshaft. If the crankshaft can be reused, lightly oil crankshaft (not the bearing) to prevent rust.

5. Grasp inner race of crankshaft ball bearing and try to work it back and forth. Replace bearing if excessive play is noted.

6. Lightly oil bearing and rotate outer race. Replace bearing if it feels or sounds rough or does not rotate smoothly.

CAUTION
Do not replace individual bearings in Step 7. If any roller bearing requires replacement, replace them all.

7. Clean center main roller bearings with solvent. Check bearings for signs of rust, galling or discoloration. Replace bearings if any of these defects are noted or if they are fractured or worn.

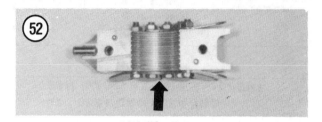

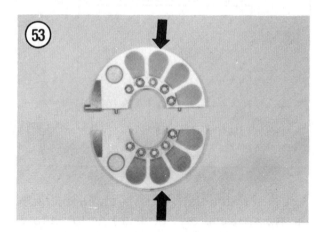

Cleaning and Inspection (Inline Engine Reed Blocks [Except 1987-on 70-115 hp])

1. Clean reed blocks and reeds thoroughly with solvent.

NOTE
Locating pins that have been subjected to overheating will adversely affect starting, idle and overall engine operation.

2. Merc 45, 500, 50, 60, 650, 700 and 70 (prior to 1984)—Check condition of nylon locating pins in reed block halves (**Figure 51**). If pin condition is not perfect, replace reed block.

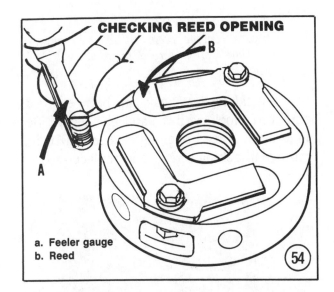

CHECKING REED OPENING

a. Feeler gauge
b. Reed

(54)

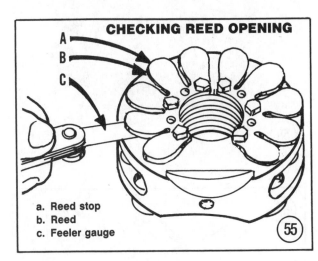

CHECKING REED OPENING

a. Reed stop
b. Reed
c. Feeler gauge

(55)

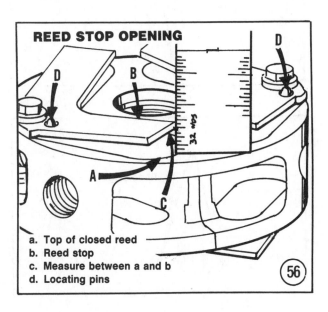

REED STOP OPENING

a. Top of closed reed
b. Reed stop
c. Measure between a and b
d. Locating pins

(56)

3. Check reed block crankshaft journal surface (**Figure 52**) for wear or damage.

4. Assemble reed block halves with screws and nuts.

5. Check each reed block face for indentations indicating wear. If reeds have indented the surface of the block, replace entire assembly.

6. Check for chipped or broken reeds. See **Figure 51** (Merc 45, 500, 50, 60, 650, 700 and 70 [prior to 1984] or **Figure 53** (all others).

NOTE
Always replace reeds in sets. Never turn a reed over for reuse.

7. Check gap between reeds and reed block with a flat feeler gauge. See **Figure 54** (Merc 45, 500, 50, 60, 650, 700 and 70 [prior to 1984] or **Figure 55** (all others). Replace reeds if they are pre-loaded (adhere tightly to reed block) or if gap exceeds 0.007 in.

8. check each reed stop opening:
   a. Merc 45, 500, 50, 60, 650, 700 and 70 (prior to 1984)—Measure from inside of reed stop to top of closed reed as shown in **Figure 56**. If reed stop opening is not 5/32 in. (Merc 45, 500 and 50) or 0.180 in. (Merc 60, 650, 700 and 70 [prior to 1984], carefully bend reed stop to bring opening within specification.
   b. All others—Measure from bottom of reed stop to top of closed reed (**Figure 57**). If reed stop opening is not 0.162 in., carefully bend reed stop to bring opening within specification.

9. If new reeds are installed, tighten retaining screws to specifications (**Table 1** or **Table 2**) and repeat Step 7.

**Cleaning and Inspection
(1987-on 70-115 hp Reed Blocks)**

The reed plate assembly is located between the intake manifold and the lower crankcase half. Do not disassemble reed valve assembly unless replacement of part is required. If

8

disassembly is required, heat may have to be applied to center bolt to ease removal procedure as Loctite was spread on bolt threads during factory installation.

CAUTION
If reed petals do not lay flat on reed plate, do not reverse reed petal assembly. Petals may brake off assembly's center hub causing serious damage to engine. Always install a new reed petal assembly.

Reed petals should not stand open more than 0.020 in. and no damage should be noted. If so, replace reed petal assembly. Center bolt should be tightened to 60 in.-lb. and tab on tab washer should be bent against bolt's head to retain torque setting.

Cleaning and Inspection (V6 Engine Reed Blocks)

1. Clean gasket surfaces of reed blocks and reed block housing thoroughly.
2. Check reed blocks and housing for distortion, cracks, deep grooves or any other defect that could cause leakage. Replace as necessary.
3. Check each reed block face for indentations indicating wear. If reeds have indented the surface of the block, replace entire assembly.
4. Check for chipped or broken reeds. See **Figure 58** (5-petal type reed shown).

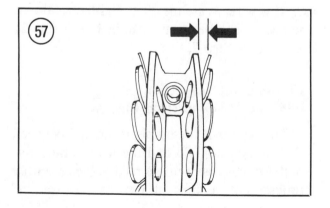

NOTE
Always replace reeds in sets. Never continue using a reed by turning it over.

5A. 5-petal type—Check gap between reeds and reed block with a flat feeler gauge. See **Figure 59**. If reed opening exceeds 0.020 in., remove attaching screws and replace reed.

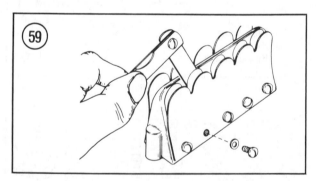

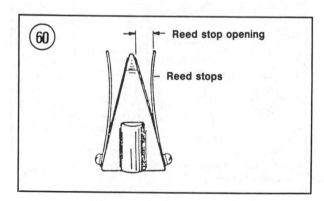

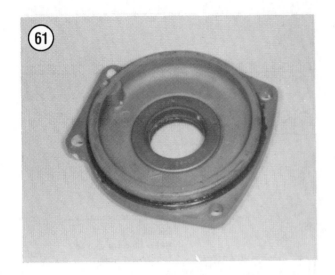

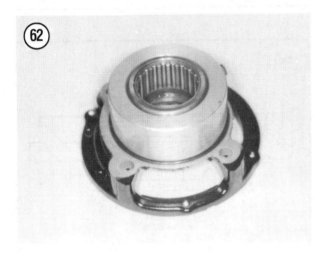

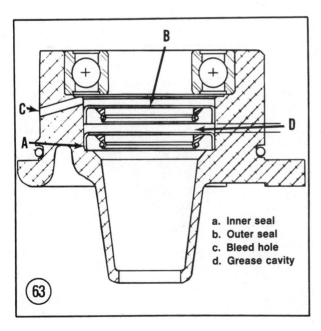

a. Inner seal
b. Outer seal
c. Bleed hole
d. Grease cavity

5B. 7-petal type—These are preloaded and must seat tightly against reed block. Replace reed if standing open.

6. If reed block is fitted with stops, measure reed stop opening as shown in **Figure 60**. It should be 0.200 in. (V150) or 0.300 in. (V175 and V200).

Cleaning and Inspection
(End Caps)

When an upper end cap bearing failure occurs on any Merc 4- or 6-cylinder inline engine, replace the upper end cap and bearing as an assembly. A loose end cap bearing may damage the bore and cause premature failing of a new bearing. See **Figure 61** (lower) and **Figure 62** (upper) for typical end caps.

1. Drive oil seal from each end cap with a punch. Discard seal.

2. Remove and discard end cap O-ring(s).

NOTE
Not all models use a lower end cap bearing. If upper cap bearing is defective on Merc V6 serial No. 5464486 and on (U.S.) or serial No. 8063935 and on (Australia), replace cap and bearing as an assembly.

3. Clean upper and lower end caps in solvent. As equipped, move bearing inner race in and out to check for excessive end play. Lubricate bearing with light oil and rotate outer race. If bearing sounds noisy or feels rough, remove from end cap with a suitable mandrel and an arbor press.

4. Wipe OD of new seal(s) with Loctite Type A (part No. C-92-32609).

5. As equipped, place oil seal in upper end cap with lip facing the bearing and press into place with an appropriate mandrel.

6A. Merc 45, 500, 50, 60, 650, 700 and 70 (prior to 1984)—Press lower end cap seal in place as shown in **Figure 63**. Inner seal lip should face inside of cylinder block; outer

8

seal lip should face outside of block. Top of second seal should be positioned just under the end cap bleed hole. Fill the space between the seals with Quicksilver Multipurpose Lubricant (part No. C-92-63250).

6B. 1987-on 70-115 hp—Press lower end cap seal in place with inner seal lip facing toward inside of cylinder block.

6C. All other inline—Press seal in upper end cap until it bottoms. Press outer seal in lower end cap with lip facing outside cylinder block. Press inner seal in lower end cap with lip facing inside block.

6D. Merc V6—Press seal in upper end cap with lip facing down until flush with top of end cap. See **Figure 64**. Press both seals in lower end cap with their lips facing down. See **Figure 65**.

7. Remove any excess Loctite. Lubricate seal lips with multipurpose lubricant.

8. Install a new O-ring on each end cap. Lubricate O-ring with multipurpose lubricant.

Cleaning and Inspection (Thermostat)

> *NOTE*
> *Some owners remove the thermostat from V6 engines and plug the block outlet hole with a pipe plug thinking this improves engine cooling. This is not true. The vent hole in the thermostat valve provides an escape path for a steam pocket if the engine gets low on water.*

1. Clean all gasket residue from thermostat and cylinder head covers.

2. Check covers for cracks or corrosion damage. Replace as required.

3. Wash thermostat (**Figure 66**) with clean water.

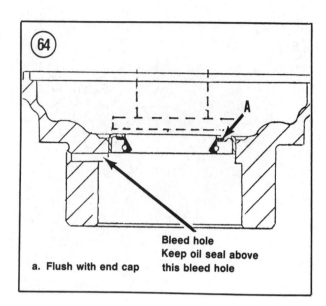

64

A

Bleed hole
Keep oil seal above
this bleed hole

a. Flush with end cap

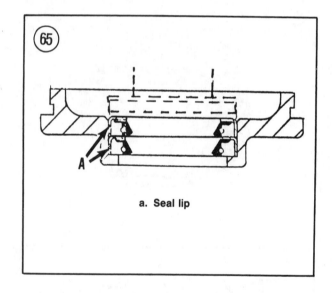

65

A

a. Seal lip

66

4. Suspend the thermostat and a thermometer in a container of water that can be heated. See **Figure 67**.

NOTE
Support the thermostat with wire so it does not touch the sides or bottom of the container.

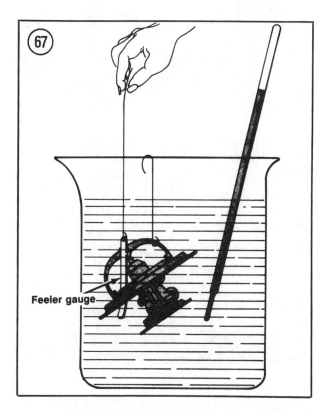

Feeler gauge

5. Heat the water and note the temperature at which the thermostat starts to open. It should be approximately 140-145° F (60-63° C). If not, replace the thermostat.

Crankshaft Assembly (Inline Engines [Except 1987-on 70-115 hp])

1. Apply a thick coat of multipurpose lubricant (part No. C-92-63250) on inside of main bearing journal. Install needle bearings on journal. Some crankshafts have a single row of bearings; others use a double row. **Figure 68** shows the double row with one bearing race installed.

2. Install bearing races on crankshaft. Install bearing race snap ring and make sure it fits into groove in race. Slide race up and insert the pointed end of an awl between the bearings at the bottom of the race halves. If the race halves separate, the correct number of bearings have been installed. On double bearing installations, slide race down and insert the awl point between the bearings at the top of the race to check the second row.

NOTE
Some main bearing supports will have the word "TOP" stamped in the support. Install the support in Step 3 with the word facing the flywheel end.

3. Install main bearing support with the oil bleed hole side facing flywheel end of crankshaft. Locating pin inside support must fit into hole in bearing race. See **Figure 69**.

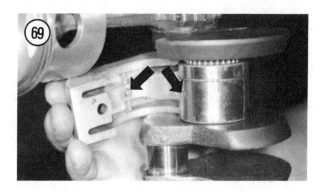

8

4. Tighten bearing support lock screws to specifications (**Table 1** or **Table 3**).

5. Wipe reed block inner bores with multipurpose lubricant. Install reed block halves to crankshaft. **Figure 70** shows one half installed. Align locating pins and holes in reed blocks and tighten fasteners to specifications (**Table 1** or **Table 3**).

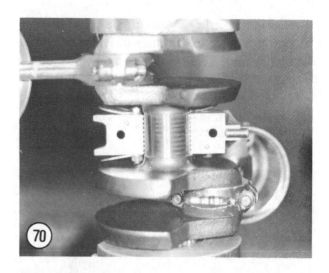

> *CAUTION*
> *Always use new connecting rod locknuts and bolts during reassembly.*

6. Clean new connecting rod bolts and locknuts with solvent. Dry with compressed air.

7. Remove rod caps from connecting rods. Discard bolts and locknuts. Work with one rod at a time.

> *NOTE*
> *Steps 8-12 apply to uncaged bearings only.*

8. Apply a thick coat of multipurpose lubricant on connecting rod crankpin bore (big end) and rod cap to hold needle bearings in position.

9. Divide the needle bearings that go with the rod you are working with into equal groups. There should be one bearing left over. Place one group of bearings around connecting rod bearing surface. Place the other group of bearings in the connecting rod cap.

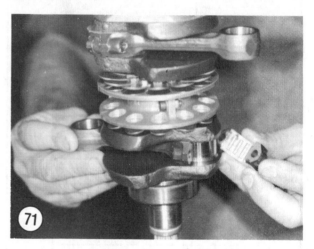

> *NOTE*
> *Make sure that connecting rod and rod cap marks are aligned as cap is installed to rod in Step 10.*

10. Carefully install connecting rod to crankpin, positioning the remaining bearing between crankpin and connecting rod bearing surface. Install cap, taking care not to disturb the bearings.

11. Install new cap bolts and locknuts, then tighten to specifications (**Table 1** or **Table 3**).

12. Spread needle bearings apart with a bent paper clip. If the correct number of bearings have been installed, they should spread the width of one bearing. Rotate connecting rod on crankpin to check for free and smooth movement. If movement is rough, remove and check bearing and race.

> *NOTE*
> *Steps 13-16 apply to caged bearings only.*

13. Apply a thick coat of multipurpose lubricant on the connecting rod crankpin bore (big end) and the rod cap to hold bearings and cages in place.

14. Install a cage in the rod crankpin bore and place a bearing in each cage slot. Repeat this step with the rod cap.

NOTE
Make sure that connecting rod and rod cap marks are aligned as cap is installed to rod in Step 15.

15. Carefully install connecting rod to crankpin. Install cap, taking care not to disturb the bearings. See **Figure 71**.

16. Install new cap bolts and locknuts, then tighten to specifications (**Table 1** or **Table 3**).

NOTE
The remaining steps apply to all installations.

17. Repeat Steps 8-12 (needle bearings) or Steps 13-16 (caged bearings) to install the remaining connecting rods.

18. Place a piece of clean paper on the workbench. Align the needle bearings removed from one piston/pin assembly in a row.

19. Install the sleeve on piston pin tool (part No. C-91-52395A1) and coat it liberally with multipurpose lubricant.

20. Roll the sleeve end of the tool over the aligned bearings. This should pick up the bearings evenly around the sleeve. If it does not, see Step 22.

21. Position the lower locating washer under the connecting rod bearing bore. Slide sleeve with attached bearings up through the washer and into the rod bore.

22. If the sleeve did not pick up all the bearings in Step 20, insert the remaining ones now. Position the upper locating washer over the piston pin tool sleeve and slide tool out of sleeve. The sleeve and washers will hold the bearings in the rod bore.

23. Install piston on connecting rod with intake side facing to the right. Align piston pin bore with sleeve, then slide pin tool through the upper pin bore and into the sleeve.

24. Lubricate the piston pin with Quicksilver Formula 50-D oil (part No. C-92-65183).

WARNING
The lamp used in Step 25 throws off an intense light. Wear the glasses provided with the lamp and do not look directly at the lamp. Wear an asbestos glove to handle the piston or wrap it in several folds of shop cloths.

8

25. Heat piston dome to approximately 190° F (88° C) with torch lamp (part No. C-91-63209).

26. Insert piston pin in lower piston boss. Insert piston pin tool through upper piston boss and into the sleeve. Hold piston pin tool with one hand and drive pin into bore with a mallet until tool and sleeve are driven out.

27A. Merc 45, 500 and 50 (prior to 1986)—Install G type lockrings in each end of piston bore with needle nose pliers. Make sure lockrings seat in their grooves.

27B. All others — Fit a C type lockring inside installer end of lockring tool part No. C-91-77109A1 (Merc 50 [3-cyl.], 60, 650, 700, and 70 [prior to 1984]) or part No. C-91-60837A1 (Merc 800-up) with needle nose pliers as shown in **Figure 72**. Assemble tool and insert in piston pin bore. Support piston with one hand and press installer handle downward quickly. See **Figure 73**. The tool will automatically expel the lockring into the piston pin bore groove. Repeat this step to install the other lockring, supporting piston with one hand and pushing installer upward quickly.

28. Repeat Steps 18-27 to install each remaining piston to its connecting rod.

29. Install piston rings on each piston with ring expander (part No. C-91-24697).

30. Lubricate piston rings with Quicksilver Formula 50-D oil and align ring ends with locating pin in each ring groove.

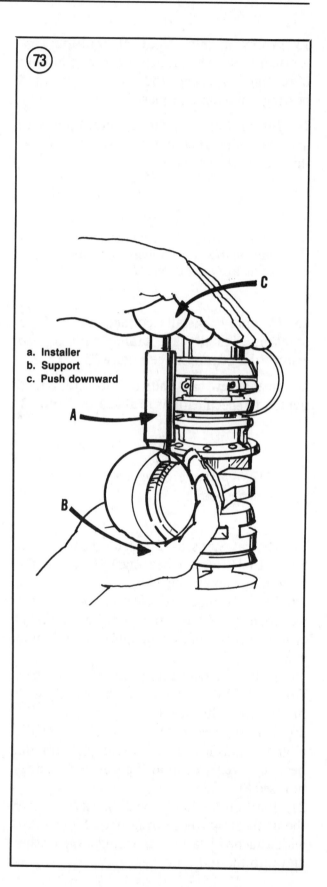

a. Installer
b. Support
c. Push downward

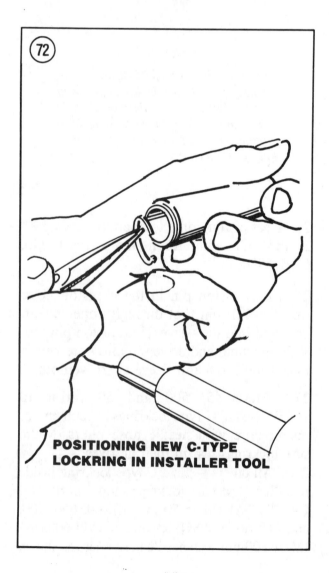

POSITIONING NEW C-TYPE
LOCKRING IN INSTALLER TOOL

Crankshaft Assembly
(1987-on 70-115 hp)

1. If oil injection pump drive gear was replaced, install drive gear on crankshaft with gear keyway and crankshaft key aligned.

2. Press lower main ball bearing onto crankshaft and secure with snap ring.

3. Each center main journal contains 2 seal rings. Replace seal rings if damage is noted and position ring gaps 180° apart.

4. Apply a liberal quantity of Quicksilver Needle Bearing Assembly Lubricant (part No. C-92-42649A-1) onto one crankshaft center main journal. Install roller bearings (32 each center main bearing) around crankshaft main journal. Install bearing races and secure with retaining ring. Repeat this step to install the remaining crankshaft center main roller bearings.

5. Place a piece of clean paper on the workbench. Align the needle bearings (29

needle bearings) removed from one piston/pin assembly in a row. Liberally coat the needle bearings with Quicksilver Needle Bearing Assembly Lubricant (part No. C-92-42649A-1).

6. Install sleeve portion of piston pin tool (part No. 91-74607A1) into connecting rod. Center tool in rod opening.

7. Install needle bearings around sleeve.

8. Position locating washers on connecting rod then install piston over connecting rod. Make sure same side of connecting rod, noted during disassembly, faces toward "UP" stamped on piston crown.

9. Insert smaller diameter end of piston pin tool (part No. 91-74607A1) through piston pin opening in piston and push out sleeve portion of tool.

10. Position piston pin on small diameter end of piston pin tool, then use a soft-faced mallet and drive piston pin into piston while driving out piston pin tool from the opposite side.

11. Fit a C type lockring inside installer end of lockring tool (part No. C-91-77109A1) with needle nose pliers as shown in **Figure 72**.

12. Assemble tool and insert in piston pin bore (**Figure 77**). Hold piston/rod assembly with one hand and press installer handle downward quickly. The tool will automatically expel the lockring into the piston pin bore groove. Turn piston over in support block and repeat this step to install the other lockring.

13. Repeat Steps 5-12 to install each remaining piston to its connecting rod.

14. Install the new piston rings onto the pistons with the side stamped with a "T" facing toward piston crown.

15. Make sure rings rotate freely in their grooves. Align each ring gap with the ring groove locating pin.

16. Match each piston with the cylinder from which it was removed.

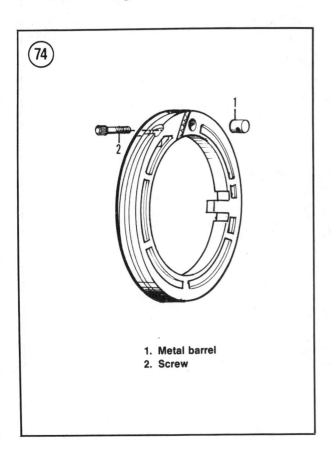

(74)

1. Metal barrel
2. Screw

8

17. Install pistons into respective cylinder bores with "UP" on piston crown facing toward flywheel end of crankshaft.

18. Insert a thin screwdriver blade through the exhaust port of each cylinder and depress each piston ring. If the ring does not return to position when the screwdriver is removed, it was probably broken during installation. Remove that piston and check ring condition.

19. Apply a liberal amount of Quicksilver Needle Bearing Assembly Lubricant (part No. C-92-42649A-1) on the rod bearing surface of each connecting rod. Install each connecting rod's bearing cage and rollers.

20. Make sure that all locating pins in the block are properly installed. If not, install new pins in block.

21. Position the center main bearing races so that the holes in the races are aligned with one edge of the cylinder block. Make a mark at the exact top of the bearing with a grease pencil, then rotate each race until the grease mark is aligned with the same cylinder block edge. This will position each race hole very close to where it should be to engage its block locating pin when the crankshaft is installed.

22. Carefully lower crankshaft into place in the block with the drive shaft end facing the drive shaft end of the block. Gently push crankshaft into place, rotating main bearing races slightly as required to engage the race holes with the locating pins.

23. Apply a liberal amount of Quicksilver Needle Bearing Assembly Lubricant (part

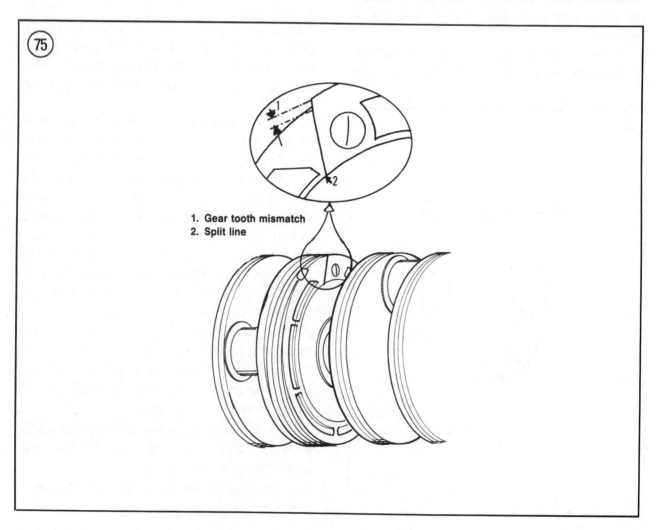

1. Gear tooth mismatch
2. Split line

No. C-92-42649A-1) on the crankshaft rod bearing surfaces.

24. Pull each connecting rod assembly into position on respective crankshaft journal, then install remaining bearing cages and rollers onto correct crankshaft journal.

25. Install each connecting rod cap on respective connecting rod making sure the rod and cap alignment mark (scribed during disassembly) align.

26. Refer to **Table 2** and tighten connecting rod cap bolts.

Crankshaft Assembly (V6 Engines)

1. If one or more sealing rings were removed, expand new ring(s) just enough to fit around crankshaft journal. Install ring(s) in crankshaft groove(s) with ring expander (part No. C-91-24697).

2. If oil injection pump drive gear was removed from crankshaft:

   a. Heat new gear in hot water for about 4 minutes, then dry gear.

   b. Spread gear at split. Install on crankshaft with lip facing crankshaft top. Gear lip should fit in crankshaft groove. Gear locating pin must fit in crankshaft slot.

   c. Install metal barrel in gear center hole, aligning barrel hole with gear hole. See **Figure 74**.

   d. Wipe retaining screw threads with Loctite Type A. Install screw and tighten to 8 in.-lb. Gear split must be drawn together completely.

   e. Measure gear tooth mismatch as shown in **Figure 75**. It should not exceed 0.030 in. or gear will fail. If mismatch is excessive, gear lip is not fully seated in crankshaft groove.

3. Apply a liberal quantity of Quicksilver Multipurpose Lubricant (part No. C-92-63250) in main bearing halves. Install bearing cages and roller bearings in bearing halves.

4. Carefully fit the bearing race halves on the crankshaft journal with the larger of the 3 holes in the race facing the drive shaft end of the crankshaft.

5. Install bearing race retaining ring. Make sure it seats fully in the race grooves.

NOTE
*This completes crankshaft assembly. The following steps will prepare the pistons for installation to the crankshaft during **Power Head Assembly**.*

6. Place a piece of clean paper on the workbench. Align the needle bearings removed from one piston/pin assembly in a row.

7. Install the sleeve on piston pin tool (part No. C-91-52395A1) and coat it liberally with multipurpose lubricant.

8. Roll the sleeve end of the tool over the aligned bearings. This should pick up the bearings evenly around the sleeve. If it does not, see Step 9.

9. Position the lower locating washer on the piston pin tool and insert the sleeve portion of tool through the connecting rod. If the sleeve did not pick up all the bearings in Step 7, insert the remaining ones now.

10. Position the upper locating washer over the piston pin tool sleeve and slide tool out of sleeve. The sleeve and washers will hold the bearings in the rod bore.

11. Lightly lubricate each piston pin with Quicksilver Formula 50-D oil (part No. C-92-65183).

12. Set piston on support block (part No. C-91-77005) with the side of the piston crown marked "UP" facing toward the block. Position block/piston assembly on an arbor press.

8

13. Hold sleeve, bearings and locating washers in place with one hand and install piston to connecting rod with the 2 alignment bumps on the crankshaft end of the rod facing in the same direction as the "UP" on the piston crown.

14. Install handle part of piston pin tool up through the hole in the bottom of the support block and into the lower piston pin boss and sleeve. See **Figure 76**.

NOTE
Use of the torch lamp (part No. C-91-63209) in Step 15 will make pin installation easier. Be sure to use the glasses furnished with the lamp and do not look directly into it. Wear an asbestos glove to handle the piston or wrap it in several folds of shop cloths.

15. Press pin into piston as far as possible with press, then insert the piston pin tool between the press and piston pin and continue pressing until pin is fully installed.

16. Fit a C type lockring inside installer end of lockring tool part No. C-91-77109A1 with needle nose pliers as shown in **Figure 72**.

17. Assemble tool and insert in piston pin bore (**Figure 77**). Hold piston/rod assembly with one hand and press installer handle downward quickly. The tool will automatically expel the lockring into the piston pin bore groove. Turn piston over in support block and repeat this step to install the other lockring.

18. Repeat Steps 5-16 to install each remaining piston to its connecting rod.

NOTE
*All V150 XR4, V175 (1985-on), V200 and V225 pistons use 2 tapered rings (**Figure 78**). V135, V150, V150 XR2 and V175 (prior to 1982) pistons may use 2 tapered rings or a tapered ring on top and a rectangular ring on the bottom (**Figure 79**). Be sure to check piston carefully and install the proper rings.*

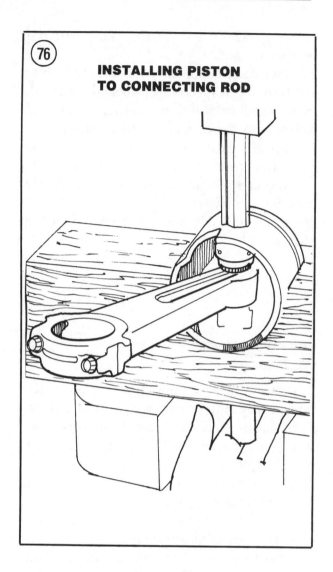

INSTALLING PISTON TO CONNECTING ROD

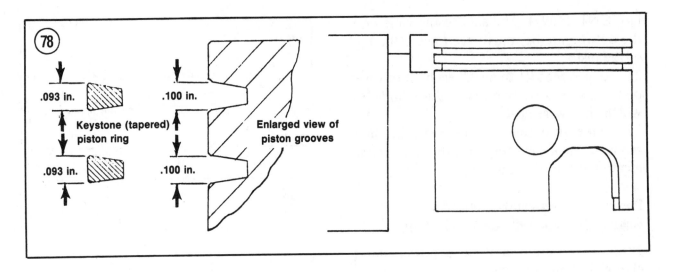

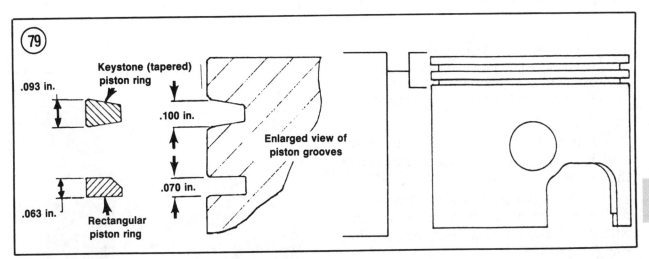

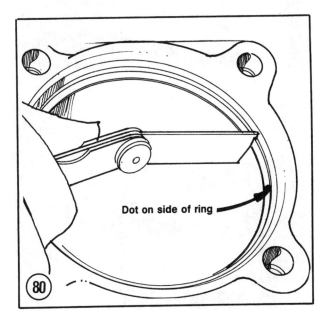

19. Insert each new piston ring (one at a time) into its respective cylinder bore. Push ring about 1/2 in. into bore with piston head. Check end gap with a flat feeler gauge as shown in **Figure 80**. It should be 0.018-0.025 in.

   a. If gap is excessive, try other rings in the cylinder until one within specifications is found.

   b. If gap is insufficient, try other rings to find one within specifications. If one cannot be found, file the piston ring end to bring the gap within specifications. Remove all rough edges after filing.

20. Install the rings checked in No. 1 cylinder on the No. 1 piston with ring expander (part

No. C-91-24697). The side of the ring with the dot (**Figure 81**) must face toward the top of the piston.

21. Repeat Step 21 to install each set of rings on the piston corresponding to the cylinder in which they were checked.

22. Make sure rings rotate freely in their grooves. Align each ring with the ring groove locating pin in the ring gap.

Power Head Assembly (Inline Engines [Except 1987-on 70-115 hp])

1. Place the crankshaft on a power stand clamped tightly in a vise.

NOTE
*Before tightening the ring compressors in Step 2 and Step 3, make sure that all piston ring end gaps are aligned with the ring groove locating pin. See **Figure 82**.*

2. Position the No. 1 and No. 2 pistons straight out from their crankpin throw and at the bottom (No. 1) and top (No. 2) of their stroke. Install straight ring compressors.

3. Position remaining pistons directly in line with No. 1 and No. 2 pistons. Install offset ring compressors.

4. Reinstall main bearing/reed cage locating pins in cylinder block, if removed.

5. Lubricate pistons, piston rings and cylinder bores with Quicksilver Formula 50-D oil (part No. C-92-65183).

6. Remove crankshaft assembly from vise with power head stand and position it over the block with the power head stand end facing the cylinder block mounting studs. See **Figure 83**.

7. Slowly lower the crankshaft assembly into the cylinder block, aligning the compressor ends with the slots in the block. Keep crankshaft horizontal and gradually ease the entire assembly in place. Remove each compressor as its piston enters the cylinder bore (**Figure 84**).

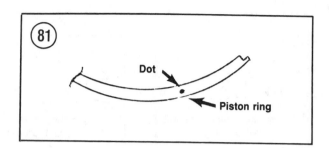

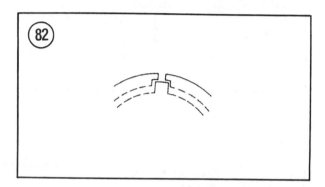

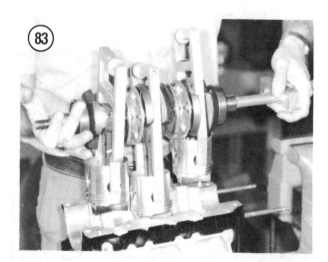

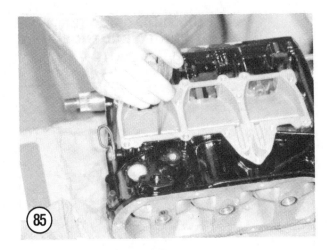

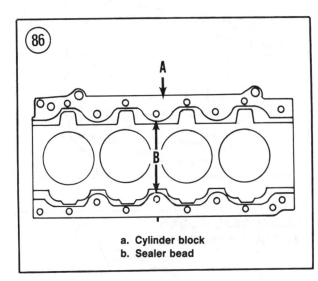

a. Cylinder block
b. Sealer bead

**CRANKCASE COVER
TORQUE SEQUENCE**

8. Align locating holes in center main bearing(s) and reed cage(s) with cylinder block locating pins. Depress bearing(s) and reed cage(s) to seat them in the block.

9. Insert a screwdriver through the exhaust or intake port of each cylinder and press inward on each ring (**Figure 85**, typical). If the ring does not return to position when the screwdriver is removed, it was probably broken during Step 7. Correct the problem before continuing.

10. Rotate crankshaft several times with the power head stand to make sure that it operates without binding.

11. Check crankshaft end play as described in this chapter.

12. Loosen end cap bolts several turns. Slide caps away from block to provide clearance for crankcase cover installation.

13. Make sure that the block and crankcase cover mating surfaces are clean, dry and oil-free. If necessary, wipe surfaces with a solvent-moistened cloth to remove any traces of oil.

14A. Merc 45, 500 and 50 (Prior to 1986)—Apply a continuous bead of Loctite Master Gasket sealant on cylinder block as shown in **Figure 86**. Lower crankcase cover onto block and install lockwashers and attaching bolts. Tighten bolts to specifications (**Table 1**) following the sequence shown in **Figure 87**.

8

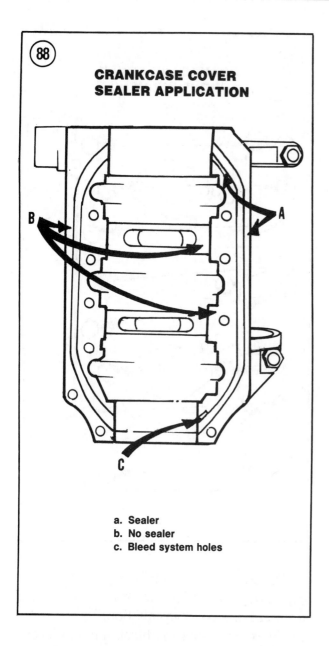

⑧

**CRANKCASE COVER
SEALER APPLICATION**

B → ← A

C

a. Sealer
b. No sealer
c. Bleed system holes

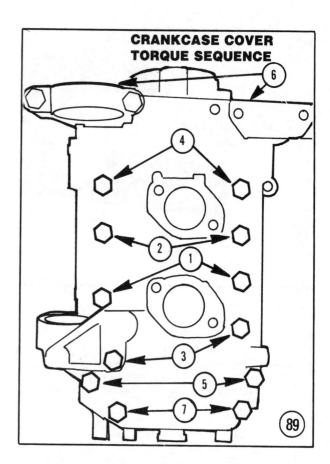

**CRANKCASE COVER
TORQUE SEQUENCE**

⑧

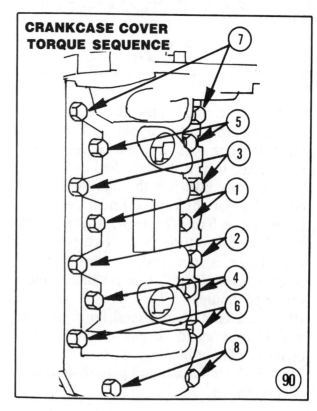

**CRANKCASE COVER
TORQUE SEQUENCE**

⑨

14B. Merc 50 (3-cyl.), 60, 650, 700 and 70 (prior to 1984) — Install gasket strip in crankcase cover groove and apply a coat of Permatex 2C-12 sealer as shown in **Figure 88**. Lower crankcase cover onto block and center reed cage in carburetor inlet. Wipe off any excess sealer that bleeds through the case splitline. Install attaching bolts and tighten to specifications (**Table 1**) following the sequence shown in **Figure 89**.

14C. All others—Install gasket strip in crankcase cover groove and apply a thin,

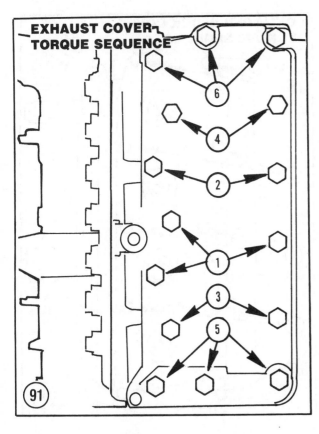

EXHAUST COVER TORQUE SEQUENCE

91

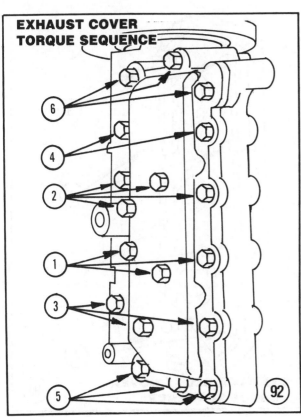

EXHAUST COVER TORQUE SEQUENCE

92

even coat of Permatex 2C-12 on crankcase cover. Lower crankcase cover onto block and wipe off any excess sealer that bleeds through the case splitline. Center valve-type main bearings in carburetor inlets. Install washers and attaching bolts. Tighten bolts to specifications (**Table 3**) following the sequence shown in **Figure 90**.

15. Install center main bearing/reed block locking tabs and mounting bolts. Tighten bolts to specifications (**Table 1** or **Table 3**). Bend locking tabs against the flat on each bolt.

16. Tighten end cap mounting bolts to specifications.

17. Rotate crankshaft several times to make sure it does not bind or catch. If it does, crankshaft was incorrectly installed. Remove cover and reinstall crankshaft.

18. Install transfer port cover(s) with new gasket(s). Tighten cover bolts to specifications (**Table 1** or **Table 3**).

NOTE
When installing a new divider plate in Step 19A on models manufactured before 1976, be sure to use part No. A-90421 only. Using the plate designed for 1976 and later models (part No. A-77161) will allow water to spray into the exhaust chamber.

19A. Merc 45, 500 and 50 (prior to 1986)—Install exhaust cover with divider plate and new gasket. Tighten fasteners to specifications (**Table 1**) following the sequence shown in **Figure 91**.

19B. All others—Put a small amount of Quicksilver Anti-Corrosion Grease (part No. C-92-63290) into each hole in the exhaust cover, baffle and gaskets to prevent corrosion. Install baffle gasket, baffle, cover gasket and cover in that order. Tighten bolts to the sequence shown in **Figure 92** (Merc 50 [3-cyl.], 60, 650, 700 and 70) or **Figure 93** (all others).

8

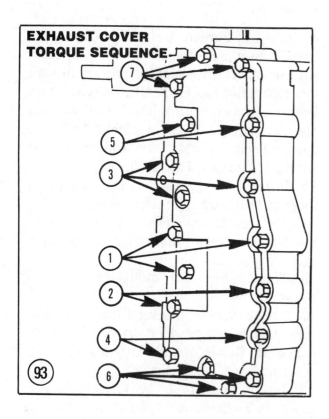

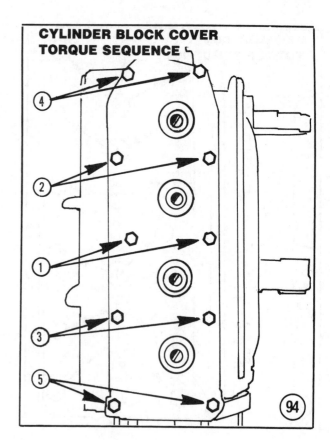

20. Install cylinder block cover with new gasket. Tighten bolts to specifications (**Table 1** or **Table 3**) following the sequence shown in **Figure 94** (Merc 45, 500 and 50 [prior to 1986]), **Figure 95** (Merc 50 [3-cyl.], 60, 650, 700 and 70) or **Figure 96** (all others).

21. Install thermostat and thermostat cover with a new gasket.

22. Install balance tube(s) and bleed line(s), if removed.

23. Install power head as described in this chapter.

Power Head Assembly
(1987-on Merc 70, 80 and 90)

1. Apply a coat of Perfect Seal on lower crankcase end cap surface where end cap and crankcase surface mate. Install end cap and finger tighten 2 cylinder block mounting bolts.

2. Apply a continous bead of Loctite Master Gasket sealant on cylinder block as shown in **Figure 86**. Lower crankcase cover onto block

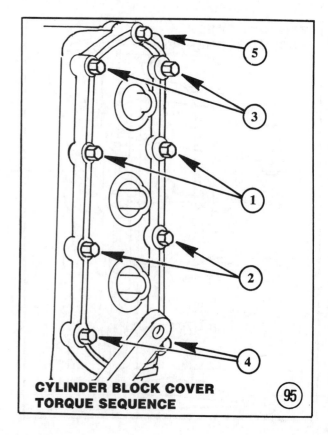

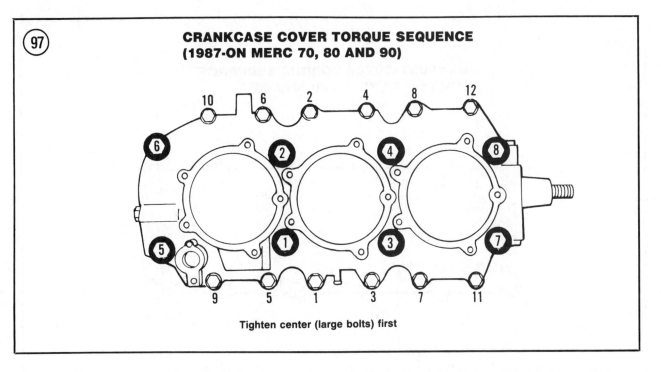

**CRANKCASE COVER TORQUE SEQUENCE
(1987-ON MERC 70, 80 AND 90)**

Tighten center (large bolts) first

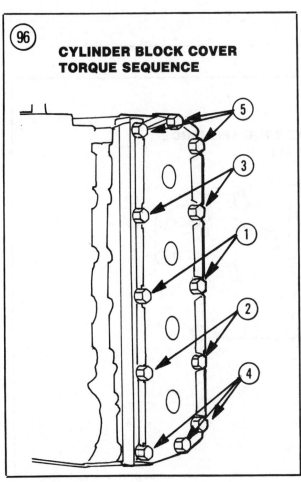

**CYLINDER BLOCK COVER
TORQUE SEQUENCE**

and install attaching bolts. Tighten bolts in 3 equal increments following sequence shown in **Figure 97** until final specification noted in **Table 2** is obtained. First tighten center crankcase bolts (large bolts) to recommended torque, then tighten outside crankcase bolts (small bolts) to recommended torque.

3. Install remaining lower crankcase cover bolt, then tighten the 3 bolts to the torque specified in **Table 2**.

4. Install exhaust cover with divider plate and new gaskets. Tighten fasteners to specification (**Table 2**) following the sequence shown in **Figure 98**.

5. Install cylinder block cover with a new gasket and finger tighten fasteners.

6. Install thermostat and poppet valve into cylinder block cover passages.

7. Install thermostat housing and gasket and finger tighten fasteners.

8. Tighten cylinder block cover fasteners to specification (**Table 2**) following the sequence shown in **Figure 99**.

9. Install fuel pump (**Table 2**) and correctly attach hoses.

8

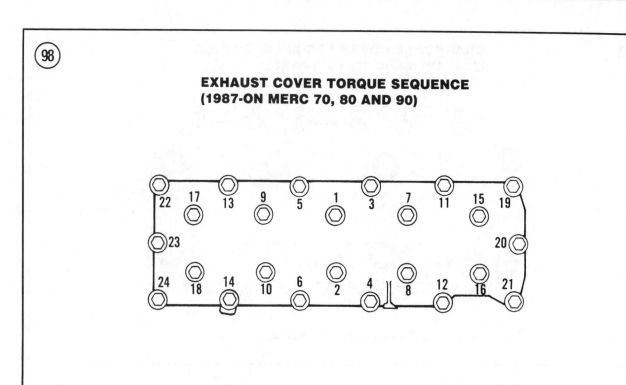

EXHAUST COVER TORQUE SEQUENCE
(1987-ON MERC 70, 80 AND 90)

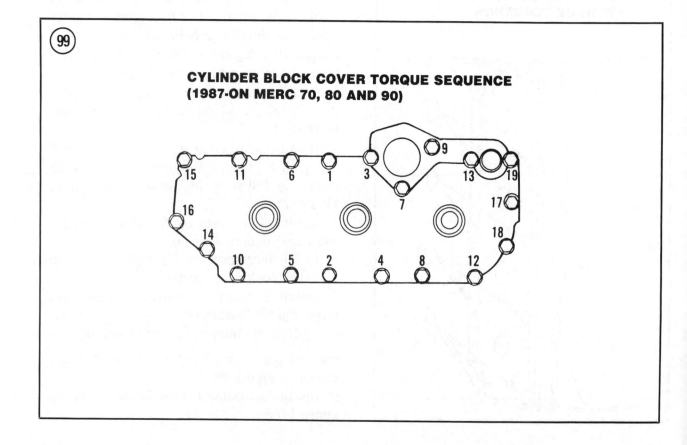

CYLINDER BLOCK COVER TORQUE SEQUENCE
(1987-ON MERC 70, 80 AND 90)

10. Install oil injection pump (**Table 2**), housing and shaft, then correctly attach hoses.

11. Install power head as described in this chapter.

Power Head Assembly
(1988-on Merc 100 and 115)

1. Apply a coat of Perfect Seal on lower crankcase end cap surface where end cap and crankcase surface mate. Install end cap and finger tighten 2 cylinder block mounting bolts.

2. Apply a continuous bead of Loctite Master Gasket sealant on cylinder block as shown in **Figure 86**. Lower crankcase cover onto block and install attaching bolts. Tighten bolts in 3 equal increments following sequence shown in **Figure 100** until final specification noted in **Table 2** is obtained. First tighten center crankcase bolts (large bolts) to recommended torque, then tighten outside crankcase bolts (small bolts) to recommended torque.

3. Install remaining lower crankcase cover bolt, then tighten the 3 bolts to the torque specified in **Table 2**.

4. Install exhaust cover with divider plate and new gaskets. Tighten fasteners to specification (**Table 2**) following the sequence shown in **Figure 101**.

5. Install cylinder block cover with a new gasket and finger tighten fasteners.

6. Install thermostat and poppet valve into cylinder block cover passages.

7. Install thermostat housing and gasket and finger tighten fasteners.

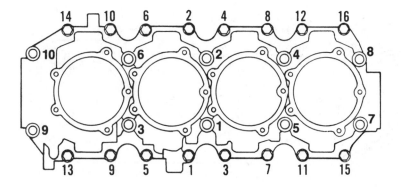

CRANKCASE COVER TORQUE SEQUENCE (1988-ON MERC 100 AND 115)

Tighten center (large bolts) first

8

8. Tighten cylinder block cover fasteners to specifications (**Table 2**) following the sequence shown in **Figure 102**.

9. Install fuel pump (**Table 2**) and correctly attach hoses.

10. Install oil injection pump (**Table 2**), housing and shaft, then correctly attach hoses.

11. Install throttle/shift bracket and securely tighten the 2 retaining bolts and lockwashers.

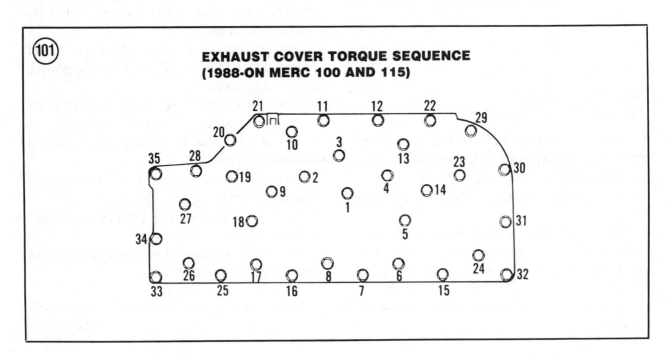

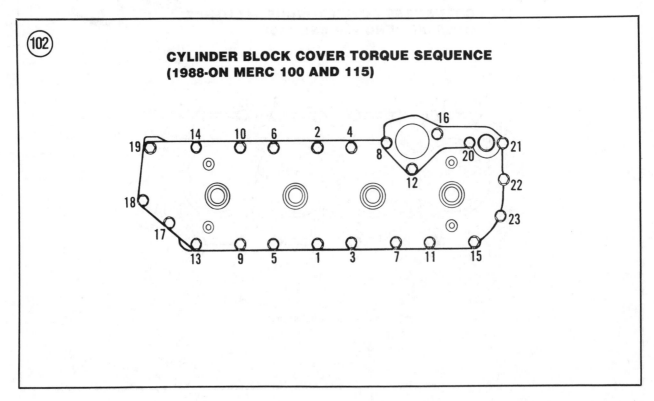

12. Install throttle arm and spark advance arm assembly and securely tighten the 17 mm retaining nut. Make sure arm assembly pivots freely after tightening retaining nut.

13. Install accelerator pump and reattach pump hoses to cylinder 3 and 4 check valve fittings.

14. Install ignition plate with electrical components and associated wiring. Apply Loctite grade A on the threads of the 4 remaining bolts then tighten the bolts to 180 in.-lb.

15. Install trigger assembly and stator assembly (**Table 2**). Attach trigger actuating linkage to throttle arm.

16. Install power head as described in this chapter.

Power Head Assembly
(V6 Engines)

When installing a new crankshaft in a previously-used cylinder block, inspect the crankshaft sealing ring mating surfaces in the block and cover. If the old crankshaft sealing rings created wear grooves in the block or cover, the rings on the new crankshaft must fit into them without binding the crankshaft or the block/cover must also be replaced.

1. Lightly lubricate the crankshaft sealing rings with Quicksilver Formula 50-D oil (part No. C-92-65183).
2. Make sure that all locating pins in the block are properly installed. If not, install new pins in block.
3. Align sealing rings so that their gaps will face up when the crankshaft is placed in the block.
4. Position the center main bearing race(s) so that the hole(s) in the race(s) are aligned with one edge of the cylinder block. Make a mark at the exact top of the bearing with a grease pencil, then rotate each race until the grease mark is aligned with the opposite edge of the block. This will position each race hole very close to where it should be to engage its block locating pin when the crankshaft is installed.
5. Carefully lower crankshaft into place in the block (**Figure 103**) with the drive shaft end facing the drive shaft end of the block. Gently push crankshaft into place, rotating main bearing races slightly as required to engage the race holes with the locating pins. Compress sealing rings and push crankshaft down until properly seated.
6. Lightly lubricate the oil seal areas on the crankshaft ends with Quicksilver Formula 50-D oil.
7. Carefully lift one end of the crankshaft up slightly and install end cap (**Figure 104**). Repeat this step to install the other end cap.

8

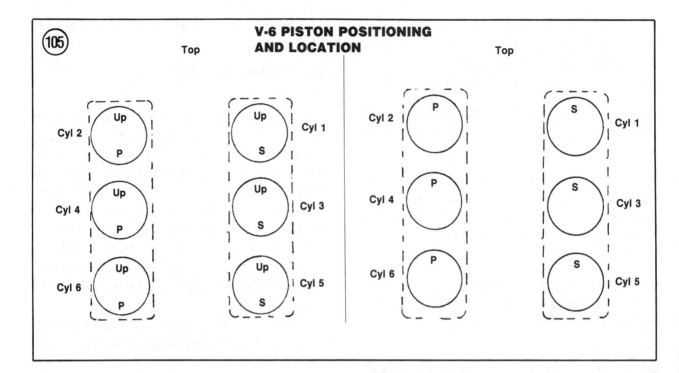

V-6 PISTON POSITIONING AND LOCATION

Top — Top

Cyl 2 — Up P
Cyl 4 — Up P
Cyl 6 — Up P

Up S — Cyl 1
Up S — Cyl 3
Up S — Cyl 5

Cyl 2 — P
Cyl 4 — P
Cyl 6 — P

S — Cyl 1
S — Cyl 3
S — Cyl 5

8. Install but do not tighten end cap bolts.

9. Lightly lubricate all pistons, rings and cylinder bores with Quicksilver Formula 50-D oil.

10. Match each piston with the cylinder from which it was removed. Position the piston as shown in **Figure 105**.

CAUTION
If ring groove locating pins are not properly centered in ring end gaps in Step 11, piston ring(s) may be broken during installation.

11. Install ring compressor part No. C-91-65494 (V150 and V175) or part No. C-91-85534 (V200 and V225) on one piston, making sure that the ring groove locating pins are centered in the ring end gaps as the compressor is tightened.

12. Remove and discard the connecting rod cap bolts. Remove the rod cap.

13. Position the piston/rod assembly as shown in **Figure 105** and fit it into the proper cylinder (**Figure 106**). Align the connecting rod with the block opening and push on

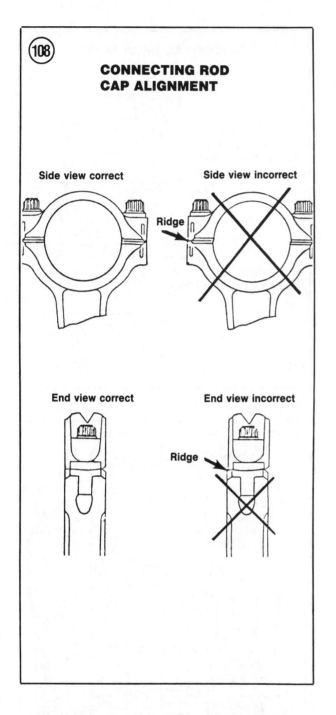

CONNECTING ROD CAP ALIGNMENT

Side view correct

Side view incorrect

Ridge

End view correct

End view incorrect

Ridge

remaining rollers. Install the connecting rod cap, making sure the rod and cap alignment marks match. See **Figure 107**.

16. Clean new rod cap bolts with solvent and blow dry. Wipe bolt threads with Loctite Type A (part No. C-92-32609). Install bolts and finger-tighten, checking for correct alignment as shown in **Figure 108**.

17. Tighten cap bolts evenly in 3 stages until torqued to specifications (**Table 4**).

18. Repeat Steps 11-17 to install each remaining piston.

19. Insert a thin screwdriver blade through the exhaust port of each cylinder and depress each piston ring. If the ring does not return to position when the screwdriver is removed, it was probably broken during installation. Remove that piston and check ring condition.

20. Install power head stand on crankshaft end and rotate crankshaft several times. If crankshaft binds or catches during rotation, remove it from the block and check for mismated locating pin and race hole or sealing ring groove burrs. Correct as required.

21. Make sure that the block and crankcase cover mating surfaces are clean, dry and oil-free. If necessary, wipe surfaces with a solvent-moistened cloth to remove any traces of oil.

NOTE
Not all engines will use all of the components described in the following steps.

piston crown until it slips into the bore and the ring compressor tool is pushed off.

14. Apply a liberal amount of multipurpose lubricant to the rod bearing surface. Install the bearing cage and rollers, then bring the rod up to the crankshaft journal.

15. Coat the rod cap with multipurpose lubricant and install the other cage and

22. Install new gasket strips in crankcase cover grooves, trimming the end of each strip flush with the cover.

23. Apply a thin, even coat of Permatex 2C-12 on the cylinder block and crankcase cover.

24. Place cover on block and install the large bolts. Tighten bolts a few turns at a time

8

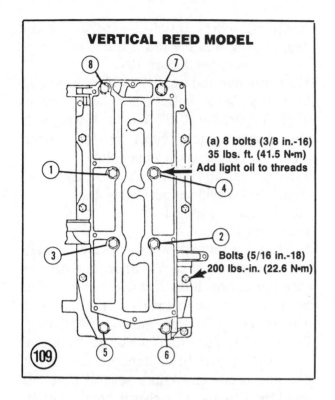

VERTICAL REED MODEL

(a) 8 bolts (3/8 in.-16)
35 lbs. ft. (41.5 N•m)
Add light oil to threads

Bolts (5/16 in.-18)
200 lbs.-in. (22.6 N•m)

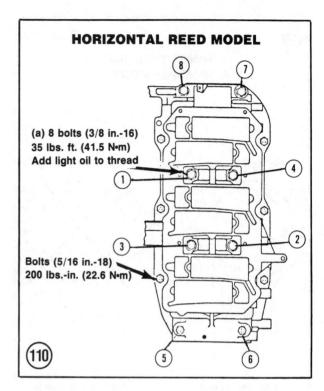

HORIZONTAL REED MODEL

(a) 8 bolts (3/8 in.-16)
35 lbs. ft. (41.5 N•m)
Add light oil to thread

Bolts (5/16 in.-18)
200 lbs.-in. (22.6 N•m)

following the sequence shown in **Figure 109** (vertical reed model) or **Figure 110** (horizontal reed model) to slowly compress sealing rings and draw cover down to block. Now tighten the bolts to specifications (**Table 4**) in 3 stages following the same sequence.

25. Install the small cover bolts. Tighten to specifications (**Table 4**) in 3 stages following **Figure 109** or **Figure 110** as appropriate.

26. Install end cap-to-cover bolts. Tighten all end cap bolts to specifications (**Table 4**).

27. Wipe off any excess sealer that may have been squeezed from the block/cover mating surfaces.

28. Install power head stand on crankshaft and rotate crankshaft several times to check for binding.

NOTE
If bleed hose routing is incorrect in Step 29, the engine will not operate properly.

29. Install and connect bleed hoses. Refer to **Figure 111** (V150 and V200 with vertical

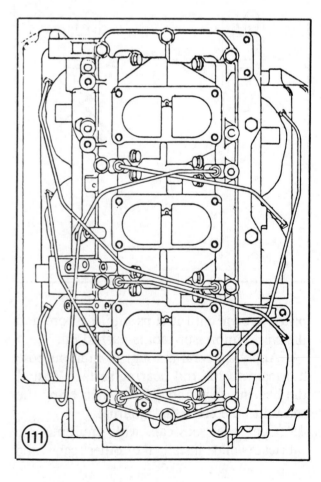

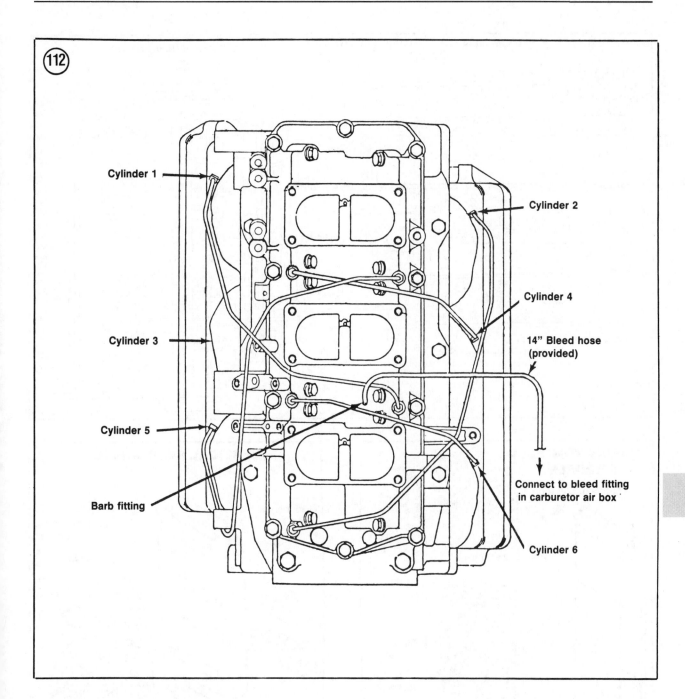

(112)

Cylinder 1

Cylinder 2

Cylinder 4

Cylinder 3

14" Bleed hose
(provided)

Cylinder 5

Connect to bleed fitting
in carburetor air box

Barb fitting

Cylinder 6

8

reeds and 6 bleed hoses), **Figure 112** (V150 and V200 with vertical reeds and 5 bleed hoses) or **Figure 113** (all V225 and some V200 with same block design).

30. Install a new gasket on the intake manifold assembly, then install reed blocks to manifold. Refer to **Figures 114-116** as appropriate and finger-tighten reed block attaching screws.

31. Install intake manifold to crankcase cover and tighten bolts to specifications (**Table 4**).

32. Tighten reed block housing screws to specifications (**Table 4**).

33. Assemble and install exhaust cover components as follows:

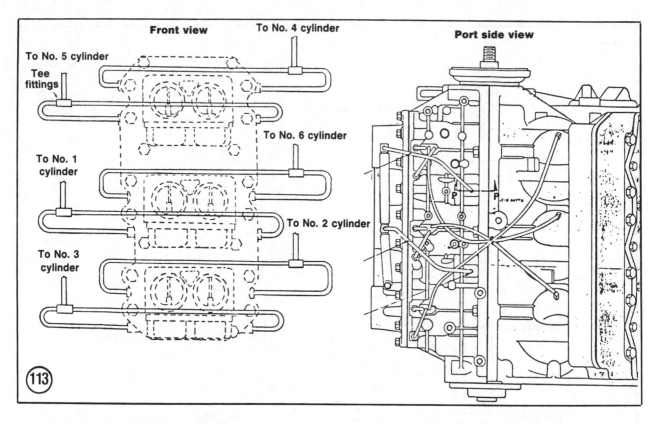

Front view   To No. 4 cylinder

To No. 5 cylinder

Tee fittings

To No. 1 cylinder

To No. 6 cylinder

To No. 3 cylinder

To No. 2 cylinder

Port side view

(113)

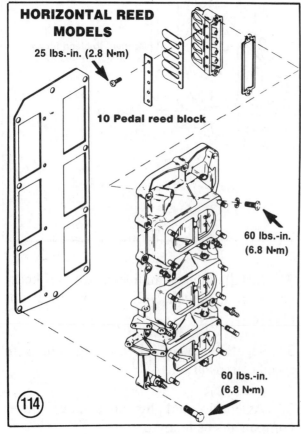

HORIZONTAL REED MODELS

25 lbs.-in. (2.8 N•m)

10 Pedal reed block

60 lbs.-in. (6.8 N•m)

60 lbs.-in. (6.8 N•m)

(114)

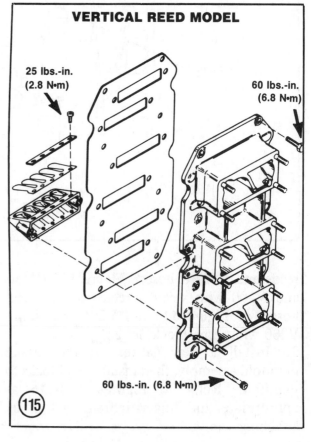

VERTICAL REED MODEL

25 lbs.-in. (2.8 N•m)

60 lbs.-in. (6.8 N•m)

60 lbs.-in. (6.8 N•m)

(115)

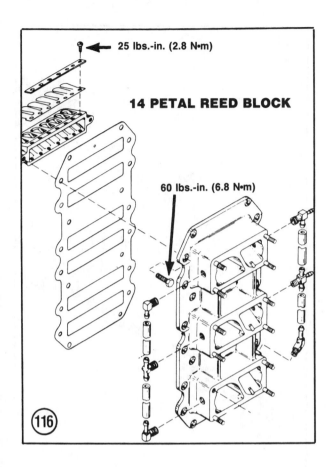

25 lbs.-in. (2.8 N•m)

14 PETAL REED BLOCK

60 lbs.-in. (6.8 N•m)

(116)

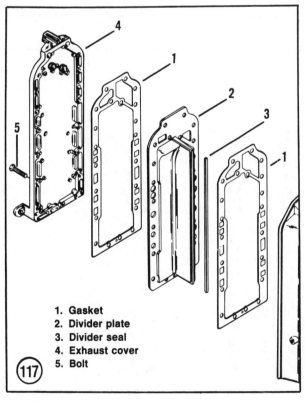

1. Gasket
2. Divider plate
3. Divider seal
4. Exhaust cover
5. Bolt

(117)

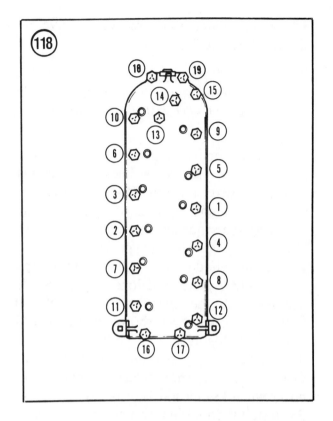

(118)

a. Install divider seal (3, **Figure 117**) in the block slot between the exhaust ports.

b. Position a new gasket on each side of the exhaust divider plate (1 and 2, **Figure 117**). Align all holes, then position on cylinder block.

c. Place exhaust cover (4, **Figure 117**) on divider plate assembly.

d. Wipe attaching bolt threads with Loctite 271 and install (5, **Figure 117**).

e. Tighten attaching bolts to specifications (**Table 4**) following the sequence shown in **Figure 118**.

NOTE
Some owners leave the valve assembly out in Step 34, thinking that water flow will increase significantly. However, running the engine without the pressure relief valve can result in engine damage. Idle quality is affected, especially in cold water areas, and water pressure is reduced by approximately 1 1/2 psi at full throttle.

8

34. Install water pressure relief valve as shown in **Figure 119**.

> *NOTE*
> *Head bolts must be retorqued to specification after engine has been run 3 hours.*

35. Install cylinder heads with new gaskets (1 and 2, **Figure 120**). Wipe head bolt threads with Quicksilver Formula 50-D oil (part No. C-92-65183) and tighten to specifications following the sequence shown in **Figure 121** (Type 1) or **Figure 122** (Type 2).

36. Install cylinder head covers with J-clips in the same bolt locations as removed. Tighten bolts to specifications (**Table 4**) following the sequence shown in **Figure 123** (Type 1) or **Figure 124** (Type 2).

37. Install a new gasket on each thermostat. Gasket shoulder should face cylinder head cover when thermostat is installed.

38. Install thermostats with covers and water distribution hoses to cylinder head cover. Tighten bolts to specifications (**Table 4**). See 3, **Figure 120**.

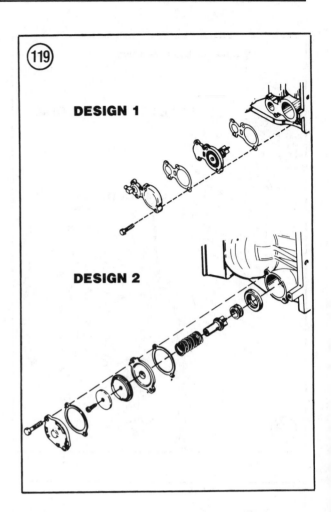

DESIGN 1

DESIGN 2

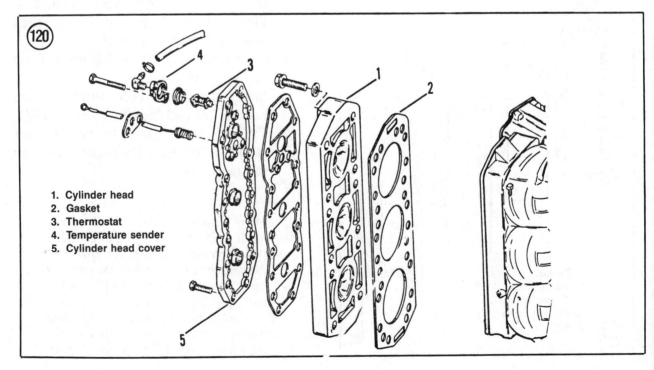

1. Cylinder head
2. Gasket
3. Thermostat
4. Temperature sender
5. Cylinder head cover

CYLINDER HEAD BOLT TORQUE SEQUENCE

Type 1

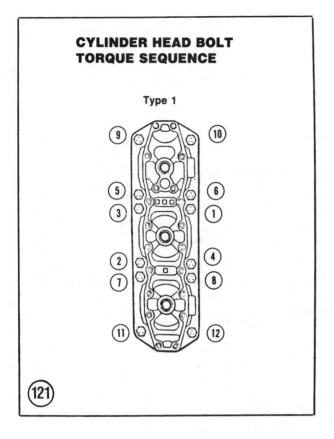

CYLINDER HEAD COVER BOLT TORQUE SEQUENCE

Type 1

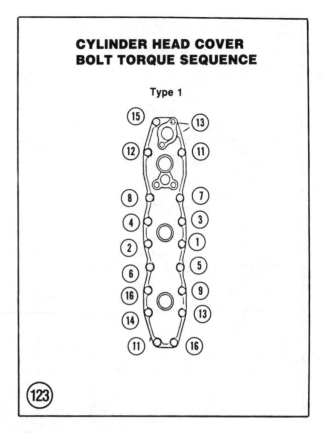

CYLINDER HEAD BOLT TORQUE SEQUENCE

Type 2

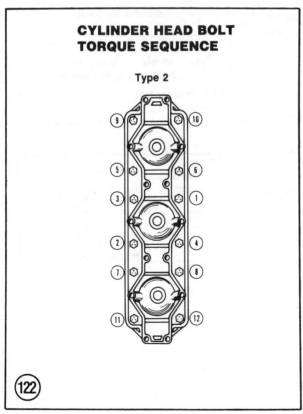

CYLINDER HEAD COVER BOLT TORQUE SEQUENCE

Type 2

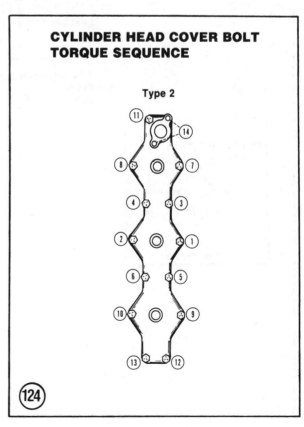

8

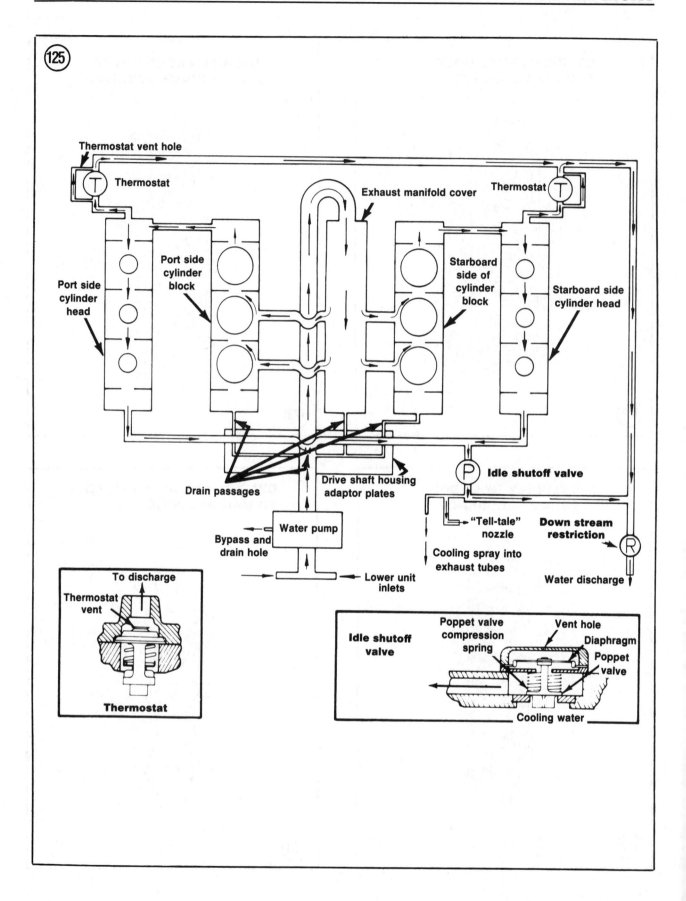

39. Connect water distribution hoses to idle shutoff valve fitting and route hoses through J-clips, then install new straps. See **Figure 125** for water flow with idle shutoff valve.

NOTE
If temperature sender replacement is necessary, be sure to use the correct unit in Step 40. Identify the sender temperature by the length of its lead. The 240° F sender has a 15 1/2 in. lead; the 190° F sender has an 18 1/2 in. lead.

40. Install the 190° F temperature sender (4, **Figure 120**) in the outer side of the cylinder head. If the engine uses a 240° F sender, it is installed below the No. 1 spark plug hole.

41. Install power head with a new gasket as described in this chapter.

Crankshaft End Play (Merc 45, 500 and 50 [Prior to 1986])

1. Install new end cap O-rings and lubricate O-ring/oil seal surfaces with Quicksilver Multipurpose Lubricant (part No. C-92-63250).

2. Temporarily install the end caps with their original shim(s). See **Figure 126**. Tighten cap bolts to specifications (**Table 1**).

3. Tap crankshaft toward drive shaft end of block with a mallet.

4. Hold crankshaft against lower end cap tightly and measure the gap between the inner race of the upper ball bearing and the crankshaft thrust face with a feeler gauge. It should be 0.008-0.012 in.

5. If end play is incorrect, add shim(s) to increase or remove shim(s) to decrease end play until it is within specification. Keep shim thicknesses within 0.005 in. of each other to maintain proper crankpin throw centering over the cylinders.

6. Loosen end cap bolts sufficiently to slide caps back for crankcase cover installation.

Crankshaft End Play (All Other Inline Engines [Except 1987-on 70-115])

1. Install new end cap O-rings and lubricate O-ring/oil seal surfaces with Quicksilver Multipurpose Lubricant (part No. C-92-63250).

2. Temporarily install the end caps with their original shim(s). Tighten cap bolts to specifications (**Table 1**).

3. Tap crankshaft toward drive shaft end of block with a mallet.

4. Hold crankshaft against lower end cap tightly and measure the gap between the inner face of the end cap and the first crankshaft counterweight with a feeler gauge. It should be approximately 0.050 in.

5. Tap crankshaft away from drive shaft end of block with a mallet and repeat Step 4.

6. Subtract Step 5 measurement from Step 4 measurement. The difference is the end play, which should be 0.004-0.012 in.

7. If end play is incorrect, add shim(s) to increase or remove shim(s) to decrease end play until it is within specification. Keep shim thicknesses within 0.005 in. of each other to maintain proper crankpin throw centering over the cylinders.

8. Loosen end cap bolts sufficiently to slide caps back for crankcase cover installation.

8

Table 1 TIGHTENING TORQUES (MERC 45, 500, 50, 60, 650, 700, 70 [Prior to 1984])

Fastener	in.-lb.	ft.-lb.
Carburetor mounting nuts		
Merc 500, 45, 50 (4-cyl.)	150	
Merc 650, 700, 50 (3-cyl.), 60, 70	110	
Center main bearing lockscrew		
Merc 500, 650, 700	200	
Merc 45, 50, 60, 70	100	
Coil terminal nuts	30	
Connecting rod nuts	180	
Crankcase cover screws	200	
Cylinder block cover	70	
Distributor		
Cap clamp	60	
Pulley flange screw	60	
Shaft nut	70	
End cap screws (upper/lower)	150	
Exhaust manifold cover screws		
5/16-18	200	
1/4-20	115	
Flywheel nut		
Merc 500, 45, 50 (4-cyl.)		65
Merc 650, 700, 50 (3-cyl.), 60, 70		85
Fuel pump screws		
Merc 500, 45, 50 (4 cyl.)	30	
Merc 650, 700, 50 (3-cyl.), 60, 70	70	
Main bearing support bolts	85	
Power head-to-drive shaft housing plate	180	
Reed block		
Attaching screws	40	
To crankcase cover lockbolt	50	
Reed stop retaining screws	30	
Spark plug		20
Starter mounting bolts		
Merc 500, 45, 50 (4-cyl.)	160	
Merc 650, 700, 50 (3-cyl.), 60, 70	180	
Stator mounting screws	60	
Throttle lever cam nut	30	
Transfer port cover screws		
Merc 500, 45, 50 (4-cyl.)	60	
Merc 650, 700, 50 (3-cyl), 60, 70	160	

Table 2 TIGHTENING TORQUES (1987-ON 70-115 HP)

Fastener	in.-lb.	ft.-lb.
Connecting rod cap screws		
First torque	15	
Second torque		30[1]
Crankcase cover		
First pattern-large screws		25[2]
Second pattern-small screws		
Merc 70, 80, 90	165[2]	
Merc 100, 115	180[2]	(continued)

Table 2 TIGHTENING TORQUES (1987-ON 70-115 HP) (continued)

Fastener	in.-lb.	ft.-lb.
Crankcase end cap screws		
Merc 70, 80, 90	150	
Merc 100, 115	180	
Cylinder block cover		
Merc 70, 80, 90	165	
Merc 100, 115	180	
Exhaust manifold cover screws		
Merc 70, 80, 90		
Merc 100, 115	180	
Flywheel		120
Fuel pump screws	40	
Ignition plate mounting screws		
Merc 70, 80, 90	165[3]	
Merc 100, 115	180[3]	
Intake manifold screws		
Merc 70, 80, 90	150	
Merc 100, 115	180	
Oil injection pump	60	
Power head-to-drive shaft housing		
Merc 70, 80, 90	165	
Merc 100, 115	350	
Spark plug		20
Starter mounting screws		
Merc 70, 80, 90	165	
Merc 100, 115	180	
Stator screws	60[4]	

1. Check connecting rod cap alignment after torqueing to 30 ft.-lb., then rotate cap screws an additional 1/4 turn if alignment is correct. Repeat torqueing sequence if connecting rod and cap are not in alignment.
2. Tighten in 3 step increments to final torque.
3. Apply Loctite grade A on screw threads prior to installation.
4. If a Patch screw is not used, apply Loctite grade A on screw threads prior to installation.

Table 3 TIGHTENING TORQUES (MERC 4- AND 6 CYLINDER INLINE)

Fastener	in.-lb.	ft.-lb.
Carburetor mounting nuts		
Merc 800, 850	100	
All others	150	
Carburetor interconnect link screws	35	
Coil terminal nuts	20	
Connecting rod nuts	180	
Crankcase cover screws	200	

(continued)

8

Table 3 TIGHTENING TORQUES (MERC 4- AND 6 CYLINDER INLINE) (continued)

Fastener	in.-lb.	ft.-lb.
Cylinder block cover	85	
Distributor		
Cap clamp	60	
Pulley flange screw	60	
Shaft nut	70	
End cap screws (upper/lower)	150	
Exhaust manifold cover screws	250	
Flywheel nut		100
Fuel pump screws	85	
Main bearing support screws	100	
Power head		
To drive shaft housing plate		45
To exhaust extension plate		20
Reed block attaching screws	85	
Reed stop retaining screws	25	
Spark plug		20
Starter mounting bolts	150	
Stator mounting screws	60	
Transfer port cover screws	85	

Table 4 TIGHTENING TORQUES (MERC V6)

Fastener	in.-lb.	ft.-lb.
Carburetor mounting nuts	180	
Coil		
Attaching screws	35	
Terminal nuts	20	
Connecting rod screws/nuts		30
Crankcase cover screws		
5/16-18	200	
3/8-16		34
Cylinder head cover screws	150	
Cylinder head bolts		
Type 1		30
Type 2		40
End cap screws		
Upper	150	
Lower	60	
Exhaust manifold cover screws	180	
Flywheel nut		100
Fuel pump screws	25	
Idle shutoff valve cover screws	150	
Power head to exhaust extension plate		45

(continued)

Table 4 TIGHTENING TORQUES (MERC V6) (continued)

Fastener	in.-lb.	ft.-lb.
Reed block		
Reed attaching screws	25	
Housing mounting bolts	60	
Reed stop retaining screws	25	
Relief valve cover bolts	150	
Spark plug		17
Starter mounting bolts	180	
Stator mounting screws	30	
Thermostat cover screws	150	

Table 5 PISTON DIAMETER AND CYLINDER BLOCK FINISH HONE

Model	Piston diameter (above rings)	Piston diameter (bottom of skirt)	Cylinder block finish hone
Merc 45, 500, 50 (prior to 1986)			
Standard piston	2.551	2.558	2.565
0.015 in. oversize	2.566	2.573	2.580
Merc 1987-on 70-115 hp			
Standard piston		3.371	3.375
0.015 in. oversize		3.383	3.390
0.030 in. oversize		3.401	3.405
All other inline			
Standard piston	2.863	2.872	2.875
0.015 in. oversize	2.878	2.878	2.890
Merc V6			
Standard	3.108	3.120	3.125
Barrel profile piston			
V135, V150, V150 XR2, V175 (prior to 1982)*			3.125
V150 XR4**			3.375
V175 (1985-on), V200, V225			Chrome finish

* 3.115 in. diameter.
** 3.372 in. diameter.

Table 6 ENGINE SPECIFICATIONS[1]

Crankshaft	
Top roller bearing journal	
V225	1.375 in.
2000, V200	1.498 in.
1750, V175	1.498 in.
1500, V150	1.498 in.
Top ball bearing journal	
1500 (1973-1977), 1500XS, 1400,	
1150, 115, 900, 90 (6 cyl.)	1.181 in.
850, 800, 80	1.181 in.
650, 700, 50 (3 cyl.), 60, 70	1.378 in.
500, 45, 50 (4-cyl.)	1.180 in.
Center main valve bearing journal	
All inline except 500, 45, 50 (4-cyl.)	1.238 in.
500, 45, 50 (4-cyl.)	0.984 in.
Main roller bearing journal	
All V6	1.375 in.
All inline except 500, 45, 50 (4-cyl.)	1.238 in.
500, 45, 50 (4-cyl.)	1.000 in.
Connecting rod journal	
V225	1.810 in.
All other V6	1.181 in.
All inline except 500, 45, 50 (4-cyl.)	1.139 in.
500, 45, 50 (4-cyl.)	0.882 in.
Bottom ball bearing journal	
All V6	1.575 in.
1500, 1500XS, 1400, 1150, 115, 850,	
800, 80	1.181 in.
900, 90	1.182 in.
650, 700, 50 (3-cyl.), 60, 70	1.378 in.
500, 45, 50 (4-cyl.)	1.180 in.
Connecting rod	
Piston pin end (ID)	
All except 500, 45, 50 (4-cyl.)	0.957 in.
500, 45, 50 (4-cyl.)	0.898 in.
Crankpin end (ID)	
All V6 except 1976-1977 1750	1.499 in.
1976-1977 1750	1.500 in.
All inline except 500, 45, 50 (4-cyl.)	1.453 in.
500, 45, 50 (4-cyl.)	1.137 in.
Piston/cylinder	
OD above ring land	
V225, 2000, V200	(See note 2)
1750 (1976-1977)	(See note 3)
All other V6	(See note 4)
1500, 1150, 900, 90 (6-cyl.)	2.863 in.
1500XS	2.860 in.
1400, 140 except 1978	2.857 in.
1978 1400	2.860 in.
115, 1972 800	2.857 in.
850, 800 (except 1972), 80	2.863 in.

(continued)

Table 6 ENGINE SPECIFICATIONS¹ (continued)

650, 700, 50 (3-cyl.), 60, 70	2.863 in.
500, 45, 50 (1975-1985)	2.553 in.
500 (1972-1974)	2.551 in.
OD @ skirt	
V225, 2000, V200	(See note 2)
1750 (1976-1977)	(See note 3)
All other V6	(See note 4)
1400 (except 1978) 800 (1972) 115	2.865 in.
500, 45, 50 (4-cyl.)	2.558 in.
All other inline	2.872 in.

1. No engine specifications available for 1987-on 70-115 hp models.
2. Measure piston OD 1/2 in. up from bottom, in line with piston pin and @ 90° angle to piston pin. Measurement should be 3.372 in.
3. Measure piston OD 29/32 in. up from bottom of piston, in line with piston pin and @ 90° angle to piston pin. Measurement should be 3.115 in.
4. Pistons with casting No. 755-6307/08 should measure 3.108 in. above ring land and 3.120 in. @ skirt. For all other pistons regardless of casting number (or lack of one), refer to Note 3.

8

Chapter Nine

Lower Unit and Drive Shaft Housing

A drive shaft transfers engine torque from the engine crankshaft through the drive shaft housing to the lower unit gear housing. A pinion gear on the drive shaft meshes with a drive gear in the lower unit gear housing to change the vertical power flow into a horizontal flow through the propeller shaft.

On outboards which have a shift capability, a sliding clutch engages a forward or reverse gear in the lower unit gear housing. This creates a direct coupling that transfers the power flow from the pinion to the propeller shaft.

The lower unit gear housing can be removed from the drive shaft housing without removing the entire outboard from the boat. This chapter covers the older standard lower unit (including the E-Z shift design) and the redesigned Model R lower unit introduced as a running change on V6 models during 1985 (including the later MR model). For user convenience, the 2 lower units are covered in separate sections.

The chapter contains removal, overhaul and installation procedures for the lower unit gear housing, drive shaft housing, water pump and propeller. **Tables 1-3** are at the end of the chapter.

SERVICE PRECAUTIONS

Whenever you work on a Mercury outboard, there are several good procedures to keep in mind that will make your work easier, faster and more accurate.

1. Never use elastic stop nuts more than twice. It is a good idea to replace such nuts with new ones each time they are removed. Never use worn-out stop nuts or non-locking nuts.

2. Use special tools where noted. In some cases, it may be possible to perform the procedure with makeshift tools, but this is not recommended. The use of makeshift tools can damage the components and may cause serious personal injury.

3. Use a vise with protective jaws to hold housings or parts. If protective jaws are not available, insert blocks of wood on either side of the part(s) before clamping them in the vise.

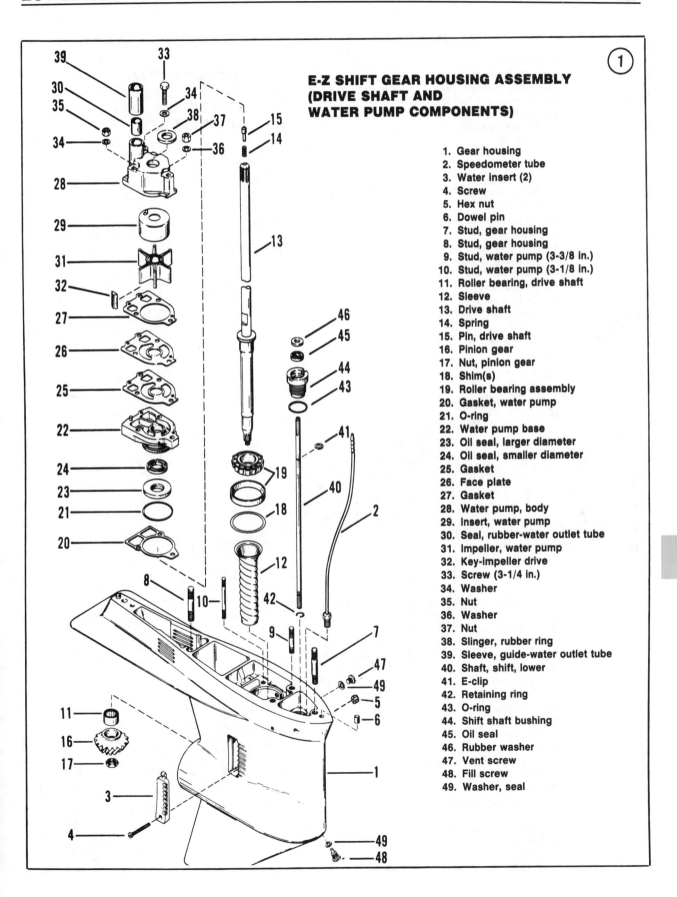

**E-Z SHIFT GEAR HOUSING ASSEMBLY
(DRIVE SHAFT AND
WATER PUMP COMPONENTS)**

1. Gear housing
2. Speedometer tube
3. Water insert (2)
4. Screw
5. Hex nut
6. Dowel pin
7. Stud, gear housing
8. Stud, gear housing
9. Stud, water pump (3-3/8 in.)
10. Stud, water pump (3-1/8 in.)
11. Roller bearing, drive shaft
12. Sleeve
13. Drive shaft
14. Spring
15. Pin, drive shaft
16. Pinion gear
17. Nut, pinion gear
18. Shim(s)
19. Roller bearing assembly
20. Gasket, water pump
21. O-ring
22. Water pump base
23. Oil seal, larger diameter
24. Oil seal, smaller diameter
25. Gasket
26. Face plate
27. Gasket
28. Water pump, body
29. Insert, water pump
30. Seal, rubber-water outlet tube
31. Impeller, water pump
32. Key-impeller drive
33. Screw (3-1/4 in.)
34. Washer
35. Nut
36. Washer
37. Nut
38. Slinger, rubber ring
39. Sleeve, guide-water outlet tube
40. Shaft, shift, lower
41. E-clip
42. Retaining ring
43. O-ring
44. Shift shaft bushing
45. Oil seal
46. Rubber washer
47. Vent screw
48. Fill screw
49. Washer, seal

9

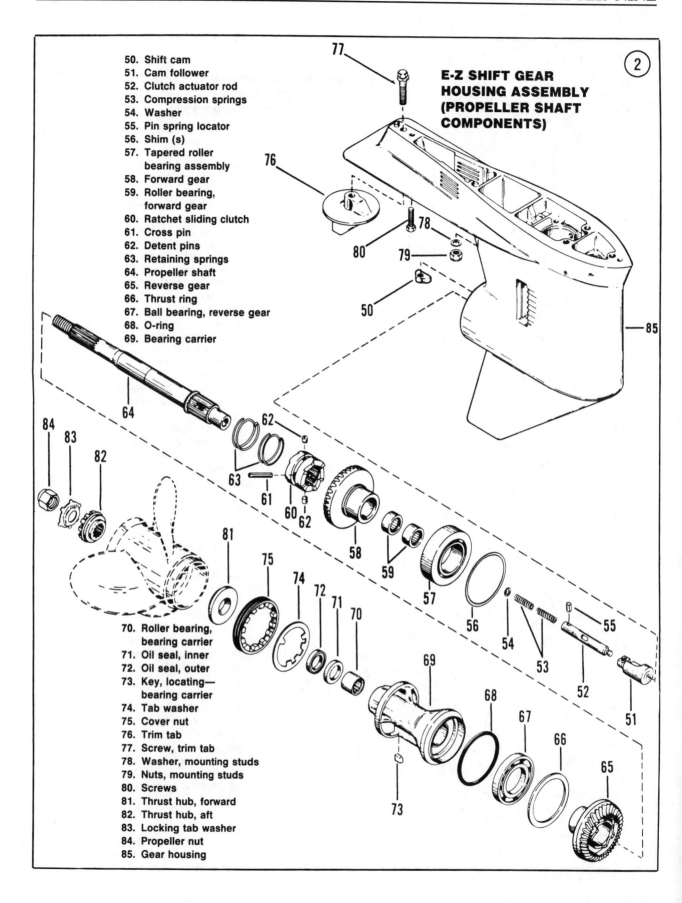

50. Shift cam
51. Cam follower
52. Clutch actuator rod
53. Compression springs
54. Washer
55. Pin spring locator
56. Shim (s)
57. Tapered roller bearing assembly
58. Forward gear
59. Roller bearing, forward gear
60. Ratchet sliding clutch
61. Cross pin
62. Detent pins
63. Retaining springs
64. Propeller shaft
65. Reverse gear
66. Thrust ring
67. Ball bearing, reverse gear
68. O-ring
69. Bearing carrier

E-Z SHIFT GEAR HOUSING ASSEMBLY (PROPELLER SHAFT COMPONENTS)

②

70. Roller bearing, bearing carrier
71. Oil seal, inner
72. Oil seal, outer
73. Key, locating— bearing carrier
74. Tab washer
75. Cover nut
76. Trim tab
77. Screw, trim tab
78. Washer, mounting studs
79. Nuts, mounting studs
80. Screws
81. Thrust hub, forward
82. Thrust hub, aft
83. Locking tab washer
84. Propeller nut
85. Gear housing

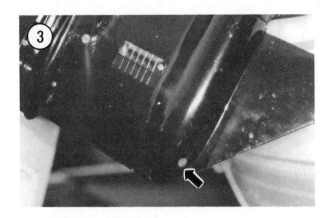

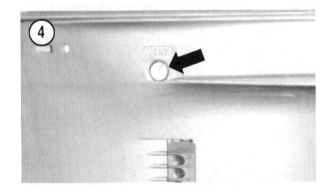

9. Keep a records of all shims and where they came from. As soon as the shims are removed, inspect them for damage and write down their thickness and location. Wire the shims together for reassembly and place them in a safe place. Follow shimming instructions closely. If gear backlash is not properly set, the unit will be noisy and suffer premature gear failure. Incorrect bearing preload will result in premature bearing failure.

10. Work in an area where there is good lighting and sufficient space for component storage. Keep an ample number of clean containers available for storing small parts. Cover parts with clean shop cloths when you are not working with them.

STANDARD GEAR HOUSING

Figure 1 and **Figure 2** are exploded views showing the components of a typical Merc outboard lower unit gear housing used on all outboards except mid-1985 and later V6 models. Since this chapter covers a large range of models over a lengthy time period, the lower units shown in the accompanying pictures are the most common ones. While it is possible that the components shown in the pictures may not be identical with those being serviced, the step-by-step procedures may be used with all models covered in this manual.

Removal

1. Disconnect spark plug leads as a safety precaution to prevent any accidental starting of the engine during Step 7.

2. Shift engine into FORWARD.

3. Tilt engine to full out position and engage tilt lock lever.

4. Shift engine into NEUTRAL.

5. Place a container under the fill plug (**Figure 3**, typical) and remove it. Remove the vent plug (**Figure 4**, typical). Drain the lubricant from the unit.

4. Remove and install pressed-on parts with an appropriate mandrel, support and hydraulic press. Do not try to pry, hammer or otherwise force them on or off.

5. Refer to the appropriate table at the end of the chapter for torque values, if not given in the text. Proper torque is essential to assure long life and satisfactory service from outboard components.

6. Apply Perfect Seal (part No. C-92-34227) to the outer surfaces of all bearing carrier, retainer and housing mating surfaces during reassembly. Do *not* allow Perfect Seal to touch O-rings or enter the bearings or gears.

7. Discard all O-rings and oil seals during disassembly. Apply Quicksilver Multipurpose Lubricant (part No. C-92-63250) to new O-rings and seal lips to prevent damage when the motor is first started.

8. Apply Loctite Type A (part No. C-92-32609) on the outside diameter of all metal case oil seals.

NOTE
If the lubricant is creamy in color or metallic particles are found in Step 6, remove and disassemble the lower unit gear housing to determine and correct the cause of the problem.

6. Wipe a small amount of lubricant on a finger and rub the finger and thumb together. Check for the presence of metallic particles in the lubricant. Note the color of the lubricant. A white or creamy color indicates water in the lubricant. Check the drain container for signs of water separation from the lubricant.

7. Remove the propeller as described in this chapter.

8. Scribe a mark on the gear housing and trim tab for reassembly reference. Pry the plastic plug from the rear of the drive shaft housing. See **Figure 5**.

9. Unbolt and remove the trim tab (**Figure 6**).

10. On Merc 45, 500 and 50 (prior to 1986) models, remove the hex head locknut from the inside of the trim tab cavity. On all other models, remove the bolt from the rear bottom of the drive shaft housing. See A, **Figure 7** (typical).

11. Remove the hex head locknut(s) from the center bottom of the anti-cavitation plate. See B, **Figure 7**, typical.

12. Remove the locknut at the front of the gear housing mounting stud (**Figure 8**).

CAUTION
Drive shaft housing damage may result in Step 13 if the locknuts are removed from one side before the opposite side is properly loosened.

13. Loosen the side mounting locknuts (**Figure 9**) on each side equally and drop the gear housing slightly. On badly corroded units, the water tubes and drive shaft may be frozen in the gear housing, making it necessary to pry the gear housing loose from the drive shaft housing.

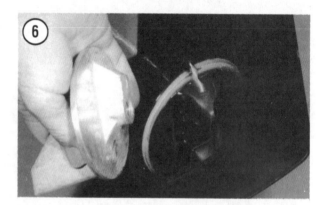

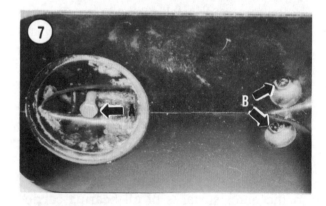

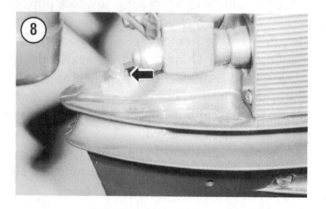

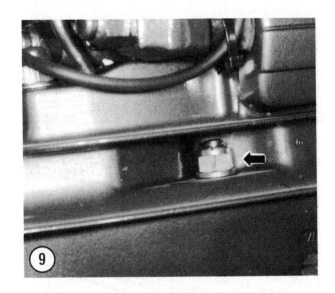

9

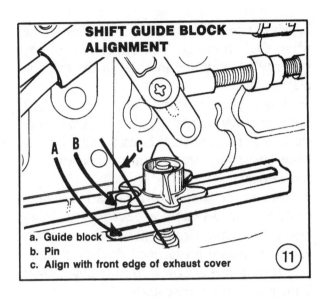

SHIFT GUIDE BLOCK ALIGNMENT

a. Guide block
b. Pin
c. Align with front edge of exhaust cover

11

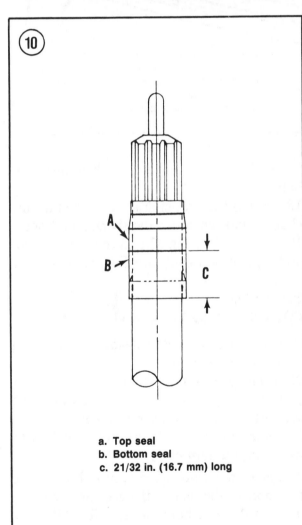

10

a. Top seal
b. Bottom seal
c. 21/32 in. (16.7 mm) long

14. Holding the gear housing firmly, remove the loosened nuts and separate the gear housing from the drive shaft housing.

15. Remove the upper reverse locking cam and nylon spool sleeve from the upper shift shaft, if so equipped.

16. Mount gear housing in a suitable holding fixture.

Installation
Merc 45-70 (Prior to 1984) hp Models

1. Install the bottom drive shaft seal on the drive shaft with its splined end facing upward. See **Figure 10**.

2. Install the top drive shaft seal on the drive shaft with its smaller OD facing upward. See **Figure 10**.

3. Install the exhaust tube support plate and tube seal in the gear housing. Ribbed side of support plate must face down.

4. Install the trim tab retaining bolt in the large diameter hole at the rear of the gear housing.

5. Shift the gear housing into NEUTRAL.

6. Make sure the upper shift shaft is positioned in neutral. The rear edge of the guide block pin should be aligned with the front edge of the exhaust plate cover. See **Figure 11**.

9

7. Make sure the water tube is installed in the drive shaft housing. The upper end of the water tube should be inserted in the exhaust plate.

8. Align gear housing with drive shaft housing studs. Insert the gear housing drive shaft into the drive shaft housing, aligning the water tube and water pump cover with a screwdriver.

9. Join lower unit to drive shaft housing, rotating the flywheel clockwise to align crankshaft and drive shaft splines while exerting upward pressure on the lower unit.

10. Install new elastic stop nuts finger-tight on drive shaft housing studs.

NOTE
If gear housing and drive shaft housing do not mate in Step 11, the 2 shift shafts are not aligned. Separate the units and repeat Steps 3-11.

11. Push upper shift shaft onto lower shift shaft with a punch or drift and seat gear housing against drive shaft housing.

NOTE
If the lower unit does not shift as described in Step 12 and Step 13, separate the units and repeat Steps 3-11.

12. Shift engine into FORWARD and make sure that the propeller shaft cannot be turned counterclockwise.

13. Shift engine into NEUTRAL. Propeller shaft should rotate freely in either direction.

14. Install the nut in the anti-cavitation plate cavity finger-tight.

15. Install the nut on the trim tab recess stud finger-tight.

16. Tighten all nuts snugly, beginning with those on the side of the drive shaft housing. Torque nuts to specifications (**Table 1**).

17. Install trim tab, align marks scribed during disassembly and tighten bolt securely.

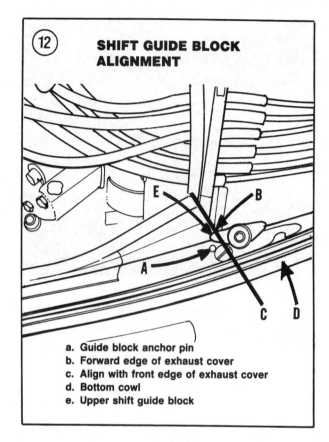

⑫ **SHIFT GUIDE BLOCK ALIGNMENT**

a. Guide block anchor pin
b. Forward edge of exhaust cover
c. Align with front edge of exhaust cover
d. Bottom cowl
e. Upper shift guide block

Press plastic cap into trim tab adjustment bolt hole.

18. Install the propeller as described in this chapter and reconnect the spark plug leads.

19. Fill gear housing with the correct amount and type of lubricant. See Chapter Four.

Installation
(Merc 80-150 hp Inline Models)

1. Install support plate flat side up in opening at rear of water pump.

2. Install exhaust tube seal above the support plate, working it into the opening between the support plate and water pump base.

3. Lubricate the exhaust tube seal with multipurpose lubricant.

4. Install the trim tab retaining bolt in the rear hole at the rear of the gear housing.

5. Shift the gear housing into NEUTRAL.

6. Install water tube guide in water pump cover above the water tube seal.

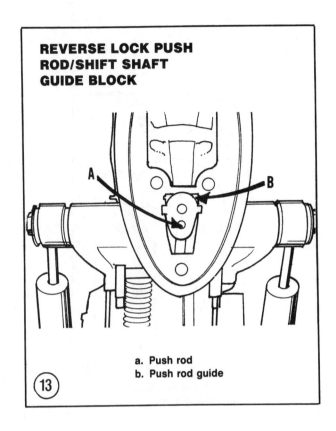

REVERSE LOCK PUSH ROD/SHIFT SHAFT GUIDE BLOCK

a. Push rod
b. Push rod guide

⑬

7. Make sure the upper shift shaft is positioned in neutral. The rear edge of the guide block pin should be aligned with the forward edge of the exhaust plate cover. See **Figure 12**.

8. Make sure the water tube is positioned in the exhaust extension plate.

9. Check reverse lock pushrod and shift shaft guide block positioning (**Figure 13**).

10. Lightly lubricate the drive shaft splines with multipurpose lubricant, then install drive shaft in drive shaft housing.

11. Insert the water tube in its guide, using a screwdriver or your fingers to assist in alignment.

12. Align gear housing with drive shaft housing studs.

13. Join lower unit to drive shaft housing, rotating the flywheel clockwise to align crankshaft and drive shaft splines while exerting upward pressure on the lower unit.

14. Install flat washers and new elastic stop nuts finger-tight on drive shaft housing studs.

15. Check position of shift shaft at exhaust extension plate bushing. If upper shift shaft was pushed upward when nuts were tightened in Step 10, the shafts are not aligned. Realign shafts with a punch and light hammer taps. When shafts are properly aligned, the gear housing should mate with the drive shaft housing.

16. Shift engine into FORWARD. Propeller shaft should not turn counterclockwise. Shift engine into NEUTRAL. Propeller shaft should rotate freely in either direction. Shift engine into REVERSE. Propeller shaft should rotate 1/3 turn in either direction.

17. Hand start the trim tab recess bolt, but do not tighten at this time.

18. Tighten the drive shaft housing side nuts evenly and torque to specifications (**Table 1**).

19. Install washers and nuts on the studs in the anti-cavitation plate cavity and tighten to specifications (**Table 1**).

20. Install the washer and nut on the stud at the leading edge of the drive shaft housing and tighten to specifications (**Table 1**).

21. Tighten the trim tab recess bolt (started in Step 17) to specifications (**Table 1**).

22. Install trim tab, align marks scribed during disassembly and tighten bolt securely. Press plastic cap into trim tab adjustment bolt hole.

23. Shift engine into FORWARD. Release tilt lock lever and lower engine to operating position.

24. Install propeller as described in this chapter and reconnect spark plug leads.

25. Fill gear housing with the correct amount and type of lubricant. See Chapter Four.

NOTE
Steps 26-29 are for engines not equipped with power trim.

26. Shift engine into NEUTRAL. Pull outward on the lower unit to check reverse

9

lock operation. The reverse lock must engage the tilt angle pin as shown in **Figure 14**.

27. Repeat Step 26 with the engine in REVERSE.

28. Shift engine into FORWARD. When the lower unit is pulled outward, it must move in that direction.

29. If the reverse lock does not operate as specified in Steps 26-28, the reverse lock cam is incorrectly indexed. Remove the lower unit as described in this chapter and index the reverse lock cam with its high part at upper end of ramp facing forward, then reinstall lower unit as described in this procedure.

Installation
(Merc V6 Models)

CAUTION
Grease on the top of the shafts in Step 1 will prevent them from fully engaging and can excessively load the drive shaft/crankshaft when the housing nuts are tightened. This will cause damage to the power head or gear housing.

1. Lightly lubricate shift shaft and drive shaft splines with multipurpose lubricant. Wipe any grease off the top of the shafts.

2. Run a thin bead of GE Silicone Sealer against the top of the exhaust divider plate.

3. Install the trim tab retaining bolt in the rear hole at the rear of the gear housing.

4. Shift the gear housing into FORWARD.

5. Make sure the guide block anchor pin is positioned as shown in **Figure 15**.

6. Position lower unit with drive shaft in drive shaft housing. Align shift shaft splines and fit water tube in water tube guide as gear housing is pushed upward toward drive shaft housing.

7. Join lower unit to drive shaft housing. If necessary, temporarily install propeller on prop shaft and rotate it counterclockwise to align crankshaft and drive shaft splines while exerting upward pressure on the lower unit.

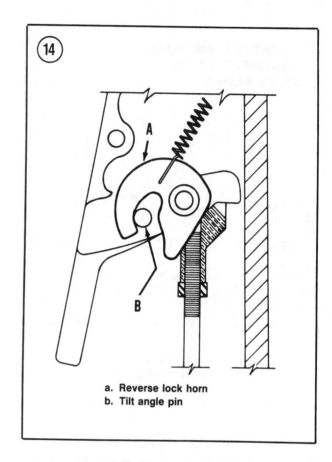

a. Reverse lock horn
b. Tilt angle pin

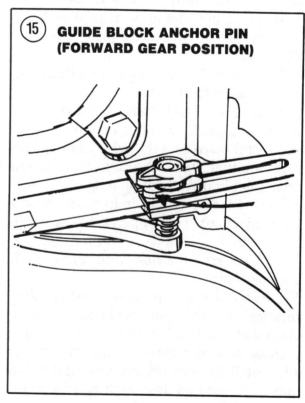

GUIDE BLOCK ANCHOR PIN (FORWARD GEAR POSITION)

16   PRESSURE TYPE WATER PUMP

1. Pump cover
2. Pump base
3. Face plate
4. Impeller
5. Insert
6. Gasket
7. Seal
8. O-ring
9. Drive shaft key

8. Install flat washers and new elastic stop nuts finger-tight on drive shaft housing studs.

9. Hand start the trim tab recess bolt, but do not tighten at this time.

10. Recheck shift shaft spline alignment and correct, if necessary.

11. Tighten the drive shaft housing side nuts evenly and torque to specifications (**Table 1**).

NOTE
If the unit does not shift as described in Step 12, the gear housing must be removed and reinstalled.

12. Move guide block anchor pin into forward gear. Rotate crankshaft clockwise; propeller shaft should turn in the same direction. Move anchor pin into neutral gear. Propeller shaft should rotate freely in either direction. Move anchor pin into reverse gear. Rotate crankshaft clockwise; propeller shaft should turn in the opposite direction.

13. Install washers and nuts on the studs in the anti-cavitation plate cavity and tighten to specifications (**Table 1**).

14. Install the special flat washer and nut on the stud at the leading edge of the drive shaft housing and tighten to specifications (**Table 1**).

15. Tighten the trim tab recess bolt (started in Step 9) to specifications (**Table 1**).

16. Install trim tab, align marks scribed during disassembly and tighten bolt securely. Press plastic cap into trim tab adjustment bolt hole.

17. Install propeller as described in this chapter and reconnect spark plug leads.

18. Fill gear housing with the correct amount and type of lubricant. See Chapter Four.

WATER PUMP

Removal and Disassembly

Mercury Marine recommends that all seals and gaskets be replaced whenever the water pump is removed. It is also a good idea to install a new impeller at this time. **Figure 16** is an exploded view of typical water pump components.

1. Secure the gear housing in a suitable holding device or a vise with protective jaws. If protective jaws are not available for the vise, position the unit upright with the skeg between wooden blocks.

9

2. Remove the rubber centrifugal slinger from the drive shaft (A, **Figure 17**).

3. Remove the water tube guide (B, **Figure 17**) and seal from the water pump cover. Discard the seal.

NOTE
Merc 50 and 70 hp models use only 3 nuts to retain water pump in Step 4.

4. Remove the 3 nuts, 1 bolt and all washers holding the pump cover to the gear housing (C, **Figure 17**).

5. Insert screwdrivers at the fore and aft ends of the pump cover and pry cover up. See **Figure 18**. Remove cover from drive shaft.

NOTE
In extreme cases, it may be necessary to split the impeller hub with a hammer and chisel to remove it in Step 6.

6. Drive impeller upward on shaft with a punch and hammer. Remove the impeller and the drive key from shaft. See **Figure 19**.

7. Remove water pump face plate with top and bottom gaskets (**Figure 20**). Separate face plate from gaskets. Discard gaskets.

8. Remove the flush plug and gasket from the upper port side of the gear housing, if so equipped.

NOTE
Units equipped with a one-piece drive shaft bearing will have shims installed underneath the pump base in Step 9. Be sure to retrieve and save the shimming for reassembly.

9. Insert screwdrivers at the fore and aft ends of the pump base. Pad the pry areas under each screwdriver with clean shop cloths and pry pump base loose. Remove base from shaft (**Figure 21**).

10. Remove and discard base-to-gear housing O-ring (A, **Figure 22**).

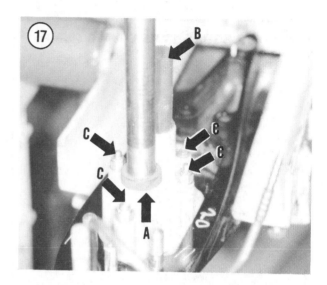

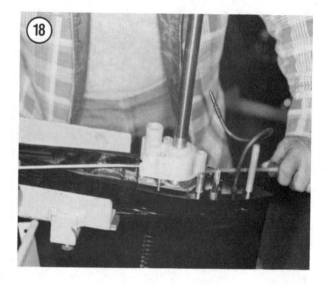

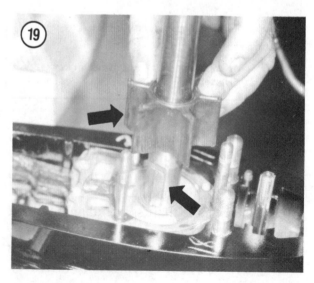

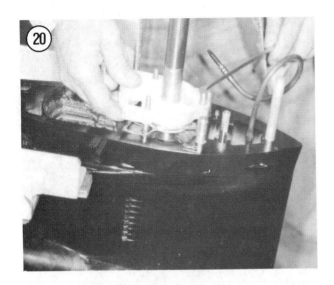

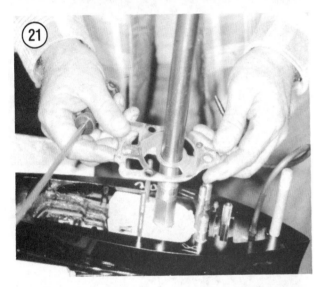

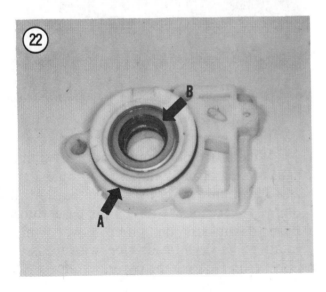

11. Working from the gear housing side of the pump base, pry the oil seals from the base (B, **Figure 22**).

Cleaning and Inspection

1. Clean all metal parts in solvent and blow dry with compressed air, if available.

2. Clean gasket residue from all mating surfaces.

3. Check pump cover and base for cracks or distortion from overheating.

4. Check face plate and water pump insert for grooves or rough surfaces. Replace if any defects are found.

5. If original impeller must be reused, check bonding to hub. Check side seal surfaces and blade ends for cracks, tears, wear or a glazed or melted appearance. If any of these defects are noted, do *not* reuse original impeller.

Assembly and Installation

1. Secure the gear housing in a suitable holding device or a vise with protective jaws. If protective jaws are not available for the vise, position the unit upright with the skeg between wooden blocks.

2. If water pump insert must be replaced, drive old insert from pump cover with a punch and hammer. If the insert refuses to come out, carefully drill a 3/16 in. hole through the top (but not through the insert) on each side of the cover and drive insert out with a hammer and punch. Coat insert area in cover with Perfect Seal and install new insert, aligning its tab with the cover recess.

NOTE
If water pump insert removal required drilling of holes in pump cover, fill holes with GE Silicone Sealer or equivalent.

3. Position the pump base on a press. Wipe the OD of each new oil seal with Loctite Type A. Press smaller diameter seal into pump

9

base with seal lip facing the impeller. Press larger diameter seal into pump base with seal lip facing gear housing. Wipe any excess Loctite from seals and pump base.

4. Install new O-ring in pump base groove.

5. Lubricate O-ring and oil seals with multipurpose lubricant.

6. If equipped with a one-piece drive shaft bearing, shim the water pump base as described in this chapter.

7. Install a new pump base gasket over pump mounting studs. Tape drive shaft O-ring groove to prevent seal damage and install pump base over drive shaft and into housing. See **Figure 23**.

8. Sandwich the face plate between new gaskets and install on pump base (**Figure 24**). Dowel pins on base must engage face plate/gasket sandwich.

9. Wipe drive shaft key flat on shaft with a small quantity of multipurpose lubricant to hold key in place. Install key to drive shaft flat and slide new impeller on drive shaft. See **Figure 25**.

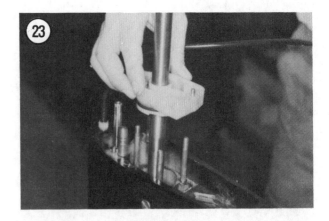

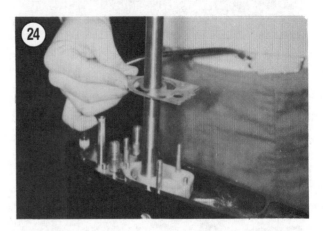

> *CAUTION*
> *If the original impeller must be reused, install it in the same rotational direction to avoid premature failure. The curl of the blades should be positioned in a counterclockwise direction, as seen from the top of the unit. See* **Figure 26**.

10. Install new impeller and rotate drive shaft clockwise to make sure the drive key is properly positioned on drive shaft flat when impeller is fully seated (impeller should rotate with drive shaft). If not, remove impeller and reposition key properly.

11. Install new water tube seal in pump cover with plastic side of seal facing downward. On Merc 45-70 (prior to 1984) hp models, install cupped washer in pump cover with recessed side facing away from face plate.

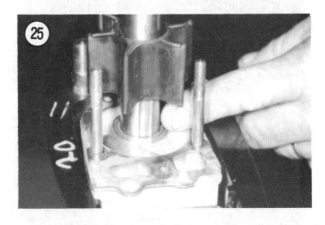

12. Install water tube guide in pump cover.

13. Wipe inside of pump cover insert with a light coating of multipurpose lubricant.

14. Slide pump cover over drive shaft. Align pump cover holes with pump base studs. Push downward on pump cover while rotating the drive shaft clockwise to assist impeller in entering the cover.

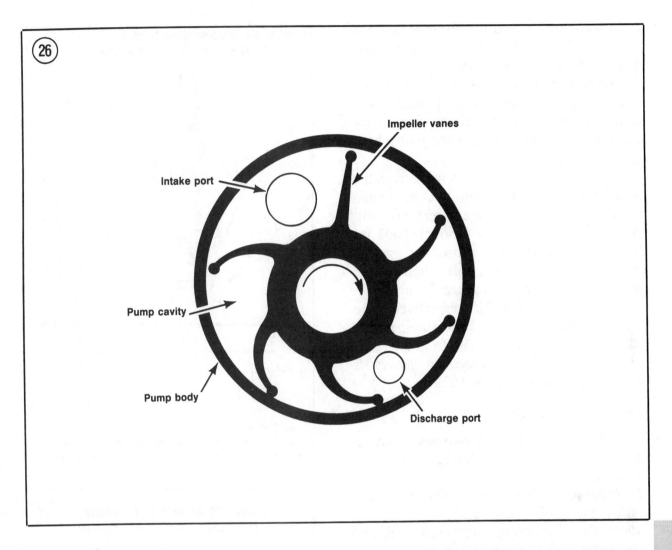

㉖

Impeller vanes

Intake port

Pump cavity

Pump body

Discharge port

9

CAUTION
Do not over-tighten fasteners in Step 15 or pump cover may crack during operation.

15. Install pump cover retainer washers, bolt and nuts. Tighten all fasteners to specifications (**Table 1**).

16. Install centrifugal slinger over drive shaft and position against pump cover.

17. Install flush plug in gear housing, if so equipped.

18. Remove tape from drive shaft splines. Clean any tape residue from splines.

Water Pump Base Shimming

If the unit is equipped with a one-piece drive shaft bearing, the water pump base must be properly shimmed to maintain the correct forward gear backlash. Proper shimming eliminates all clearance between the drive shaft ball bearing and pump base and provides 0.002 in. compression of the pump base gasket. The depth micrometer method is the most accurate, but shimming can be accomplished with a feeler gauge if a micrometer is not available.

Depth micrometer method

1. Install a new pump base-to-gear housing gasket over the drive shaft and seat in the gear housing.

2. Measure and record the distance between the top of the gasket and the outer race of the drive shaft bearing. See **Figure 27**.

3. Invert pump base. Measure and record the distance between that part of the pump base which enters the drive shaft bearing cavity and the surface that touches the pump base gasket.

4. Subtract the Step 3 measurement from the Step 2 measurement. A shim thickness equal to the difference in measurements will eliminate clearance. Now subtract 0.002 in. from that figure to allow for gasket compression. As an example, suppose the measurements obtained in Step 2 and Step 3 were 0.515 in. and 0.490 in. respectively. The difference between these 2 measurements is 0.025 in. Subtracting 0.002 in. from 0.025 in. to provide gasket compression leaves a required shim thickness of 0.023 in.

Feeler gauge method

1. Install a new pump base-to-gear housing gasket over the drive shaft and seat in the gear housing.

2. Remove O-ring from pump base for measurement purposes.

3. Install shimming removed during disassembly plus an extra 0.020 in.

4. Install water pump base over drive shaft and push firmly into gear housing.

5. Hold pump base against gear housing and measure the gap between the base and gasket with a feeler gauge (**Figure 28**).

6. Add 0.002 in. to the gap measured in Step 5 to obtain the correct shim thickness. Subtract that figure from the 0.020 in. extra shimming added in Step 3, then remove the difference from the shim pack. For example, suppose the gap measured 0.009 in. Adding 0.002 to 0.009 gives us a total of 0.011 in. Since 0.020 in. was added in Step 3, subtract 0.011 in. from that figure. The difference (0.009 in.) must be removed from the shim pack.

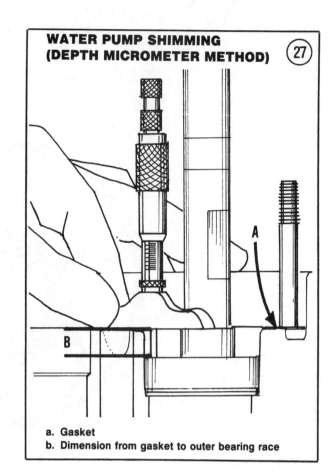

WATER PUMP SHIMMING (DEPTH MICROMETER METHOD) 27

a. Gasket
b. Dimension from gasket to outer bearing race

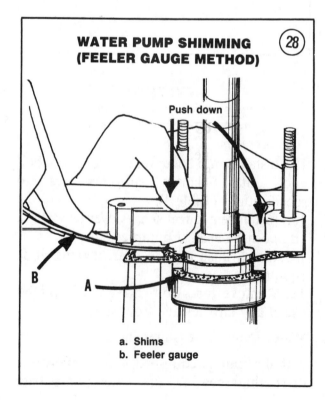

WATER PUMP SHIMMING (FEELER GAUGE METHOD) 28

Push down

a. Shims
b. Feeler gauge

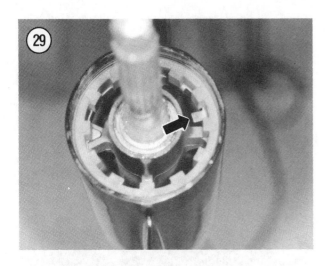

7. Remove the pump base and reinstall the O-ring.

BEARING CARRIER AND PROPELLER SHAFT

Merc V6 engines may be equipped either with a Cam-Shift or E-Z Shift gear housing. Externally, these 2 housings appear identical but the internal components are different. For this reason, disassembly procedures differ according to type. If you do not know which type you are working on, shift the gear housing into neutral and turn the shift shaft to either side of the neutral position. The shift shaft in a Cam-Shift housing will rotate 360° counterclockwise, while the shift shaft in an E-Z Shift housing will only turn 30° either side of the neutral position.

Removal (Except Merc V6 E-Z Shift Models)

1. Secure the gear housing in a suitable holding device or a vise with protective jaws. If protective jaws are not available for the vise, position the unit upright with the skeg between wooden blocks.

2. On Merc 45-70 (prior to 1984) hp models, check and record reverse gear backlash as described in this chapter.

3. Bend the tab on the cover nut lock out of the cover nut recess with a screwdriver or punch and a hammer. See **Figure 29**.

NOTE
If the cover nut is frozen in place and cannot be moved in Step 4 even with the assistance of heat and tapping on the tool, use an electric drill to drill out one side of the nut. This will permit removal of the nut without damage to the housing.

4. Install cover nut remover and remove cover nut. With Merc 45-70 (prior to 1984) hp, use remover part No. C-91-74241. Use remover part No. C-91-73688 with all others. See **Figure 30**, typical.

NOTE
Late-model Merc 80, 90 and 115 hp bearing carriers may have 2 lube fittings which will prevent use of remover part No. C-91-73688 in Step 4 until it is modified by machining the inside diameter.

5. Remove lock tab washer from gear housing.

6A. Merc 45-70 (prior to 1984) hp—remove gear housing from vise. Clamp propeller shaft in vise (use protective jaws or wood blocks) and strike gear housing at a point between the propeller shaft and anti-cavitation plate with a mallet to drive the housing off the bearing carrier/propeller shaft assembly. Do not drop

9

gear housing or lose the carrier alignment key. Remove propeller shaft from bearing carrier.

> *CAUTION*
> *Two different types of bearing carriers are used with Merc 80 hp and larger gear housings. With one type, the reverse gear is not secured to the carrier. It may or may not come out of the housing with the carrier. Perform Step 6B carefully and do not allow the reverse gear to fall from the housing/carrier and strike the floor.*

6B. All others—install puller jaws part No. C-91-46086A1 and puller bolt (part No. C-91-85716) or equivalent and remove bearing carrier (**Figure 31**, typical). If necessary, use propeller thrust hub to exert outward pressure on the puller jaws. Check carrier to make sure alignment key is with it. Remove propeller shaft from gear housing (**Figure 32**).

Removal (Merc V6 E-Z Shift Models)

1. Secure the gear housing in a suitable holding device or a vise with protective jaws. If protective jaws are not available for the vise, position the unit upright with the skeg between wooden blocks.
2. Shift gear housing into NEUTRAL.
3. Unthread (but do not remove) shift shaft bushing with bushing tool part No. C-91-31107.

> *NOTE*
> *Do not rotate shift shaft in either direction during removal in Step 4.*

4. Pull shift shaft from gear housing (**Figure 33**). If it is necessary to use pliers, wrap a strip of aluminum around the shaft splines for a clamping surface.
5. Bend the tab on the cover nut lock out of the cover nut recess with a screwdriver or punch and a hammer. See **Figure 29**.

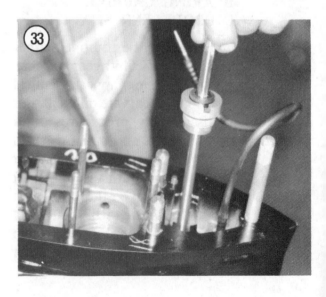

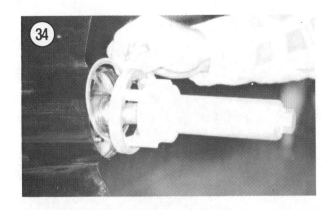

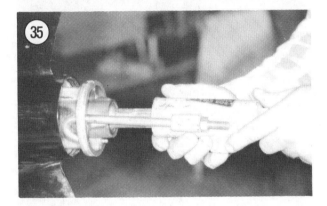

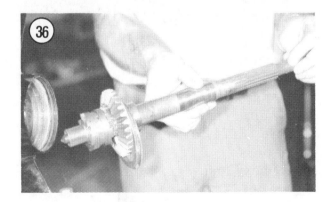

NOTE
If the cover nut is frozen in place and cannot be moved in Step 6 even with the assistance of heat and tapping on the tool, use an electric drill to drill out one side of the nut. This will permit removal of the nut without damage to the housing.

6. Install cover nut remover (part No. C-91-61069) and remove cover nut. See **Figure 34**.

7. Remove lock tab washer from gear housing. See **Figure 34**.

8. Install puller jaws part No. C-91-46086A1 and puller bolt (part No. C-91-85716) or equivalent and remove bearing carrier (**Figure 35**). If necessary, use propeller thrust hub to exert outward pressure on the puller jaws. Check carrier to make sure alignment key is with it.

CAUTION
*At this point, side force must **not** be applied to propeller shaft or it may break the clutch actuator rod neck.*

9. Pull propeller shaft, cam follower and shift cam straight out of the gear housing with a single smooth movement (**Figure 36**). If shaft will not come easily, proceed as follows:

　a. Push shaft back in place against the forward gear. Look into the shift shaft hole with a flashlight. If you can see the splined hole in the shift cam, reinstall the shift shaft and rotate to the neutral position. Remove shift shaft and remove shaft, cam follower and shift cam.

　b. If propeller shaft will not come out smoothly after step a, push the shaft back in place against the forward gear. Reinstall the bearing carrier sufficiently to support the propeller shaft. Remove gear housing from vise and lay on its port side. Strike the upper leading edge of the housing with a rubber mallet to dislodge shift cam from cam follower. Remove bearing carrier and pull propeller shaft from housing. To remove the shift cam and follower, remove the forward gear as described in this chapter.

Cleaning and Inspection

1. Clean all parts in fresh solvent. Blow dry with compressed air, if available.

9

2. Check bearing carrier roller/needle bearing contact points on propeller shaft. If shaft shows signs of pitting, grooves, scoring, heat discoloration or embedded metallic particles, replace shaft and bearings.

3. Check propeller shaft surface where oil seal lips touch shaft. If grooved, replace the shaft and oil seals.

4. Check propeller shaft splines for wear, rust or corrosion damage. Replace shaft as necessary.

5. Apply a light coat of oil to reverse gear ball bearing and rotate bearing to check for rough spots. Push and pull on reverse gear to check for side wear. If movement is excessive, replace bearing using an arbor press.

6. Check reverse gear teeth and clutch jaws (**Figure 37**). If teeth are pitted, chipped, broken or excessively worn, replace gear. If clutch jaw surfaces are chipped or rounded off, replace gear and check for improper shifting cable adjustment, excessive rpm during idling or poor shift habits (shifting too slowly from NEUTRAL to REVERSE).

7. Check reverse gear shift dogs on sliding clutch (**Figure 38**) for the same defects as in Step 6. If shift dogs are rounded off, replace sliding clutch assembly.

8. Check reverse gear to pinion gear wear pattern. If it is not smooth and even, replace reverse and pinion gears.

9. Check cam follower for wear, pitting, scoring or a rough surface. If any of these defects are found, replace the cam follower and shift cam.

10. Inspect cover nut for cracks and broken or corroded threads. Replace as required.

Bearing Carrier Disassembly/Assembly

1. If inspection determines that bearing carrier component replacement is necessary, clamp carrier in a vise with protective jaws or between wood blocks.

2. Remove reverse gear with a slide hammer.

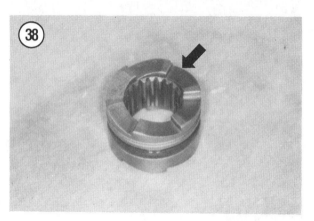

3. If reverse gear bearing remains in the carrier, remove with the slide hammer. If reverse gear is fitted with a ball bearing and the bearing remained on the gear (**Figure 39**), remove with a universal puller plate and arbor press.

4. Remove and discard carrier O-ring (A, **Figure 40**).

5. If needle bearing replacement is not necessary, pry oil seals (B, **Figure 40**) from carrier with a screwdriver.

NOTE
Some bearing carriers are designed to function without a needle bearing. On such carriers, pry oil seal out with a screwdriver and proceed with Step 7.

6. If needle bearing requires replacement, press bearing and oil seals from carrier with a suitable bearing and seal remover.

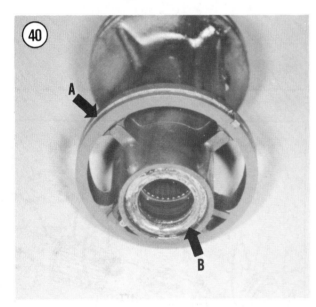

8. Wipe ID of reverse gear ball bearing with a light coat of multipurpose lubricant. Position bearing on gear with its numbered side facing upward.

9. Press bearing onto gear until fully seated using a mandrel which will apply pressure only on the inner race.

10. Wipe OD of propeller shaft needle bearing with a light coat of multipurpose lubricant. Position needle bearing in aft end of carrier with numbered side facing aft end and press in place with a suitable mandrel.

11. Wipe OD of reverse gear ball bearing with multipurpose lubricant. Position carrier assembly over ball bearing and press into place with a suitable mandrel and arbor press.

12. Wipe OD of propeller shaft oil seals with Loctite Type A. Install one seal on longer shoulder of driver part No. C-91-31108 with lip facing *away* from shoulder of tool. Press seal into carrier until driver bottoms.

13. Install the other seal on the short shoulder of driver part No. C-91-31108 with lip facing *toward* shoulder of tool. Press seal into carrier until driver bottoms.

14. Wipe excess Loctite from seals. Lubricate seals with multipurpose lubricant.

15. Install new O-ring and lubricate with multipurpose lubricant.

7. To reassemble, position reverse gear on a press with the teeth facing downward. Install thrust washer with bevel side toward gear.

NOTE
Some bearing carriers are designed to function without a ball bearing. On such carriers, install the thrust washer with its bevel side facing away from the carrier, wipe carrier bore with multipurpose lubricant and press gear/thrust washer into carrier. Proceed with Step 12.

Propeller Shaft Disassembly/Assembly (V6 EZ-Shift and Inline Engines)

1. Remove shift cam from cam follower, if so equipped.

2. Insert a thin-bladed screwdriver or awl under the front coil of the cross pin retainer spring. Lift coil up and rotate propeller shaft to unwind spring from sliding clutch. Take care not to stretch the spring excessively.

9

3. Repeat Step 2 to remove the second cross pin retainer spring. Remove detent pins from the sliding clutch. See **Figure 41**.

4. Push cross pin from sliding clutch and propeller shaft with an appropriate punch. Remove sliding clutch from shaft.

5. Pull cam follower and clutch actuator rod straight out of propeller shaft. Do not move cam follower up and down or side-to-side during removal.

6. Separate clutch actuator rod from cam follower.

7. To reassemble, partially install clutch actuator rod in propeller shaft end. Install cam follower on end of actuator rod and push rod fully into the propeller shaft. Align shaft and rod cross pin slots.

8. Install sliding clutch on propeller shaft. Grooved rings on clutch should face prop end of shaft. Align cross pin and detent holes in clutch with slot and notches on propeller shaft. See **Figure 42**.

9. Insert cross pin tool (part No. C-91-86642) or an appropriate size dummy shaft through the sliding clutch, propeller shaft and actuator rod. Tool or dummy shaft must pass *between* compression springs.

10. Install cross pin through the sliding clutch, propeller shaft and actuator rod with flat sides facing compression springs, forcing the tool or dummy shaft out.

11. Apply a small quantity of multipurpose lubricant on each detent pin. Install detent pins in sliding clutch pin holes with rounded ends toward propeller shaft.

12. Insert tang end of first retaining spring in a detent pin. Spiral the spring into the sliding clutch groove and position spring with straight end against side of groove.

13. Insert tang end of second retaining spring in the other detent pin. Spiral the spring in the sliding clutch groove in a direction opposite to that of the first spring. Position spring with straight end against side of groove but not overlapping the first spring.

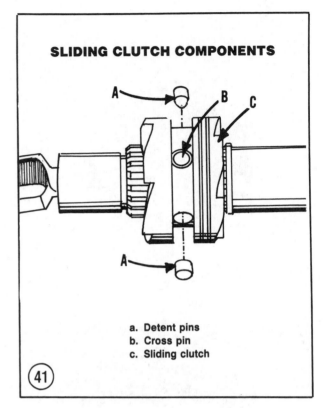

SLIDING CLUTCH COMPONENTS

a. Detent pins
b. Cross pin
c. Sliding clutch

(41)

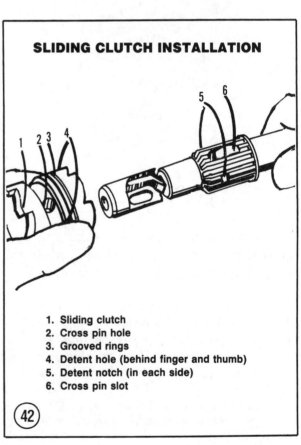

SLIDING CLUTCH INSTALLATION

1. Sliding clutch
2. Cross pin hole
3. Grooved rings
4. Detent hole (behind finger and thumb)
5. Detent notch (in each side)
6. Cross pin slot

(42)

Propeller Shaft
Disassembly/Assembly
(V6 Cam Shift and Inline Engines)

1. Push cam follower assembly against a solid object. Insert a thin-bladed screwdriver or awl under the front coil of the cross pin retainer spring. Lift coil up and rotate propeller shaft to unwind spring from sliding clutch. Take care not to stretch the spring excessively.

2. Push cam follower against the solid object and hold the pressure. Remove the cross pin from the sliding clutch and propeller shaft with an appropriate punch. Release pressure and remove sliding clutch from shaft.

3. Tilt propeller shaft and catch cam follower, guide block and spring assembly as it slides off the shaft.

4. To reassemble, install sliding clutch and align cross pin hole in clutch with corresponding slot in propeller shaft.

5. Insert spring in end of propeller shaft, then insert the stepped end of the guide block into the front end of the shaft. Align the guide block cross pin hole with the sliding clutch cross pin hole.

NOTE
It may be necessary to realign cross pin holes with a punch while applying pressure in Step 6.

6. Insert flat end of cam follower in propeller shaft. Push cam follower against a solid object to compress spring and hold pressure while installing the cross pin.

7. Release pressure and install retainer spring over sliding clutch. Do not stretch spring excessively during installation.

8. Remove cam follower. Place a small amount of multipurpose lubricant in propeller shaft end and reinstall cam follower with its flat end first.

Installation
(Except Merc V6 E-Z Shift Models)

1. Insert propeller shaft in center of forward gear assembly.

2. Make sure bearing carrier O-ring is lubricated with multipurpose lubricant.

NOTE
Step 3A and Step 3B apply only to Merc 50 and 70 hp models.

3A. If shimming removed during disassembly was correct, install on gear housing shoulder behind pinion gear. See *Pinion Depth/ Gear Backlash* in this chapter.

3B. If shimming removed during disassembly was not correct, add shim(s) to increase or subtract shim(s) to decrease backlash until it is within specifications. See *Pinion Depth/ Gear Backlash* in this chapter. Each 0.001 in. change in shimming will change backlash about 0.0015 in.

CAUTION
Do not let Perfect Seal touch O-ring or oil seals in Step 4.

4. Apply a light coat of Perfect Seal (part No. C-92-34227) to the OD of the bearing carrier at all points where carrier touches gear housing.

5. Carefully slide bearing carrier over propeller shaft to prevent oil seal damage and insert into gear housing. At the same time, rotate the drive shaft clockwise to mesh the pinion and reverse gears. Make sure the bearing carrier keyway aligns with the gear housing keyway.

9

6. Push bearing carrier into gear housing as far as possible and install key in keyway with a small punch (**Figure 43**).

7. Install a new tab washer against bearing carrier. If the washer has a "V" portion, position it opposite the keyway.

8. Wipe cover nut threads with Perfect Seal. Install cover nut in housing. Any writing and/or arrows on cover nut must face outward.

9. Hand-start cover nut in gear housing, then install tool part No. C-91-74241 (50 and 70 hp) or part No. C-91-73688 (all others) and tighten to specifications (**Table 1**).

10. Determine which lock tab on washer will align with cover nut slots. Bend that tab flush with slot in nut.

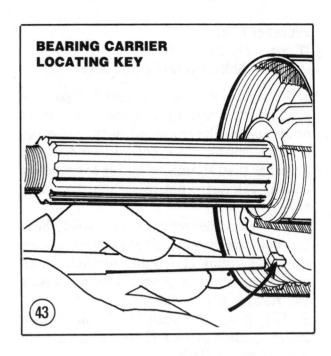

BEARING CARRIER LOCATING KEY

43

Installation (Merc V6 E-Z Shift Models)

1. Coat the cam follower pocket with multipurpose lubricant. See **Figure 44**.

2. Position shift cam in cam follower pocket (**Figure 44**) with numbered side facing upward.

3. Make sure the retaining and E-rings are properly positioned on the shift shaft (**Figure 45**). Install shift shaft in gear housing and through the shift cam and cam follower. If necessary, rotate shift shaft back and forth slightly until it engages the shift cam hole.

NOTE
Do not let Perfect Seal touch bushing oil seals or O-ring in Step 4.

4. Wipe shift shaft bushing threads with a light coat of Perfect Seal (part No. C-92-34227). Thread bushing in place but do not tighten at this time.

5. Make sure bearing carrier O-ring is lubricated with multipurpose lubricant.

NOTE
Do not let Perfect Seal touch bearings or O-ring in Step 6.

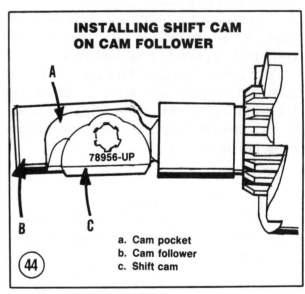

INSTALLING SHIFT CAM ON CAM FOLLOWER

A

78956-UP

B   C

44

a. Cam pocket
b. Cam follower
c. Shift cam

6. Apply a light coat of Perfect Seal to the OD of the bearing carrier at all points where carrier touches gear housing.

7. Carefully slide bearing carrier over propeller shaft to prevent oil seal damage and insert into gear housing. At the same time, rotate the drive shaft clockwise to mesh the pinion and reverse gears. Make sure the bearing carrier keyway aligns with the gear housing keyway.

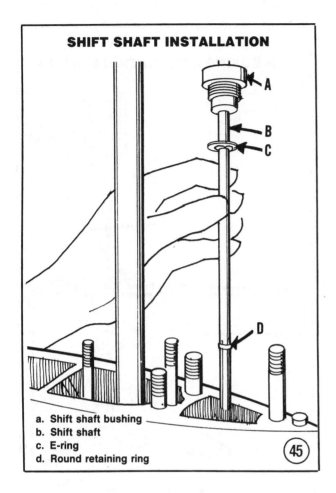

SHIFT SHAFT INSTALLATION

a. Shift shaft bushing
b. Shift shaft
c. E-ring
d. Round retaining ring

(45)

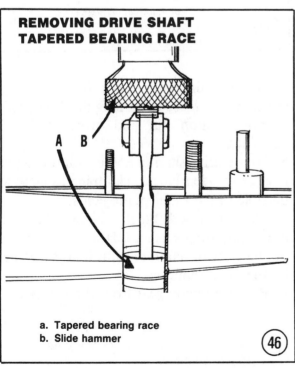

**REMOVING DRIVE SHAFT
TAPERED BEARING RACE**

a. Tapered bearing race
b. Slide hammer

(46)

8. Push bearing carrier into gear housing as far as possible and install key in keyways with a small punch (**Figure 43**).

9. Install a new tab washer against bearing carrier.

10. Wipe cover nut threads with Perfect Seal. Install cover nut in housing. Any writing and/or arrows on cover nut must face outward.

11. Hand-start cover nut in gear housing, then install tool part No. C-91-61069 and tighten to specifications (**Table 1**).

12. Determine which lock tab on washer will align with cover nut slots. Bend that tab flush with slot in nut.

13. Tighten shift shaft bushing securely with bushing tool part No. C-91-31107.

PINION GEAR, DRIVE SHAFT AND FORWARD GEAR

**Removal
(Merc 45-70 [Prior to 1984] hp Models)**

1. Remove bearing carrier and propeller shaft as described in this chapter.

2. Secure drive shaft in a vise with protective jaws or wood blocks as close as possible to water pump studs.

3. Remove pinion gear retainer nut with an appropriate size box end wrench or socket.

4. Place a wood block against the gear housing mating surfaces. Hold housing and tap block with hammer until housing comes off the drive shaft.

5. Remove pinion and forward gears from housing.

6. Remove drive shaft from vise. Secure gear housing in the vise and remove the drive shaft tapered bearing race with a slide hammer (**Figure 46**). Retrieve shims under bearing race.

9

7. Remove gear housing lubrication sleeve with water pump cartridge puller part No. C-91-27780 as shown in **Figure 47**.

Removal
(All Other Inline; V6 Cam-Shift Models)

1. Remove bearing carrier and propeller shaft as described in this chapter.
2. Install drive shaft nut wrench (part No. C-91-34377A1), socket and flex handle on drive shaft splines.
3. Hold pinion nut with a socket and flex handle. Pad that part of the gear housing where the flex handle will hit with shop cloths to prevent housing damage.
4. Holding the pinion nut from moving, break the nut loose by turning the drive shaft. Remove pinion nut and drive shaft nut wrenches.
5. Secure drive shaft in a vise with protective jaws or wooden blocks, clamping as close as possible to the water pump studs.
6. Place a wood block against the gear housing mating surfaces. Hold housing and tap block with hammer until housing comes off the drive shaft.
7. Remove shims installed between drive shaft bearing and housing.
8. Remove pinion and forward gears from the housing.

Removal
(Merc V6 E-Z Shift Models)

1. Remove bearing retainer and propeller shaft as described in this chapter.
2. Install drive shaft nut wrench (part No. C-91-34377A1), socket and flex handle on drive shaft splines.
3. Hold pinion nut with a socket and flex handle. Pad that part of the gear housing where the flex handle will hit with shop cloths to prevent housing damage.

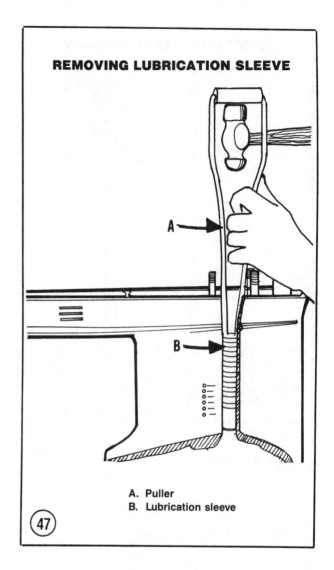

REMOVING LUBRICATION SLEEVE

A. Puller
B. Lubrication sleeve

(47)

4. Holding the pinion nut from moving, break the nut loose by turning the drive shaft. Remove pinion nut and drive shaft nut wrenches.
5. Secure drive shaft in a vise with protective jaws or wooden blocks, clamping as close as possible to the water pump studs.
6. Place a wood block against the gear housing mating surfaces. Hold housing and tap block with hammer until housing comes off the drive shaft.
7. Remove pinion gear from the housing.

NOTE
Sleeve removal tool used in Step 8 has a left-hand thread.

8. Remove gear housing lubrication sleeve with sleeve removal tool (part No. C-91-39281) and a slide hammer.

9. Remove forward gear from the housing (**Figure 48**).

Cleaning and Inspection

1. Clean drive shaft, pinion and forward gears with a clean shop cloth moistened with solvent. Blow dry with compressed air.

2. Check pinion and forward gears for pitting, grooving, scoring, uneven or excessive wear and heat discoloration. Replace the gear(s) if any of these defects are noted.

3. Check forward gear bearing for the defects described in Step 2. Replace bearing and race if any defects are noted.

NOTE
Merc 45-70 (prior to 1984) hp models use a roller bearing instead of needle bearing. Step 4 inspection is the same.

4. Check drive shaft needle bearing contact surfaces for the defects described in Step 2. Replace drive shaft and needle bearing if any defects are noted.

5. Check for excessive wear or damage to the drive shaft splines. Replace shaft as required.

6. Check the oil seal in the water pump base for grooving. Replace the drive shaft if grooves are found.

NOTE
Do not remove drive shaft bearing from drive shaft unless replacement is required.

7. Lightly lubricate drive shaft bearing with oil. Rotate bearing to check for rough spots or other defects. Check bearing for side wear. Replace bearing if any of these conditions are noted.

Drive Shaft Bearing Replacement

1. If the inspection procedures indicate that bearing replacement is necessary, remove bearing from drive shaft with a universal puller plate and arbor press. Press new bearing on shaft.

2. Remove bearing race from gear housing with a slide hammer. Install new bearing race with a suitable mandrel.

NOTE
Merc 45-70 (prior to 1984) hp models use a roller bearing instead of a needle bearing. Step 3 and Step 4 replacement procedures are the same.

3. If the inspection procedures indicate that needle bearing replacement is necessary, secure gear housing in a vise with protective jaws or wooden blocks and remove bearing

9

with a suitable driver head, pilot and mandrel. See **Figure 49**.

4. Lubricate needle bearing contact area in drive shaft cavity with Quicksilver Formula 50-D oil (part No. C-92-65183). Install new bearing with a suitable drive head, pilot and mandrel. Bearing is properly installed when it is about 1/16 in. above the bottom end of the drive shaft cavity in the housing.

Installation
(Merc 45-70 [Prior to 1984] hp Models)

CAUTION
Do not use excessive force in Step 1 or lubrication sleeve may be distorted.

1. Insert lubrication sleeve in gear housing drive shaft cavity with anti-rotation tab toward the front of the housing (**Figure 50**). Seat sleeve below shim shoulder of drive shaft bearing race.
2. Install forward gear in gear housing.
3. Position pinion gear in gear housing below drive shaft bore. Mesh pinion and forward gear teeth.
4. Hold pinion gear in position and install drive shaft in gear housing with a rotating motion to align shaft splines with gear ID splines.
5. Lightly lubricate pinion gear nut threads with Loctite Type A (part No. C-92-32609). Install nut to drive shaft with flat side facing away from pinion gear.
6. Clamp drive shaft in a vise with protective jaws or wooden blocks and tighten pinion nut to specifications (**Table 1**). Wipe any excess Loctite from pinion nut and gear.

Installation
(All Other Inline; V6 Cam-Shift Models)

1. Install forward gear in gear housing.
2. Position pinion gear in gear housing below drive shaft bore. Mesh pinion and forward gear teeth.

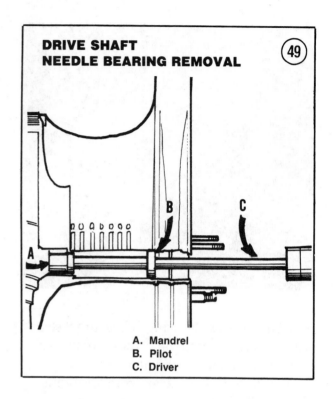

DRIVE SHAFT NEEDLE BEARING REMOVAL (49)

A. Mandrel
B. Pilot
C. Driver

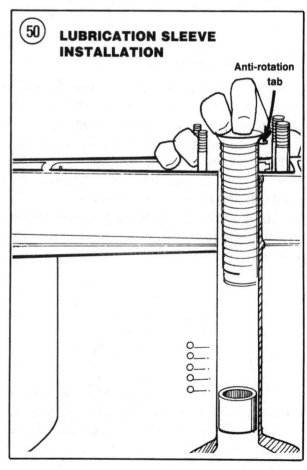

(50) **LUBRICATION SLEEVE INSTALLATION**

Anti-rotation tab

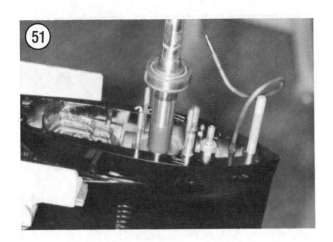

3. Hold pinion gear in position and install drive shaft in gear housing (**Figure 51**). Tap end of drive shaft with a mallet to seat bearing in housing, then rotate drive shaft to align and engage shaft and gear splines. Several tap/rotational sequences will be required.

4. Once drive shaft has entered the pinion gear splines, wipe retainer nut threads with Loctite Type A (part No.C-92-32609). Install nut on drive shaft with grooved side facing the pinion gear.

5. Hold pinion gear nut with a socket and flex handle. Pad the gear housing area where the flex handle will rest with shop cloths to prevent housing damage.

6. Install drive shaft nut tool (part No. C-91-34377A1), socket and torque wrench on drive shaft end.

7. Tighten drive shaft to torque pinion nut to specifications (**Table 1**). Wipe any excess Loctite from pinion nut and gear.

Installation
(Merc V6 E-Z Shift Models)

1. Install forward gear in gear housing.

2. Insert lubrication sleeve in drive shaft bore, aligning flats in bore with flats on the sleeve. The notch in the top of the sleeve should face the leading edge of the gear housing.

CAUTION
Do not use excessive force in Step 3 or lubrication sleeve may be distorted.

3. Install lubrication sleeve in housing with sleeve driver part No. C-91-39238 and a mallet. Tap sleeve until it is just below the tapered bearing shim surface.

4. Position pinion gear in gear housing below drive shaft bore. Mesh pinion and forward gear teeth.

5. Hold pinion gear in position and install drive shaft in gear housing with a rotating motion to align shaft splines with gear ID splines. Drive shaft is fully installed when its tapered bearing rests against the bearing race.

6. Lightly lubricate pinion gear nut threads with Loctite Type A (part No. C-92-32609). Install nut to drive shaft with flat side facing away from pinion gear.

7. Hold pinion gear nut with a socket and flex handle. Pad the gear housing area where the flex handle will rest with shop cloths to prevent housing damage.

8. Install drive shaft nut tool (part No. C-91-34377A1), socket and torque wrench on drive shaft end.

9. Tighten drive shaft to torque pinion nut to specifications (**Table 1**). Wipe any excess Loctite from pinion nut and gear.

LOWER SHIFT SHAFT, BUSHING AND CAM

Removal and Disassembly (All Inline Models)

1. Remove propeller shaft, drive shaft and forward gear as described in this chapter.

2. Secure gear housing in a vise with protective jaws or wooden blocks.

3. Pry reverse locking cam and spacer from shift shaft, if so equipped.

4. Install shift shaft bushing tool part No. C-91-23033 (Merc 45-70 [prior to 1984] hp) or part No. C-91-31107 (all others) over shift

9

shaft, engaging tool tangs with bushing slots. Slip an appropriate size box end wrench over tool and turn counterclockwise to remove the bushing.

5. Remove shift shaft from gear housing. Reach inside propeller shaft cavity in housing and remove shift cam. See **Figure 52**.

6. Slide bushing up and off shift shaft.

7. Remove and discard shift shaft bushing O-ring.

8A. Merc 45-70 (prior to 1984) hp—drive oil seals from gear housing side of bushing with a punch and hammer. Discard seals.

8B. All others-if shift shaft bushing has one seal, remove with a punch and hammer. If bushing has 2 seals, replace bushing and seals as an assembly.

Cleaning and Inspection

1. Clean all parts with solvent. Blow dry with compressed air, if available.

2. Check shift shaft splines and seal surface for excessive or uneven wear or corrosion. Replace as required.

3. Check E-clip (**Figure 52**) and replace if bent.

4. Check shift cam for excessive wear. Replace if wear can be seen.

Assembly and Installation
(All Inline Models)

1A. Merc 45-70 (prior to 1984) hp—coat outer surface of new bushing oil seals with Loctite Type A (part No. C-92-32609). Install small seal in bushing with seal lip facing away from the bushing top. Install larger seal with seal lip facing away from the bushing top. Remove any excess Loctite.

1B. All others—if one-seal bushing, install seal as in Step 1A. If 2-seal bushing, obtain a new bushing/seal assembly.

2. Install a new bushing O-ring. Lubricate O-ring and oil seals with Quicksilver

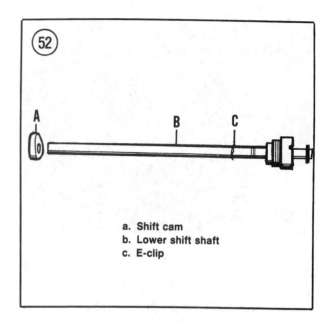

(52)

a. Shift cam
b. Lower shift shaft
c. E-clip

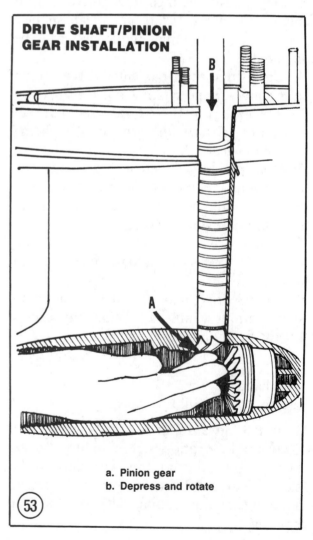

DRIVE SHAFT/PINION GEAR INSTALLATION

a. Pinion gear
b. Depress and rotate

(53)

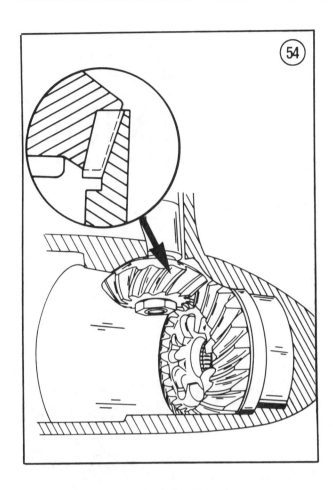

Multipurpose Lubricant (part No. C-92-63250).

3. Make sure E-clip is installed in shift shaft groove (**Figure 52**).

4A. Merc 50 and 70 hp—install shift cam in gear housing. Long side of cam should face grease FILL hole. When properly installed, shift cam ramps can be seen through bearing carrier cavity.

4B. All others—install shift cam between cast webbing in gear housing. Long side of cam should face port side of housing. When properly installed, shift cam ramps can be seen through the bearing carrier cavity.

5. Install shift shaft in gear housing and engage shift cam by slightly rotating shaft to align its splines with those in the cam.

6. Coat bushing threads with Perfect Seal (part No. C-92-34227). Fit bushing over shaft and thread into gear housing.

7. Tighten bushing securely with bushing tool part No. C-92-23033 (Merc 45-70 [prior to 1984] hp) or part No. C-92-31107 (all others).

8. Install rubber washer on shift shaft (if so equipped) and slide down against the oil seal.

PINION DEPTH/GEAR BACKLASH

Proper pinion gear engagement and forward/reverse gear backlash is important for smooth operation and long service life. Two or three shimming procedures must be performed to properly set up the lower unit gear housing. The pinion gear must be shimmed to a correct depth; the forward gear must be shimmed to the pinion gear for proper backlash and, on Merc 45-70 (prior to 1984) hp models, the reverse gear must be shimmed to the pinion gear for proper backlash.

Merc 45-70 (Prior to 1984) hp Models

Pinion gear depth

1. Secure the gear housing in a suitable fixture or a vise with protective jaws or wooden blocks.

2. Depress drive shaft and check pinion gear depth (**Figure 53**).

3. If pinion gear teeth do not engage forward gear teeth fully (**Figure 54**), remove drive shaft as described in this chapter.

NOTE
Any changes made to pinion gear depth in Step 4 will affect forward gear backlash.

4. Remove drive shaft tapered bearing race with a slide hammer puller and add or subtract shims as required to bring pinion gear teeth into full engagement with forward gear teeth.

9

Forward gear backlash

1. Depress drive shaft and move forward gear back and forth (**Figure 55**). Amount of free play should be 0.003-0.005 in.

> *NOTE*
> *A change in shim thickness of 0.001 in. will change backlash approximately 0.0015 in. in Step 2.*

2. If backlash is not within specifications, remove pinion gear, drive shaft, forward gear and forward gear bearing race. Add shims to reduce or remove shims to increase backlash.

Reverse gear backlash

Reverse gear backlash should be checked and recorded prior to disassembly of the lower unit gear housing as a reference for shimming during reassembly. If backlash is satisfactory before disassembly, the same amount of shimming can be used for reassembly, unless the reverse gear or pinion gear is replaced.

1. Shift lower unit into REVERSE.

2. Rotate propeller shaft counterclockwise to take up any free play between the reverse gear and clutch dogs.

3. Shift lower unit into NEUTRAL and rotate propeller shaft 1/8 in. counterclockwise.

4. It should not be possible at this point to shift the lower unit back into REVERSE. If it can be shifted, repeat Steps 1-3.

5. Maintain pressure on the lower shift shaft in the direction of reverse gear. Push drive shaft downward. Pull out on the propeller shaft and rock it from side to side at the same time.

6. If reverse gear-to-pinion gear backlash is correct, the propeller shaft should move 0.003-0.005 in. Record the reading for reassembly reference.

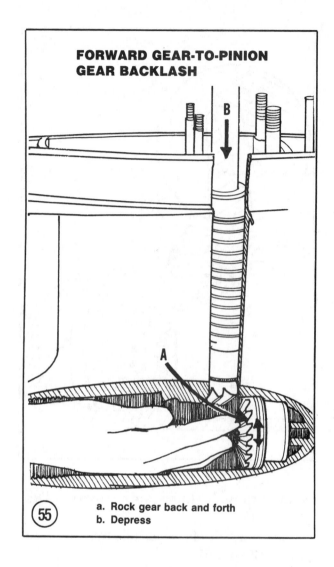

FORWARD GEAR-TO-PINION GEAR BACKLASH

(55)
a. Rock gear back and forth
b. Depress

> *NOTE*
> *A change in shim thickness of 0.001 in. will change backlash approximately 0.0015 in. in Step 7.*

7. If backlash is not correct, add sufficient shimming on gear housing shoulder at rear of pinion gear to increase (or remove to decrease) backlash during reassembly.

All Other Inline Models

Pinion gear depth/forward gear backlash

1. Install water pump base (without O-ring) and cover (without impeller) with correct shimming as described in this chapter. Tighten fasteners to specifications.

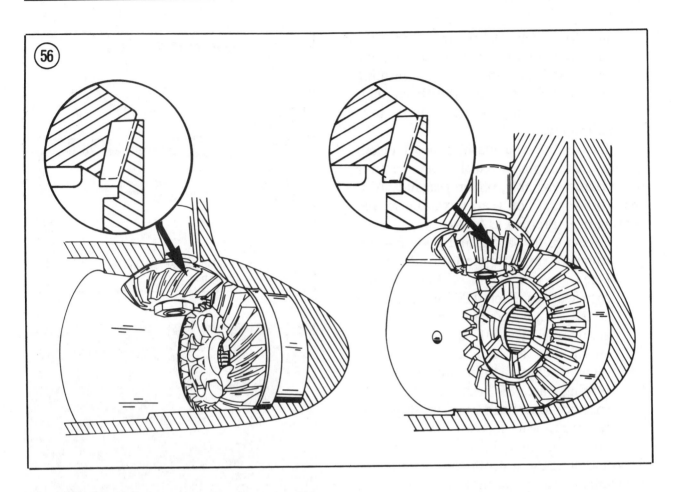

2. Pull drive shaft up and hold stationary during Steps 3-5.

3. Check pinion gear depth (**Figure 53**, typical). Pinion gear teeth must engage forward gear teeth according to cut of gear as shown in **Figure 56**. If they do not, complete this procedure before making any corrections.

4. Reach inside the propeller shaft cavity and place a finger at the 3 and 9 o'clock positions on the forward gear.

5. Push forward gear toward front of housing, then lightly rock it back and forth. The amount of free play felt is the forward gear backlash. If correct, backlash will be 0.008-0.0012 (Merc 80 and 85 hp) or 0.014-0.016 in. (all others).

6. If pinion gear depth and/or forward gear backlash is incorrect, remove the water pump assembly, pinion gear nut, drive shaft, bearing and pinion gear. Proceed as follows:

a. Insufficient forward gear backlash and pinion gear too deep—add sufficient shimming in drive shaft bore to correct pinion gear depth. Each 0.001 in. shimming added will increase forward gear backlash by 0.0015 in. Remove the equivalent amount of shimming added here from that used under the water pump base.

b. Insufficient forward gear backlash and pinion gear too shallow—remove sufficient shimming in drive shaft bore to correct pinion gear depth. Remove forward gear and bearing race. Remove the same amount of forward gear shimming as that removed to correct pinion gear depth plus the additional amount necessary to bring forward gear backlash within specifications. Forward gear backlash will increase about 0.0015 in. for each 0.001 in. shimming removed from the front of the bearing race. Add the amount of shimming removed from under the drive shaft bearing to the water pump base shimming.

7. If forward gear backlash is incorrect but pinion gear depth is satisfactory, remove water pump assembly, pinion gear nut, drive shaft, bearing, pinion gear, forward gear and bearing race. Proceed as follows:

   a. Excessive forward gear backlash—add sufficient shimming in front of bearing race to bring backlash into specifications. Each 0.001 in. shimming added will decrease backlash by approximately 0.0015 in.

   b. Insufficient forward gear backlash—remove sufficient shimming in front of bearing race to bring backlash into specifications. Each 0.001 in. shimming removed will increase backlash by approximately 0.0015 in.

8. When pinion gear depth and forward gear backlash are within specifications, reassemble components as described in this chapter.

Merc V6 Models

Pinion gear depth

1. Clean reverse gear shoulder in propeller shaft cavity. Clean inner diameter of cavity.

2. Insert shimming tool (part No. C-91-74776) in cavity until it bottoms on reverse gear shoulder.

3. Align shimming tool access slot with pinion gear nose.

4. Rotate drive shaft several times while applying downward pressure to seat tapered bearing.

5. Apply and hold 15 lb. pressure on drive shaft. Insert a feeler gauge through the shimming tool access slot to determine clearance. It should be 0.025 in.

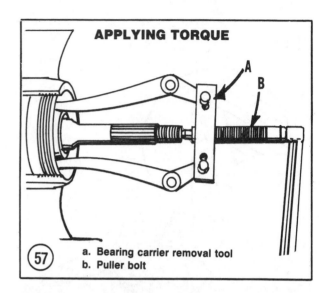

APPLYING TORQUE

A

B

57
a. Bearing carrier removal tool
b. Puller bolt

58

6. If clearance is not 0.025 in., reshim drive shaft tapered bearing race to raise/lower pinion gear as required.

   a. Remove pinion gear nut.

   b. Remove drive shaft.

   c. Remove drive shaft tapered bearing race.

   d. Add or remove shimming as required to bring clearance within specifications. Adding shims will lower the pinion gear; removing them will raise it.

Forward gear backlash

1. Insert propeller shaft without shift cam in gear housing.

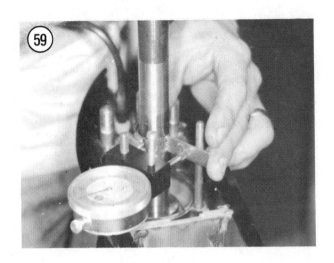

2. Install bearing carrier in gear housing. Thread cover nut against carrier.

3. Attach carrier removal tool (part No. C-91-46086A1) with puller bolt (part No. C-91-85716) as shown in **Figure 57**.

4. Tighten puller bolt to 45 in.-lb., then rotate drive shaft 2-3 times with load applied on propeller shaft to seat forward gear bearing.

5. Install a dial indicator to gear housing. Install backlash indicator tool part No. C-91-78473 to drive shaft. See **Figure 58**.

6. Recheck puller bolt torque at 45 in.-lb.

NOTE
To determine gear ratio in Step 7, count pinion gear teeth. There should be 14 teeth (1.86:1) or 15 teeth (2:1).

7. Align dial indicator plunger with "No. 1" (1.86:1 ratio) or "No. 2" (2:1 ratio) on backlash indicator tool and zero indicator gauge.

8. Apply downward pressure on drive shaft and rotate shaft back and forth lightly (**Figure 59**).

9. Check dial indicator gauge. It should read 0.008-0.013 in.

10. If backlash is not 0.008-0.013 in., reshim forward gear as follows:

    a. Remove dial indicator, backlash tool and bearing carrier removal tool.

    b. Remove cover nut, bearing carrier and propeller shaft as described in this chapter.

    c. Remove pinion gear nut and drive shaft as described in this chapter.

    d. Remove forward gear and bearing race. Remove or add sufficient shimming to bring backlash within specifications. Every 0.001 in. change in shimming will change backlash approximately 0.0015 in.

    e. Reassemble components as described in this chapter.

Propeller Removal/Installation

Old-style 4- and 6-cylinder Merc 650-800 model propeller shafts have a square thrust hub shoulder instead of the tapered shoulder used on later thrust hubs. To install a new-style propeller and thrust hub (part No. A-75282) on such motors, install spacer part No. C-23-86918. Refer to **Figure 60** and **Figure 61** for this procedure.

WARNING
To prevent accidental engine starting during this procedure, disconnect all spark plug leads from the plugs on manual and electric start models. In addition, Mercury Marine recommends that electric start models be shifted into NEUTRAL and the key removed from the ignition as further safety precautions.

1. Install a block of wood between the propeller blade and anti-cavitation plate to prevent propeller from rotating.

2. Straighten bent tab(s) on tab washer with a punch and hammer.

3. Remove propeller nut, splined washer/rear thrust hub, tab washer and propeller.

4. Remove propeller shaft thrust hub. If necessary, loosen thrust hub by prying with 2

9

screwdrivers. Be sure to pad areas on gear housing where screwdrivers will apply pressure.

5. Check propeller shaft splines for wear and/or corrosion. If worn excessively or badly corroded, replace shaft as described in this chapter.

6. Coat propeller shaft splines liberally with Perfect Seal (part No. C-92-34227).

7. Install forward thrust hub on propeller shaft.

8. Align propeller and drive shaft splines. Install propeller on drive shaft. Install splined washer/rear thrust hub and tab washer.

9. Install propeller nut. Install the block of wood between the propeller blade and anti-cavitation plate, then tighten nut to specifications (**Table 1**).

10A. Merc 50 and 70 hp—bend one tab on washer against side of nut to lock nut in place.

10B. All others—bend 3 washer tabs into propeller thrust hub grooves to lock nut in place (**Figure 62**). If washer tabs do not align with grooves, tighten nut until they do.

11. After engine has been run the first time, straighten the washer tab(s) and retorque propeller nut to specifications (**Table 1**), then bend tab(s) back against nut or propeller hub grooves.

MODEL R
DRIVE GEAR HOUSING

A redesigned gear housing was introduced as a running change on 1985 V175/V200 and 1986 V150 models. The new housing can be identified by the lack of a preload pin at the top of the drive shaft and the model designation R.

Figure 63 is an exploded view of the R gear housing. Service procedures which differ from those provided under *Standard Gear Housing* in this chapter are given below. Torque specifications and required lubricants,

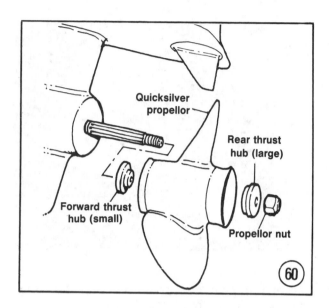

Quicksilver propellor

Forward thrust hub (small)

Rear thrust hub (large)

Propellor nut

60

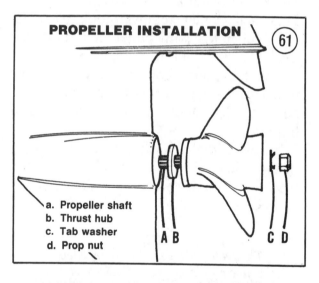

PROPELLER INSTALLATION   61

a. Propeller shaft
b. Thrust hub
c. Tab washer
d. Prop nut

A B   C D

62

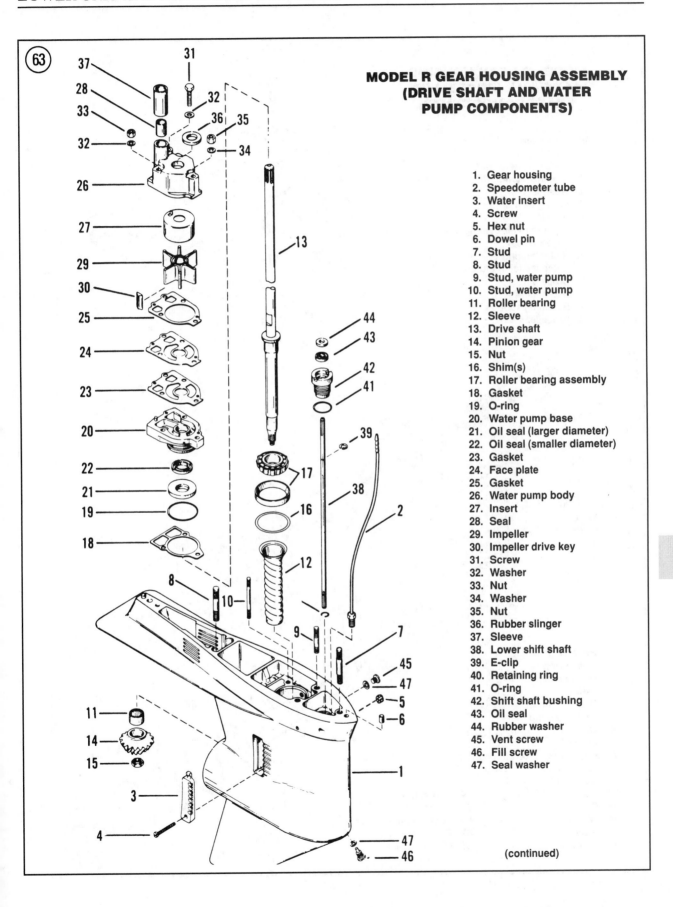

MODEL R GEAR HOUSING ASSEMBLY (DRIVE SHAFT AND WATER PUMP COMPONENTS)

1. Gear housing
2. Speedometer tube
3. Water insert
4. Screw
5. Hex nut
6. Dowel pin
7. Stud
8. Stud
9. Stud, water pump
10. Stud, water pump
11. Roller bearing
12. Sleeve
13. Drive shaft
14. Pinion gear
15. Nut
16. Shim(s)
17. Roller bearing assembly
18. Gasket
19. O-ring
20. Water pump base
21. Oil seal (larger diameter)
22. Oil seal (smaller diameter)
23. Gasket
24. Face plate
25. Gasket
26. Water pump body
27. Insert
28. Seal
29. Impeller
30. Impeller drive key
31. Screw
32. Washer
33. Nut
34. Washer
35. Nut
36. Rubber slinger
37. Sleeve
38. Lower shift shaft
39. E-clip
40. Retaining ring
41. O-ring
42. Shift shaft bushing
43. Oil seal
44. Rubber washer
45. Vent screw
46. Fill screw
47. Seal washer

9

(continued)

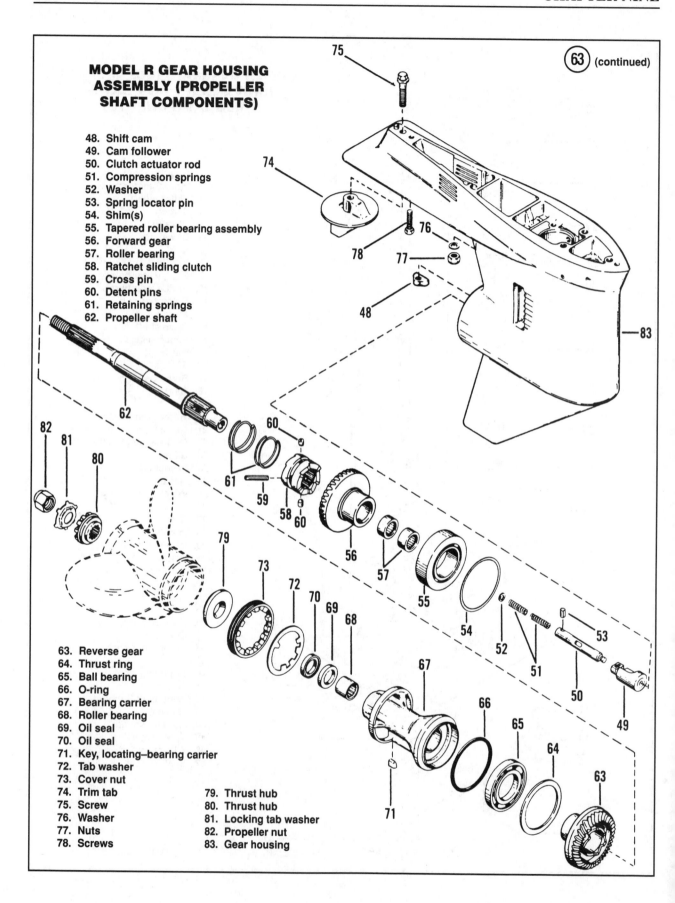

63 (continued)

MODEL R GEAR HOUSING ASSEMBLY (PROPELLER SHAFT COMPONENTS)

48. Shift cam
49. Cam follower
50. Clutch actuator rod
51. Compression springs
52. Washer
53. Spring locator pin
54. Shim(s)
55. Tapered roller bearing assembly
56. Forward gear
57. Roller bearing
58. Ratchet sliding clutch
59. Cross pin
60. Detent pins
61. Retaining springs
62. Propeller shaft

63. Reverse gear
64. Thrust ring
65. Ball bearing
66. O-ring
67. Bearing carrier
68. Roller bearing
69. Oil seal
70. Oil seal
71. Key, locating–bearing carrier
72. Tab washer
73. Cover nut
74. Trim tab
75. Screw
76. Washer
77. Nuts
78. Screws
79. Thrust hub
80. Thrust hub
81. Locking tab washer
82. Propeller nut
83. Gear housing

adhesives and sealers are provided in **Table 2** and **Table 3** at the end of this chapter.

Special Tools

New special tools are required to service the R gear housing as follows:

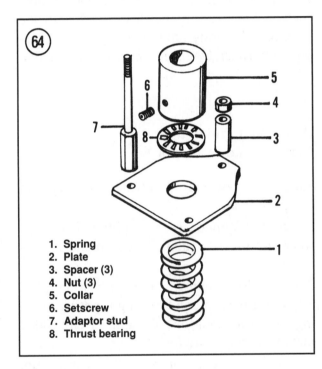

1. Spring
2. Plate
3. Spacer (3)
4. Nut (3)
5. Collar
6. Setscrew
7. Adaptor stud
8. Thrust bearing

a. Drive shaft bearing preload tool (part No. 91-44307A1). This tool provides the necessary upward pressure on the drive shaft to seat the bearing when pinion gear height and gear backlash is checked. See **Figure 64**.

b. Drive shaft bearing retainer tool (part No. 91-43506). This tool is necessary to remove and install the threaded retainer. See **Figure 65**.

c. Pinion nut adapter wrench (part No. 91-61067A2). This tool supersedes the previous wrench (part No. 91-61607A1) and can be used with older gear housings as well as the Model R. See **Figure 66**.

Gear Housing Removal/Installation

The procedure is essentially the same as given under *Standard Gear Housing* with the following exceptions:

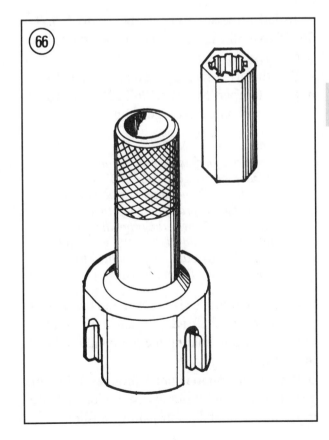

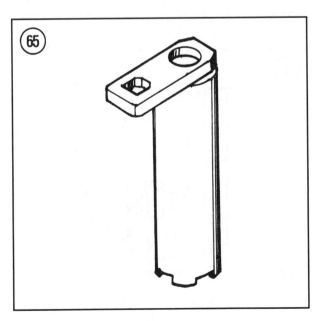

9

a. Trim the lower unit to its full out position for removal/installation.

b. A 3/8 in. Allen wrench is required to remove the trim tab screw.

c. Use Quicksilver 2-4-C Multi-Lube on the end of the water tube and drive shaft splines.

d. Coat gear housing oil seal with Quicksilver Special Lubricant 101, 2-4-C Multi-Lube or Perfect Seal.

e. Rotate shift shaft *clockwise* to shift gear housing into FORWARD gear.

Drive Shaft/Pinion Gear Removal

1. Remove the bearing carrier retainer/reverse gear as described under *Standard Gear Housing* in this chapter.

2. Install the drive shaft bearing retainer tool (part No. 91-43506) and loosen the bearing retainer at least 2 full turns (do not remove the retainer at this time).

3. Install drive shaft nut wrench (part No. 91-56775) over the drive shaft to protect the splines from possible damage.

4. Pull the drive shaft upward and install pinion nut adapter (part No. 91-61067A2) over propeller shaft and onto pinion gear nut.

NOTE
If the drive shaft is broken, install pinion nut adaptor (part No. 61067A2) over the propeller shaft and onto the pinion gear nut. Install the propeller shaft tool (part No. 91-61077) over the propeller shaft. Shift the unit into FORWARD gear and rotate the propeller shaft counterclockwise to remove the pinion nut.

5. Fit an appropriate size socket and breaker bar over the drive shaft adaptor and turn counterclockwise while holding the pinion nut to break the nut free.

6. Remove the pinion nut adaptor, reach into the gear housing and unscrew the pinion nut. Remove the nut and the anti-galling washer.

NOTE
The 18 pinion roller bearings may fall out of the outer bearing race in Step 7. If so, be sure to retrieve all 18 or a new set will have to be installed during reassembly. Do not substitute a roller bearing from another unit for one that is missing.

7. Remove the drive shaft bearing retainer loosened in Step 2. Lift the drive shaft with the bearing and bearing cup from the gearcase housing. Remove and tag the shims for reinstallation reference.

Drive Shaft/Pinion Gear Cleaning and Inspection

1. Clean all parts in fresh solvent. Blow dry with compressed air.

2. Check the pinion gear for pitting, excessive wear or broken or chipped teeth; replace as required.

3. Check drive shaft where roller bearing rides. Replace drive shaft and bearing if pitting, scoring, grooving, heat discoloration or embedded metallic particles are found.

4. Check drive shaft tapered roller bearing cup. Replace bearing and cup if pitting, scoring,

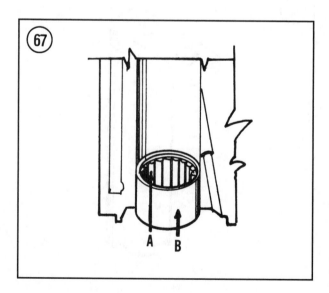

grooving, heat discoloration or embedded metallic particles are found.

5. Check splines on each end of drive shaft for excessive wear, twisting or damage.

6. Suspend drive shaft between V-blocks and check straightness with a dial indicator.

Drive Shaft/Pinion Gear Installation

The unit does not require reshimming if no new parts are installed.

1. If rollers (A, **Figure 67**) fell out of the drive shaft roller bearing race (B, **Figure 67**) during

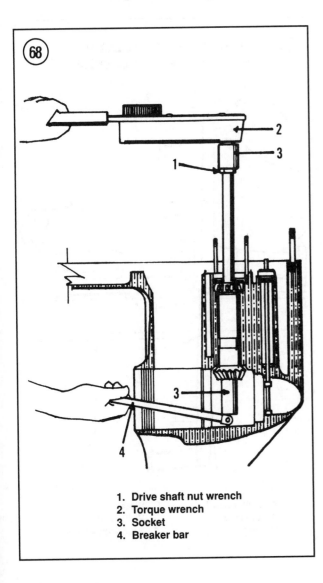

1. **Drive shaft nut wrench**
2. **Torque wrench**
3. **Socket**
4. **Breaker bar**

removal, coat all 18 rollers with Quicksilver Needle Bearing Assembly Lubricant and reinstall.

2. Reinstall any shim(s) removed from the drive shaft housing bore during disassembly. If shim(s) were lost or if the pinion gear, drive shaft, drive shaft roller bearing or gearcase housing were replaced, install a 0.015 in. shim as a starting point.

3. Grease the pinion gear washer and attach it to the pinion gear nut.

4. Position the pinion gear in the gear housing. Gear teeth must mesh with the forward gear teeth.

5. Hold pinion gear in place and insert the drive shaft in the housing bore. Rotate the drive shaft to align and engage its splines with those of the pinion gear. Install but do not tighten pinion gear washer and nut.

6. Install the drive shaft bearing cup over the tapered roller bearings, then thread the retainer in place until all threads are engaged.

7. Install drive shaft bearing retainer tool (part No. 91-43506) and tighten the retainer to specifications (**Table 2**).

8. Install adaptor (part No. 91-56775) on the drive shaft, then tighten the pinion gear nut to specifications (**Table 2**) using appropriate sockets, a breaker bar and a torque wrench. See **Figure 68**.

9. Check pinion gear height as described in this chapter.

CAUTION
Loctite sets up in 3 hours, but does not dry completely for 24 hours. If the Loctite applied to the nut threads in Step 10 is not dry, the nut may back off during operation at a later date especially if the torque applied to the nut is incorrect.

10. Remove pinion gear nut and washer. Wipe the nut threads with Loctite Type A. Reinstall the washer and nut and tighten to specifications (**Table 2**).

9

11. Reinstall the bearing carrier retainer/reverse gear as described under *Standard Gear Housing* in this chapter.

Propeller Shaft/Forward Gear Removal/Disassembly

The procedure is essentially the same as given under *Standard Gear Housing* in this chapter with the following exceptions:

a. Disassembly of the spool assembly can result in damage to the assembly and is not recommended unless its components show obvious signs of damage. The spool assembly can be cleaned satisfactorily without disassembly.

b. The forward gear needle bearing case is manufactured of a very high tensile steel and cannot be easily split with a chisel and hammer. If replacement is required, use a high-speed grinder to cut one or more notches in the bearing case as required for removal.

Shift Shaft Removal

1. Remove the bearing carrier retainer/reverse gear as described under *Standard Gear Housing* in this chapter.

2. Remove the drive shaft/pinion gear as described in this chapter.

3. Remove the propeller shaft/forward gear as described under *Standard Gear Housing* in this chapter.

4. Remove the metal and rubber washers from the shift shaft.

5. Remove the shift shaft bushing with bushing remover (part No. C-91-31107).

6. Pull shift shaft from gearcase housing.

7. Reach inside gear housing and remove the shift crank from its locating pin.

Shift Shaft Cleaning and Inspection

Refer to **Figure 63** for this procedure.

1. Remove and discard the shift shaft O-ring. Remove the clip, washer and bushing from the shift shaft.

2. Clean all parts in fresh solvent. Blow dry with compressed air.

3. Check shift shaft splines for wear and/or corrosion.

4. Check shift shaft bushing for corrosion.

5. Check shift crank for excessive wear in shift spool contact areas.

6. Install a new O-ring on bushing.

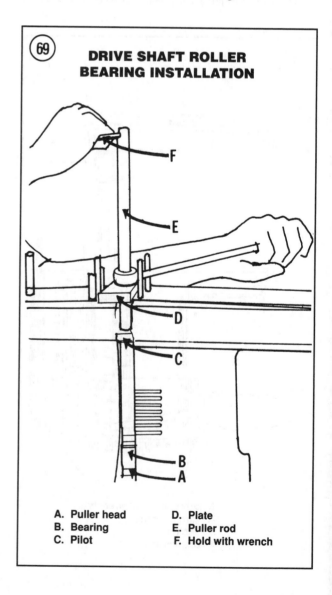

(69) DRIVE SHAFT ROLLER BEARING INSTALLATION

A. Puller head
B. Bearing
C. Pilot
D. Plate
E. Puller rod
F. Hold with wrench

Shift Shaft Installation

1. Drive oil seal through top of bushing and install a new seal with its lip facing upward.

2. Install the retaining clip in the shift shaft groove.

3. Reach all the way into the gearcase housing and position the shift crank on the locating pin. The "throw" side of the crank should face the oil fill side of the gear case housing.

4. Insert the shift shaft with retaining clip in gearcase housing and engage with shift actuating crank splines.

5. Position the retaining washer over the shift shaft on the top side of the retaining clip.

6. Thread the shift shaft into the gearcase housing.

7. Lubricate shift shaft bushing threads, oil seal lip and O-ring with Quicksilver 2-4-C Multi-Lube.

8. Install the shift shaft busing int he gearcase housing and tighten to 50 ft.-lb. (68 N·m) with shift shaft tool (part No. C-91-31107).

9. Install the rubber washer on the shift shaft, then install the stainless steel washer.

Gearcase Housing Inspection

1. Clean housing in fresh solvent. Blow dry with compressed air.

2. Check housing for signs of impact damage.

WARNING
If the drive shaft roller bearing has failed and the original bearing case has turned in the housing, replace the housing. Loose fitting roller bearings will move out of position and cause continuous premature failure.

3. Check the bearings and cups for looseness or signs that they have spun.

4. Check the gearcase housing carrier retainer threads for corrosion or stripped threads. Do *not* wire brush the threads.

5. Check the 2 alignment pins on the gearcase housing mating surface. These should engage the drive shaft housing when the 2 units are assembled. If the pins are damaged, distorted or loose, replace the gearcase housing.

Drive Shaft Roller Bearing, Drive Shaft and Forward Gear Bearing Cups

Gearcase housing bearings or cups should only be removed if they have failed. None should be reused after removal.

1. Remove the drive shaft roller bearing from the gearcase housing with special tool (part No. C-91-36569) and a suitable driver.

NOTE
New bearings come with a cardboard shipping sleeve which holds the bearings in the race. Leave the shipping sleeve in place during bearing installation to prevent the rollers from falling out.

2. Wipe a new bearing with Quicksilver 2-4-C Multi-Lube and install in drive shaft bore with its numbered side facing upward.

3. Install and pull roller baring in place with puller rod and nut (part No. C-91-31229), pilot (part No. C-91-36571), plate (part No. C-91-29310) and puller head (part No. C-91-38628). See **Figure 69**. Pull bearing up into bore until it bottoms on the gearcase housing shoulder.

4. Install the forward gear bearing cup shim(s) in the gearcase housing.

5. Place the bearing cup in the housing and install with driver cup (part No. C-91-36577), drive rod (part No. C-91-37323) and adaptor (part No. C-91-37263). See **Figure 70**.

6. Repeat Step 5 with drive cup (part No. C-91-34379), driver rod (part No. C-91-37323) and adaptor (part No. C-91-37263) to install drive shaft tapered roller bearing cup and shims.

9

Gear Housing Shimming

Three shimming procedures must be performed to properly set up the gear housing components. The pinion gear height must be shimmed to a correct depth, the forward gear must be shimmed to the pinion gear for proper backlash and the reverse gear must be shimmed to the pinion gear for proper backlash.

Pinion gear height

1. Push inward on the propeller shaft and rotate it to seat the bearings.

2. Install bearing preload tool (part No. 91-44307A1) components over the drive shaft in the order shown in **Figure 71**.

3. Install and tighten the water pump stud nuts until they just bottom.

4. Fit the collar from tool (part No. 91-44307A1) over the drive shaft with setscrew facing downward. Align setscrew with water pump impeller keyway.

5. Pull upward on the drive shaft and push downward on the collar at the same time. Holding both assemblies in this position, tighten the setscrew securely.

6. Back off the water pump stud nuts 3-4 turns, then rotate the drive shaft clockwise at least 2 full turns to seat its bearings.

7. Insert pinion gear shimming tool (part No. 91-56048) in gearcase housing. See A, **Figure 72**.

8. Insert a 0.025 in. flat feeler gauge between the high point of the shimming tool and one of the pinion gear teeth. See B, **Figure 72**. The feeler gauge should just fit.

9. Repeat Step 8 to take 2 more readings, rotating the drive shaft 120° between each reading. This will provide 3 readings taken at 120° intervals or one full turn of the drive shaft.

NOTE
Before removing the preload tool, tighten the water pump stud nuts until

they bottom, then loosen the tool setscrew.

10. If the clearance is not exactly 0.025 in. at each reading, determine how much clearance exists, then remove the shimming tool, pinion gear, drive shaft and bearing cup. Add shims if clearance is too great; remove shims if clearance is insufficient. Reinstall bearing cup, drive shaft and pinion gear, then repeat procedure to recheck clearance.

Forward gear backlash

1. Perform Steps 1-6 of *Pinion Gear Height* in this chapter.

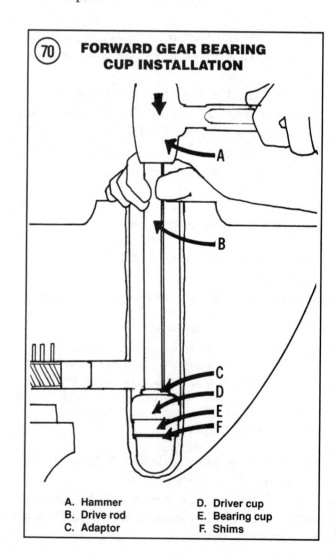

70 **FORWARD GEAR BEARING CUP INSTALLATION**

A. Hammer	D. Driver cup
B. Drive rod	E. Bearing cup
C. Adaptor	F. Shims

2. Thread the stud adaptor from tool (part No. 91-44307A1) onto the rear water pump stud (starboard side) and install a dial indicator to the adaptor.

3. Install backlash indicator rod (part No. 91-53459) to the drive shaft.

4. Move the dial indicator plunger to the "I" line on the backlash indicator rod. Set indicator scale to zero.

5. Install puller jaws (part No. 46086A1) and puller bolts (part No. 91-85716) to the bearing

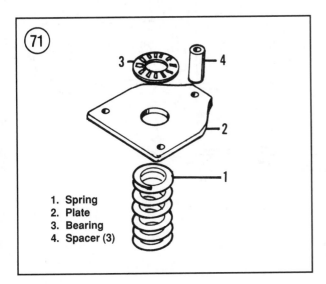

71

1. Spring
2. Plate
3. Bearing
4. Spacer (3)

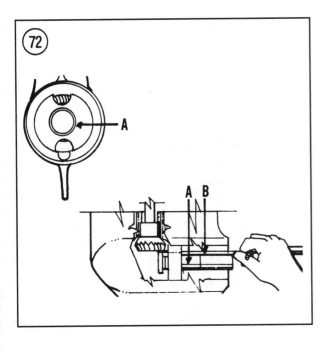

72

carrier and propeller shaft. Tighten the puller bolt to 45 in.-lb. (5 N•m).

6. Rotate drive shaft back and forth lightly without allowing propeller shaft to turn. The dial indicator should read 0.017-0.028 in. (0.43-0.71 mm).

7. Repeat Step 6 to take 3 more readings, rotating the drive shaft 90° between each reading. Be sure to realign the dial indicator plunger to the "I" line on the backlash indicator rod for each reading. This will provide 4 readings taken at 90° intervals or one full rotation of the drive shaft.

8. If backlash readings are within specifications, continue with procedure. If backlash is too small, remove shim(s) from the forward gear bearing; if too great, add shim(s) as required. A 0.001 in. (0.025 mm) shim change will change backlash approximately 0.0008 in. (0.020 mm).

9. Remove puller assembly installed in Step 5.

Reverse gear backlash

1. Perform Steps 1-6 of *Pinion Gear Height* in this chapter.

2. Shift the gearcase housing into full reverse position and rotate the drive shaft clockwise to make sure the sliding clutch dog engages fully.

3. Install pinion nut adaptor (part No. 91-61067A2) on the propeller shaft. Install TR belleville washer (part No. 12-54048) with its concave side facing away from the gearcase housing. Install propeller nut and tighten to 45 in.-lb. (5 N•m).

4. Rotate the drive shaft back and forth lightly without allowing the propeller shaft to turn. The dial indicator should read 0.028-0.052 in. (0.71-1.32 mm).

5. If backlash is correct, continue with assembly. If backlash is too small, add shims between the gearcase housing and bearing carrier; if too great, check for improper installation of bearing carrier.

9

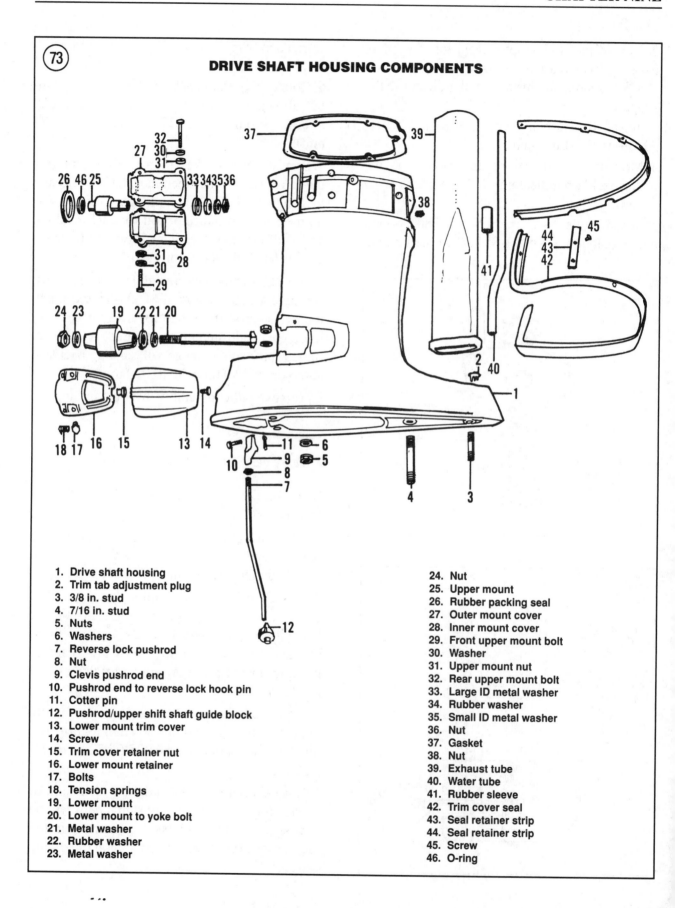

(73) **DRIVE SHAFT HOUSING COMPONENTS**

1. Drive shaft housing
2. Trim tab adjustment plug
3. 3/8 in. stud
4. 7/16 in. stud
5. Nuts
6. Washers
7. Reverse lock pushrod
8. Nut
9. Clevis pushrod end
10. Pushrod end to reverse lock hook pin
11. Cotter pin
12. Pushrod/upper shift shaft guide block
13. Lower mount trim cover
14. Screw
15. Trim cover retainer nut
16. Lower mount retainer
17. Bolts
18. Tension springs
19. Lower mount
20. Lower mount to yoke bolt
21. Metal washer
22. Rubber washer
23. Metal washer
24. Nut
25. Upper mount
26. Rubber packing seal
27. Outer mount cover
28. Inner mount cover
29. Front upper mount bolt
30. Washer
31. Upper mount nut
32. Rear upper mount bolt
33. Large ID metal washer
34. Rubber washer
35. Small ID metal washer
36. Nut
37. Gasket
38. Nut
39. Exhaust tube
40. Water tube
41. Rubber sleeve
42. Trim cover seal
43. Seal retainer strip
44. Seal retainer strip
45. Screw
46. O-ring

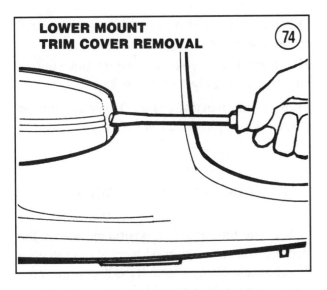

LOWER MOUNT TRIM COVER REMOVAL (74)

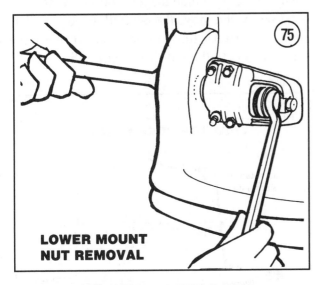

LOWER MOUNT NUT REMOVAL (75)

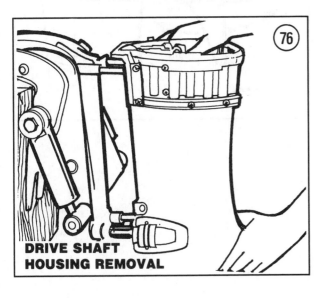

DRIVE SHAFT HOUSING REMOVAL (76)

DRIVE SHAFT HOUSING

Figure 73 is an exploded view of the drive shaft housing with Dyna-Float suspension and mounting yoke.

Removal

1. Remove cross pins holding reverse lock lever in drive shaft housing (**Figure 73**).

2. Remove trim cover screws and trim cover (**Figure 74**, typical).

3. Remove rubber bumpers from mounting bolt heads. Remove nuts from lower mounting bolts (**Figure 75**, typical).

4. Remove rubber caps from upper mounts. Remove nuts from upper swivel pin bolts.

5. Remove drive shaft housing by pulling from top and bottom (**Figure 76**, typical).

6. Remove 4 screws and pull the top mounts. Remove the U-cup packing seal. Separate the inner and outer halves.

7. On Merc 45, 500 and 50 (prior to 1986) models, remove 2 cap screws and the mount clamp. Remove the rubber mount (**Figure 77**).

9

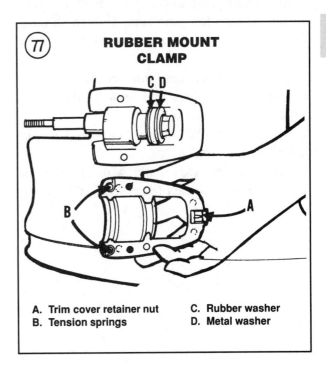

(77) **RUBBER MOUNT CLAMP**

A. Trim cover retainer nut
B. Tension springs
C. Rubber washer
D. Metal washer

8. Remove the self-locking nut from the bottom of the swivel pin. Earlier models may use a snap ring instead of a locknut.

9. Tap the lower yoke from the swivel pin with a mallet.

10. Tap or pull the swivel pin from the swivel bracket. On earlier motors, the co-pilot assembly must be removed first.

Installation

1. Place the top mounts in the inside and outside covers. Install the U-cup seal.

2. Install the upper mount assemblies in the drive shaft housing but do not tighten all screws at this time.

3. Place lower mounts on the bolts and position in the drive shaft housing recesses. Install washers on the threaded ends of the bolts. On Merc 45, 500 and 50 (prior to 1986) models, install the mount clamp.

4. After positioning the upper and lower yoke bracket, place the drive shaft housing on the yoke brackets.

5. Install large ID steel washer, spacer, rubber washer and (where applicable) small ID steel washer on each top yoke stud. Tighten all nuts. Tighten 4 screws and nuts on each top mount cover.

6. Insert the rubber caps on upper mounts.

7. Install the washers and nuts on the lower mounts. Tighten securely.

8. Install the rubber bumper caps and mount covers, if so equipped.

9. Lubricate the swivel pin with Quicksilver Multipurpose Lubricant (part No. C-92-63250).

Drive swivel pin into swivel bracket. Reinstall co-pilot assembly on earlier models.

10. Insert lower yoke on swivel pin splines, aligning it squarely with top yoke.

11. Reinstall snap ring or nut. Do *not* overtighten nut, as swivel pin must rotate freely.

TRIM TAB ADJUSTMENT

The trim tab should be positioned so that the steering wheel will turn with equal ease in each direction at cruising speed. If the boat turns more easily to the right than the left, loosen the socket head screw and move the tab trailing edge to the right. If the boat turns more easily to the left, move the tab to the left. See **Figure 78**.

(78) TRIM TAB POSITIONING

Trim retainer screw cap

Left   Right

Table 1 TIGHTENING TORQUES

Fastener	in.-lb.	ft.-lb.
Bearing carrier nut		
Merc 500, 650, 700		110
Merc 45, 50, 60, 70		100
All others		210
Gear housing to drive shaft housing nuts		
3/8-16		55
3/8-24		55
7/16-20		65
Pinion nut		
Merc 500, 650, 700		50
All others		70
Trim tab screw		25
Water pump		
1/4-28 nuts	30	
5/16-24 nuts	40	
1/4-20 screw	20	

Table 2 V150/175/200 GEAR HOUSING TORQUE SPECIFICATIONS

Fastener	in.-lb.	ft.-lb.	N•m
Bearing carrier retainer nut		210	285
Drive shaft bearing retainer		100	136
Gear housing			
Nuts		35	47
Screw		28	38
Pinion gear nut		60-80	81-108
Shift shaft bushing		50	68
Trim tab screw		23	31
Water pump body			
Nuts	60-90		7-10
Screw	30-40		3-5

Table 3 RECOMMENDED LUBRICANTS, ADHESIVES AND SEALERS

Material	Part No.
2-4-C Multi-Lube	92-90018A12
3M Adhesive	92-25234
Bellows adhesive	92-86166
Needle Bearing Assembly Lubricant	92-42649A1
Perfect Seal	92-34227-1
RTV Sealer	92-91600-1
Special Lubricant 101	92-79214A1
Super Duty Lower Unit Lubricant	92-75580A24

9

Chapter Ten

Power Trim and Tilt System

The usual method of raising and lowering the outboard lower unit is a mechanical one, consisting of a series of holes in the transom mounting bracket. To trim the engine, an adjustment stud is removed from the bracket, the outboard is repositioned and the stud reinserted in the proper holes to hold the unit in place.

Power trim provides low-effort control whether the boat is underway or at rest. The Mercury outboard power trim system is designed for Merc 45 hp and larger engines. It is optional on the Merc 45-115 hp and standard on all V6 models.

Two types of power trim systems have been used: the external and integral power trim assemblies. The integral system (designated as Design 2) was introduced on 1985 inline engines and as a running change on 1986 V6 engines. All previous models used the external system.

This chapter includes maintenance, trim cylinder replacement and troubleshooting procedures for external power trim systems with dual or single solenoid trim pump and for Design 2 power trim systems.

EXTERNAL POWER TRIM SYSTEM

Components

The Mercury power trim system consists of a hydraulic pump (containing an electric motor, oil reservoir, oil pump and valve body), a hydraulic trim cylinder mounted on each side of the engine and necessary connecting lines. The switches which operate the system are contained within the remote control or control panel.

Power trim systems used on the models covered in this manual differ according to the pump type and trim cylinders used. The trim pump may be a Prestolite or Oildyne. Inline trim cylinders are a single ram design. The V6 trim cylinders may be a single or twin ram design. System operation is basically the same, but troubleshooting procedures will vary.

Operation

Depressing the UP trim switch closes the pump motor circuit. The motor drives the oil pump, forcing oil into the up side of the trim

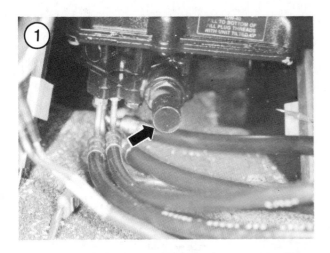

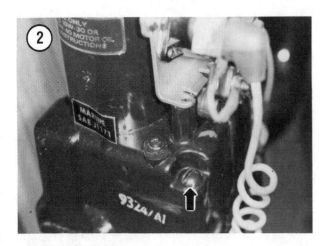

cylinders. The engine will trim upward until the switch is released or the trim limit cutout switch opens the circuit to keep the swivel bracket within the supporting flanges of the clamp bracket.

Depressing the IN or DOWN trim switch also closes the pump motor circuit. The motor runs in the opposite direction, driving the oil pump to force oil into the "down" side of the trim cylinders and trimming the engine to the desired position. If the switch is not released when the engine reaches the limit of its downward travel, an overload cutout switch opens to shut the pump motor off and prevent system damage.

Depressing the TRAILERING or UP/OUT switch trims the engine upward and bypasses the trim limit switch to permit the engine to be tilted up for trailering, docking or shallow water operation.

Manual Trim

The V6 power trim system allows the engine to be manually tilted up or down. Inline engines with a power trim system can be manually tilted up but not down. To operate either system manually:

1. Shift remote control into NEUTRAL.

2. Remove ignition key from switch.

3. Turn trim pump control knob (**Figure 1**) fully clockwise to disengage reverse lock valve in pump motor.

4. Lift up (inline or V6) or push down (V6 only) on engine and rotate tilt lock lever.

5. When engine is in desired position, turn control knob (**Figure 1**) fully counterclockwise to engage reverse lock valve in pump motor.

NOTE
If a power trim system failure is experienced on inline engines when trimmed up, remove the bleed screw from the "up" side of each trim cylinder. See **Bleeding the System** *in this chapter. This allows hydraulic fluid to escape as the engine weight forces the engine downward. When engine reaches tilt pin, reinstall bleed screws. Have power trim system serviced as soon as possible.*

HYDRAULIC PUMP

Fluid Check

1. Tilt outboard to its full UP (DOWN if equipped with a square motor) position.

2. Clean area around pump fill screw (**Figure 2**). Remove the screw and visually check the fluid level in the pump reservoir. It should be at the bottom of the fill hole threads.

10

NOTE
*V6 trim pumps with a square motor housing use a combination fill/vent screw. Remove screw and check the fluid level in the pump reservoir with the dipstick portion of the screw (**Figure 3**). It should be on the FULL mark.*

3. Top up if necessary with SAE 10W-30 or 10W-40 automotive oil rated API service SE.

NOTE
SAE 30W engine oil can be used instead of a multi-viscosity oil in the tropics.

4. If equipped with a fill screw, install and tighten screw snugly. If equipped with a fill/vent screw, install and tighten screw snugly, then back off 1 1/2 turns to allow the reservoir vent to function.

Bleeding the System

The hydraulic system should be bled whenever air enters it. Air in the power trim system will compress, rather than transmit pressure to the trim cylinders. If the engine will not trim in either direction, trims with an erratic motion, thumps when shifted or trails out when backing throttle off at high speed, bleeding is usually called for. Bleeding is also necessary whenever a hydraulic line is disconnected.

Inline engine

1. Tilt the engine to its full UP position.
2. Rotate the tilt lock lever to engage it.
3. Shift remote control into NEUTRAL and remove ignition key.
4. Remove both trim cylinders as described in this chapter.
5. Clean area around "DOWN" bleed screw at front of trim cylinder (**Figure 4**). Remove screw and O-ring.
6. Depress and hold "DOWN" or "IN" button for several seconds. Release button

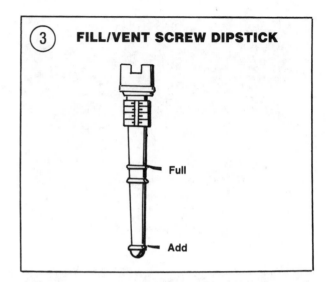

③ **FILL/VENT SCREW DIPSTICK**

Full

Add

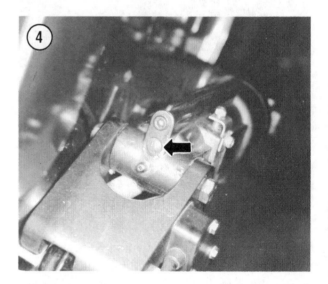

④

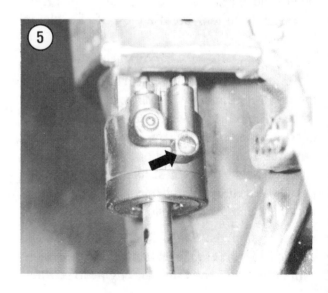

⑤

and wait about one minute. Repeat this step until there are no air bubbles in the oil flowing from the bleed port.

7. Install bleed screw with O-ring and tighten securely.

8. Repeat Steps 5-7 to bleed the other cylinder.

9. Clean area around "Up" bleed screw at rear of trim cylinder (**Figure 5**). Remove screw and O-ring.

10. Position trim cylinder horizontally with bleed port facing upward.

11. Depress and hold "UP" or "UP/OUT" buttons for several seconds. Release button and wait about one minute. Repeat this step until there are no air bubbles in the oil flowing from the bleed port.

12. Install bleed screw with O-ring and tighten securely.

13. Repeat Steps 9-12 to bleed the other cylinder.

14. Install trim cylinders as described in this chapter.

15. Check and refill pump reservoir, if necessary, as described in this chapter.

16. Check trim limit switch adjustment as described in this chapter.

Early V6 (round motor housing)

The V6 hydraulic system has a self-bleeding feature. To bleed the system:

1. Tilt the engine to its full UP position.

2. Remove the pump "FILL" screw and top up the reservoir, if necessary.

3. Operate the power trim up and down several times.

4. Refill the reservoir, if necessary.

5. Install and tighten the "FILL" screw.

Late V6 (square motor housing)

The V6 hydraulic system has a self-bleeding feature. To bleed the system:

1. Check manual release knob to make sure it is turned as far clockwise as possible.

2. Make sure "FILL/VENT" screw is backed out 1 1/2 turns from a fully seated position to vent the reservoir.

3. Operate the "TRAILER" circuit to trim engine to its full up position. Refill pump to "ADD" line on dipstick, if necessary, to bring engine fully up.

4. Operate the "DOWN" circuit to trim engine to its full down position. Refill pump to "ADD" line on dipstick, if necessary, to bring engine fully down.

5. Trim the engine up and down several times. Each time engine reaches its full down position, check dipstick and refill pump to "FULL" line, if necessary.

6. Install and seat "FILL/VENT" screw, then back off 1 1/2 turns to vent the pump reservoir.

7. Check system for leaks.

TROUBLESHOOTING

Whenever a problem develops in the power trim system, the initial step is to determine whether the problem is in the electrical or hydraulic system. Refer to Chapter Three to make this determination. Electrical tests are given in this chapter. If the problem appears to be in the hydraulic system and cannot be corrected by bleeding the system, refer it to a dealer or qualified specialist for necessary service.

Before troubleshooting any electrical circuit:

1. Make sure the plug-in connectors are properly engaged and that all terminals and wires are free of corrosion. Tighten and clean as required.

2. Make sure the battery is fully charged. Charge or replace as required.

**Inline Engine Dual
Solenoid Trim System**

All circuits inoperative

Refer to **Figure 6** and **Figure 7** for this procedure.

10

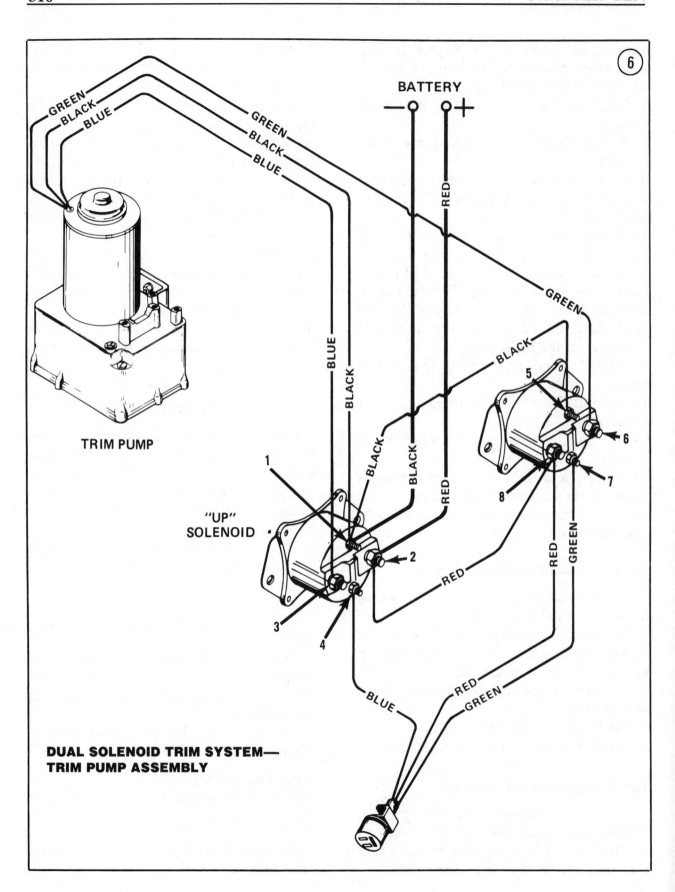

6

BATTERY

GREEN
BLACK
BLUE

GREEN
BLACK
BLUE

RED

GREEN

BLACK

BLUE

BLACK

BLACK

BLACK

RED

5

6

7

8

TRIM PUMP

"UP"
SOLENOID

1

2

3

4

RED

RED

GREEN

BLUE

RED

GREEN

**DUAL SOLENOID TRIM SYSTEM—
TRIM PUMP ASSEMBLY**

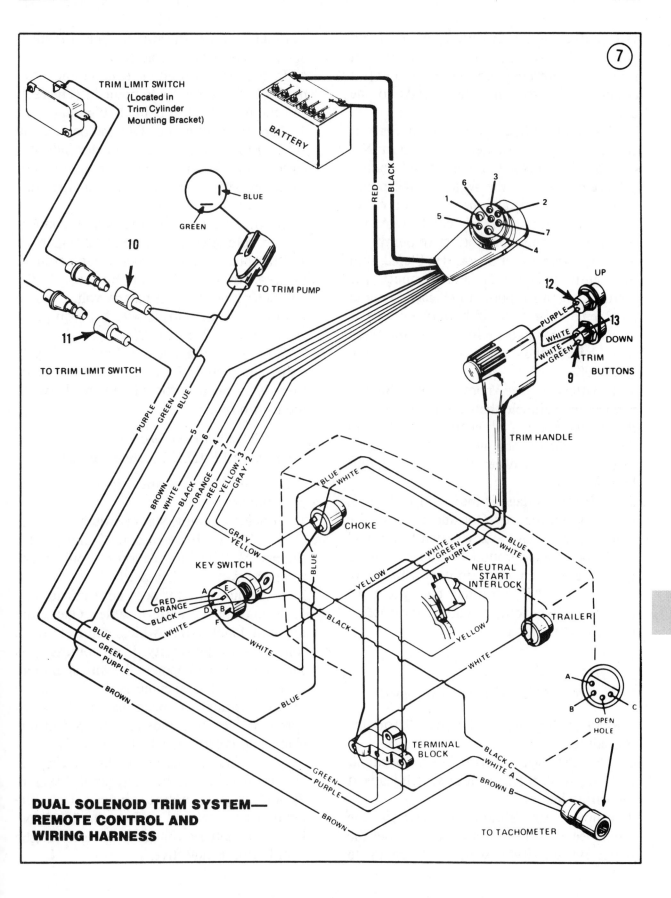

**DUAL SOLENOID TRIM SYSTEM—
REMOTE CONTROL AND
WIRING HARNESS**

1. Connect a voltmeter between point 11 and point 12 (**Figure 7**). If battery voltage is not shown, look for poor connections or an open circuit in the red and black leads to the battery.

2. If battery voltage is shown in Step 1, connect a remote starter switch (part No. C-91-52024A1) between point 2 and point 4 (**Figure 6**). Depress the switch. If the pump motor does not operate, the problem is either an open circuit in the black lead between the motor and solenoid or a defective pump.

3. If the pump motor operates in Step 2, turn the ignition key ON and connect the voltmeter between point 13 (**Figure 7**) and a good engine ground. If battery voltage is shown, look for an open in the blue and green wire between the remote control and pump solenoids.

4. If battery voltage is not shown in Step 3, connect the voltmeter between the key switch A terminal and a good engine ground. If no voltage reading is obtained, look for an open in the red lead between the key switch and harness connector.

5. If battery voltage is indicated in Step 4, turn the ignition key ON and connect the voltmeter between the key switch F terminal and a good engine ground. If voltage is shown now, there is an open in the white wire between the "F" terminal and point 13 (**Figure 7**). No voltage reading indicates a defective key switch.

"UP" circuit ("TRAILER" circuit good)

Refer to **Figure 6** and **Figure 7** for this procedure.

1. Trim the engine to its full down position.
2. Disconnect the trim limit switch leads at the wiring harness.
3. Connect an ohmmeter between the disconnected trim limit switch leads. Set the meter on the R×1 scale. If there is no

continuity shown, the switch plunger is stuck open or the switch is defective.

4. If there is continuity shown, connect the red lead of a voltmeter to point 11 (**Figure 7**) and the black lead to point 1 (**Figure 6**).

5. Turn the ignition key ON and depress the "UP" trim button. If the voltmeter indicates battery voltage but the "UP" circuit does not work properly, the problem is in the trim limit switch connections.

6. If no voltage is shown in Step 5, connect the red voltmeter lead to point 12 (**Figure 7**) and the black lead to a good engine ground. Depress the "UP" trim button. If the voltmeter now indicates battery voltage, there is an open in the purple wire between point 11 and point 12 (**Figure 7**).

7. If battery voltage is not shown in Step 6, either the trim "UP" button is defective or there is an open in the white wires between the trim buttons.

"DOWN" circuit inoperative ("UP and "TRAILER" circuits good)

Refer to **Figure 6** and **Figure 7** for this procedure.

1. Connect a remote starter switch (part No. C-91-52024A1) between point 7 and point 8 (**Figure 6**). The pump motor should work when the switch is depressed.

2. If the pump motor does not work in Step 1, disconnect the battery cables. Check the red and black wires which connect the 2 solenoids for continuity. If no continuity is shown, there in an open in the wire(s). If there is continuity, the solenoid is either defective or its terminal connections are loose or corroded. Test solenoids as described in this chapter to determine which is defective.

3. If the pump motor works in Step 2, connect a voltmeter between point 9 (**Figure 7**) and a good engine ground. Turn the ignition key ON and operate the "DOWN" button. If battery voltage is not shown, the trim button is defective.

4. If battery voltage is shown in Step 3, there is an open in the green wire between point 7 (**Figure 6**) and point 9 (**Figure 7**).

"UP and "TRAILER" circuit inoperative ("DOWN" circuit good)

Refer to **Figure 6** and **Figure 7** for this procedure.
1. Connect a remote starter switch (part No. C-91-52024A1) between point 2 and point 4 (**Figure 6**). The pump motor should work when the switch is depressed.
2. If the pump motor does not work in Step 1, check for loose or corroded connections at the "UP" solenoid or a defective solenoid.
3. If the pump motor works in Step 1, there is an open in the blue wire between point 4 (**Figure 6**) and point 10 (**Figure 7**).

"TRAILER" circuit inoperative ("UP" circuit good)

The problem is either a defective "TRAILER" button or an open in the blue lead between the trim limit switch connector and the "TRAILER" button.

Inline Engine Single Solenoid Trim System

All circuits inoperative

Refer to **Figure 8** or **Figure 9** for this procedure.
1. Connect a voltmeter between point 1 and point 2. If battery voltage is not shown, look for poor connections or an open circuit in the red and black leads to the battery.
2. If battery voltage is shown in Step 1, connect a remote starter switch (part No. C-91-52024A1) between point 1 and point 5. Depress the switch. If the pump motor does not operate, the problem is either an open circuit in the black lead between the motor and solenoid or a defective pump.

3. If the pump motor operates in Step 2, there is an open in the red wire between point 1 and point 12 or an open in the blue and green wires between point 4 and point 5 and the trim buttons.

"OUT" and "UP" circuit inoperative ("IN" circuit good)

Refer to **Figure 8** or **Figure 9** for this procedure.
1. Trim the engine to its full down position.
2. Connect a remote starter switch (part No. C-91-52024A1) between point 1 and point 4. If the pump motor does not work when the switch is activated, check for a loose or corroded connection at point 3. If none is found, replace the solenoid.
3. If the pump operates in Step 2, connect a voltmeter between point 10 and a good engine ground. If battery voltage is not shown when the "UP" and "UP/OUT" buttons are depressed, there is either an open in the red wire between point 11 and point 12 or the "UP/OUT" trim button is defective.
4. If battery voltage is shown in Step 3, connect a voltmeter between point 8 and a good engine ground. If battery voltage is not shown when the "UP" and "UP/OUT" buttons are depressed, there is an open in the blue and purple wires between the trim buttons and the trim limit switch.
5. If battery voltage is shown in Step 4, there is an open in the blue wire between point 4 and point 8.

"OUT" circuit inoperative ("IN" and "UP" circuits good)

Refer to **Figure 8** or **Figure 9** for this procedure.
1. Trim the engine to its full down position.
2. Disconnect the trim limit switch leads at the wiring harness.
3. Connect an ohmmeter between the disconnected trim limit switch leads. Set the

10

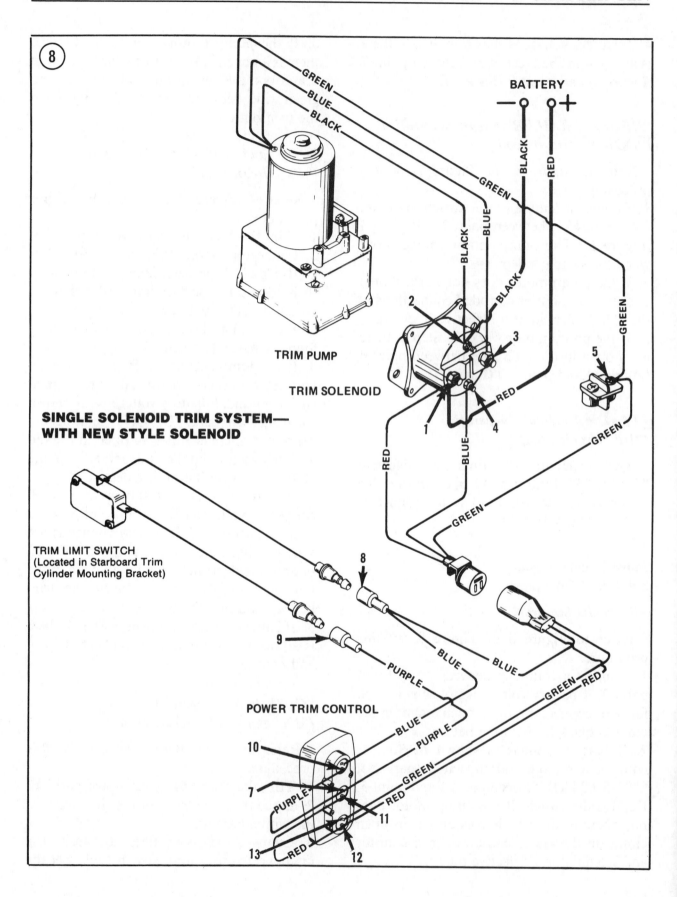

⑧

GREEN
BLUE
BLACK

BATTERY

TRIM PUMP

TRIM SOLENOID

BLACK

GREEN

BLUE

BLACK

BLACK

RED

BLACK

RED

GREEN

2

3

1

4

5

GREEN

GREEN

RED

BLUE

**SINGLE SOLENOID TRIM SYSTEM—
WITH NEW STYLE SOLENOID**

GREEN

TRIM LIMIT SWITCH
(Located in Starboard Trim
Cylinder Mounting Bracket)

8

9

BLUE

BLUE

PURPLE

POWER TRIM CONTROL

GREEN RED

BLUE

PURPLE

10

7

PURPLE

GREEN

RED

11

13

RED

12

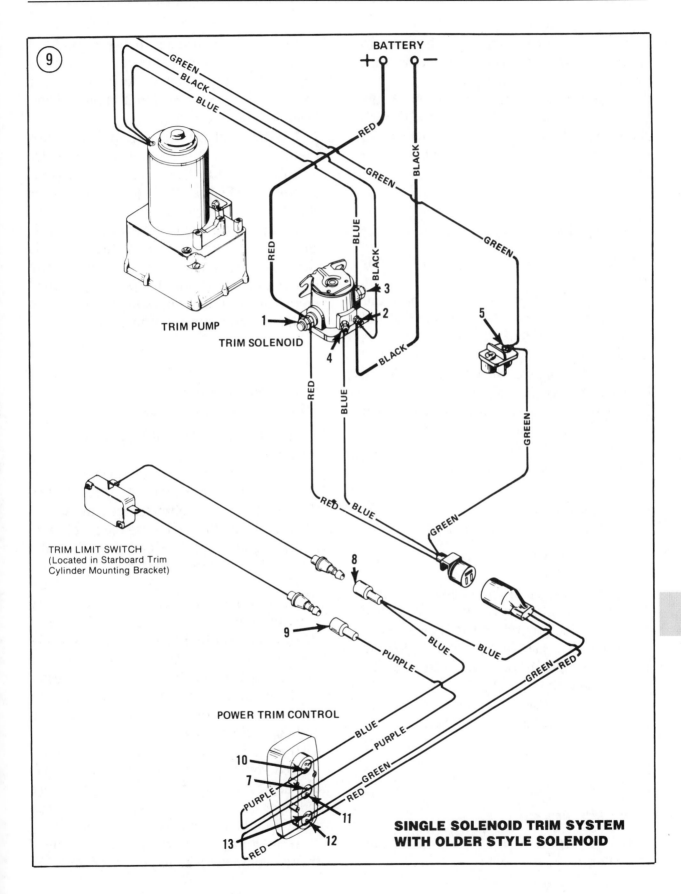

BATTERY

GREEN
BLACK
BLUE

RED

GREEN

BLACK

GREEN

RED

BLUE

BLACK

3

2

BLACK

TRIM PUMP

1

TRIM SOLENOID

4

5

BLACK

GREEN

RED

BLUE

RED BLUE

GREEN

GREEN

TRIM LIMIT SWITCH
(Located in Starboard Trim
Cylinder Mounting Bracket)

8

9

BLUE

BLUE

BLUE

PURPLE

GREEN RED

POWER TRIM CONTROL

BLUE

PURPLE

10

7

GREEN

RED

PURPLE

11

13

RED

12

**SINGLE SOLENOID TRIM SYSTEM
WITH OLDER STYLE SOLENOID**

10

meter on the R×1 scale. If there is no continuity shown, the switch plunger is stuck open or the switch is defective.

4. If there is continuity shown, check the trim limit switch for poor or corroded connection. If none are found, there is an open in the purple wire between point 7 and point 8.

"UP" circuit
("OUT" and "IN" circuits good)

Refer to **Figure 8** or **Figure 9** for this procedure.

1. Trim the engine to its full down position.
2. Connect a voltmeter between point 10 and a good engine ground. If battery voltage is indicated when the "UP" and "UP/OUT" buttons are depressed, there is an open in the blue wire between point 8 and point 10.
3. If battery voltage is not indicated in Step 2, the "UP" trim button is defective or there is an open in the purple wire between the "UP" and "UP/OUT" buttons.

"IN" circuit
("OUT" and "UP" circuits good)

Refer to **Figure 8** or **Figure 9** for this procedure.

1. Trim the engine to its full down position.
2. Connect a voltmeter between point 13 and a good engine ground. If battery voltage is indicated when the "IN" button is depressed, there is an open in the green wire between point 13 and the trim pump.
3. If battery voltage is not indicated in Step 2, the "IN" trim button is defective.

Early V6 Trim System
(Round Motor Housing)

All circuits inoperative

Refer to **Figure 10** and **Figure 11** for this procedure.

1. Connect a voltmeter between point 9 (**Figure 10**) and point 7 (**Figure 11**). If battery voltage is not shown, look for poor connections or an open circuit in the red and black leads to the battery.
2. If battery voltage is shown in Step 1, turn the ignition key ON. Remove the voltmeter lead from point 9 (**Figure 10**) and connect it to point 10 (**Figure 10**). If battery voltage is still shown, the pump motor requires service.
3. If battery voltage is not shown in Step 2, check the ignition switch. If the switch is good, there is either an open in the red wire between the switch and the positive terminal on the engine or or an open in the white wires in the remote control housing.

"UP" circuit inoperative
("TRAILER" circuit good)

Refer to **Figure 10** and **Figure 11** for this procedure.

1. Trim the engine to its full down position.
2. Disconnect connector A (**Figure 10**). Connect the black voltmeter lead to point 3 (**Figure 10**) and the red lead to the purple wire receptacle at point 6 (**Figure 10**). Turn the ignition key on and depress the UP button.
3. If battery voltage is shown in Step 2, check the trim sender/limit switch for continuity with an ohmmeter set on the R×1 scale. If there is no continuity, the switch is either defective or there is an open in the blue or purple wire between the switch and connector A. If continuity is shown, there is an open in the blue wire between the "OUT" solenoid and connector A.
4. If no voltage is shown in Step 2, connect the red voltmeter lead to point 7 (**Figure 11**) and depress the "UP" button. Battery voltage indicates an open in the purple wire between point 7 and connector A.
5. If no voltage is shown in Step 4, connect the red voltmeter lead to point 8 (**Figure 11**).

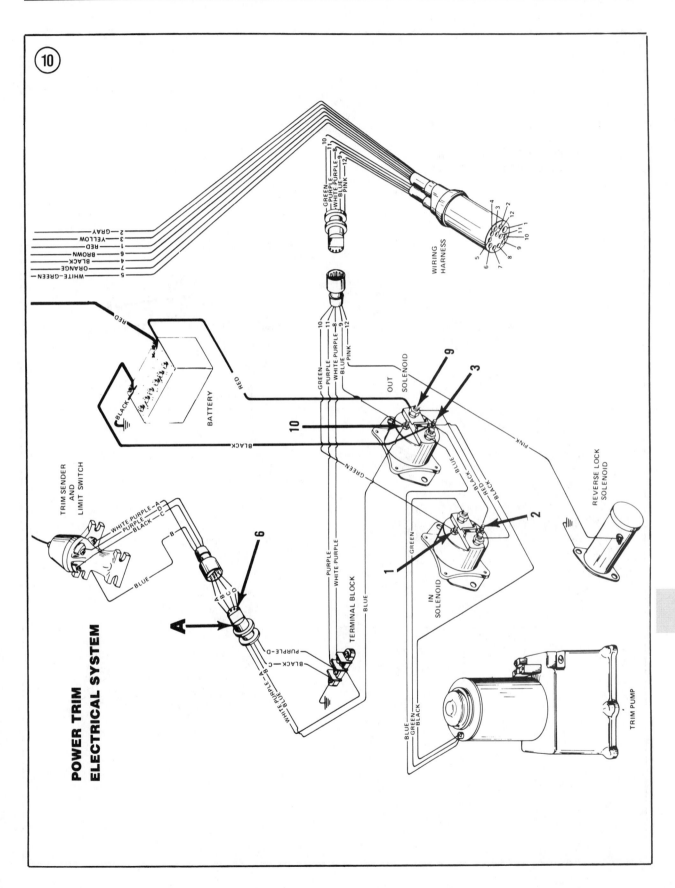

**POWER TRIM
ELECTRICAL SYSTEM**

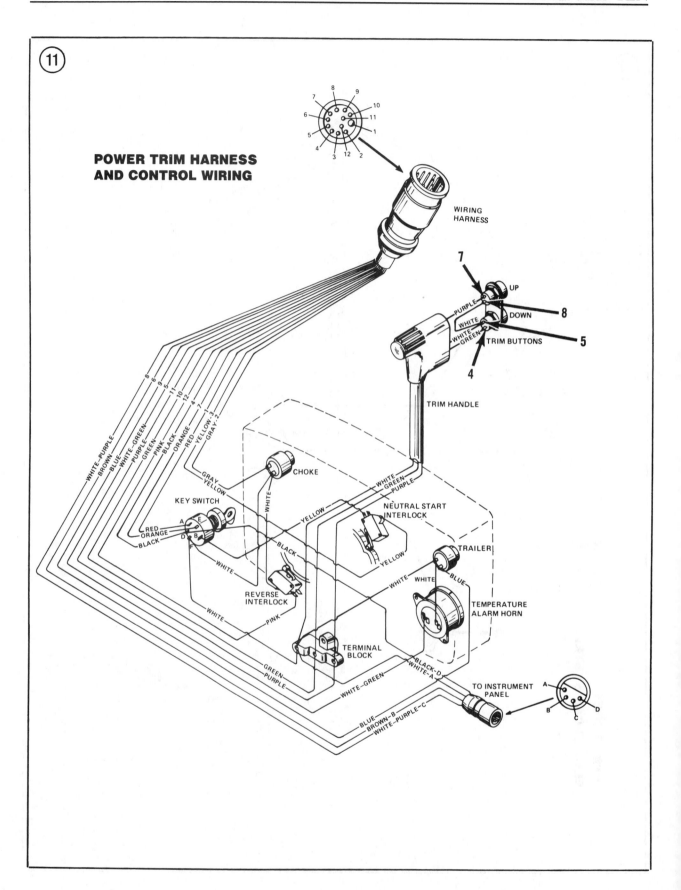

**POWER TRiM HARNESS
AND CONTROL WIRING**

Voltage indicates a defective trim button; no voltage indicates an open in the white wire between the switches.

"DOWN" circuit inoperative ("UP" circuit good)

Refer to **Figure 10** and **Figure 11** for this procedure.
1. Connect the red voltmeter lead to point 1 (**Figure 10**) and the black lead to point 2 (**Figure 10**). Turn the ignition key ON and depress the "DOWN" button. If battery voltage is shown, check for loose or corroded connections at the "IN" solenoid. If none are found, replace the solenoid.
2. If no voltage is shown in Step 1, connect the black voltmeter lead to point 3 (**Figure 10**) and depress the "DOWN" button. A voltage reading indicates an open in the black wire connecting the solenoids.
3. If no voltage is shown in Step 2, connect the red voltmeter lead to point 4 (**Figure 11**) and depress the "DOWN" button. A voltage reading indicates an open in the green wire between point 1 (**Figure 10**) and point 4 (**Figure 11**).
4. If not voltage is shown in Step 3, connect the red voltmeter lead to point 5 (**Figure 11**). A voltage reading indicates a defective trim button. If no voltage is shown, there is an open in the white wire between the trim switches.

"TRAILER" circuit inoperative ("UP" circuit good)

Refer to **Figure 10** for this procedure.
1. Connect an ohmmeter between the "TRAILER" button and point 10. If there is no continuity shown, there is an open in the blue wire.
2. If continuity is shown in Step 1, test for continuity between the "TRAILER" button terminals with the button depressed. No continuity indicates a defective button.

3. If continuity is shown in Step 2, there is an open in the white wire leading to the "TRAILER" button.

"UP" and "TRAILER" circuits inoperative ("DOWN" circuit good)

Refer to **Figure 10** for this procedure.
1. Connect the red voltmeter lead to point 10 and the black lead to point 3. Turn the ignition key ON and depress the "TRAILER" button. If battery voltage is shown, check for loose or corroded connections at the "OUT" solenoid. If none are found, replace the solenoid.
2. If voltage is shown in Step 1, there is an open in the blue and purple wires between the control housing and "OUT" solenoid.

Late V6 Trim System (Square Motor Housing)

All circuits inoperative

Refer to **Figures 12-14** for this procedure.
1. Connect the red voltmeter lead to point 9 and the black lead to point 3. If battery voltage is not shown, check the battery cables for poor connections or an open circuit. Check the trim pump fuse, if so equipped. If this does not locate the problem, the pump thermal overload switch is defective.
2. If battery voltage is shown in Step 1, move the red voltmeter lead to point 10 and depress the "TRAILER" button. If battery voltage is still shown, the pump motor is defective.
3. If battery voltage is not shown in Step 2, connect the red voltmeter lead to point 11 and the black lead to a good engine ground. If battery voltage is shown, there is an open in the green/white, blue/white and purple/white wires between the trim pump and trim buttons.
4. If battery voltage is not shown in Step 3, turn the ignition switch to "RUN" (do not

10

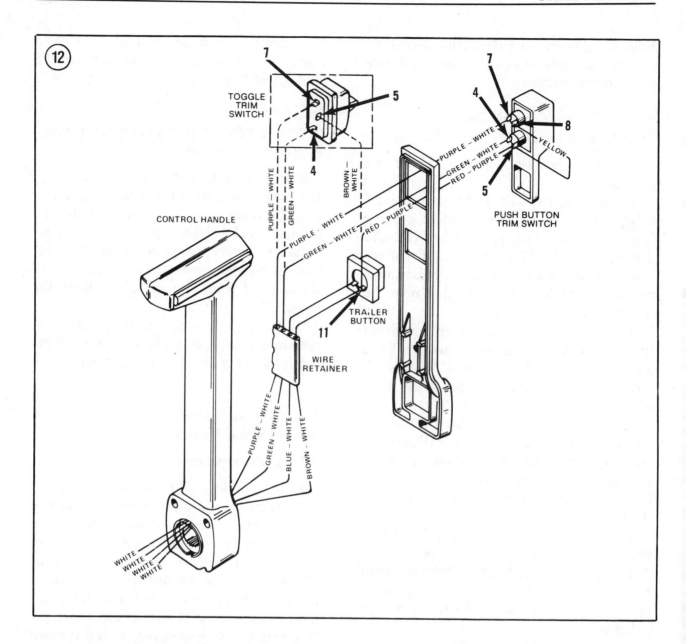

⑫

TOGGLE TRIM SWITCH

7

5

4

PURPLE — WHITE

GREEN — WHITE

BROWN — WHITE

CONTROL HANDLE

PURPLE — WHITE

GREEN — WHITE RED — PURPLE

7

4

8

5

PURPLE — WHITE

GREEN — WHITE

RED — PURPLE

YELLOW

PUSH BUTTON TRIM SWITCH

TRAILER BUTTON

11

WIRE RETAINER

PURPLE — WHITE

GREEN — WHITE

BLUE — WHITE

BROWN — WHITE

WHITE
WHITE
WHITE
WHITE

start motor) and check for voltage at any instrument. If voltage is shown, there is an open in the wire between point 11 and the ignition switch B terminal.

5. If battery voltage is not shown in Step 4, connect the red voltmeter lead to terminal where red wires connect to starter solenoid and the black lead to a good engine ground. If battery voltage is shown, there is either an open in the red wire between the starter solenoid and ignition switch B terminal or a poor connection.

6. If battery voltage is not shown in Step 5, there is an open in the cable between the positive battery terminal and the terminal where the red wires connect to the starter solenoid.

"UP" circuit inoperative ("DOWN" circuit good)

Refer to **Figures 12-14** for this procedure.
1. Trim the engine to its full down position.
2. Disconnect the purple/white wire from the black wire at point 6. Connect the red

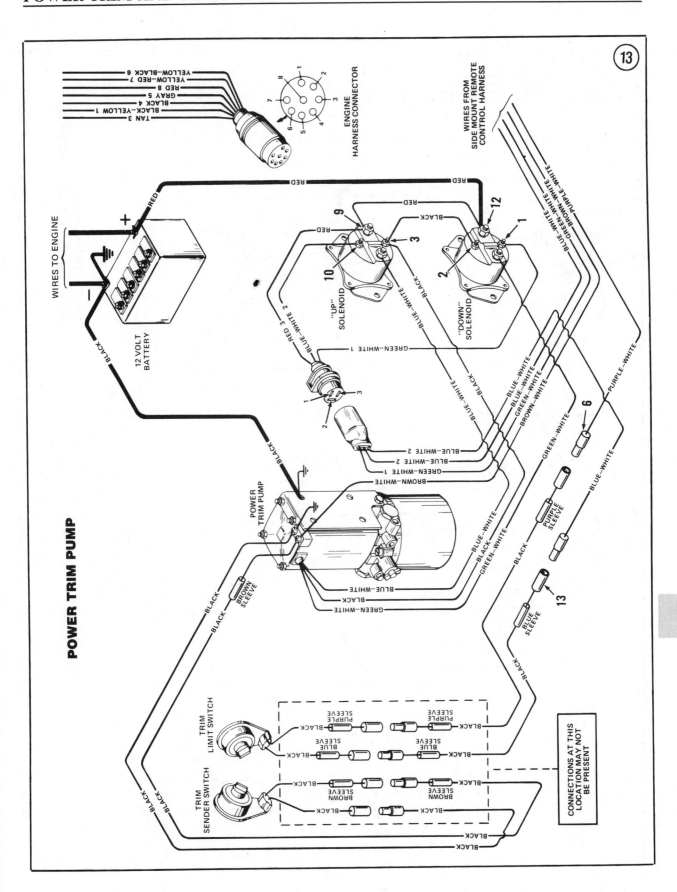

POWER TRIM PUMP

13

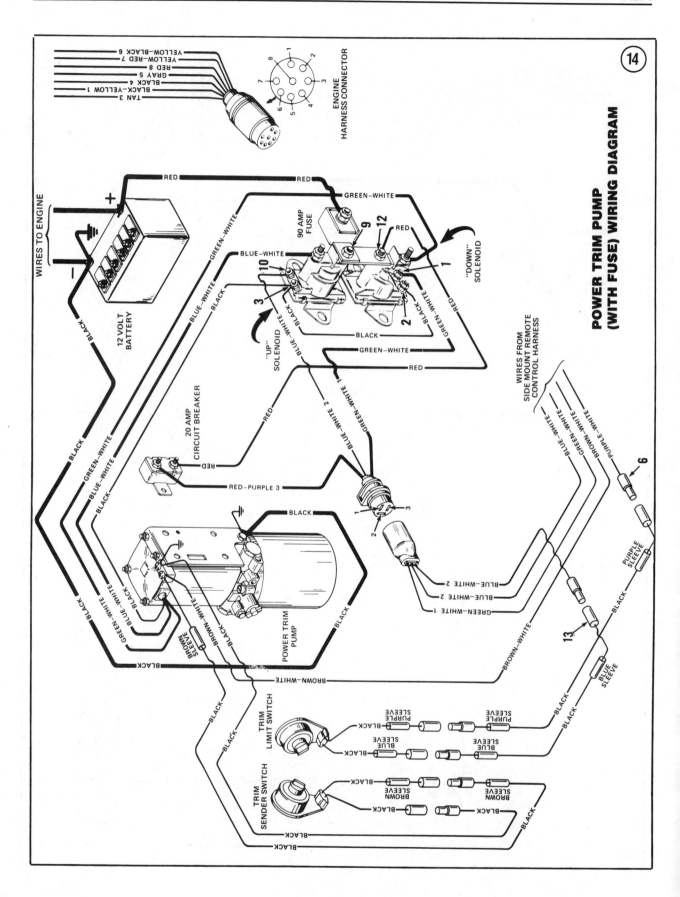

POWER TRIM PUMP (WITH FUSE) WIRING DIAGRAM

voltmeter lead to point 6 and the black lead to point 3. Battery voltage should be shown when the "UP" trim switch is depressed.

3. If battery voltage is not shown in Step 2, connect the red voltmeter lead to point 8 (push button trim switch) or point 5 (toggle trim switch). If battery voltage still is not shown, there is an open in the wiring between the "TRAILER" button and the push button or toggle trim switch.

4. If battery voltage is shown in Step 3, connect the red voltmeter lead to point 7. A voltage reading when the "UP" switch is depressed indicates an open in the white/purple wire between point 6 and point 7. No voltage reading indicates a defective trim switch.

5. If battery voltage is shown in Step 2, reconnect the purple/white and black wires at point 6. Disconnect the blue/white wire from the black wire with blue sleeve at point 13. Connect the red voltmeter lead to the black wire with blue sleeve. If battery voltage is shown when the "UP" switch is depressed, there is an open in the blue/white wire between point 13 and the 3-pronged harness connector at the trim pump.

6. If battery voltage is not shown in Step 5, check for loose or corroded connections between point 6 and point 13. If none are found, check trim limit switch adjustment. If satisfactory, the switch is defective.

"DOWN circuit inoperative ("UP" circuit good)

Refer to **Figures 12-14** for this procedure.
1. Connect the red voltmeter lead to point 1 and the black lead to point 2. If battery voltage is shown when the "DOWN" button is depressed, proceed with Step 5.
2. If battery voltage is not shown in Step 1, move the black voltmeter lead to point 3. If battery voltage is now shown, there is an open in the black wire connecting the solenoids.

3. If battery voltage is not shown in Step 2, move the red voltmeter lead to point 4 and depress the "DOWN" button. If battery voltage is shown, there is an open in the green/white wire between point 1 and point 4.

4. If battery voltage is not shown in Step 3, move the red voltmeter lead to point 5. Battery voltage indicates a defective trim switch; no voltage indicates an open in the wire supplying current to point 5 or a loose/corroded connection at point 5.

5. If battery voltage is shown in Step 1, connect the red voltmeter lead to point 12. Battery voltage indicates loose or corroded connections at the "DOWN" solenoid. If none are found, replace the solenoid.

6. If battery voltage is not shown in Step 5, look for loose or corroded connections in the circuit between point 12 and the positive battery terminal. If none are found, there is either an open in that circuit or the trim pump fuse is defective (if so equipped).

"TRAILER" circuit inoperative ("UP" circuit good)

Refer to **Figures 12-14** for this procedure.
1. Connect an ohmmeter between point 10 and the "TRAILER" button. If continuity is not shown, there is an open in the blue/white wire.
2. If continuity is shown in Step 1, disconnect the battery cables. Check for continuity between the "TRAILER" button terminals with the button depressed. If there is no continuity, replace the button.

"UP" and "TRAILER" circuits inoperative ("DOWN" circuit good)

Refer to **Figures 12-14** for this procedure.
1. Connect the red voltmeter lead to point 10 and the black lead to point 3. If battery voltage is not indicated when the "TRAILER" button is depressed, there is an

10

open in the blue/white and purple/white wires between the "UP" solenoid and the trim buttons.

2. If battery voltage is shown in Step 1, check for loose or corroded connections at the "UP" solenoid. If none are found, replace the solenoid.

SOLENOID TEST

1. Disconnect all solenoid terminal wires.
2. With an ohmmeter set on the R×1 scale, connect the test leads between the 2 large solenoid terminals.
3. Connect a 12-volt battery between the 2 small threaded solenoid terminals.
4. If the solenoid does not click and the meter scale reads zero ohms, the solenoid is defective.

TRIM LIMIT ADJUSTMENTS

Inline Engine Switch Adjustment

This is a trial-and-error adjustment procedure that may have to be repeated several times to obtain the specified trim limit.

1. Depress and hold "IN" or "DOWN" switch until engine trims to the bottom of its travel.
2. Depress and hold "UP" or "UP/OUT" button until pump motor stops.
3. The distance between the swivel and clamp bracket flanges should be 1/2 in. See **Figure 15**.
4. Manually pull lower unit outward to remove any slack in the trim cylinders. If pistons retract into cylinders more than 1/8 in., bleed the system as described in this chapter.
5. If trim limit travel is not 1/2 in., loosen the trim limit switch adjustment nut (**Figure 16**). Turn nut counterclockwise if engine tilts out too far or clockwise if it does not tilt out far enough. Tighten screw and repeat procedure

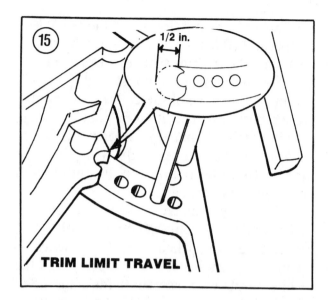

TRIM LIMIT TRAVEL

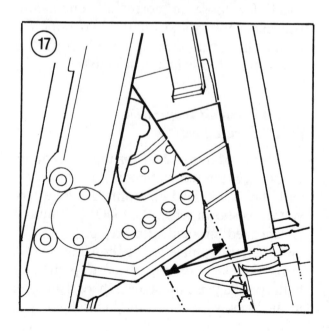

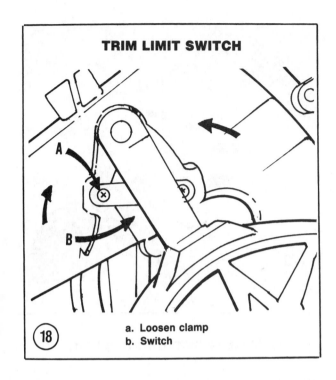

TRIM LIMIT SWITCH

a. Loosen clamp
b. Switch

⑱

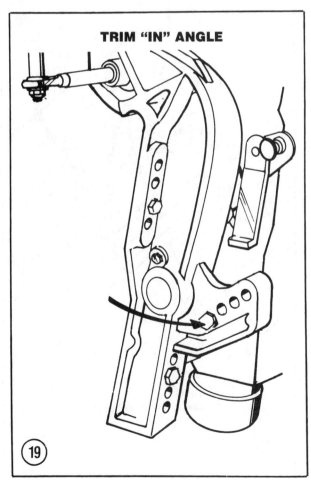

TRIM "IN" ANGLE

⑲

as required to bring trim limit within specifications.

V6 Switch Adjustment

Always water-test the boat after making a trim angle adjustment. If handling characteristics are not good, readjust the trim angle to reduce the "IN" or "OUT" trim limit.

1. Depress and hold "DOWN" switch until engine trims to the bottom of its travel.

2. Depress and hold "UP" button until pump motor stops.

3. If trim limit travel is not 1 1/2 in. (**Figure 17**), adjust the trim "IN" or "OUT" angle as necessary.

NOTE
The "OUT" limit switch is factory-adjusted for maximum allowable travel.

4. If trim "OUT" adjustment is required, loosen the clamp (A, **Figure 18**). Rotate the switch (B, **Figure 18**) clockwise to reduce outward trim travel or counterclockwise to increase it.

NOTE
Boat/motor combinations without a trim adjustment bolt are trimmed to the full "IN" angle.

5. If trim adjustment bolt (**Figure 19**) is installed and the "IN" angle requires adjustment, relocate bolt one hole and water-test to make sure the boat handles properly at planing speeds. Tighten locknut sufficiently to remove any play but *do not* over-tighten or transom brackets will be pulled inward and interfere with swivel bracket movement.

Trim Switch Replacement

1. Disconnect trim limit switch leads.

10

2. Remove the switch cover screws (**Figure 20**). Remove cover and gasket from mounting bracket.

3. Remove and save the spring (A, **Figure 21**) from the actuating plunger. Depress plunger several times to make sure it moves freely. If not, remove from mounting bracket and clean, then reinstall.

4. Remove trim limit switch screws (B, **Figure 21**). Remove switch and leads from mounting bracket.

5. Make sure actuating plunger is in place.

6. Install switch in mounting bracket and route wire harness over hydraulic hoses and through bracket hole.

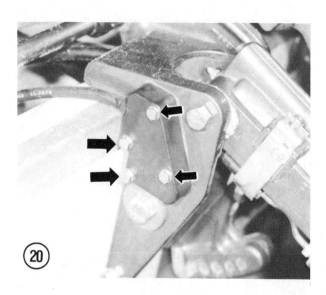

NOTE
If switch corrosion is a problem, fill entire mounting bracket cavity with anti-corrosion grease or silicone compound in Step 7.

7. Coat entire switch and wires with Quicksilver Anti-Corrosion Grease (part No. C-92-63290) or a silicone compound.

8. Fit spring into actuating plunger. Install cover and gasket on mounting bracket.

9. Depress actuating plunger and make sure the switch clicks on and off.

TRIM CYLINDERS

Removal/Installation (Inline Engines)

1. Disconnect the 2 trim hoses at the cylinder. Cap the hoses and plug the cylinder holes to prevent leakage and keep contamination out of the system.

2. Remove the mounting bolts (**Figure 22**) at each end of the cylinder. Remove the cylinder.

3. Installation is the reverse of removal. Tighten mounting bolts to 50 ft.-lb. Bleed the system as described in this chapter.

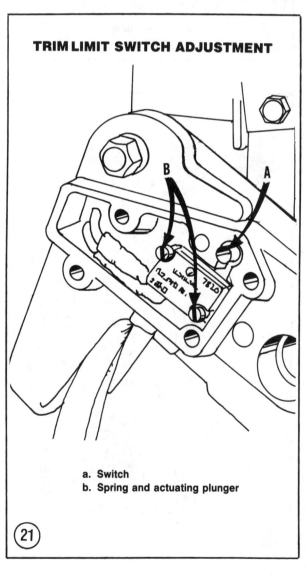

TRIM LIMIT SWITCH ADJUSTMENT

a. Switch
b. Spring and actuating plunger

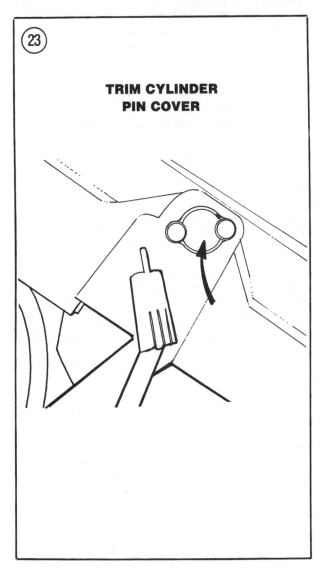

TRIM CYLINDER PIN COVER

**Removal/Installation
(Early V6 Engines With
Round Motor Housing)**

1. Shift the engine into NEUTRAL.
2. Tilt engine to full up position. Engage tilt lock lever.
3. Rotate control knob fully counterclockwise to release hydraulic pressure.
4. Disconnect the negative battery cable, then the positive cable.
5. Position a large drain pan under the trim cylinders and disconnect the hydraulic hoses from the clamp bracket connectors. Let cylinders drain.

*NOTE
Discard this fluid. Do not re-use it.*

6. Remove the trim cylinder pin covers from the swivel brackets. See **Figure 23**.
7. Have an assistant hold the trim cylinders to prevent them from swinging down and striking the boat. Thread a bolt into each trim cylinder pin and pull out of swivel bracket.
8. Disconnect steering cable and remove tilt tube nut.
9. Remove tilt limit switch connector from starboard clamp bracket.
10. Insert a wooden or metal wedge between the transom and swivel bracket.
11. Remove the bolts/washers holding the trim cylinder shaft to the clamp brackets.
12. Have an assistant hold the trim cylinders to prevent them from falling to the ground. Remove starboard clamp bracket mounting bolt and hydraulic connector.
13. Remove starboard clamp bracket from engine.
14. Remove trim cylinders from port clamp bracket. Remove cylinder shafts from cylinders.
15. Remove screws holding hydraulic manifold cover and trim cylinder spacer

10

between cylinders. Remove hydraulic tubes from cylinders.

16. To reinstall, connect hydraulic lines and hoses to manifold and trim cylinders. Tighten all nuts to 60 in.-lb.

17. Place trim cylinder spacer on same side of cylinders as hydraulic hoses.

18. Place manifold cover spacers on manifold, then install attaching screws and thread into trim cylinder spacer. Tighten 2 large screws (A, **Figure 24**) to 60 in.-lb. and small screw (B, **Figure 24**) to 24 in.-lb.

19. Wipe large OD of trim cylinder shaft with a thin coat of Quicksilver Multipurpose Lubricant (part No. C-92-63250). Insert shaft through trim cylinders until slotted end protrudes through starboard cylinder.

20. Install a shim on each end of shaft and insert Woodruff key in shaft slot.

21. Install the other end of the shaft in the port clamp bracket. Wipe shaft bolt threads with Loctite No. 35 (part No. C-92-59328). Thread bolt with washer into port clamp bracket shaft but do not tighten.

22. Install starboard clamp bracket, aligning shaft key with clamp bracket keyway.

23. Wipe shaft bolt threads with Loctite No. 35 and thread bolt into starboard clamp bracket shaft. Tighten both shaft bolts to 40 ft.-lb.

24. Apply marine sealer to unthreaded portion of hydraulic connector. Apply engine oil to threaded portion.

25. Separate starboard clamp bracket from transom enough to insert a new O-ring. Carefully install the hydraulic connector through the bracket, O-ring and transom.

26. Install a flat washer and locknut on hydraulic connector. Tighten locknut securely.

27. Reconnect trim pump lines to hydraulic connector.

28. Install tilt tube nut, tighten to 20 ft.-lb. and back off 1/4 turn.

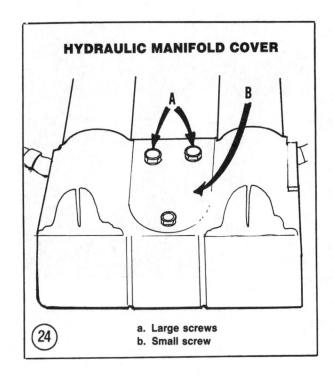

HYDRAULIC MANIFOLD COVER

(24)
a. Large screws
b. Small screw

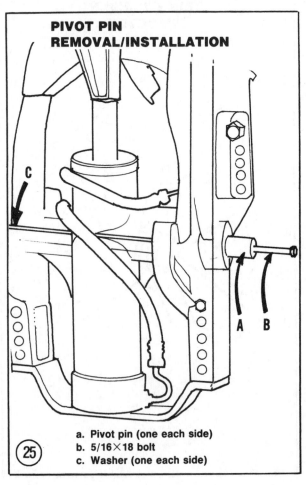

PIVOT PIN REMOVAL/INSTALLATION

(25)
a. Pivot pin (one each side)
b. 5/16 × 18 bolt
c. Washer (one each side)

29. Install trim limit switch connector to starboard clamp bracket.

30. Install steering cable.

31. Pull trim cylinder rams outward until they reach up into the swivel bracket.

32. Coat each trim cylinder pin with multipurpose lubricant, then insert in swivel bracket and through cylinder ram.

33. Install trim cylinder pin cover. Tighten bolts to 60 in.-lb.

34. Connect remaining lines to hydraulic connectors. Tighten attaching nuts to 60 in.-lb.

Removal/Installation
(Late V6 Engines
With Square Motor Housing)

1. Rotate trim pump manual release knob fully counterclockwise to release hydraulic pressure.

2. Manually tilt engine to full up position and insert a solid metal bar between the engine and clamp bracket to keep it in position.

3. Disconnect the negative battery cable, then the positive cable.

4. Remove trim adjustment bolt from clamp bracket.

5. Position a large drain pan under the trim cylinders and disconnect the hydraulic hoses from the clamp bracket connectors. Let cylinders drain.

NOTE
Discard this fluid. Do not re-use it.

6. Remove the trim cylinder pivot pin covers from the clamp brackets.

7. Thread a 5/16×18 bolt into the pivot pin on each side of the engine. Remove pivot pin, washers and springs. See **Figure 25**.

8. Remove trim sender/limit switches as described in this chapter.

9. Drive out the retaining pin holding each trim cylinder pin in place with a hammer and blunt punch.

10. Have an assistant support the trim cylinder. Drive out the upper trim cylinder pin from the swivel bracket and remove the trim cylinder.

11. To install, coat upper trim cylinder pin with 2-4-C multilube (part No. C-92-90018A12). Position trim cylinder in swivel bracket and install pin, then install the retaining pin.

12. Align trim cylinder and clamp bracket lower pin holes. Insert springs in holes. Position washers between cylinder and bracket.

13. Coat pivot pins with 2-4-C multilube and install through clamp bracket and trim cylinder. Install cover plates.

14. Connect hydraulic lines to trim cylinder.

15. Install trim sender/limit switches as described in this chapter.

16. Install trim adjustment bolt in clamp bracket and tighten just enough to remove any play.

17. Grasp engine firmly and remove metal bar. Lower engine carefully.

18. Rotate trim pump manual release valve fully clockwise.

19. Fill trim pump reservoir with oil and bleed system as described in this chapter.

INTEGRAL POWER TRIM SYSTEM

10

An integral power trim assembly mounted between the engine transom brackets (**Figure 26**) was introduced on 1985 inline engines and as a running change on 1986 V6 outboards. This system is designated as Design 2 and replaces the external system described above.

Components

The integral power trim assembly consists of an electric motor, pressurized fluid reservoir, pump, 2 trim cylinders, 1 tilt ram and necessary connecting electrical and hydraulic lines. The switches which operate the system are contained within the remote control or control panel. An anode plate is installed on the underside of the transom/power trim assembly and should be replaced when reduced to approximately 50 percent of its original size.

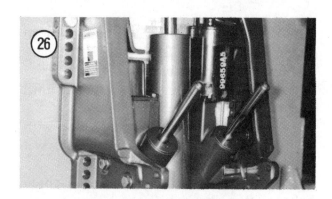

Operation

Depressing the UP trim switch energizes the UP solenoid under the engine cowl to close the pump motor circuit. The motor drives the pump, forcing automatic transmission fluid into the up side of the trim cylinders. The trim cylinders position the engine at the desired angle within the maximum 20° trim range. The engine can be trimmed beyond this maximum by keeping engine speed below approximately 2,000 rpm. Any increase in speed causes the trim system to automatically lower the engine back within the maximum range.

Depressing the DOWN trim switch energizes the DOWN solenoid and closes the pump motor circuit. The motor runs in the opposite direction, driving the pump to force automatic transmission fluid into the down side of the tilt ram, which moves the engine downward to the desired angle.

To trailer the engine, depress and hold the UP trim switch. The trim cylinders will extend fully, then the tilt ram will continue to raise the engine to the full up position for trailering.

Manual Trim

The integral power trim system allows the engine to be manually tilted up or down by opening the manual release valve (**Figure 27**) 3-4 turns counterclockwise and lifting up or pushing down on engine as required.

HYDRAULIC PUMP

Fluid Check

1. Trim outboard to its full UP position and engage tilt lock lever.

NOTE
The trim system is pressurized and fill screw should only be removed with engine positioned as in Step 1.

2. Clean area around fill screw (**Figure 28**). Slowly remove the screw and visually check the fluid level in the fill tube.
3. If fluid is not visible, top up as required with Type A or Type AF automatic transmission fluid.
4. Install and tighten fill screw securely. Wipe off any excess fluid.
5. Disengage tilt lock lever and lower outboard to its normal running position.

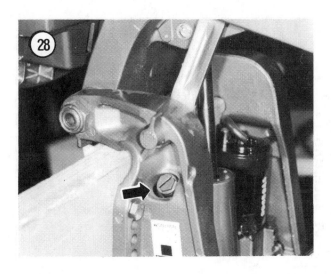

Bleeding the System

The hydraulic system should be bled whenever air enters it. Air in the power trim system will compress, rather than transmit pressure to the trim cylinders. To determine if bleeding is necessary, trim engine up until both trim rods are slightly extended. Tilt ram must not be extended. Apply downward pressure on the gear housing. If trim rods retract into cylinders more than 1/8 in., bleed the system. Bleeding is also necessary whenever a hydraulic line is disconnected.

1. Trim outboard to its full UP position and engage tilt lock lever.

NOTE
The trim system is pressurized and fill screw should only be removed with engine positioned as in Step 1.

2. Clean area around fill screw (**Figure 28**). Slowly remove the screw and visually check the fluid level in the fill tube.

3. If fluid is not visible, top up as required with Type A or Type AF automatic transmission fluid.

4. Install and tighten fill screw securely. Wipe off any excess fluid.

5. Disengage tilt lock lever and trim engine through its entire range.

6. Repeat Steps 1-5 several times, checking the fluid level and topping up each time if necessary.

TROUBLESHOOTING

Whenever a problem develops in the integral power trim system, the initial step is to determine whether the problem is in the electrical or hydraulic system. Electrical tests are given in this Supplement. If the problem appears to be in the hydraulic system and cannot be corrected by bleeding the system, refer it to a dealer or qualified specialist for necessary service.

Before troubleshooting any electrical circuit:

1. Make sure the plug-in connectors are properly engaged and that all terminals and wires are free of corrosion. Tighten and clean as required.

2. Make sure the battery is fully charged. Charge or replace as required.

All Circuits Inoperative

Refer to **Figure 29** (75 hp), **Figure 30** (90-115 hp), **Figure 31** (V6) and **Figure 32** (remote control) for this procedure.

1. Remove the engine cover and check the condition of the 2 power trim fuses.

2. If the fuses are good, connect a voltmeter between point 3 and ground. If battery voltage is not shown, look for poor connections or an open circuit in the red and black leads to the battery or the red leads between the starter motor solenoid and point 3.

3. If battery voltage is shown in Step 2, connect the voltmeter between point 10 and ground. Depress the TRAILER or UP trim button and note the meter reading.

4. If battery voltage is shown in Step 3, check the black ground leads for a poor connection at the power trim solenoids. If this ground is

10

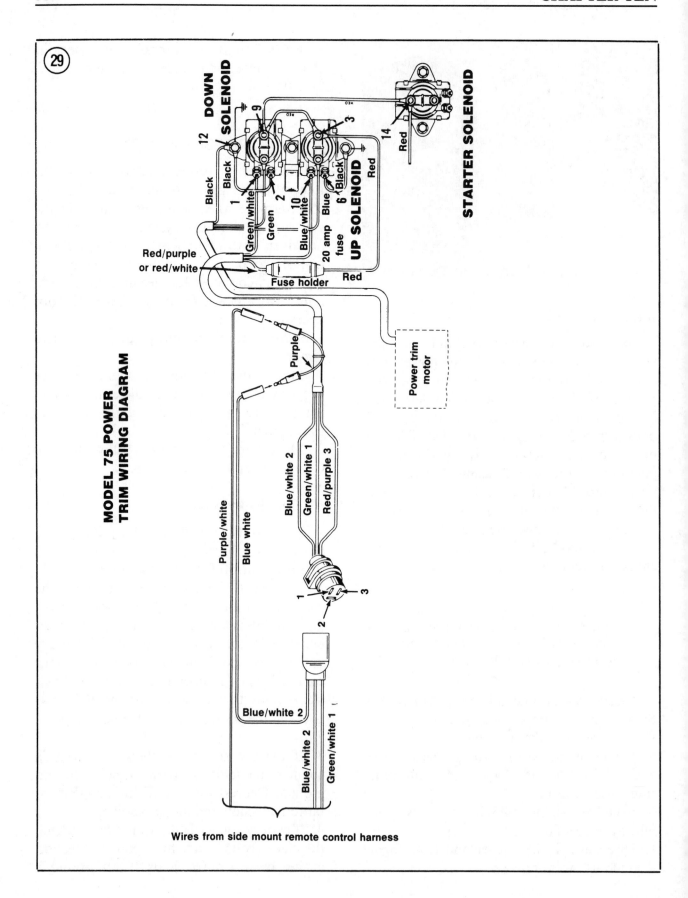

MODEL 75 POWER TRIM WIRING DIAGRAM

DOWN SOLENOID

UP SOLENOID

STARTER SOLENOID

Black

Black

Green/white

Green

Blue/white

Blue

Black

Red

Red

Red

Red/purple or red/white

20 amp fuse

Fuse holder

Power trim motor

Purple

Blue/white 2

Green/white 1

Red/purple 3

Purple/white

Blue white

Blue/white 2

Green/white 1

Blue/white 2

Green/white 1

Wires from side mount remote control harness

MODELS 90 AND 115
POWER TRIM WIRING DIAGRAM

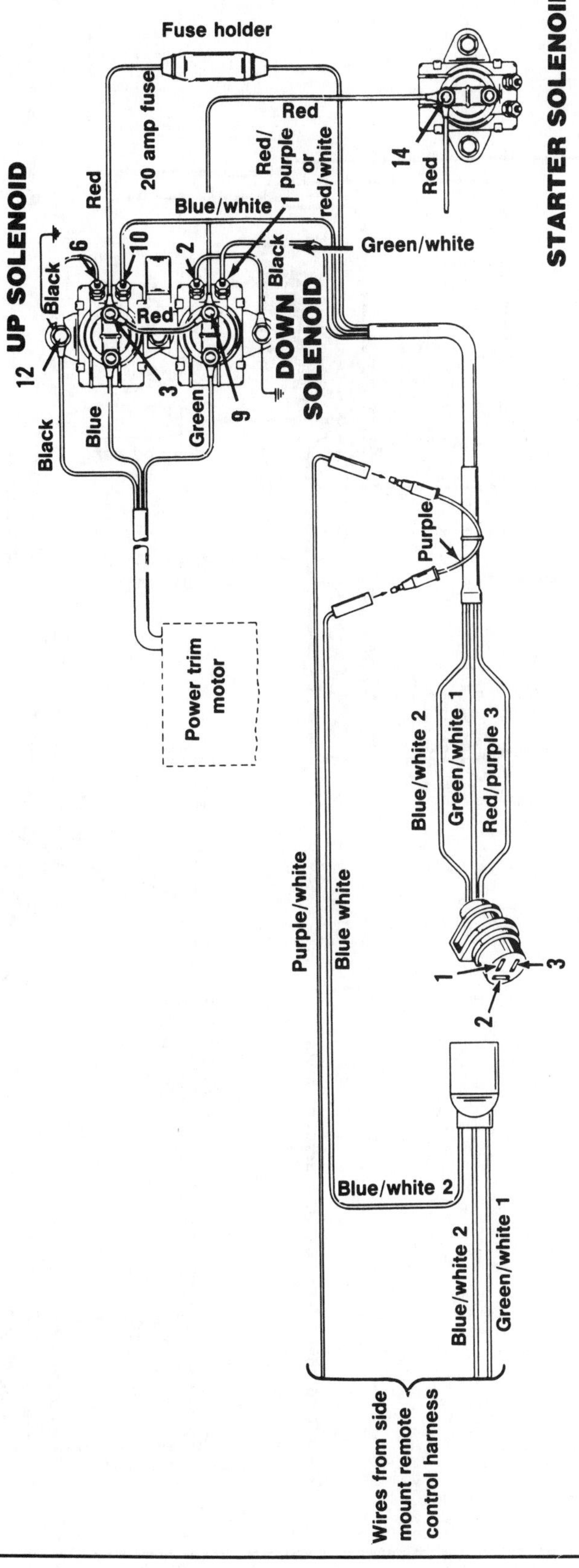

Fuse holder

UP SOLENOID

DOWN SOLENOID

STARTER SOLENOID

Power trim motor

Wires from side mount remote control harness

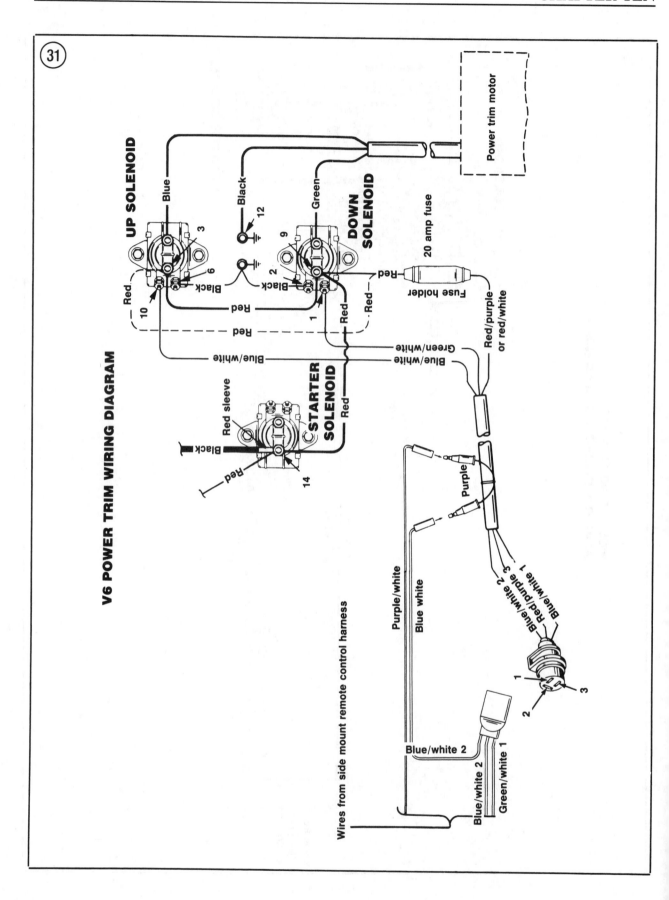

V6 POWER TRIM WIRING DIAGRAM

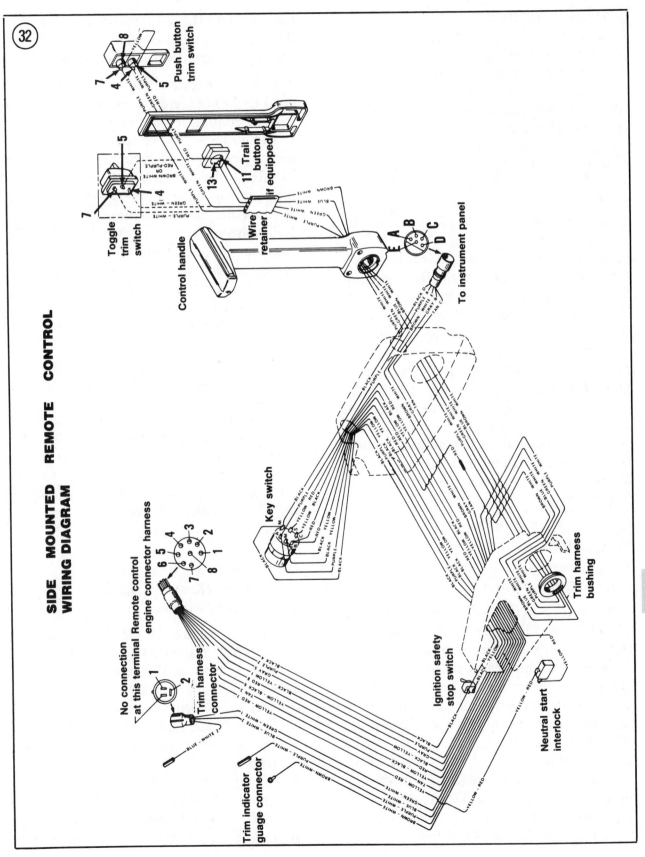

SIDE MOUNTED REMOTE CONTROL WIRING DIAGRAM

good, check the black motor lead at point 12 for a poor ground. If ground is also good, the pump motor is defective.

5. If battery voltage is not shown in Step 3, connect the voltmeter between point 11 (if equipped with TRAILER button) or point 5 (no TRAILER button) and ground. If battery voltage is shown, there is an open circuit in each of the wires between the trim buttons and pump or the trim switch is defective (if not equipped with a TRAILER button). Check for pinched/severed wires or for loose/corroded connections.

6. If battery voltage is not shown in Step 5, turn the ignition switch to the RUN position and connect the voltmeter across any instrument to check for voltage. If no voltage is shown, look for a loose/corroded connection or an open in the wire between point 14 and terminal "b" on the back of the ignition switch.

7. If battery voltage is shown in Step 6, look for an open in the wire between point 11 (if equipped with TRAILER button) or point 5 (no TRAILER button) and terminal "b" on the back of the ignition switch.

TRAILER Circuit—UP Circuit Good (Remote Control With Trailer Button)

Refer to **Figure 29** (75 hp), **Figure 30** (90-115 hp), **Figure 31** (V6) or **Figure 32** (remote control) for this procedure.

1. With an ohmmeter set on the R×1 scale, connect it between point 10 and point 13. If continuity is not shown, there is an open in the wiring between the UP trim solenoid and the TRAILER button.

2. If continuity is shown in Step 1, disconnect battery leads. Connect the ohmmeter across the TRAILER button terminals and depress button. If continuity is not shown, the button is defective.

UP And TRAILER Circuit Inoperative But DOWN Circuit Good (Remote Control With Trailer Button)

Refer to **Figure 29** (75 hp), **Figure 30** (90-115 hp), **Figure 31** (V6) or **Figure 32** (remote control) for this procedure.

1. Connect a voltmeter red lead to point 10 and black lead to ground. Depress the TRAILER button. If no voltage is shown, there is an open between the UP trim solenoid and the trim buttons.

2. If voltage is shown in Step 1, connect the voltmeter between point 3 and ground. If no voltage is shown, check for loose/corroded connections at point 3 or point 9. If connections are good, look for an open in the red wire between point 3 and point 9.

3. If voltage is shown in Step 2, connect the red voltmeter lead to point 6 and depress the TRAILER button. If no voltage is shown, replace the UP solenoid.

4. If voltage is shown in Step 3, check for loose/corroded connections at the UP solenoid terminals. If connections are good, check UP solenoid black ground lead for corrosion or an open. If this is satisfactory, the UP trim solenoid is defective.

UP Circuit Inoperative—TRAILER Circuit Good (Remote Control With Trailer Button)

Refer to **Figure 29** (75 hp), **Figure 30** (90-115 hp), **Figure 31** (V6) or **Figure 32** (remote control) for this procedure.

1. With an ohmmeter set on the R×1 scale, connect it between point 10 and point 7. If continuity is not shown, there is an open in the wiring between the UP trim solenoid and the trim button.

2. If continuity is shown in Step 1, connect a voltmeter between point 8 (push button trim switch) or point 5 (toggle trim switch) and ground. If no voltage is shown, there is an

open in the circuit between point 11 and point 8 or point 5.

3. If voltage is shown in Step 2, move the red voltmeter lead to point 7 and depress the UP trim button. If no voltage is shown, the trim switch is defective.

4. If voltage is shown in Step 3, look for a poor connection at point 7.

DOWN Circuit Inoperative— UP Circuit Good (Remote Control Without Trailer Button)

Refer to **Figure 29** (75 hp), **Figure 30** (90-115 hp), **Figure 31** (V6) or **Figure 32** (remote control) for this procedure.

1. Connect a voltmeter between point 1 and ground. Depress the DOWN trim button.

   a. If no voltage is shown at point 1, move the red voltmeter lead to point 4 and depress the DOWN trim button. If no voltage is shown at point 4, look for an open in the circuit between point 4 and point 1.

   b. If the circuit is good, move the red voltmeter lead to point 5. If voltage is shown at point 5, replace the trim switch. If no voltage is shown, look for loose/correded connections at point 5 or an open circuit in the lead supplying current to point 5.

2. If voltage is shown at point 1 in Step 1, move the red voltmeter lead to point 9. If no voltage is shown at point 9, check for loose/corroded connections or an open in the circuit between point 9 and the positive battery terminal.

3. If voltage is shown at point 9 in Step 2, move the red voltmeter lead to point 2 and depress the DOWN trim button. If no voltage is shown, replace the DOWN trim solenoid. If voltage is shown, check for loose/corroded connections at the DOWN trim solenoid terminals. If the connections are good, look for corrosion or an open in the black ground

wire at the DOWN trim solenoid. If the circuit is good, replace the DOWN trim solenoid.

UP Circuit Inoperative—DOWN Circuit Good (Remote Control Without Trailer Button)

Refer to **Figure 29** (75 hp), **Figure 30** (90-115 hp), **Figure 31** (V6) or **Figure 32** (remote control) for this procedure.

1. Connect the voltmeter between point 10 and ground. Depress the UP trim button. If no voltage is shown, there is an open in the circuit between the UP trim solenoid and trim switch.

2. If voltage is shown in Step 1, move the red voltmeter lead to point 3. If no voltage is shown, look for loose/corroded connections at point 9 or point 3. If the connections are good, look for an open in the red circuit between point 9 and point 3.

3. If voltage is shown in Step 2, move the red voltmeter lead to point 6 and depress the UP trim button. If no voltage is shown, replace the UP trim solenoid. If voltage is shown, check for loose/corroded connections at the UP trim solenoid terminals. If the connections are good, look for corrosion or an open in the black ground wire at the UP trim solenoid. If the circuit is good, replace the UP trim solenoid.

Solenoid Test

1. Disconnect all solenoid terminal wires.

2. With an ohmmeter set on the R×1 scale, connect the test leads between the 2 large solenoid terminals.

3. Connect a 12-volt battery between the 2 small threaded solenoid terminals.

4. If the solenoid does not click and the meter scale read zero ohms, the solenoid is defective.

10

Trim Sender Test

The trim sender is an optional accessory. If so equipped, refer to **Figure 33** and check trim sender operation as follows:

1. Make sure the black trim sender lead has a good ground.

2. Trim the engine to its full DOWN position and turn the ignition switch to the OFF position.

3. Connect an ohmmeter (set on R×1 scale) between a good engine ground and point 1, **Figure 33**.

4. Depress the UP trim button. If the meter needle does not move as the engine trims up, replace the trim sender.

Trim Sender Replacement

Refer to **Figure 34** for this procedure.

1. Raise the engine to its full UP trim position to provide access to the sender.

2. Disconnect the trim sender leads.

3. Remove the sender attaching screws. Remove the sender.

4. Installation is the reverse of removal. Check trim indicator gauge needle position and adjust as described under *Trim Indicator Gauge Needle Adjustment* if required.

Trim Indicator Gauge Needle Adjustment

Refer to **Figure 34** for this procedure.

1. With the engine in the full DOWN trim position, the trim indicator gauge needle should rest at the bottom of the green area on its face. If it does not, trim the engine to its full UP position.

2. Loosen the trim sender attaching screws. Rotate the sender unit counterclockwise to raise or clockwise to lower the needle on the gauge face.

3. When needle is properly positioned, tighten trim sender screws.

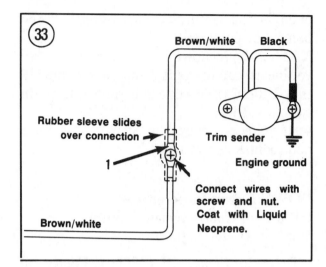

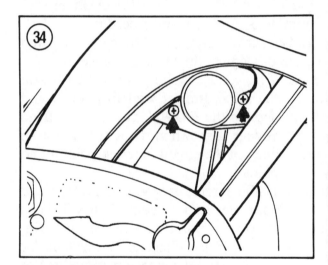

Integral Power Trim Assembly Removal

For safety's sake, this procedure requires the use of a hoist or the fabrication of a support tool made from a used shift shaft or other 3/8 in. metal rod as shown in **Figure 35**.

1. Remove the engine cover.

2. Remove the power trim harness retainer, clamps and straps. Exact location on engine depends upon model.

3. If a hoist is to be used, remove the propeller and flywheel nut. Install lifting eye (part No. 91-90455) on the crankshaft and connect a length of suitable rope between the propeller shaft and lifting eye.

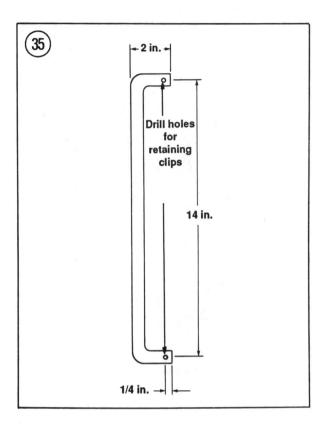

Drill holes for retaining clips

2 in.

14 in.

1/4 in.

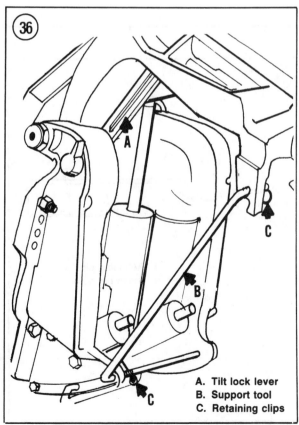

A. Tilt lock lever
B. Support tool
C. Retaining clips

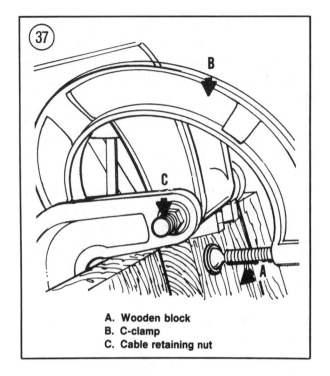

A. Wooden block
B. C-clamp
C. Cable retaining nut

4. Raise the engine to its full UP trim position and engage the tilt lock lever. See A, **Figure 36**.

5A. If a hoist is to be used, attach the rope installed in Step 3 and apply tension to the hoist to prevent the engine from tipping forward into the engine well or backward toward the transom.

5B. If the fabricated tool is to be used, install it between the top hole in the transom bracket and the swivel bracket hole on one side of the engine. Install retaining clips or cotter pins in the holes drilled at each end of the tool to prevent it from slipping out by accident during the remaining steps. See **Figure 36**.

6. Disconnect the trim pump motor leads at the trim solenoids.

7. Attach a suitable block of wood under the engine swivel bracket with a large C-clamp to support the starboard side of the engine. See **Figure 37**.

8. If equipped with thru-the-tilt tube steering, remove the cable retaining nut from the end of the tilt tube. See C, **Figure 37**.

10

9. On the starboard side of the engine, remove the 2 transom bracket mounting bolts. Remove the tilt tube nut and the 3 bolts holding the transom bracket to the power trim assembly.

10. Move the starboard transom bracket away from the power trim assembly far enough to let manual release valve clear the bracket when the assembly is removed.

11. Drive out the cross pin holding the tilt cylinder retaining pin with a suitable punch. Remove the retaining pin. See **Figure 38**.

12. Remove the 3 bolts holding the power trim assembly to the port transom bracket. Remove the power trim assembly.

Integral Power Trim Assembly Installation

1. Coat port transom bracket bolt threads with Loctite Type A and loosely install the power trim assembly to the port bracket with the bolts and lockwashers.

2. Install wave washer on tilt tube.

3. Route wiring harness through the starboard transom bracket.

4. Repeat Step 1 to install the starboard transom bracket. Work carefully to prevent damage to the manual release valve. Tighten port and starboard bolts to 30 ft.-lb. (41 N•m).

5. Coat shanks (not threads) of engine mounting bolts with marine sealer and reinstall starboard transom bracket to boat transom with bolts, flat washers and locknuts. Installation must be watertight.

6. Install tilt tube nut and tighten securely.

7. Remove the C-clamp and wooden block.

8. If equipped with thru-the-tilt tube steering, reinstall the cable retaining nut on tilt tube and tighten securely.

NOTE
If tilt ram overextends in Step 9, retract it by connecting the green wire to the positive battery terminal.

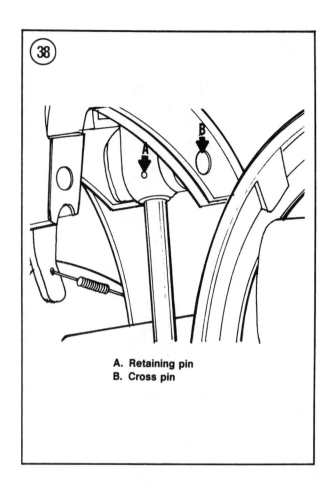

A. Retaining pin
B. Cross pin

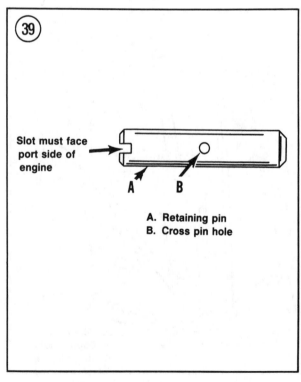

Slot must face port side of engine

A. Retaining pin
B. Cross pin hole

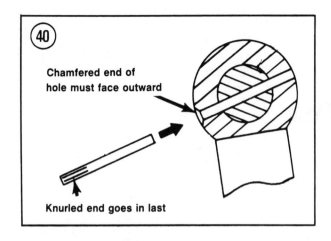

Chamfered end of hole must face outward

Knurled end goes in last

9. Connect the trim motor blue wire to the positive battery terminal and the black wire to the negative battery terminal with jumper cables to extend the end of the tilt ram enough to install the retaining pin. When alignment is correct, disconnect the jumper cables.

10. Align cross pin hole in retaining pin with the hole in the end of the tilt ram (**Figure 39**) and install retaining pin. The slot in the end of the pin can be used to move it back and forth. A suitable punch installed in the tilt ram cross pin hole will engage the retaining pin as it is moved. Once holes are aligned, remove punch and install cross pin as shown in **Figure 40**.

11. Route and connect trim motor wires to solenoids. Install all retainers, clamps and straps removed. Coat all electrical connections with Quicksilver Liquid Neoprene.

Index

11

Wiring Diagrams

MERC 500 THUNDERBOLT IGNITION THROUGH 1974

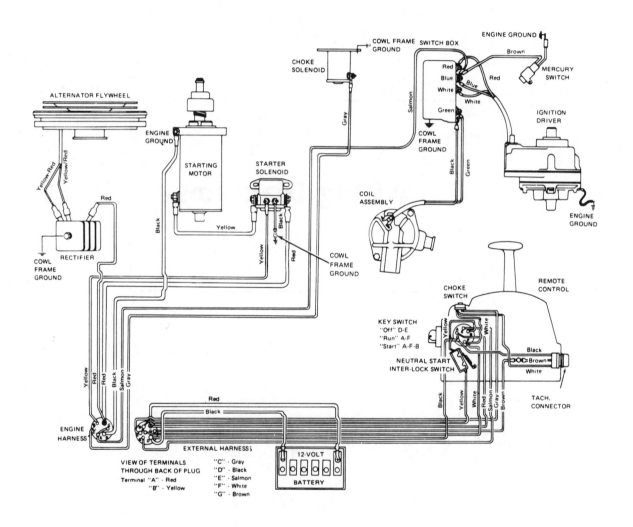

MERC 650S AND 500S BREAKERLESS WITH IGNITION DRIVER THROUGH 1974

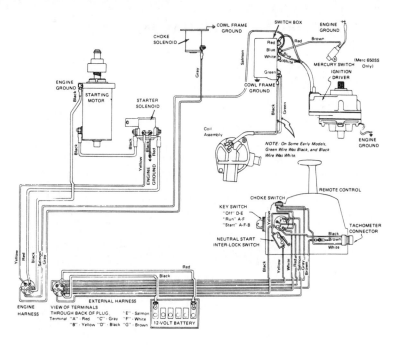

MERC 650SS AND 500SS BREAKERLESS THROUGH 1974

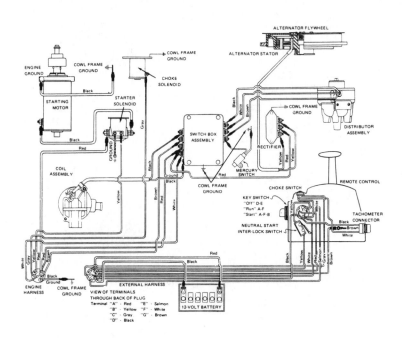

12

MERC 500 (1975) MANUAL START

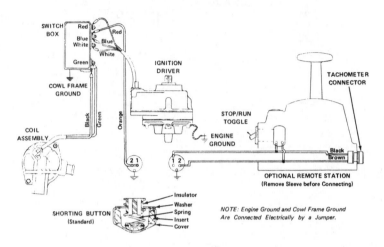

MERC 500 (1975) ELECTRIC START AD-CD IGNITION

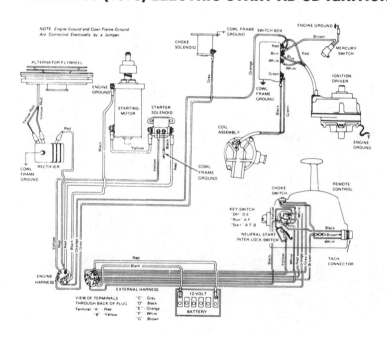

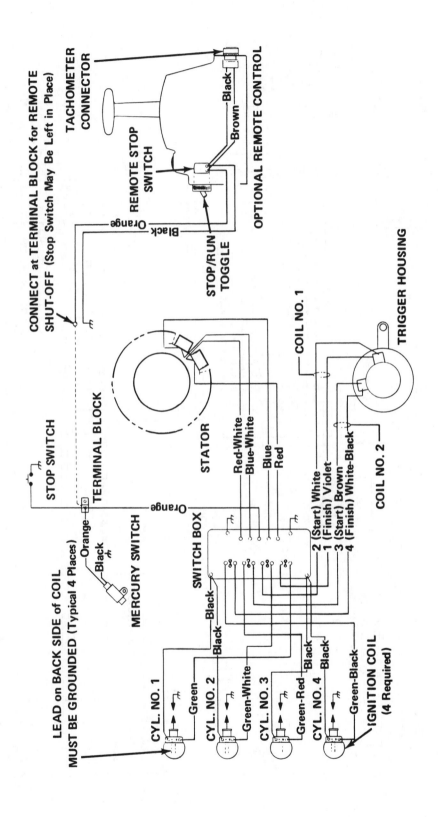

MERC 500 (1976-77-78) MANUAL START

CONNECT at TERMINAL BLOCK for REMOTE
SHUT-OFF (Stop Switch May Be Left in Place)

TACHOMETER CONNECTOR

Black

Brown

REMOTE STOP SWITCH

OPTIONAL REMOTE CONTROL

Black Orange

STOP/RUN TOGGLE

TRIGGER HOUSING

COIL NO. 1

STOP SWITCH

TERMINAL BLOCK

Orange

Black

MERCURY SWITCH

LEAD on BACK SIDE of COIL
MUST BE GROUNDED (Typical 4 Places)

STATOR

Red-White
Blue-White
Blue
Red

Orange

SWITCH BOX

2 (Start) White
1 (Finish) Violet
3 (Start) Brown
4 (Finish) White-Black

COIL NO. 2

Black

Green

CYL. NO. 1

Black

Green-White

CYL. NO. 2

Green-Red

Black

CYL. NO. 3

Black

Green-Black

CYL. NO. 4

IGNITION COIL
(4 Required)

12

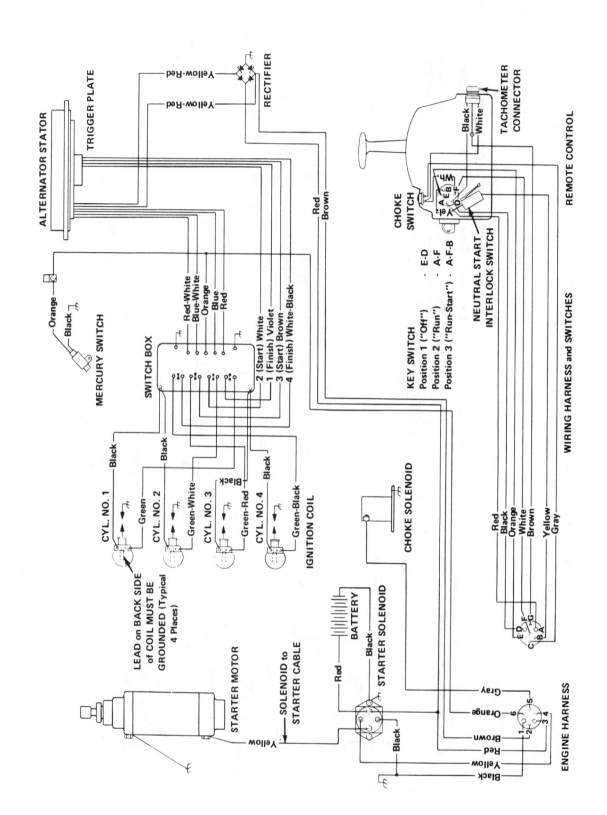

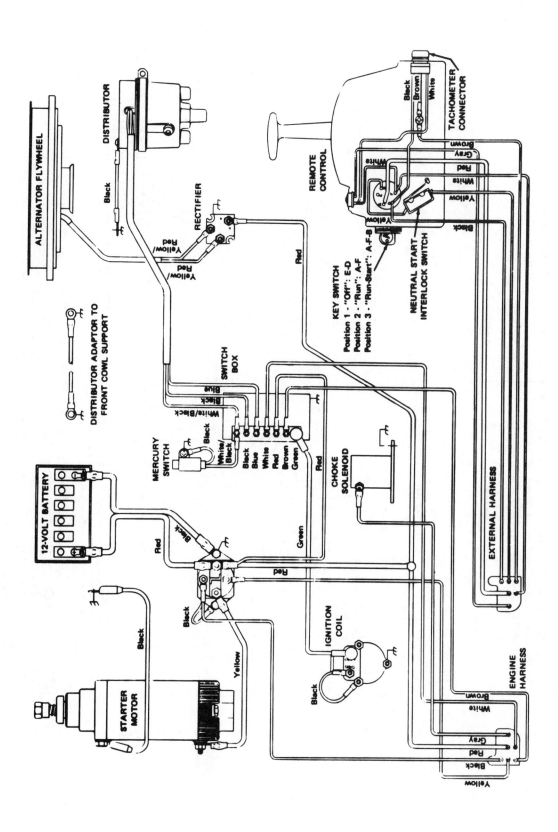

MERC 650 (3-CYL.) THROUGH 1974

ALTERNATOR FLYWHEEL

DISTRIBUTOR

Black

RECTIFIER

Yellow/Red

Yellow/Red

DISTRIBUTOR ADAPTOR TO FRONT COWL SUPPORT

REMOTE CONTROL

TACHOMETER CONNECTOR

Black Brown White

Brown

Gray

Red

White

Yellow

Yellow

Black

White

Red

KEY SWITCH

Position 1 - "Off": E-D
Position 2 - "Run": A-F
Position 3 - "Run-Start": A-F-B

NEUTRAL START INTERLOCK SWITCH

SWITCH BOX

Blue

Black

White/Black

Black
Blue
White
Red
Brown
Green

MERCURY SWITCH

Black

White/Black

Red

Green

Red

CHOKE SOLENOID

EXTERNAL HARNESS

12-VOLT BATTERY

Red

Black

Black

Red

IGNITION COIL

Black

STARTER MOTOR

Black

Yellow

ENGINE HARNESS

Brown

White

Gray

Red

Black

Yellow

12

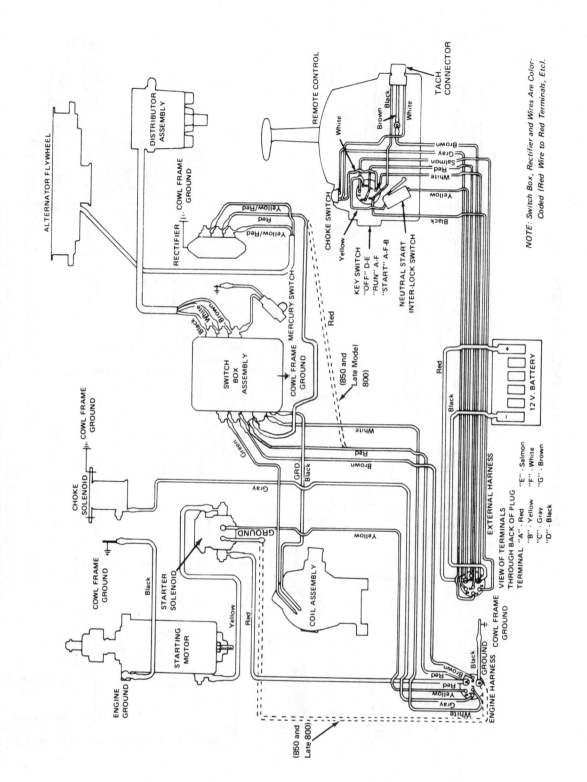

MERC 850-800*-650 (4-CYL.) THUNDERBOLT IGNITION THROUGH 1974

(*Serial No. 2991033 and below; Serial No. 3052381 thru 3059821; and Serial No. 3307347 and up)

NOTE: Switch Box, Rectifier and Wires Are Color-Coded (Red Wire to Red Terminals, Etc).

VIEW OF TERMINALS
THROUGH BACK OF PLUG

TERMINAL "A" - Red   "E" - Salmon
          "B" - Yellow   "F" - White
          "C" - Gray   "G" - Brown
          "D" - Black

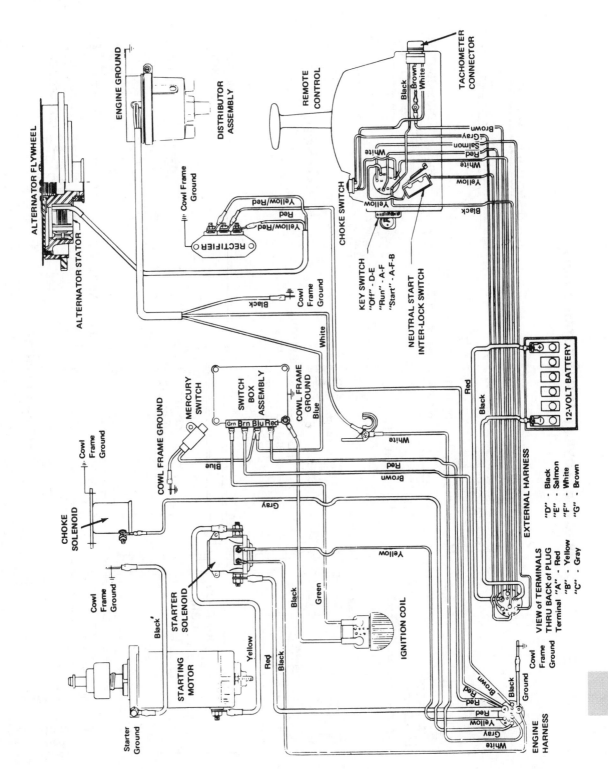

MERC 800 THUNDERBOLT IGNITION THROUGH 1974
(With Serial Nos. 2991034-3052380; 3059822-3307346)

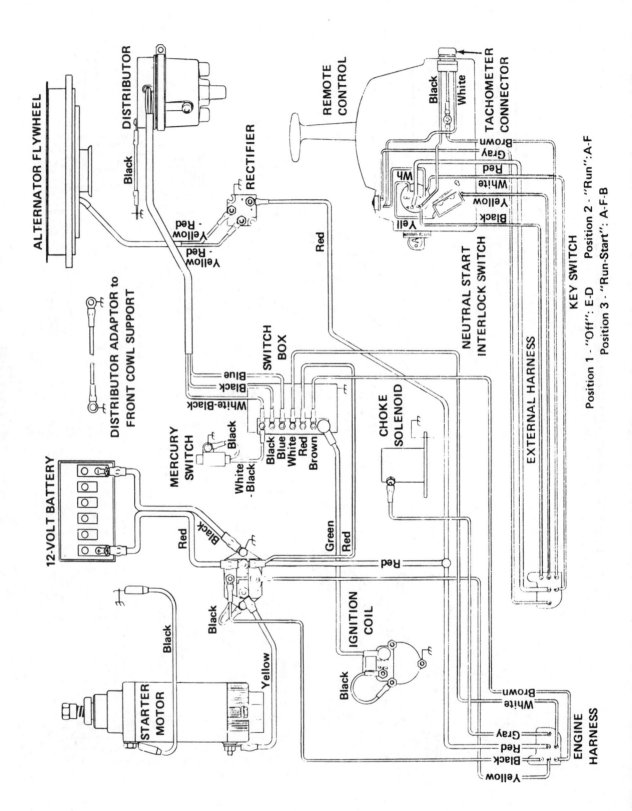

MERC 650 (3-CYL.) (1975) ELECTRIC START

ALTERNATOR FLYWHEEL

DISTRIBUTOR

Black

RECTIFIER

Yellow - Red

Yellow - Red

DISTRIBUTOR ADAPTOR to FRONT COWL SUPPORT

12-VOLT BATTERY

Red

Black

MERCURY SWITCH

Black

White - Black

SWITCH BOX

Blue

Black

White-Black

Black Blue White Red Brown

Red

CHOKE SOLENOID

Green

Red

Red

STARTER MOTOR

Black

Black

Yellow

IGNITION COIL

Black

REMOTE CONTROL

Black

White

TACHOMETER CONNECTOR

Brown
Gray
Red
White
Yellow
Black

Yell

WH

NEUTRAL START INTERLOCK SWITCH

EXTERNAL HARNESS

KEY SWITCH

Position 1 - "Off": E-D   Position 2 - "Run": A-F
Position 3 - "Run-Start": A-F-B

Brown
White
Gray
Red
Black
Yellow

ENGINE HARNESS

MERC 650 (3 CYL.) (1976) AND MERC 700 (3-CYL.) (1977-78)

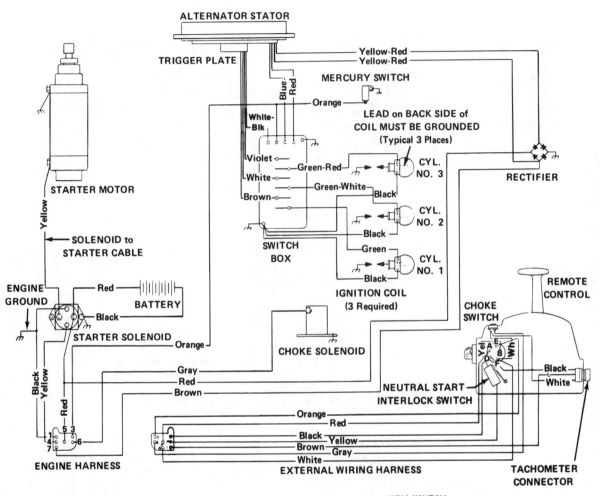

ALTERNATOR STATOR

TRIGGER PLATE

MERCURY SWITCH

Yellow-Red
Yellow-Red

Blue-Red

Orange

White-Blk

LEAD on BACK SIDE of
COIL MUST BE GROUNDED
(Typical 3 Places)

Violet
White
Brown

Green-Red

Green-White
Black

Black

Green
Black

CYL. NO. 3

CYL. NO. 2

CYL. NO. 1

RECTIFIER

STARTER MOTOR

Yellow

SOLENOID to
STARTER CABLE

SWITCH BOX

IGNITION COIL
(3 Required)

ENGINE GROUND

Red

Black

BATTERY

STARTER SOLENOID

Orange

CHOKE SOLENOID

CHOKE SWITCH

REMOTE CONTROL

Black
Yellow

Red

Gray
Red
Brown

NEUTRAL START
INTERLOCK SWITCH

Yel
A E
D B
F

Wh

Black
White

1 5 3
4   6
7

Orange
Red
Black
Brown
White

Yellow
Gray

ENGINE HARNESS

EXTERNAL WIRING HARNESS

TACHOMETER
CONNECTOR

KEY SWITCH
Position 1 ("Off") - E-D
Position 2 ("Run") - A-F
Position 3 ("Run-
Start") - A-F-B

12

MERC 1100SS AND 950SS THROUGH 1974

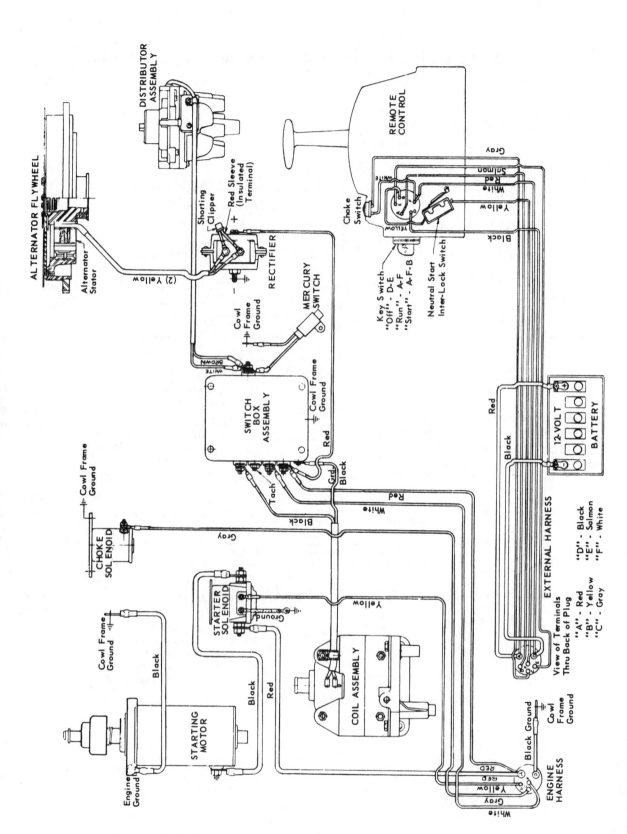

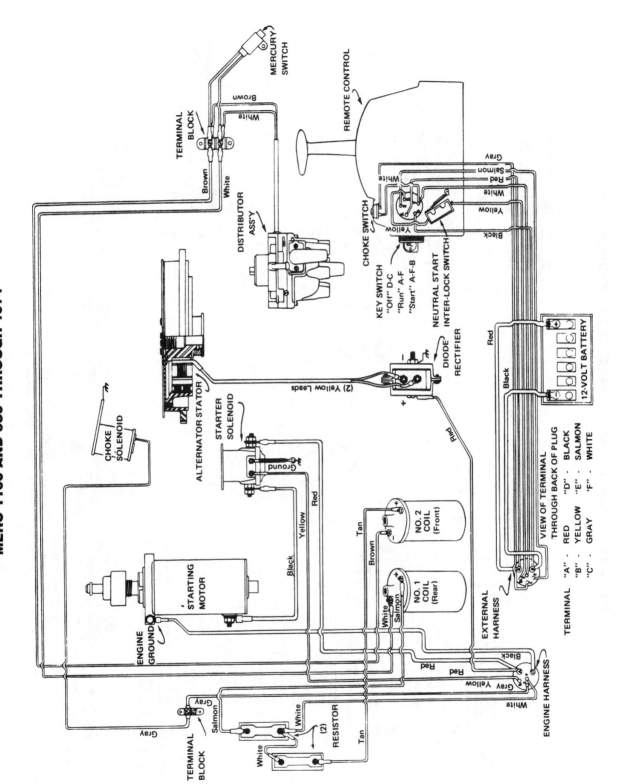

MERC 1100 AND 950 THROUGH 1974

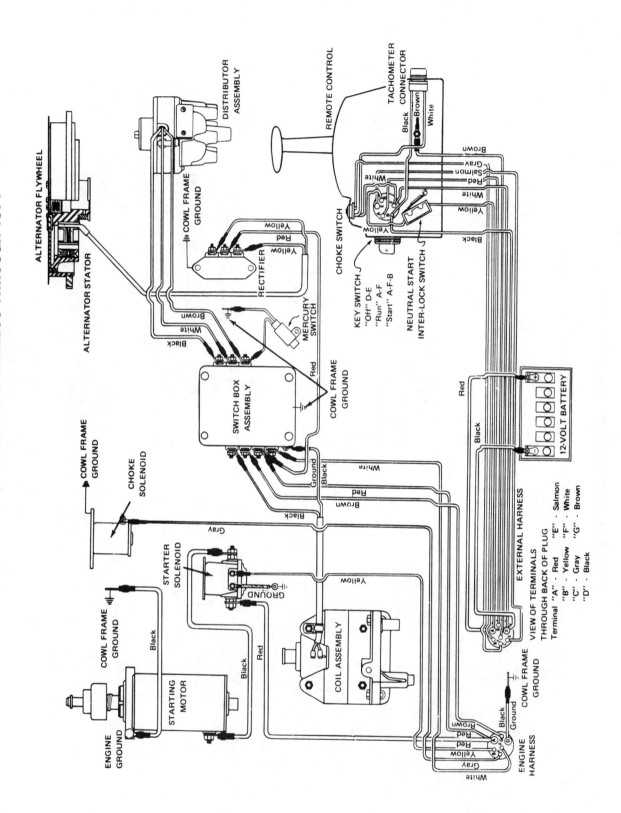

MERC 1250-1100-1000-950 BREAKERLESS THROUGH 1974

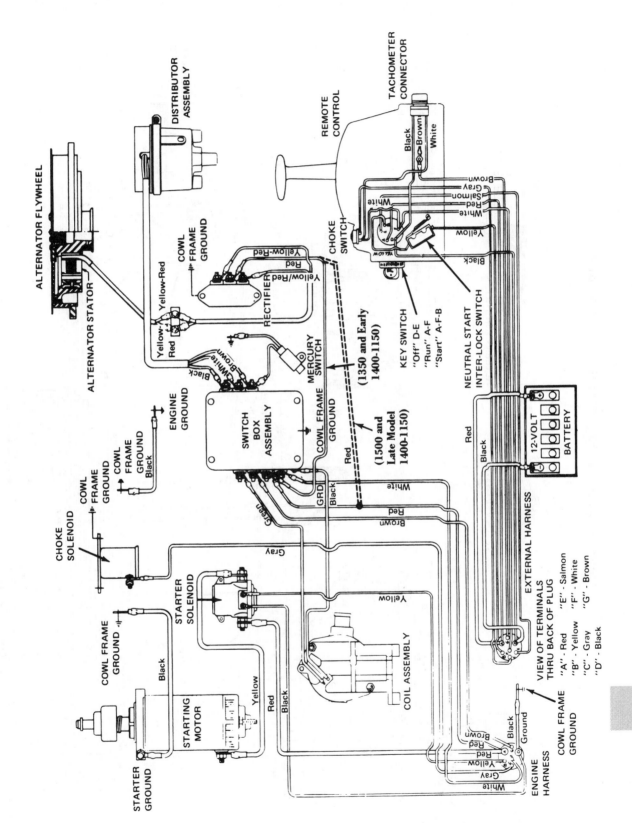

MERC 1500-1400-1350-1150 THUNDERBOLT IGNITION THROUGH 1974

12

MERC 850-1150-1500 (1975) ELECTRIC START

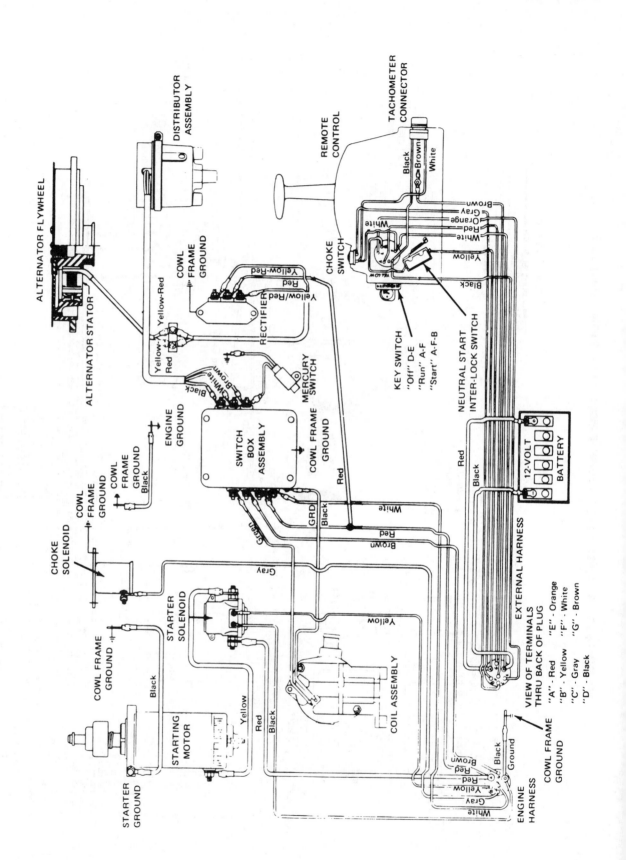

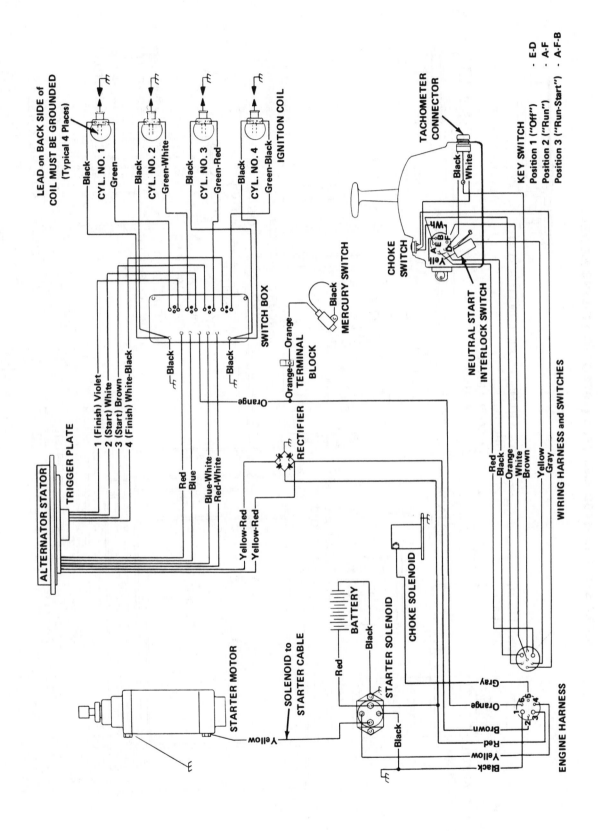

MERC 850 (1976-77) AND 800 (1978)

12

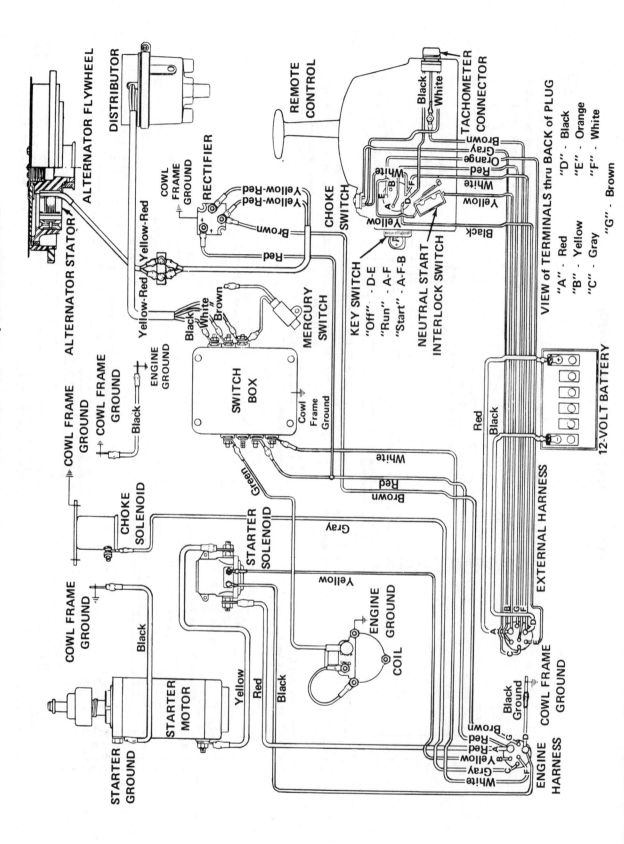

MERC 900-1150-1400 AND 1500 (1976-77-78) INLINE MODELS

KEY SWITCH
"Off" - D-E
"Run" - A-F
"Start" - A-F-B

VIEW of TERMINALS thru BACK of PLUG

"A" - Red   "D" - Black
"B" - Yellow   "E" - Orange
"C" - Gray   "F" - White
                 "G" - Brown

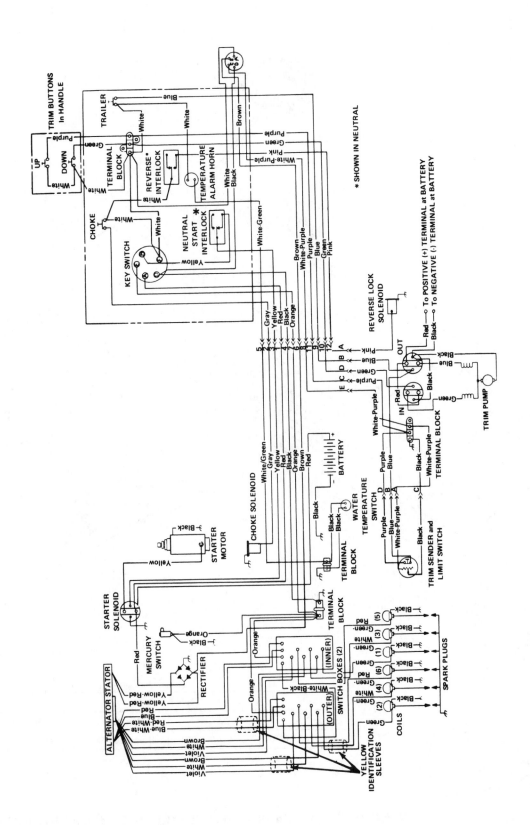

MERC V-6 (1976-77-78)

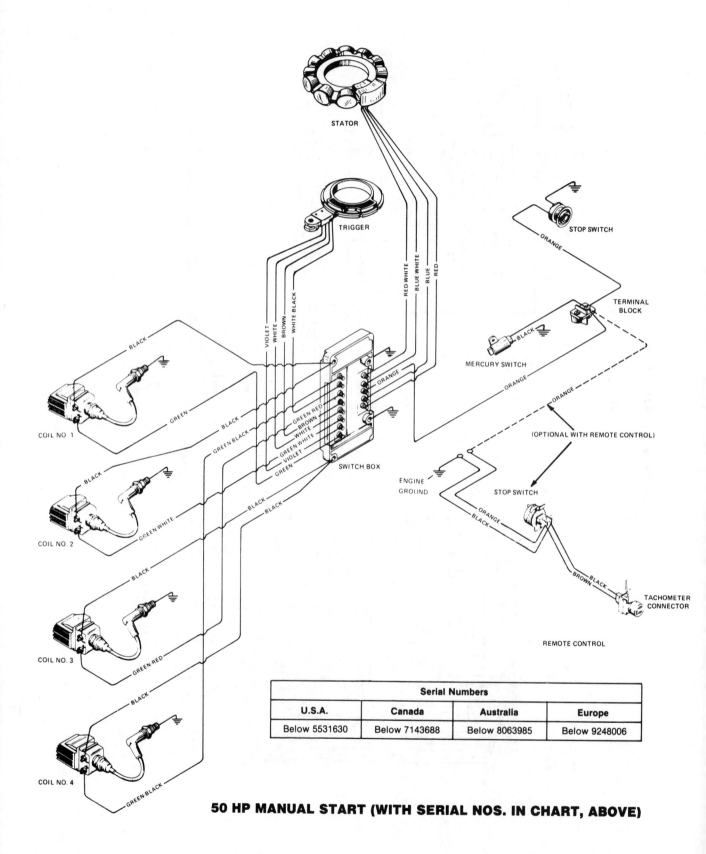

STATOR

TRIGGER

STOP SWITCH

ORANGE

TERMINAL
BLOCK

BLACK

MERCURY SWITCH

ORANGE

ORANGE

(OPTIONAL WITH REMOTE CONTROL)

RED WHITE
BLUE WHITE
BLUE
RED

VIOLET
WHITE
BROWN
WHITE BLACK

ORANGE

BLACK

BLACK

GREEN RED
BROWN
WHITE
GREEN WHITE
VIOLET
GREEN

SWITCH BOX

ENGINE
GROUND

STOP SWITCH

ORANGE

BLACK

BLACK
BLACK

GREEN

COIL NO. 1

BLACK

GREEN WHITE

COIL NO. 2

BLACK

GREEN RED

COIL NO. 3

BLACK

GREEN BLACK

COIL NO. 4

BROWN

BLACK

TACHOMETER
CONNECTOR

REMOTE CONTROL

Serial Numbers			
U.S.A.	**Canada**	**Australia**	**Europe**
Below 5531630	Below 7143688	Below 8063985	Below 9248006

50 HP MANUAL START (WITH SERIAL NOS. IN CHART, ABOVE)

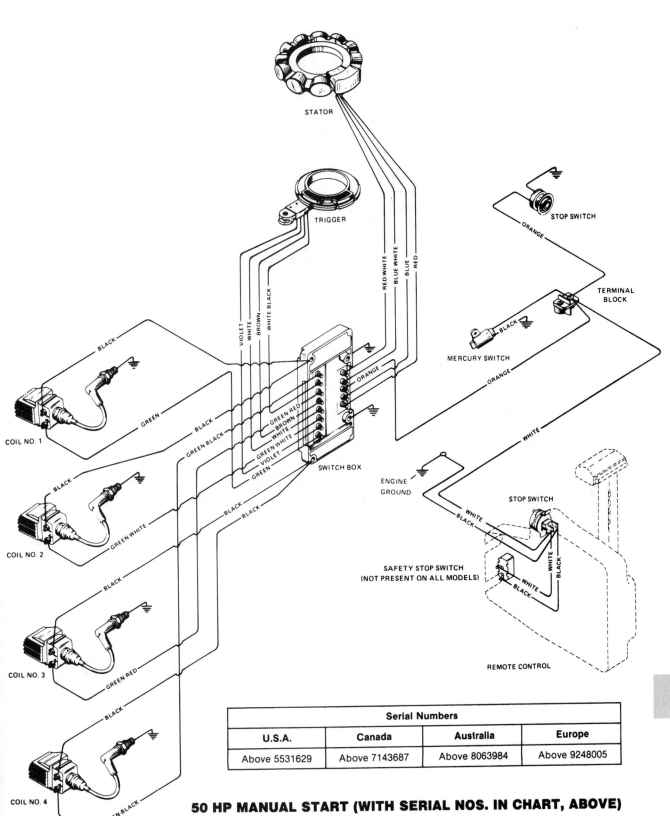

STATOR

TRIGGER

STOP SWITCH

ORANGE

TERMINAL
BLOCK

BLACK

MERCURY SWITCH

ORANGE

RED WHITE

BLUE WHITE

BLUE

RED

VIOLET

WHITE

BROWN

WHITE BLACK

BLACK

GREEN

BLACK

GREEN BLACK

ORANGE

GREEN RED

BROWN

WHITE

GREEN WHITE

VIOLET

GREEN

SWITCH BOX

WHITE

COIL NO. 1

BLACK

GREEN WHITE

COIL NO. 2

BLACK

ENGINE
GROUND

STOP SWITCH

WHITE

BLACK

WHITE

BLACK

SAFETY STOP SWITCH
(NOT PRESENT ON ALL MODELS)

WHITE

BLACK

BLACK

GREEN RED

COIL NO. 3

BLACK

REMOTE CONTROL

BLACK

GREEN BLACK

COIL NO. 4

12

Serial Numbers			
U.S.A.	**Canada**	**Australia**	**Europe**
Above 5531629	Above 7143687	Above 8063984	Above 9248005

50 HP MANUAL START (WITH SERIAL NOS. IN CHART, ABOVE)

50 HP ELECTRIC START
(WITH SERIAL NOS. IN CHART, BELOW)

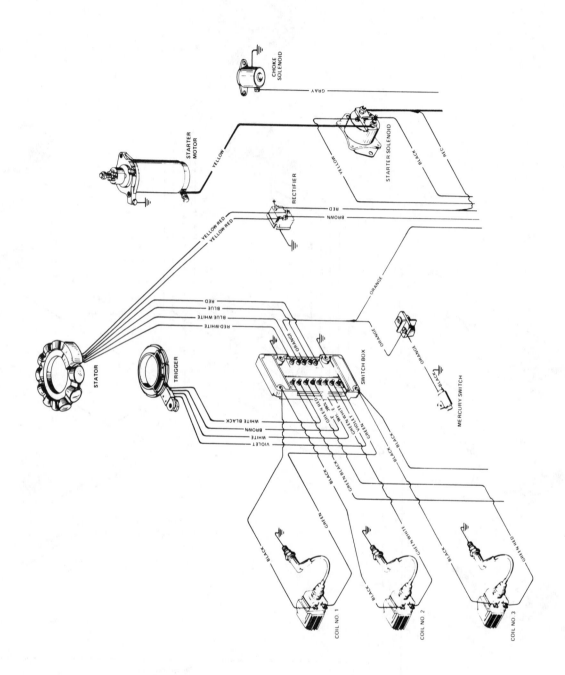

CHOKE SOLENOID

STARTER MOTOR

STARTER SOLENOID

GRAY

YELLOW

BLACK

RED

RECTIFIER

YELLOW

YELLOW RED

YELLOW RED

RED

BROWN

ORANGE

RED
BLUE
BLUE WHITE
RED-WHITE

STATOR

TRIGGER

SWITCH BOX

ORANGE

ORANGE

ORANGE

BLACK

MERCURY SWITCH

WHITE BLACK
BROWN
WHITE
VIOLET

GREEN/BLACK
GREEN/WHITE
VIOLET
GREEN/WHITE
GREEN
BLACK
BLACK

BLACK

GREEN/BLACK

BLACK

GREEN

WHITE

BLACK

COIL NO. 1

WHITE

BLACK

WHITE

COIL NO. 2

BLACK

GREEN RED

COIL NO. 3

50 HP ELECTRIC START
(WITH SERIAL NOS. IN CHART, BELOW) (continued)

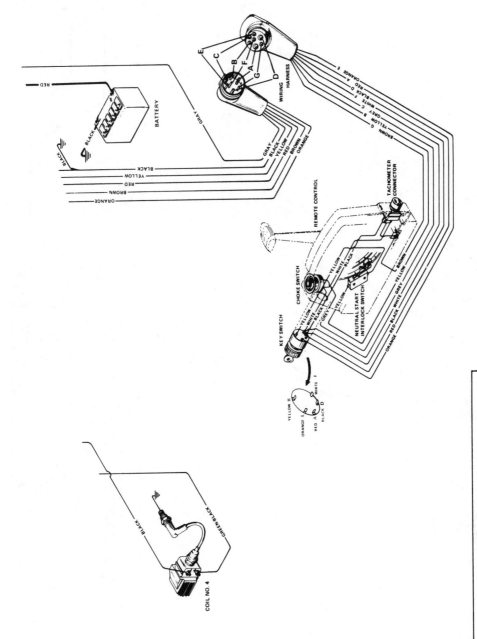

Serial Numbers			
U.S.A.	Canada	Australia	Europe
Below 5531630	Below 7143688	Below 8063985	Below 9248006

12

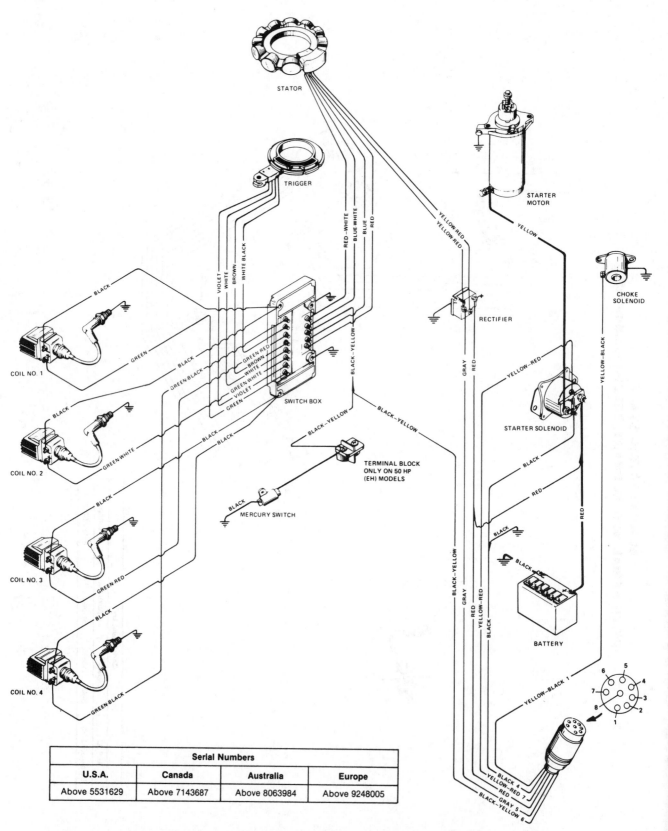

Serial Numbers			
U.S.A.	**Canada**	**Australia**	**Europe**
Above 5531629	Above 7143687	Above 8063984	Above 9248005

50 HP ELECTRIC START (WITH SERIAL NOS. IN CHART, ABOVE)

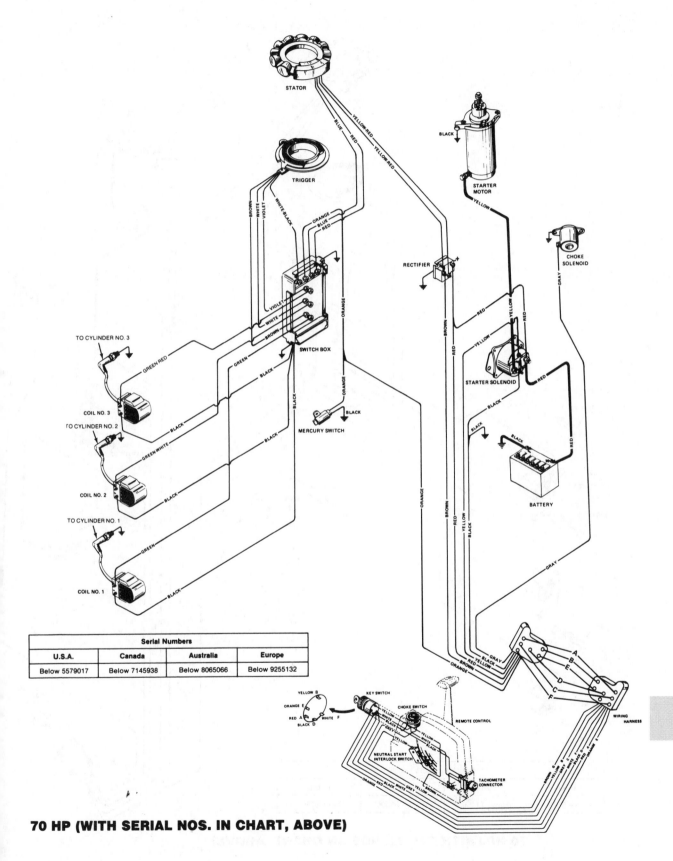

STATOR

TRIGGER

BLACK

STARTER
MOTOR

YELLOW-RED

BLUE

RED

YELLOW-RED

YELLOW

CHOKE
SOLENOID

BROWN
WHITE
VIOLET
WHITE-BLACK

ORANGE
BLUE
RED

GRAY

RECTIFIER

VIOLET
WHITE
BROWN

ORANGE

RED

YELLOW

TO CYLINDER NO. 3

SWITCH BOX

YELLOW

RED

GREEN RED

GREEN

BLACK

STARTER SOLENOID

RED

COIL NO. 3

BLACK

BLACK

TO CYLINDER NO. 2

ORANGE

BLACK

GREEN-WHITE

BLACK

MERCURY SWITCH

BLACK

BLACK

RED

COIL NO. 2

BLACK

BATTERY

TO CYLINDER NO. 1

GREEN

ORANGE

BROWN

RED

YELLOW

BLACK

COIL NO. 1

BLACK

GRAY

Serial Numbers			
U.S.A.	Canada	Australia	Europe
Below 5579017	Below 7145938	Below 8065066	Below 9255132

YELLOW B
ORANGE E
RED A
BLACK D
WHITE F

KEY SWITCH

CHOKE SWITCH

REMOTE CONTROL

BL GRAY
RED BLACK
YELLOW
BROWN
ORANGE

A
B
E
D
C
F

WIRING
HARNESS

NEUTRAL START
INTERLOCK SWITCH

TACHOMETER
CONNECTOR

ORANGE RED BLACK WHITE GREY YELLOW BROWN

12

70 HP (WITH SERIAL NOS. IN CHART, ABOVE)

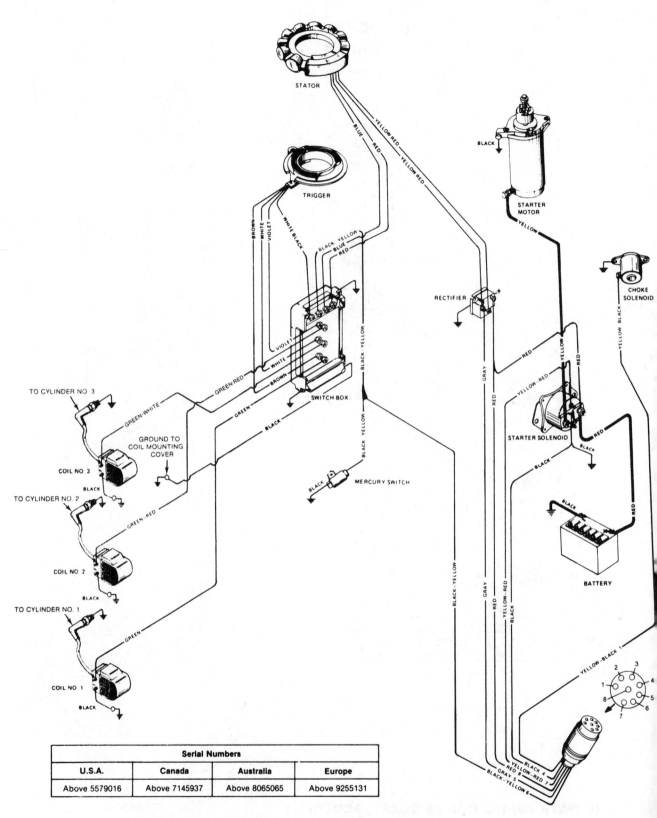

Serial Numbers			
U.S.A.	**Canada**	**Australia**	**Europe**
Above 5579016	Above 7145937	Above 8065065	Above 9255131

70 HP (WITH SERIAL NOS. IN CHART, ABOVE)

90 HP THRU 150 HP (INLINE ENGINES) WITH DISTRIBUTOR TYPE IGNITION SYSTEM

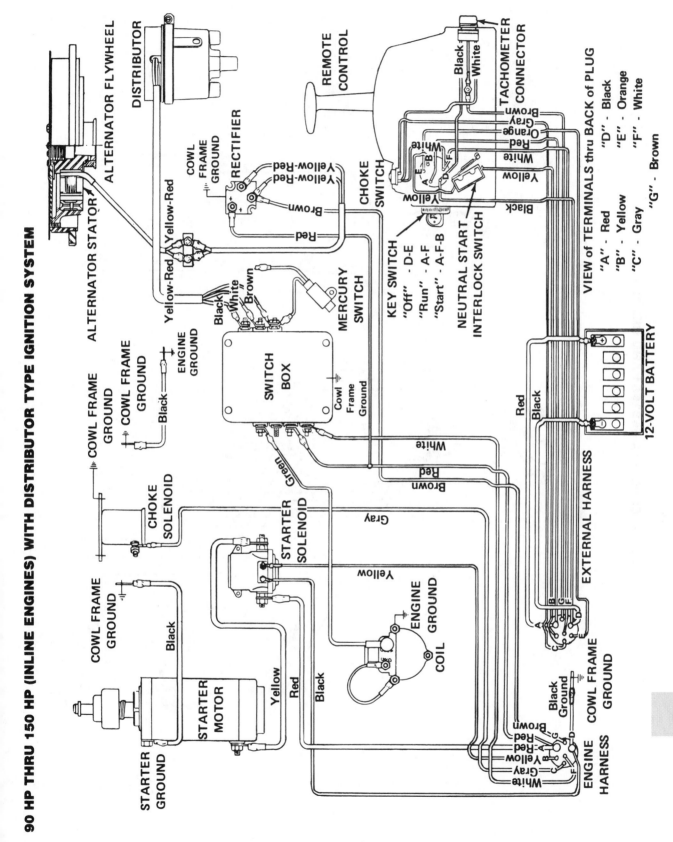

12

80 HP (SERIAL NO. 5582561 AND BELOW)

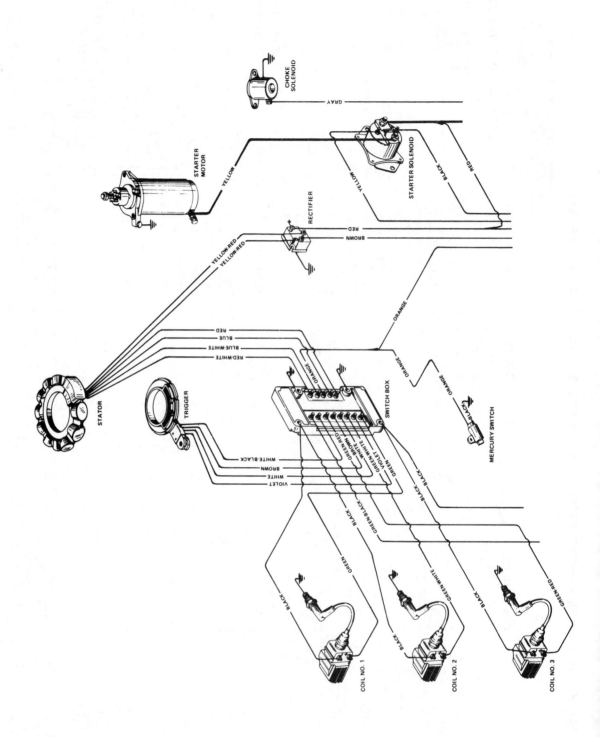

80 HP (SERIAL NO. 5582561 AND BELOW) (continued)

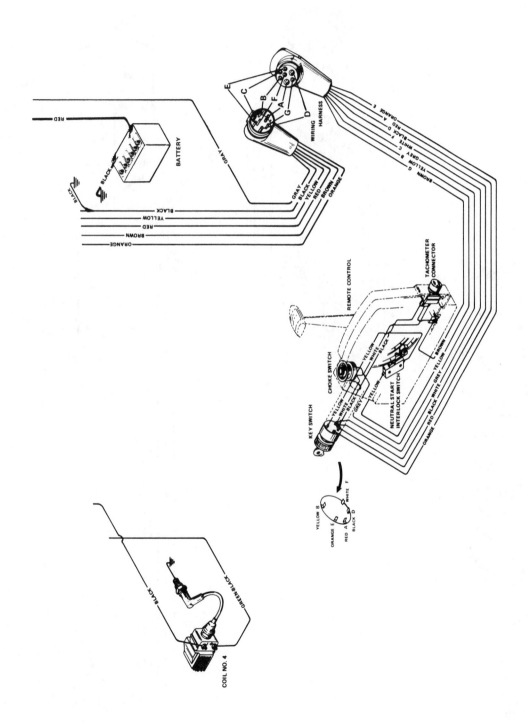

80 HP (SERIAL NO. 5582562 AND ABOVE)

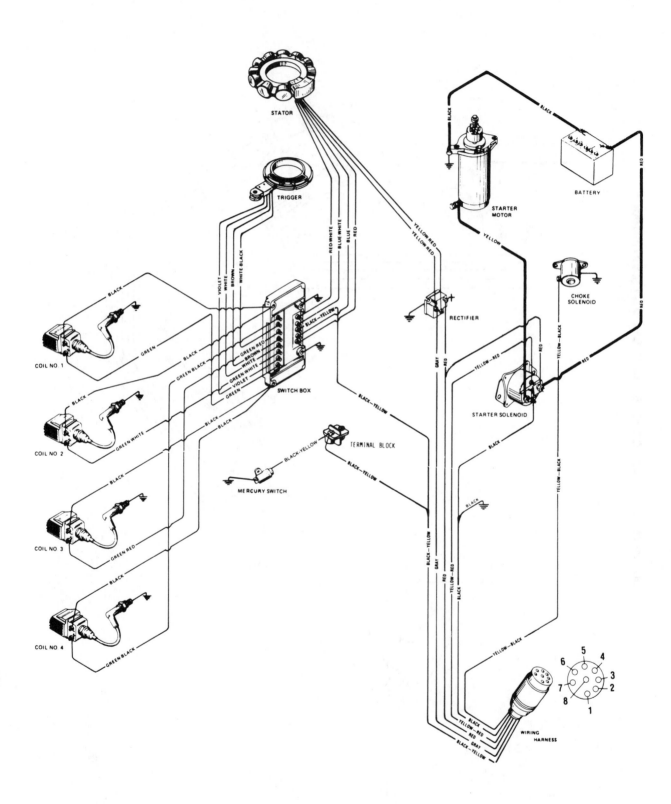

90 HP, 115 HP AND 140 HP (SERIAL NOS. 5594656 AND BELOW) WITH ADI IGNITION SYSTEM

90 HP, 115 HP AND 140 HP (SERIAL NOS. 5594656 AND BELOW) WITH ADI IGNITION SYSTEM (continued)

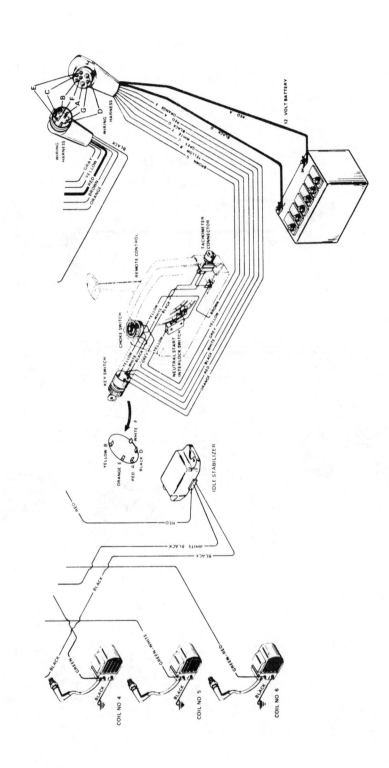

90 HP, 115 HP and 140 HP (SERIAL NOS. 5594657 AND ABOVE)

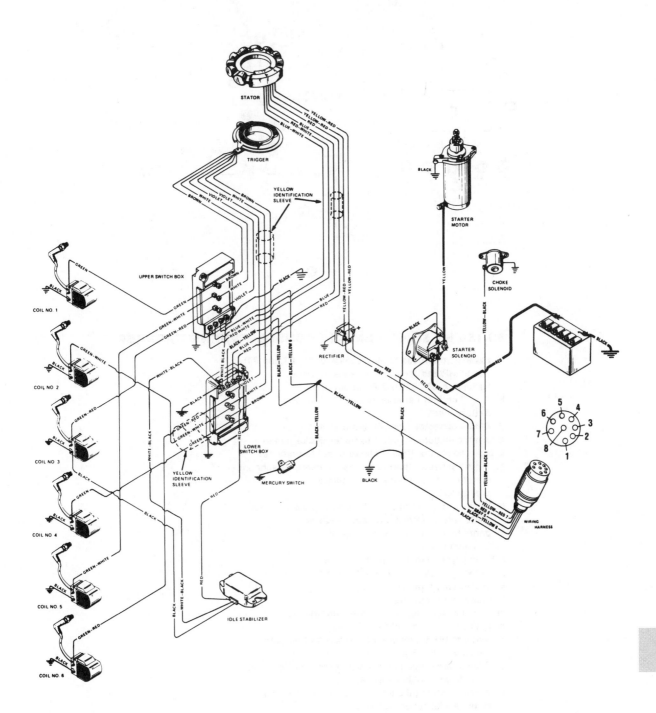

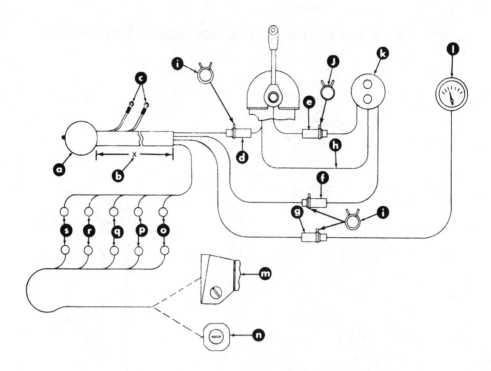

50-150 HP SINGLE ENGINE CONSOLE WIRING HARNESS

a. Extension harness (A-84-76954A10, 15, 20 and 40)
   (for 65 HP and for 70 HP models, adaptor
   harness A-84-75291A2 is required)

b. X = length of harness in feet

c. Battery leads

d. 4-pin connector (control to harness)

e. 3-pin connector (control to trailer/choke panel)

f. 5-pin connector (trailer/choke panel to harness)

g. 4-pin connector (harness to tachometer, if tachometer
   is not used, tape back and insulate
   connector)

h. White wire (control to trailer/choke panel) connect
   white wire to terminal on back side of
   panel that already has a white wire
   connected to it.

i. Spring-type clamp 13/16 in. (20.6 mm)

j. Spring-type clamp 3/4 in. (19.1 mm)

k. Trailer/choke panel

l. Tachometer (optional)

m. Locking steering mount (A-66786A3)

n. Ignition switch panel (A-54211A2)

o. Black to black (secure with screw and nut and
   insulate with rubber sleeve)

p. Orange to orange (secure with screw and nut and
   insulate with rubber sleeve)

q. White to white (secure with screw and nut and
   insulate with rubber sleeve)

r. Yellow to yellow (secure with screw and nut and
   insulate with rubber sleeve)

s. Red to red/white (secure with screw and nut and
   insulate with rubber sleeve)

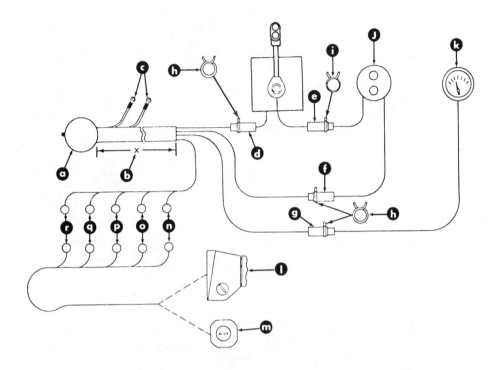

50-150 HP PANEL CONTROL WIRING HARNESS

a. Extension harness (A-84-76954A10, 15, 20 and 40)
   (for 65 HP and for 70 HP models, adaptor
   A-84-75291A2harness is required)
b. X = length of harness in feet
c. Battery cables
d. 4-pin connector (control to harness)
e. 3-pin connector (control to trailer/choke panel)
f. 5-pin connector (trailer/choke panel to harness)
g. 4-pin connector (harness to tachometer, if tachometer
   is not used, tape back and insulate
   connector wire connected to it.)
h. Spring-type clamp 13/16 in. (20.6 mm)
i. Spring-type clamp 3/4 in. (19.1 mm)
j. Trailer/ choke panel
k. Tachometer (optional)
l. Locking steering mount (A-66786A3)
m. Ignition switch panel (A-54211A2)
n. Black to black (secure with screw and nut and
   insulate with rubber sleeve)
o. Orange to orange (secure with screw and nut and
   insulate with rubber sleeve)
p. White to white (secure with screw and nut and
   insulate with rubber sleeve)
q. Yellow to yellow (secure with screw and nut and
   insulate with rubber sleeve)
r. Red to red/white (secure with screw and nut and
   insulate with rubber sleeve)

12

150 HP, 175 HP AND 200 HP V-6 MODELS WITH SERIAL NO. 5363918 AND BELOW (U.S.A.) OR 8061595 AND BELOW (AUSTRALIA)

Serial No.	
U.S.A.	Below 5363918
Australia	Below 8061595

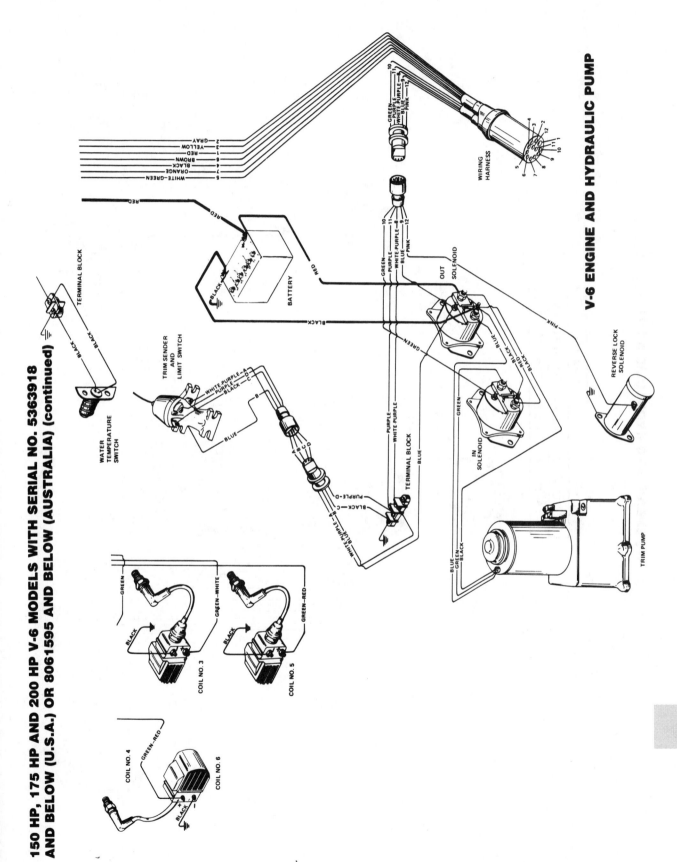

150 HP, 175 HP AND 200 HP V-6 MODELS WITH SERIAL NO. 5363918 AND BELOW (U.S.A.) OR 8061595 AND BELOW (AUSTRALIA) (continued)

V-6 ENGINE AND HYDRAULIC PUMP

12

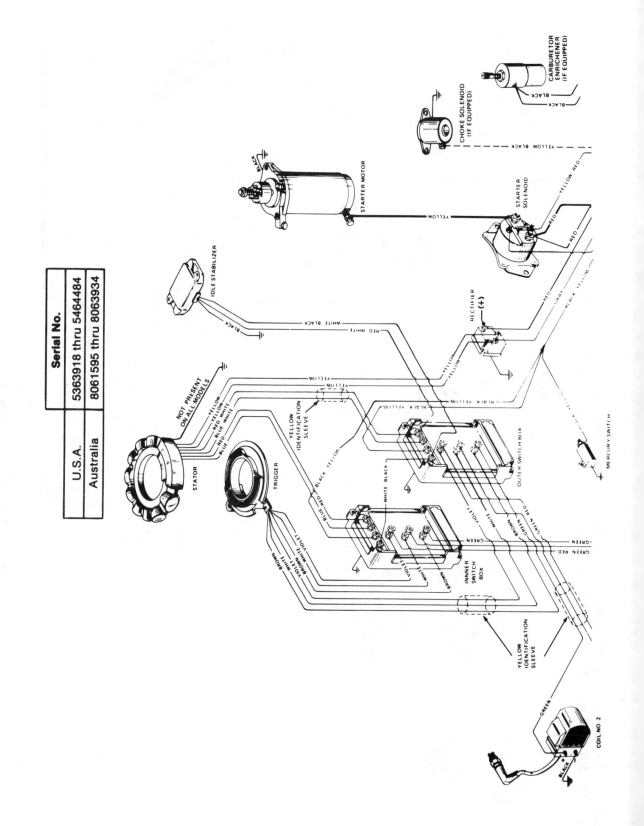

V-6 ENGINE AND HYDRAULIC PUMP

Serial No.	
U.S.A.	5363918 thru 5464484
Australia	8061595 thru 8063934

V-6 ENGINE AND HYDRAULIC PUMP (continued)

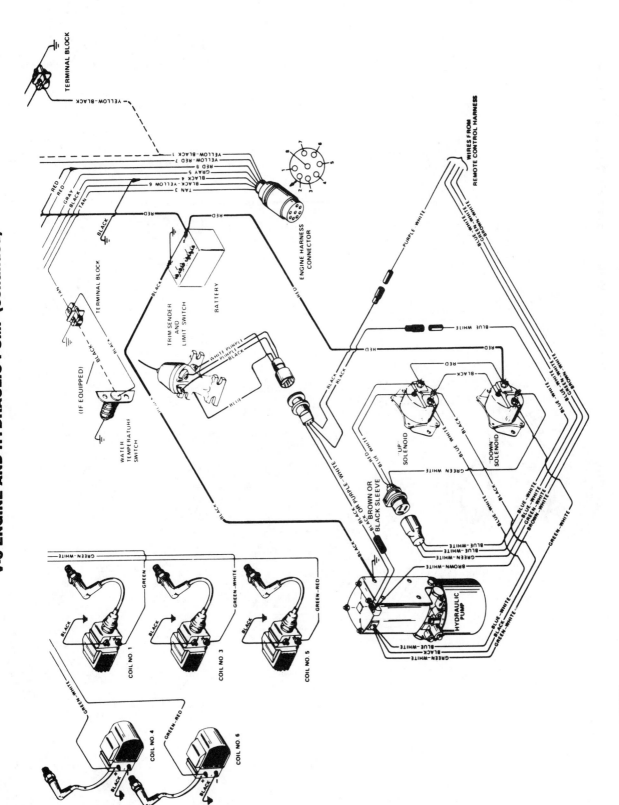

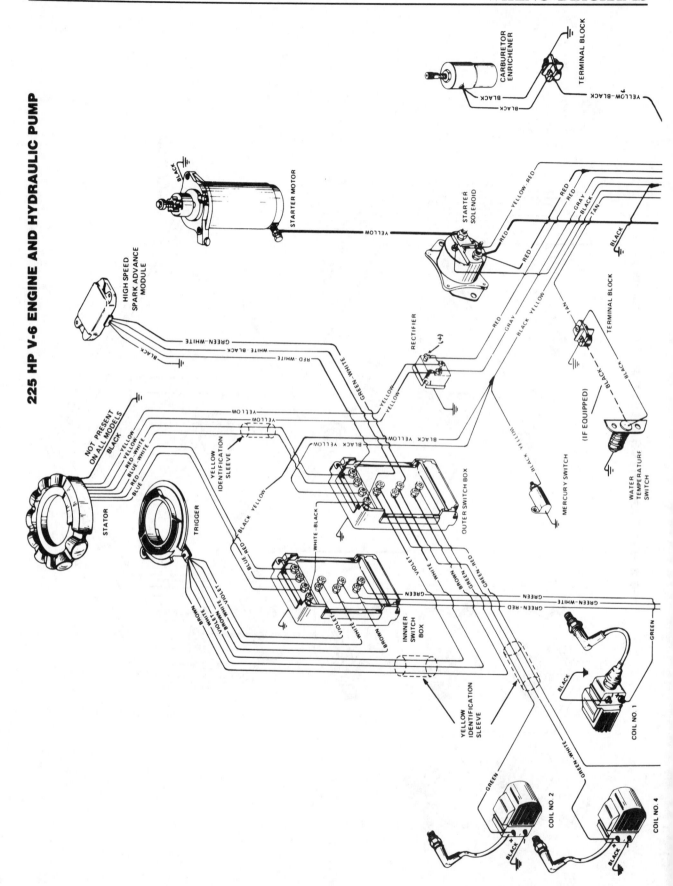

225 HP V-6 ENGINE AND HYDRAULIC PUMP

225 HP V-6 ENGINE AND HYDRAULIC PUMP (continued)

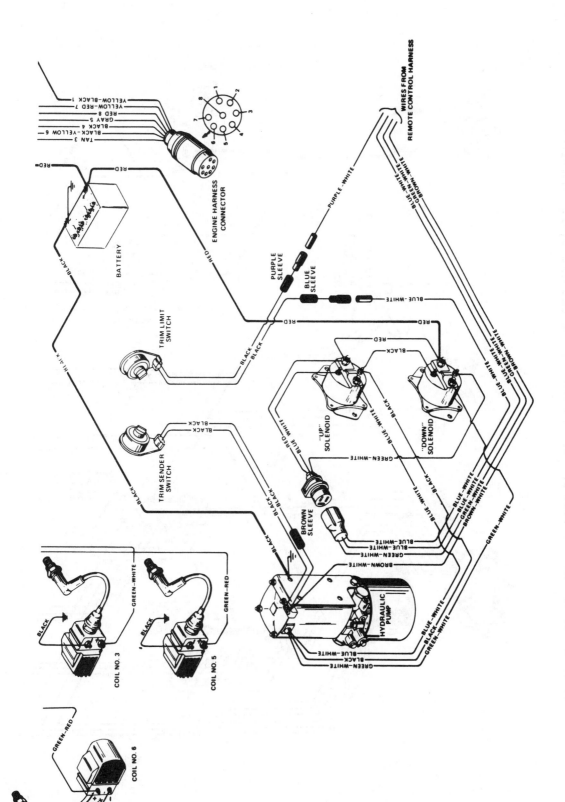

12

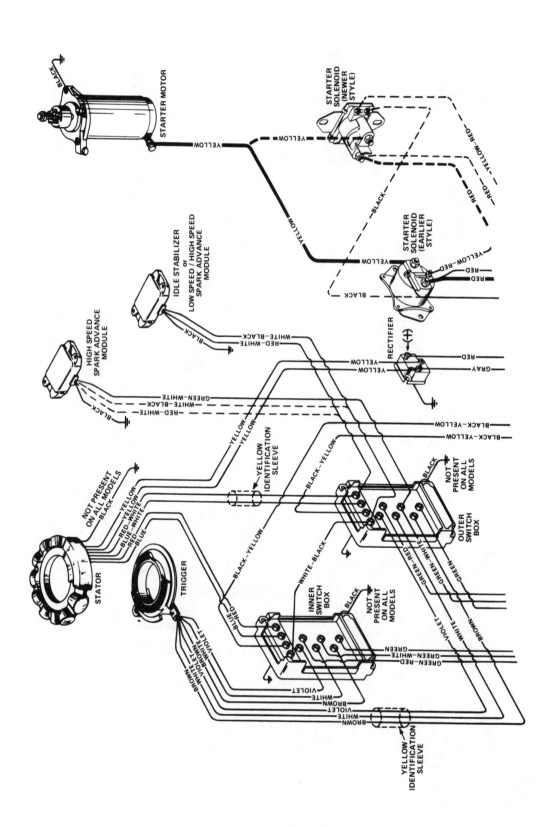

V-6 ENGINE SERIAL NO. 5464486 and UP (U.S.A.) OR 8063935 AND UP (AUSTRALIA)

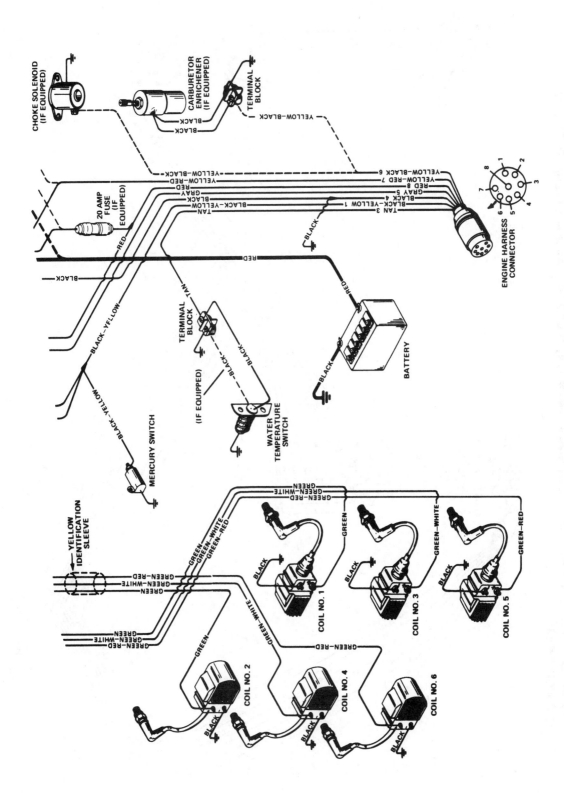

V-6 ENGINE SERIAL NO. 5464486 and UP (U.S.A.) OR 8063935 AND UP (AUSTRALIA) (continued)

"COMMANDER" SIDE MOUNT CONTROLS A-87953A, A-87954A, AND A-87729A WITHOUT POWER TRIM

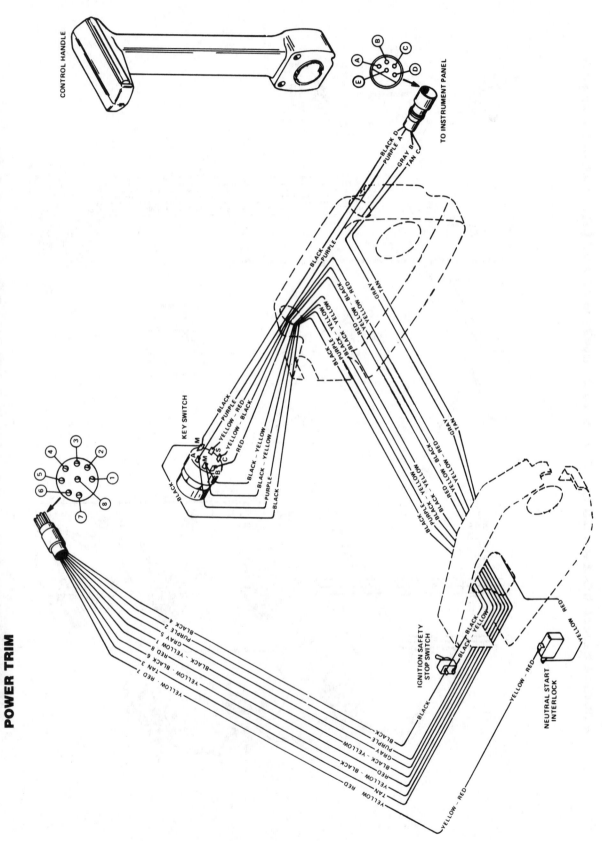

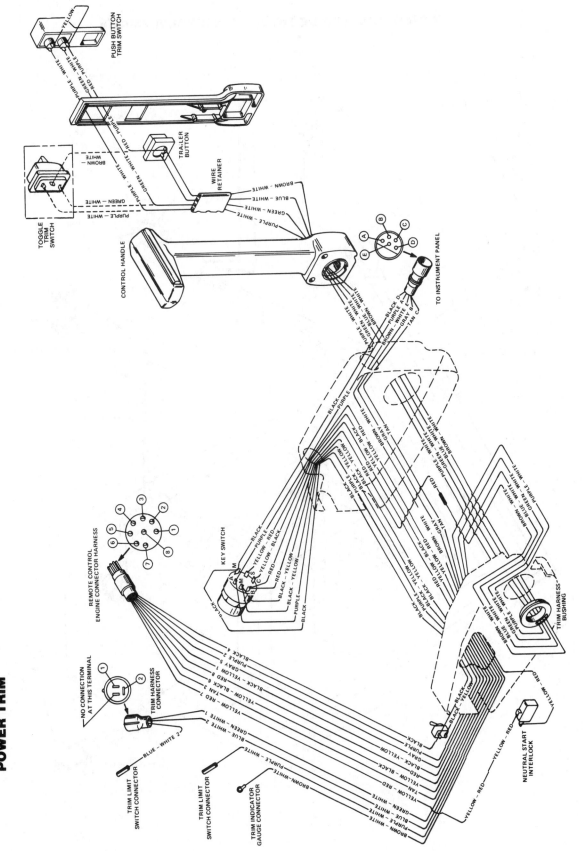

"COMMANDER" SIDE MOUNT CONTROLS A-85800A, A-87273A, AND A-87317A WITH POWER TRIM

"COMMANDER" SIDE MOUNT CONTROL A-76334A

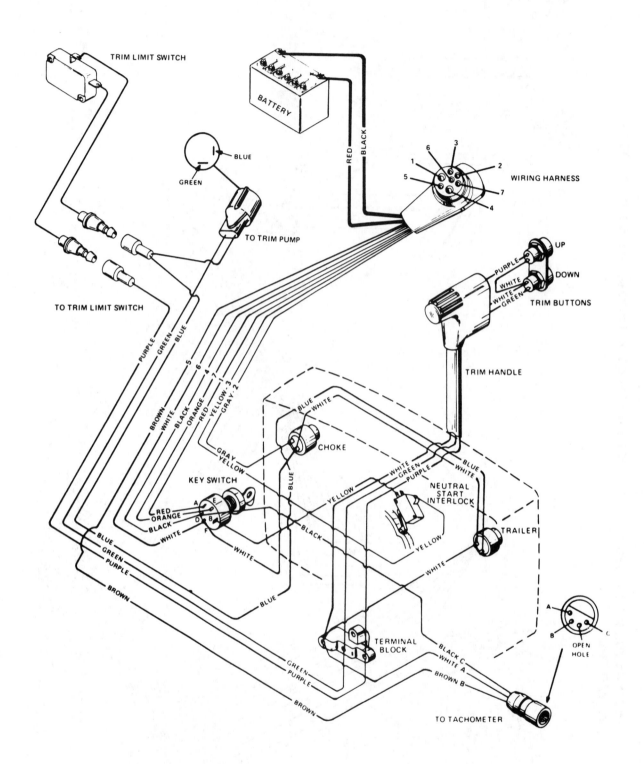

V-6 REMOTE CONTROL WITH ALARM HORN

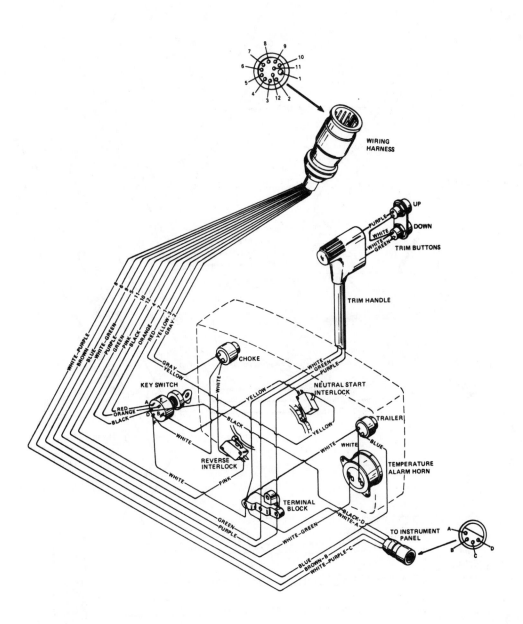

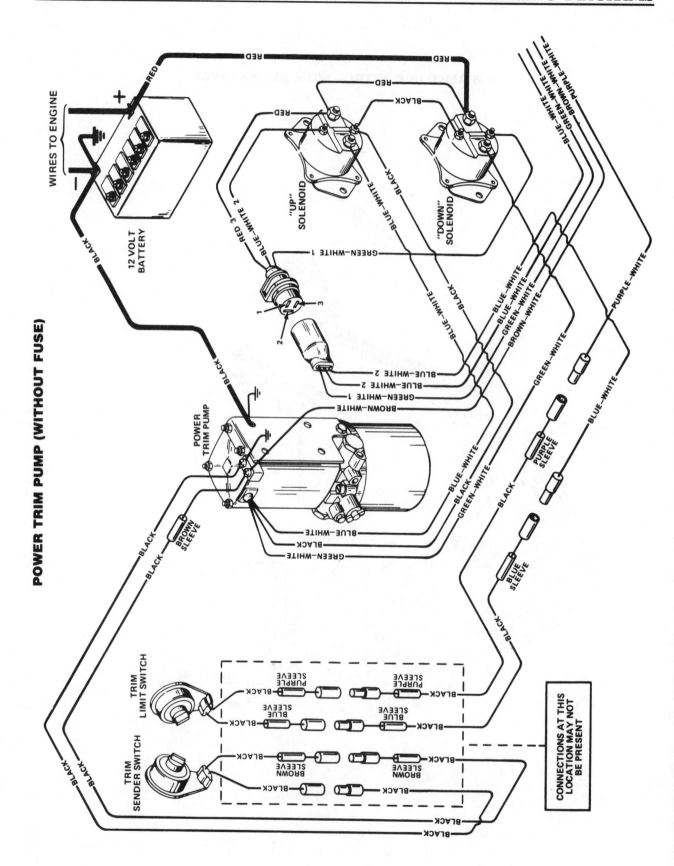

POWER TRIM PUMP (WITHOUT FUSE)

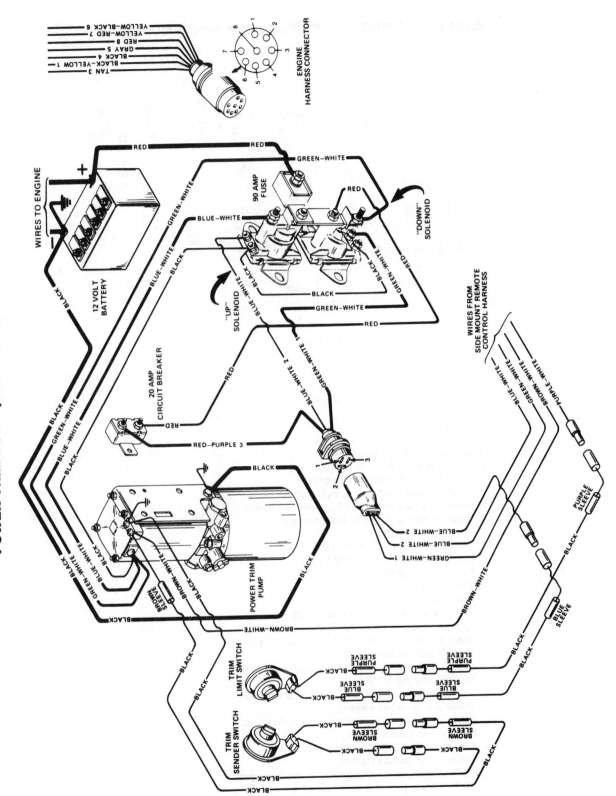

POWER TRIM PUMP (WITH FUSE)

12

HARNESS WIRING V-6 MODELS WITH PANEL CONTROL

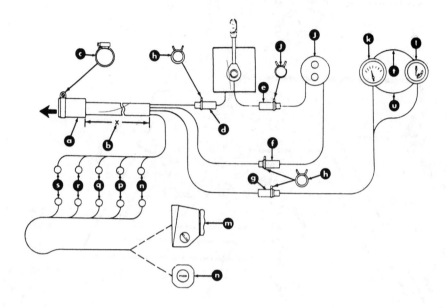

a. Extension harness
   (A-84-66005A10, A15, A20, A40)
b. X = Length of harness in feet
c. Screw-type clamp 1-5/8 in. (43.3 mm)
d. 4-pin connector (control harness)
e. 3-pin connector (control to trailer/choke panel)
f. 5-pin connector (trailer/choke panel to harness
g. 4-pin connector (harness to tachometer
   and trim indicator)
h. Spring-type clamp 13/16 in. (20.6 mm)
i. Spring-type clamp 3/4 in. (19.1 mm)
j. Trailer/choke panel
k. Tachometer
l. Trim indicator
m. Locking steering mount (A-66786A3)
n. Ignition switch (A-54211A2)
o. Black to black (secure with screw and nut and
   insulate with rubber sleeve)
p. Orange to orange (secure with screw and nut and
   insulate with rubber sleeve)
q. White to white (secure with screw and nut and
   insulate with rubber sleeve)
r. Yellow to yellow (secure with screw and nut and
   insulate with rubber sleeve)
s. Red to red (secure with screw and nut and
   insulate with rubber sleeve)
t. Black jumper (connect to ground on both gauges)
u. White jumper (connect to + 12V on both gauges)

HARNESS WIRING V-6 MODELS WITH SINGLE ENGINE CONSOLE CONTROL

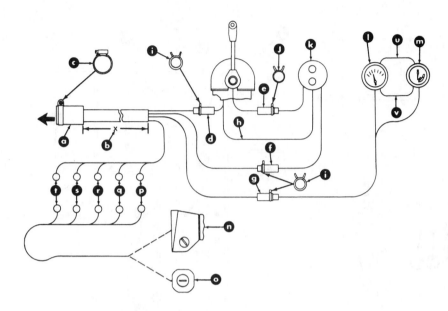

a. Extension harness (A-84-66005A10, A15, A20, A40)
b. X = Length of harness in feet
c. Screw-type clamp 1-5/8 in. (43.3 mm)
d. 4-pin connector (control harness)
e. 3-pin connector (control to trailer/choke panel)
f. 5-pin connector (trailer/choke panel to harness
g. 4-pin connector (harness to tachometer
   and trim indicator)
h. White wire (control to trailer/choke panel)
   connect white wire to terminal on back side
   of panel that already has a wire connected to it.
i. Spring-type clamp 13/16 in. (20.6 mm)
j. Spring-type clamp 3/4 in. (19.1 mm)
k. Trailer/choke panel
l. Tachometer
m. Trim indicator
n. Locking steering mount (A-66786A3)
o. Ignition switch (A-54211A2)
p. Black to black (secure with screw and nut and
   insulate with rubber sleeve)
q. Orange to orange (secure with screw and nut and
   insulate with rubber sleeve)
r. White to white (secure with screw and nut and
   insulate with rubber sleeve)
s. Yellow to yellow (secure with screw and nut and
   insulate with rubber sleeve)
t. Red to red (secure with screw and nut and insulate
   with rubber sleeve)
u. Black jumper (connect to ground on both gauges)
v White jumper (connect to + 12V on both gauges)

12

HARNESS WIRING V-6 MODELS WITH DUAL ENGINE CONSOLE CONTROL

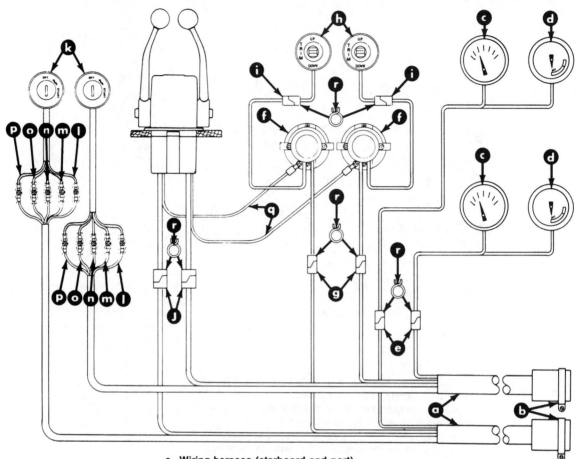

a. Wiring harness (starboard and port)
b. Screw-type clamps 1-5/8 in. (41.3 mm)
c. Tachometer
d. Trim indicator
e. 4-pin connector (tachometer/trim indicator to harness)
f. Choke/trailer panel (rear view of panels)
g. 5-pin connector (choke/trailer panel to harness)
h. Trim switch
i. 3-pin connector (trim switch to choke/trailer panel)
j. 4-pin connector (control harness)
k. Ignition switch panel
l. Black to black (secure with screw and nut and insulate with rubber sleeve)
m. Orange to orange (secure with screw and nut and insulate with rubber sleeve)
n. White to white (secure with screw and nut and insulate with rubber sleeve)
o. Yellow to yellow (secure with screw and nut and insulate with rubber sleeve)
p. Red to red/white (secure with screw and nut and insulate with rubber sleeve)
q. White wire (control to choke/trailer panel) connect white wire to terminal on back side of panel that already has a white wire connected to it.
r. Spring-type clamp (secure wiring connections with clamp)

TRIM INDICATOR GAUGE (WITH LAMP WIRE)

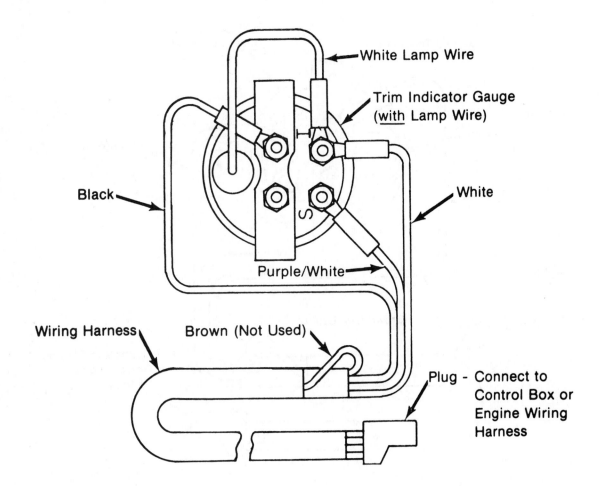

White Lamp Wire

Trim Indicator Gauge
(<u>with</u> Lamp Wire)

White

Black

Purple/White

Wiring Harness   Brown (Not Used)

Plug - Connect to
Control Box or
Engine Wiring
Harness

12

TRIM INDICATOR GAUGE (WITHOUT LAMP WIRE)

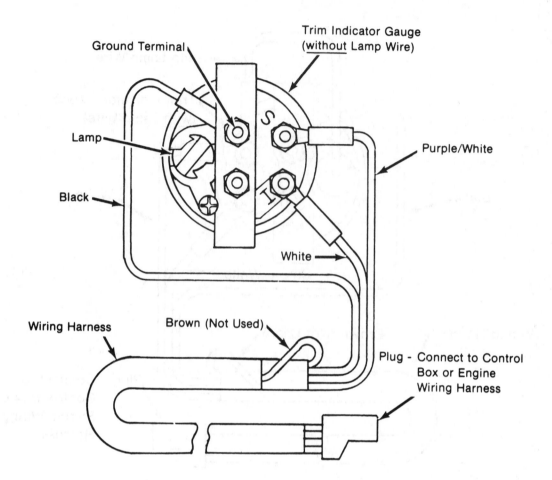

Trim Indicator Gauge
(without Lamp Wire)

Ground Terminal

Lamp

Black

Purple/White

White

Wiring Harness

Brown (Not Used)

Plug - Connect to Control
Box or Engine
Wiring Harness

TACHOMETER WITH TRIM INDICATOR GAUGE (WITH LAMP WIRE)

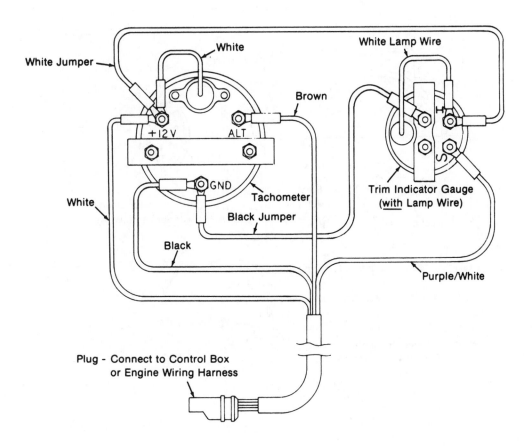

White Jumper

White

White Lamp Wire

Brown

+12V

ALT

GND

Tachometer

White

Black Jumper

Black

Trim Indicator Gauge
(with Lamp Wire)

Purple/White

Plug - Connect to Control Box
or Engine Wiring Harness

12

TACHOMETER WITH TRIM INDICATOR GAUGE (WITH LAMP WIRE)

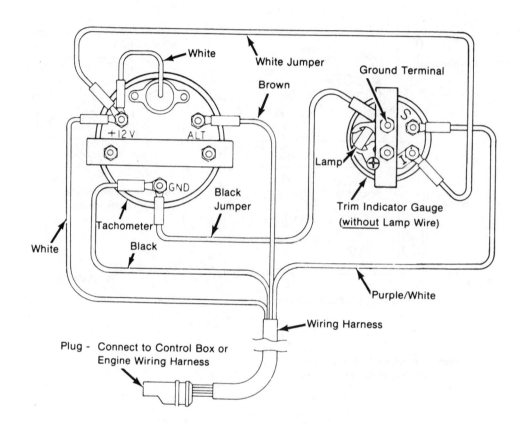

TRIM INDICATOR GAUGE AND ALARM HORN

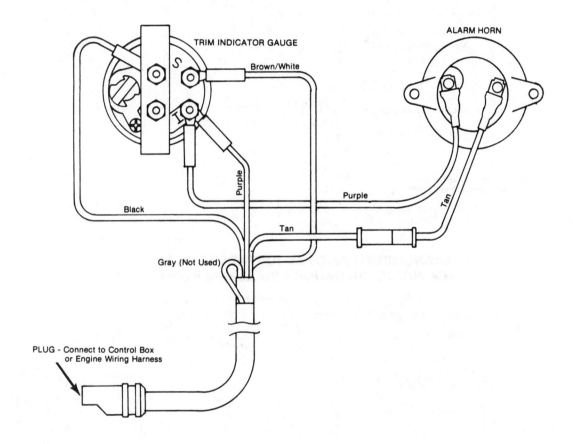

TRIM INDICATOR GAUGE

ALARM HORN

Brown/White

S

I

Purple

Black

Purple

Tan

Tan

Gray (Not Used)

PLUG - Connect to Control Box
or Engine Wiring Harness

12

TACHOMETER (WITHOUT ADJUSTABLE DIAL), TRIM INDICATOR GAUGE AND ALARM HORN

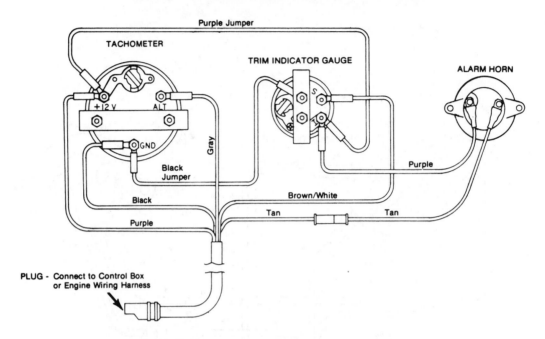

TACHOMETER (WITH ADJUSTABLE DIAL), TRIM INDICATOR GAUGE AND ALARM HORN

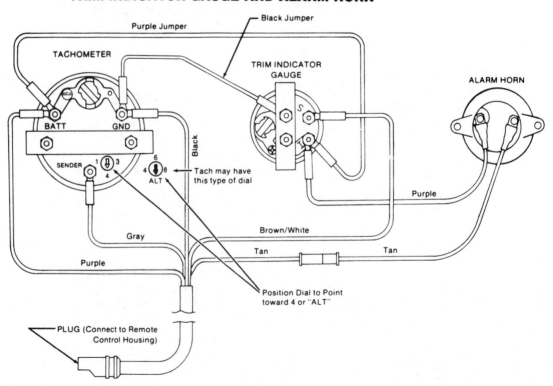

NOTES

NOTES

NOTES

NOTES

MAINTENANCE LOG

Service Performed	Mileage Reading				
Oil change (example)	2,836	5,782	8,601		